Lands of the Shamans

Archaeology, Cosmology and Landscape

Edited by

Dragoş Gheorghiu, George Nash,
Herman Bender and Emília Pásztor

Published in the United Kingdom in 2018 by
OXBOW BOOKS
The Old Music Hall, 106–108 Cowley Road, Oxford OX4 1JE

and in the United States by
OXBOW BOOKS
1950 Lawrence Road, Havertown, PA 19083

Paperback Edition: ISBN 978-1-78570-954-8
Digital Edition: ISBN 978-1-78570-955-5 (epub)

A CIP record for this book is available from the British Library

Library of Congress Control Number: 2018951275

Typeset in India by Versatile PreMedia Services. www.versatilepremedia.com

For a complete list of Oxbow titles, please contact:

UNITED KINGDOM
Oxbow Books
Telephone (01865) 241249, Fax (01865) 794449
Email: oxbow@oxbowbooks.com
www.oxbowbooks.com

UNITED STATES OF AMERICA
Oxbow Books
Telephone (800) 791-9354, Fax (610) 853-9146
Email: queries@casemateacademic.com
www.casemateacademic.com/oxbow

Oxbow Books is part of the Casemate Group

Back cover image: The deer panel, located on the 'elbow' of the Ocreza River. (Photo by D. Gheorghiu)

Contents

Contributors v

Introduction: Towards a Landscape for Shamans vi
The Editors

1. The Horse as a Shamanic Landscape Device: The Distribution of *Equus* on Upper Palaeolithic Open-Air Rock Art Sites of the Iberian Peninsula 1
George Nash and Sara Garcês

2. Göbekli Tepe – A Shamanic Landscape 21
Dragoş Gheorghiu

3. Caves and the Sacral Landscape: A Case Study on the Neolithic and Early Aeneolithic Periods in South-east Central Europe 46
Vladimír Peša

4. As Above, So Below: St Melangell and the Celestial Journey 89
Caroline Malim

5. Songs of the Shamans? Acoustical Studies in European Prehistory 111
Chris Scarre

6. Sights and Sounds of Selected Sacred and Shamanic Landscapes 123
Paul Devereux

7. Bronze Age Deposits in the Carpathian Basin – Markers for Spirit-Animated Landscape? The Role of Structured Deposition in Understanding the Worldview of Bronze Age Europe 144
Emília Pásztor

8. Landscape Transformation and Continuity in Shamanic Rock Art of Northern Asia 168
Ekaterina Devlet

9. Shamans' Landscapes: note sur la psychologie du shaman pre et protohistorique plus particulierement en Eurasie 191
Michel Louis Sériadès

10. The Mystery of the Bird-Nester: The Shaman Which Lévi-Strauss Did Not Recognise 206
Enrico Comba

11. Bear Myths and Traditions: The Moon and Mounds in North America 226
Herman Bender

12. To Re-Enact Is to Remember: Envisioning a Shamanic Research Protocol in Archaeology 258
Apela Colorado and Ryan Hurd

Contributors

HERMAN BENDER
Hanwakan Center for Archeoastronomy, Cosmology and Cultural Landscape Studies, Inc. USA

APELA COLORADO
Worldwide Indigenous Science Network, USA

ENRICO COMBA
Università degli Studi di Torino, Dipartimento di Culture, Politica e Società, Turin, Italy

PAUL DEVEREUX
(i)Royal College of Art; (ii)Time & Mind journal, UK

EKATERINA DEVLET
Institute of Archaeology Russian Academy of Sciences, Centre of Paleoart Studies, Moscow, Russia

SARA GARCÊS
Trás-os-Montes e Alto Douro University, UTAD, Quinta de Prados, 5000-801 Vila Real, Portugal; Earth and Memory Institute (ITM), Quaternary and Prehistory Group of the Geosciences Centre (u. ID73 – FCT). FCT Scholarship (SFRH/BD/69625/2010), Portugal

DRAGOȘ GHEORGHIU
Doctoral School, National University of Arts, Bucharest, Romania;
Earth and Memory Institute (ITM), Quaternary and Prehistory Group of the Geosciences Centre (u. ID73 – FCT), Portugal

RYAN HURD
Worldwide Indigenous Science Network, USA

CAROLINE MALIM
SLR Consulting Limited, Hermes House, Oxon Business Park, Shrewsbury, UK

GEORGE NASH
Department of Archaeology and Anthropology of University of Bristol, UK

EMÍLIA PÁSZTOR
Türr István Museum, Baja, Hungary

VLADIMÍR PEŠA
Regional Museum and Gallery at *Česká* Lípa, Czech Republic

CHRIS SCARRE
Department of Archaeology, Durham University, UK

MICHEL LOUIS SÉFÉRIADÈS
Anthropologue et archéologue honoraire au Centre National de la Recherche Scientifique (CNRS), Paris, France

Introduction: Towards a Landscape for Shamans

The Editors

Setting the Scene

Over the past 20 years, shamanism has become an emerging topic in archaeology – see Price (2001); David Lewis-Williams (2002), Guba & Szevereny (2007), Mannermaa (2008), Pásztor (2011), Reymann (2015), Gheorghiu *et al.* (2017), Rozwadowski (2017). It has begun to emerge that shamanism can take on many guises; from the potential shamanism of the very ancient world of our Palaeolithic ancestors to the Neoshamanic practices of the Counterculture of the late 20th century (Lewis-Williams 2002; Nash 2017). The various strands recognised within this subject clearly shows that shamanism, like other subjects, relies on many mechanisms in order to survive and flourish; one of these is landscape. As far as we the authors are concerned, this edited volume is the first of its kind to associate shamanism with landscape as clearly, the two interact.[1]

If we accept shamanism (or a belief-system best described with a shamanistic world view, see Winkelman 2004) was already a generic phenomenon in the prehistoric times, then we should be able to use shamanism as an ethnographic analogy in order to analyse certain archaeological artefacts. Reconstructing a belief-system with the help of archaeological artefacts is often difficult and rarely straightforward (see Gheorghiu *et al.* 2017). However, we cannot overlook the possibility of shamanism being used, regardless the sceptics, as a possible analogy during the research of prehistoric beliefs.

The most characteristic element of shamanic ritual is the way special individuals would enter into an altered state of consciousness (ASC). There can be many explanations behind this, even physiological, as confirmed through anthropological research. Thanks to this even one of the richest graves from the Mesolithic period, discovered in 1930 in Bad Dürrenberg, Germany was considered to belong to a shaman. Anatomical changes to the female skull intimated frequent shifts into transient state.

Based on fragmentary archaeological evidence and documentary ethnographic accounts, shamans often used hallucinogen substances to reach altered states of consciousness. Trace elements of opium poppy have been found among archaeological artefacts on the eastern and southern slopes of the Jura Mountain from almost every period (Merlin 2003); here, the landscape plays a significant role in the shamanistic beliefs.

Many scientists trace back the origin of shamanism to later prehistory. However, as far back as the 1950s, Russian scientists have claimed that Siberian shamanism, in fact, originates from a much earlier period and can be regarded as an ideological background for the analysis of rock art (Okladnikov & Martinov 1972); sentiments that were later supported by Lewis-Williams and Dowson (1988, 1990), Clottes and Lewis-Williams (1998) and Whitley (1998). The eminent Russian prehistoric historian Okladnikov considered the origin of shamanism to date to the Neolithic, around 3000–4000 BCE (Okladnyikov 1972). Bronze Age craftsmanship among the Western-Siberian Obi-Ugrians, dating between the 8th century BCE and 17th century CE, supports the concept of belief-systems being influenced by ASC. Many archaeologists working within this geographical area regard the figurines found at the Achmylovo site (on the Upper-Volga and dating back to between 8th and 6th century BCE) as devices used in shamanistic practices (Schwerin von Krosigk 1992). They believe that recovered artefacts such as amulets, jewellery and other items of dwelling adornment would have assisted in warding away evil spirits within the house; a practice that is recorded within both the anthropological and ethnographic records (Fedorova 2001; Patrushev 2000). Interestingly, the geographical range of these amulets is replicated in the present day, suggesting that the ancient practices are still in use.

If the term *shaman* represents a special perception of the world, then shamans are 'creators of interaction between this world and the other world through the ecstatic role-taking technique' (Siikala 1978, 28–30). This definition suggests that we are not witnessing a world of chaos rather more a world of order whereby the shaman would have had control of the community; but at the same time, would have been the direct device between the community and spirit world. The spirit world would have been comprised of things us mortals cannot and should not see. In prehistoric times until relatively recent times, sections of landscape would have been ritualised and strictly taboo. This is witnessed in the way prehistoric ritualised monuments, burial or landscape markers are concentrated in clusters and are located away from settlements. The organisation of space – sacred and profane occurs in all areas of the world and one considered the segregation of these spaces as being a fundamental human trait that evokes social and political control in hierarchies (e.g. using landscape to segregate class and gender).

Onto Landscape

The *Land of the Shamans* presents a landscape narrative that involves all the ingredients for shamanistic practices such as underworlds, over (or upper) worlds and the *scapes* between and above. This (collective) cosmos is at the same time both physical and metaphysical. The physicality of the rock surface not only creates a platform for rock art but also absorbs sounds from when the art was created and performed. On a more subtle observation, the rock surface also creates shadows that are dominated by the ambiance of light. In a similar vein, buried hoards are physical in form yet at the same time are hidden below the ground with only its owner knowing its whereabouts. Such interplay between physical and metaphysical space could have been the source for trance and ASC; thus artificial light such as fire and sounds such as chanting and dancing in, say, darkness, under the nightly sky, within the dreary vaults of megalithic structures or the underworld voids of the cave could have been points of reference for shamanic performance (as evidenced in the archaeological record – see Peša, this volume).

This book intends to provide the reader with a novel account of how landscape is viewed through the eyes and mindset of the shaman. Clearly, this is not a simple narrative that involve male shamans delving into a landscape; far more complex patterns of interplay between people and community and their landscape is going on; however, the archaeological evidence is somewhat fragmentary.

Current archaeological approaches to shamanism are restricted to experiments and ethnographic analogies that restrict the complexity of *the empirical nature of shamanism* (Winkelman 1989, 161). The editors are aware that we cannot clearly demonstrate archaeologically a relationship between the essence of shamanism and ASC and landscape (see Eliade 1951; Winkelman 1989; 2006, 91; Wautischer 1998, 163–190). We are content with the notion that some traits of the landscape could have assisted in producing some psychological states of ritualised stress and disorientation; the most obvious of spaces being the cave or rock shelter (e.g. Peša; Séfériadès, this volume). One should also consider how elements of diverse landscapes guided and helped the shamans during their vision quest, examples of which are found all over the modern world.

To understand the connection between shamanism and landscape, ethnographic studies have played a significant role in creating a meaningful contribution. Indigenous cultures worldwide suggest that 'nature and culture are part of the same socio- cosmic field' (Viveiros de Castro 2005, 148). And:

> 'All shamanism [...] are particularly linked to what we define as sacred landscapes both in the human and physical as well as in the other-than- human world. The physical and non- physical landscapes in shamanism are deeply interrelated and interconnected, and constitute an inseparable unity. This is the reason why these territories are not just landscapes but "sacred landscapes"' (Fotiou *et al.* 2017, 7)

Here, Fotiou intimates that 'shamans are the main actors in shaping and preserving them [landscapes]'.

Sacred places in the landscape are socially and culturally constructed; these scapes are unordered, unmade and uncontrollable (Zola 2017, 193). Sacred landscapes could also be metaphysical, formed by the vibration of sounds, smell, taste – a sensory cacophony of emotions, many of which are intangible in terms of physical evidence. There is however, tangible evidence in the form of, for example, shaman drums which are adorned with maps or diagrammed landscapes portraying all manner of social and ritual life.

As we will see throughout this book, sacred natural space such as mountains, plateaus and ravines involve many different world views; what one landscape means to one may not have the same meaning to another – no two mindsets are the same (Children & Nash 1997). To the shaman, scape can mean a number of things – below and above and the troposphere; a time continuum can also feature, creating a multiphased and multifaceted entity. The aptly-named *sky-dome* viewed in non-western tribal terms as a huge bowl or cauldron covers the troposphere – our earth and is the barrier between us and the upper world. Above the *sky-dome*, the *skyscape* is the realm where celestial phenomena exist. At the same time the underworld forms a mysterious, sometimes dangerous *scape* where cave entrances or springs issuing forth from the earth are the gateways to this realm where the shaman can experience ASC. The cave entrance and probably the cave itself form a luminal space. According to Levi-Struassian theory (1963), the cave acts as a pivotal contradiction to binary or polar oppositions between the living and the dead (e.g. light: dark, life: death, warm: cold etc.). Similarly, buried hoards also form part of the underworld, sometimes hiding special and magical objects though these objects may have been buried for a variety of reasons (Bradley 1998). Rituals for celestial beings were performed along the riverside for example, but also in elevated places, such as mountains. Therefore, structured deposition could have been also offered to the spirits of different shamanistic worlds other than to supernatural beings of the underworld.

In terms of archaeology, a shamanic landscape can reveal itself as a series of palimpsests that overlap the natural forms; therefore, we recognise *skyscapes* (e.g. Malim; Bender), *soundscapes* (e.g. Devereux, Scarre), *zoomorphic-scapes* (e.g. Nash and Garcês, Gheorghiu, Comba), *subterranean-scapes*, such as caves (Peša) and springs and subterranean water courses which emit their *richness* from inner earth (e.g. Bender; Peša), or those produced by hidden deposits (e.g. Pásztor). Besides identifying various shamanistic landscapes, this volume also explains the psychology of the shaman's environment (e.g. Séfériadès), and the sacredness of the land (e.g. Pásztor).

All these types of shamanistic landscape described are not isolated or separated, but co-exist and interconnect; for example the association with Palaeolithic rock art and various landscape forms (e.g. Nash and Garcês), the quarried stone that constructs the Early Pre-pottery Neolithic monument of Göbekli Tepe (e.g. Gheorghiu), or prehistoric imagery associated with soundscapes (e.g. Devereux; Devlet; Scarre). In addition, we must consider more subtle and fragmentary pieces of evidence such as the Neolithic and Bronze Age deposits that are hidden below the surface of the land – i.e. the realm of the underworld (e.g. Séfériadès; Pásztor). The upper or over-world is represented by the terrestrial realm, the *scape* that is in control of us mortals (e.g. Malim; Bender). It is here that we mortals, through an intermediary, would revere animals and animal spirits (e.g. Gheorghiu), some of which are suspended between the different worlds of being including the cosmos above (e.g. Bender).

Interestingly, similar narratives to the cosmologies were to be found in Eurasia, Europe and the Americas (e.g. Nash and Garcês, Gheorghiu, Bender, Séfériadès, Comba) demonstrating the existence of a unity of the human mind and the underlying mechanisms that control and manipulate society.

Editorial Responsibilities

This book, organised into 12 chapters, guides the reader from the Palaeolithic banks of the Tagus River, the Early Neolithic enclosures at Gobekli Tepe, the Chalcolithic caves of Central Europe, the Neolithic-Medieval palimpsests in Wales, the prehistoric acoustic sites of Europe, the Bronze Age deposits and imagery of Eurasia, to the cosmologies of the New World.

For this volume, we have attempted to subtly create an intellectual thread between chapters; for example, the information about animism (e.g. Séfériadès; Comba) could be used to analyse the chapters on acoustics (e.g. Devereux; Scarre) or the underworld objects (e.g. Pasztor). It would appear that many of the *isms* and themes embracing shamanism and landscape have much wider implications, including semantics associated with modernity (e.g. Colorado and Hurd).

The role of this book is to sensitise the reader with a prehistoric vision of the world before the emergence of the major historical religions, a vision which could be attributed to shamanism and to offer a new vision on how landscapes played a vital role in manoeuvring prehistoric communities into organising and dividing various *scapes*. The book ends with a proposal of a holistic method of re-enactment to remember the past proposed from a Native American perspective (Colorado & Hurd) that can be interpreted as a key to read the book as a holistic account to the landscapes of the shaman.

Landscapes are animated when stones, water, mythical beasts, light and sound could and would have created an out-of-this-world experience in the viewer's mind. Therefore, certain rock surfaces could have been animated with engravings and paintings (e.g. Nash & Garcês, Gheorghiu, Devlet) or with percussion sounds (e.g. Devereux, Scarre). Running water, for example, would have produced distinct sounds in places where animals congregated (e.g. Nash & Garcês), or to reflect solar and stellar entities (e.g. Malim). Such animation of the world offers the reader the image of a living cosmos which was by and large revealed through the uses of artistic endeavour. What do we mean by *art*? Rather than the concept of 'art for arts' sake', we take the meaning of art as being visual representations and acoustic productions that overlap the natural landscape with *artscapes*. Here, art acts as a device which turns a space into a place. The act of converting a space into a place was and is an artificial one and, in terms of ritualising such a *scape*, veneration was probably via a shaman.

If we accept the concept of artistic endeavour as a shamanistic device that bridges reality with fantasy, the so-called artificial landscapes presented in this book could be seen as a product of magical-animistic productions with a strong emotional impact, generating an out-of-this-world state of rapture.

What on Earth Do the Chapters Have to Say?

The book is divided into 12 chapters, each discussing the role of how landscape plays in shamanism. The editors have been careful in how the term *landscape* is used. In a previous volume by the editors – Gheorghiu *et al.* (2017), the emphasis was firmly placed on the artefact. The over-riding theme of this book was assessing the rather fragmentary evidence to suggest that shamanistic practices actually existed; in this book, the editors share a similar concern, albeit using different approaches to tease out the available evidence. Despite these issues, Tilley (1994; 2005) has gone some way to suggest that landscape (or the perceptions of landscape) is fundamental to the way we as modern humans live our lives. Even within the modern world there are many pockets of landscape that are considered sacred and special. Some of areas are restricted, some evoke deep and meaningful memories and stories that sometimes involve supernatural beings; creatures that are not of this world. These places of sacredness, such as the Dreamtime sites of the indigenous peoples of Australia are so powerful that successive communities over many thousands of years have seen fit to add their signature, thus ensuring that the stories and memories never go away.

In the first chapter Nash and Garcês discuss the relationship between Palaeolithic horse images and the riverine landscape of the Upper Ocreza Valley in Portugal. They suggest that the symbolic present may have replicated various zones within a ritualised landscape. The rock art is perceived as a mnemonic process that represents special events. In this case special events may have involved the actual process of engraving alongside the river. An interpretation of the horse image and of the river exposes common symbolic traits, revealing the metaphorical basis for engraving. It is conceivable that the act of engraving would have been in hands of an artist involved in shamanistic practices, in this case he or she being the mediator between spirit world – the metaphysical landscape, the engraved rock panels and the recipients of the narrative – the audience.

In Chapter 2, Dragoş Gheorghiu analyses the iconography from Enclosure D at Gobekli Tepe focusing on the form of the early pre-pottery, the Neolithic landscape and the engraved zoomorphic images. The animal species and their biotopes appear to reveal a series of water landscapes. The author suggests the iconography was a sort of visual story that involved a disastrous natural event, such as flooding. Archaeological analogies, with the inventory of a shaman's tomb from the same period and region, and the symbolism of animals depicted are used as arguments for a shamanic link to the iconography present.

Fig. 0.1: Landscape view showing the final section of the Ocreza River before it flows into the Tagus (photo: D. Gheorghiu)

Fig. 0.2: The deer panel, located on the 'elbow' of the Ocreza River (photo: D. Gheorghiu)

Fig. 0.3: The deer panel, located on the 'elbow' of the Ocreza River (photo: G. Nash)

Vladimír Peša in Chapter 3 approaches the metaphysical underworld of the cave from the perspective of *speleoarchaeology.* Here, the cave space becomes a repository for communication with deities and important cult and religious centres elsewhere within the sacred landscape. The use of caves from Palaeolithic to the Neolithic and protohistorical periods was both sacred and profane and was divided into public and privates spaces. This division of cave space may reveal a relationship between culture and nature; crossing the divide would have been power and special people such as shamans. According to the author, the natural features of the cave, such as the numerous speleothems, niches and cracks were revered, and in recent times, the calcite was used as a medicine, thus demonstrating the powerful substances that lie within the cave.

In the next chapter, Caroline Malim investigates the sacred nature of overlapped sites, using St Melangell in Berwyn Range in Powys, Wales as an example. From this site archaeology and history reveals rituals associated with death and resurrection, and a belief system that could have had a shamanic background since it incorporated landscape, animals, divination, shape-shifting and astronomical alignments in various forms. Historic tales and the iconography associated with St Melangell reveal pagan symbols of lunar worship such as the hare. This animal is associated with the moon, the otherworld, rebirth and everlasting life. The narrative of the legend of St Melangell illustrates the position of constellations at the Autumn Equinox, and a relationship between the local landscape and the celestial one which is perceived in the reflection of the Milky Way over the nearby River Tanat.

In Chapter 5, Chris Scarre examines the influence of the natural world, in particular the wind and water on the sensory qualities of certain settings or spaces, and provides an extensive discussion of the archaeoacoustic qualities in different periods and regions of the world. Examples discussed include the relationship between the sounds of the rushing water of surface and underground rivers and rock-art or Parietal art, and the acoustic influence of wind and rain on Neolithic megaliths. Particular attention is placed on the acoustic qualities in caves that contain Palaeolithic painted rock art.

In a similar vein, Paul Devereux in Chapter 6 discusses the sacred geography of where the physical world and *otherworlds* meet. According to Devereux, ancient and traditional peoples have found many different ways to integrate their home territories with spiritual or mythical meaning. Such geographies of the soul could be small and intimate or cover large tracts of ground and involve communities. These *scapes* could be natural or socially-constructed, or a combination of both. Physical and virtual features via human agency would have been superimposed on the physical topography, allowing visible and invisible routes for spirits to travel along, establishing large scale ground markings (what Devereux terms geoglyphs), and choreographed routes for pilgrimages to sacred places, whether natural or built. Based on these sacred routes, this chapter will explore many parts of the world where sacred landscapes were created and used by special people engaged as mediators between the spirit world and the real world.

In Chapter 7, Emília Pásztor investigates Bronze Age ritualised deposition. The act of creating *place* significantly characterises this period throughout most of Europe.

However, unlike other areas of European, watery sites appear not to have been the preferred places for deposition. In the Carpathian Basin, the ratio between sacred dry and watery places is more balanced. Many ancient and indigenous mythologies are characterized by animated elements of nature, including natural surroundings which were probably essential elements of their cosmological belief system. Bronze Age depositional customs and the ethnographical analogies appear to be replicated. Based on this assumption, Pásztor argues that deposition could have served similar purpose during the Bronze Age to ensure the welfare of the community by token offerings in order to please the spirits. This close and strong connection with nature also supports the theoretical assumption of the existence of shamanism during the Bronze Age, in the Carpathian Basin.

Similarly, Katerina Devlet in Chapter 8 raises questions of how and why particular places were chosen for rock art. Devlet argues that image-complexity is linked to site hierarchies or they are core sites forming the centre of a sacral landscape. The most significant shamanist activities were held near cliffs marked by petroglyphs. The sites also have a long-lasting tradition of veneration and ritual activity. These factors support her argument that many scenes on the rock surface, the juxtaposition and even superimposition could be interpreted in keeping with a shamanistic worldview and activities.

Michel Séfériadès approaches shamanism in Chapter 9 as an ageless religion that is dependent on environment, ecosystems and biotopes. According to preconceived anthropological and ethnographic sources, a shaman is related to an animated (and magical) world, terrestrial and celestial, augmenting his or her body with the physical and spiritual attributes of different animals (e.g. Keesing 1981). This is witnessed when a shaman, through ASC, becomes an intermediary between the human world and the spirit world, representing the symbiosis between humans and nature. Such qualities are illustrated in the various cultures that date from the Upper Palaeolithic to proto-historical times, represented usually as parietal or portable art.

In Chapter 10, Enrico Comba advances a hypothesis that the bird-nester myth from the Bororo Indians of Central Brazil, used by anthropologist Claude Lévi-Strauss, describes the initiation of an apprentice shaman with variants representing a general pattern that is common to most of the shamanic experiences of Amerindian people (Lévi-Strauss 1963; 1964). Other variants describe the cosmological structure of a multi-layered universe that is strictly related to the practice of shamanism and shared by most Native American cultures.

In the penultimate chapter Herman Bender examines the relationship between the bear, the moon, other cosmological entities such as the stars and the terrestrial world. Here, Bender places an emphasis on the relationship between the night sky and the ability of the shaman (or, as a more accurate description in American Indian tradition and practice, a medicine man) to act as a psychopomp. Two geographic areas and times are represented, the Ohio River Valley giant earthworks which are approximately 2000 years old and the effigy mounds in Wisconsin which are approximately 800–1000 years old. Even though they are not coeval, surprising similarities exist with alignments of bear related features toward a lunar maximum rise or set point and likely Milky Way affiliations. There are also traditional bear star similarities that may have transcended the millennium which separates the two loci and a function or purpose that is certainly related to the upper world and ability of the medicine person (shaman) to travel between worlds (in full consciousness or deep concentration) assisted by the bear as a spirit guide.

Within the final chapter, Apela Colorado and Ryan Hurd take on the semantics of the world of the shaman, focusing on current views of what shamanism represents and how it fits within non-western indigenous societies around the globe, and the effects on spiritual knowledge from external factors. Contentious issues such as climate change, sea rise, extreme weather events, food inequity and global health challenges intervene. These issues along with the threat of social change through neoliberal economics has, in many cases, diluted the potential powerbase of hierarchal societies in terms of (community) religion, which itself is firmly tied into the *politik* of a tribal group. Colorado and Hurd question how the tradition and modernity coexist. Here, indigenous science is presented in a dynamic and reciprocal relationship of contextualization with landscape archaeology, performance, narratives and community education being the main foci for discussion. This paper identifies the deepening levels of contemporary shamanism where ancestral site are present including the Kurgans (burial mounds) of Karakol Valley, Altai Republic and the oral and pictorial living traditions in South-eastern Alaska.

Acknowledgements

The editors thank Oxbow Publisher Dr Julie Gardiner for the kind help and patience during the process of writing and editing this volume. Thanks also to the Production and Design Assistant Katie Allen for the wonderful cover design that illustrates the structure of the book, and to Professor Mihály Hoppál for useful suggestions. Last, but not least, many thanks to Mrs. Cornelia Cătuna for the editorial help.

Note

1 Prior to the publication of this volume, archaeological approaches to shamanism and landscape was briefly discussed in the studies on cave imagery (e.g. Clottes & Lewis-Williams 2001; Lewis-Williams 2002; Lewis-Williams & Challis 2011; Gheorghiu *et al.* 2017). Other related texts include studies on rock art and landscape (Rozwadowski 2001; Price 2001; Nash & Chippindale 2002), archaeoacoustics and landscape (Devereux & Nash 2014), as well as pioneering approaches by various authors contributing to the journal of *Time and Mind* (Taylor & Frances).

References

Bradley, R. 1998. *The Passage of Arms: An Archaeological Analysis of Prehistoric Hoards and Votive Deposits.* Oxford: Oxbow Books.

Children, G. & Nash, G. H. 1997. Establishing a discourse: The language of landscape. In G. H. Nash (ed.), *Semiotics of Landscape: The Archaeology of Mind.* British Archaeological Report S661. Oxford: Archaeopress.

Clottes, J. & Lewis-Williams, D. 1998. *The Shamans of Prehistory: Trance and Magic in the Painted Caves.* New York: Abrams.

Clottes, J. & Lewis-Williams, D. 2001. *Les chamanes de la préhistoire.* Paris: La Maison des Roches.

Devereux, P. & Nash, G. 2014. Indications of an Acoustic Landscape at Bryn Celli Ddu, Anglesey, North Wales. *Time and Mind, The Journal of Archaeology, Consciousness and Culture* 7(4), 385–390.

Fedorova, N., 2001. Shamans, heroes and ancestors in the bronze castings of western Siberia. In N. S. Price, (ed.) *The Archaeology of Shamanism.* London, New York: Routledge, 56–65.

Fotiou, E., Riboli, D., & Torri, D. 2017. The First Conference of the International Society for Academic Research on Shamanism (ISARS), Delphi, Greece, in 2015. *Shaman* 25(1–2), 5–14.

Gheorghiu, D., Pásztor, E., Bender, H. & Nash, G. H. 2017. *Archaeological Approaches to Shamanism: Mind-Body, Nature, and Culture.* Newcastle-upon-Tyne: Cambridge Scholarly Publishing.

Guba, Sz. & Szeverény, V. 2007. Bronze Age bird representations from the Carpathian Basin. *Communicationes Archaeologicae Hungariae,* 75–110.

Keesing, R. M. 1981. *Cultural Anthropology: A Contemporary Perspective.* New York: Holt, Rinehart & Winston.

Lévi-Strauss, C. 1963. *Structural Anthropology.* London: Nicholson.

Lévi-Strauss, C. 1964. *Mythologiques.* Paris: Plon.

Lewis-Williams, J. D. 2002. *A Cosmos in Stone.* Walnut Creek, CA: Altamira Press.

Lewis-Williams, D. & Challis, S. 2011. *Deciphering Ancient Minds. The Mystery of San Bushman Rock Art,* London: Thames and Hudson.

Lewis-Williams, D. J. & Dowson, T. A. 1988. The signs of all times: entoptic phenomena in Upper Palaeolithic art. *Current Anthropology,* 29(2), 201–245.

Lewis-Williams, J. D. & Dowson, T. A. 1990. Palaeolithic art and the neuropsychological model. *Current Anthropology* 31, 407–408.

Mannermaa K., 2008. The archaeology of wings. Birds and people in the Baltic Sea region during the Stone Age. Unpublished dissertation. Helsinki: Gummerus kirjapaino.

Merlin, M. D., 2003, Archaeological evidence for the tradition of Psychoactive plant use in the Old World. *Economic Botany* 57(3), 295–323.

Nash, G. H., 2017. Shamanism as a product of modernity: The archaeology of the Ecstasy [MDMA] culture of the late 20th century. In D. Gheorghiu, E. Pasztor, H. Bender & G. H. Nash (eds) *Archaeological Approaches to Shamanism: Mind-body, Nature & Culture.* Newcastle-upon-Tyne: Cambridge Scholarly Publishing, 116–131.

Nash, G. & Chippindale, C. 2002. *European Landscapes of Rock-Art.* London and New York: Routledge.

Okladnikov, A. P. 1972. *Der Hirsch mit dem goldenen Geweih. Vorgeschichtliche Velsbilder Sibiriens.* Wiesbaden: Brockhaus.

Okladnikov, A. P. & Martinov, A. I. 1972. *The Richness of Rock Carvings in Tomsk region* (in Russian). Moskow: Iskustvo.

Pásztor, E., 2011. Prehistoric sky lore and spirituality. In D. Gheorghiu (ed.) *Archaeology Experimenting Spirituality?* Newcastle-upon-Tyne: Cambridge Scholars Publishing, 89–117.

Patrushev, V. 2000. *The Early History of the Finno-Ugric Peoples of European Russia.* Studia Archaeologica Finno-Ugrica 1. Oulu: Societas historiae Fenno-Ugricae, 124 & 170.

Price, N. (ed.). 2001. *Archaeology of Shamanism.* Routledge: London.

Reymann, A. 2015. *Das religions-ethnologische Konzept des Schamanen in der prähistorischen Archäologie.* Frankfurter Archäologische Schriften/Frankfurter Archaeological Studies 28. Bonn: Habelt.
Rozwadowski, A. 2001. From semiotics to phenomenology: Central Asian petrogliphs and the Indo-Iranian mythology. In K. Helskog (ed.) *Theoretical Perspectives on Rock Art Research.* Oslo: Novus Press, 155–174.
Rozwadowski, A. 2017. *Rocks, Cracks and Drums. In Search of Ancient Shamanism in Siberia and Central Asia.* Budapest: Molnar & Kelemen Oriental Publishers.
Schwerin von Krosigk, H. G. 1992. Bemerkung zu elf Idolen des 8.– 6. Jahrhunderts v. Chr. Aus der älteren Nekropole von Achmylovo am linken Wolgaufer in Mittelrussland. *Prähistorische Zeitschrift* 67, 43–66.
Siikala, A-L. 1978. *The Rite Technique of the Siberian Shaman.* Helsinki: Suomalainen tiedeakatemia, FF Communications 220.
Tilley, C. 1994. *A Phenomenology of Landscape: Places, Paths and Monuments.* Oxford: Berg.
Tilley, C. 2005. *The Materiality of Stone: Explorations in Landscape Phenomenology.* London: Berg.
Viveiros de Castro, E. 2005. From multiculturalism to multiculturalism. In O. Malik & J-C. Eoyoux (eds) *Cosmograms*, New York: Lukes and Sternberg, 136–156.
Whitley, D. 1998. Cognitive neuroscience, shamanism and the rock art of Native California. *Anthropology of Consciousness* 9, 22–37. Doi: 10.1525/ac.1998.9.1.22.
Winkelman, M. 1989. Shamanism and altered states of consciousness: An introduction, *Journal of Psychoactive Drugs*, 159–180.
Winkelman, M. 2002. Shamanism and cognitive evolution. *Cambridge Archaeological Journal* 12(1), 71–101.
Winkelman, M. 2006. Shamanism and biological origins of religiosity. *Shaman* 14(1–2), 89–116.
Zola, L. 2017. The making and unmaking of a sacred place: A case-study in the Sakha Republic (Yakutia). *Shaman* 25(1–2), 181–196.

Chapter 1

The Horse as a Shamanic Landscape Device: The Distribution of *Equus* on Upper Palaeolithic Open-Air Rock Art Sites of the Iberian Peninsula

George Nash and Sara Garcês

Abstract *Throughout early prehistory the horse is featured in rock art, none more so than within the steep-sided valleys of the western Iberian Peninsula. The engravings are of a generic style, found within a limited number of locations across central and northern Portugal, in particular, along the major river systems of the Côa, Douro, Zêzere, and Tagus. Based on fieldwork between 2010 and 2014 a geoprospection team from ITM, Mação, central Portugal explored one particular river valley – the Ocreza.*

Within a 450 m section of the river was small but significant assemblage of engravings that were found to date from the Upper Palaeolithic to the Bronze Age. Among this assemblage is the now famous Upper Palaeolithic Ocreza horse. The location of this and other engraved horses throughout this part of south-western Europe appears to be a deliberate act.

In this chapter, we suggest that the horse would have acted as a metaphor for various elements of this sometimes dangerous and rugged landscape. Here, the artist would have been concerned with the complex world of ritual and symbolism of the horse and what its relationship with the hunter-gatherers groups. Special people, possibly with shamanistic tendencies would have mediated between the rock on which the horse is engraved, the horse and the audience, thus providing a direct association between the landscape and the community.

Introduction: Contextual Considerations

Within the Upper Palaeolithic rock art record of the western Iberian Peninsula (including Portugal) the engraved horse is featured most prominently, in particular along the major river systems and its tributaries of the Côa, Douro, Zêzere, and Tagus Rivers. Fieldwork and desk-based GIS research by the authors suggest that the location of horse engravings from this period was an intentional act; artists appear to be concerned with certain landscape elements and the prominence of each engraving. Moreover, the horse appears to act as a metaphor for various elements of the landscape, suggesting maleness, potency and untamed wildness. The artists/storyteller concerned would have been bound-up in a complex world of ritual, symbolic behaviour, probably extracting the magic and potency of the horse from the rocks on which they were engraved upon. Here, special people within the community, possibly shamans would have been the mediators between the rock, the image and the audience (e.g. Bradley 2009).

The Upper Ocreza Valley, or what we term the Ocreza Valley Catchment (OVC), is located within a kilometre of the confluence of the Ocreza/Tagus Rivers in Central Portugal. This section of the valley, extending *c.* 450 m, comprises a steep-sided V-shaped terrain constructed from exposed jagged schist rocks and loose boulders, covered by a veneer of parent-rock related soils. It is within this landscape that five authenticated rock art panels stand (referenced as Nos. OCR001 to OCR005). In the summer of 2014 a team from ITM (Mação) discovered a further three panels; however, these have yet to be traced and fully analysed.

During the winter months, the water of the Ocreza River forms a series of powerful rapids.[1] It is at these points that strategically-placed prehistoric engraved rock art is located (Fig. 1.1). During summer months, the Ocreza waters usually form stagnant rock pools and the rock art arguably becomes redundant, potentially losing its potency; this redundancy is assisted by an abundance of vegetation and the overhead sunlight which makes viewing the rock art difficult. The engraving assemblage of the five sites includes cervids, a horse and abstract designs; the date range is between the Upper Palaeolithic and the Bronze Age. The horse engraving is probably Upper Palaeolithic and is one of a small number of panels of this type within the western Iberian Peninsula. Ironically, the first discoveries of open-air Palaeolithic rock art made in Iberian Peninsula included single representations of the horse; however, because of their scarcity, the archaeological community did not consider them as genuine.

The horse, along with other megafauna has been the focus of a number of in-depth Pleistocene-and Holocene-based studies, including that of Leroi-Gourhan (1965), Stuart (1977; 1982) and Kaagan (2000). Based on archaeological evidence, the horse is one of four megafauna within this region of Europe that dominate the rock art narrative; others include cervids, wild bovines and caprids. Throughout prehistory the horse has arguably become a potent symbol, possibly representing hunting magic, maleness, warriorship and wildness. Engraved and painted horses feature extensively within Western European Upper Palaeolithic cave and open-air art. Until relatively recently, such a tradition was largely absent from the Iberian Peninsula. However, during the later part of the 20th century significant open-air rock art was discovered in north-eastern Portugal (Rebanda, 1995). Until these discoveries were made, the horse representation was mainly confined to the caves of south-western France and northern Spain, although several engravings were known of but were not considered important. For example, in 1981 in the Mazouco parish (Freixo-de-Espada-à-Cinta council) in north-east Portugal, a set of figures (three horses) was discovered that

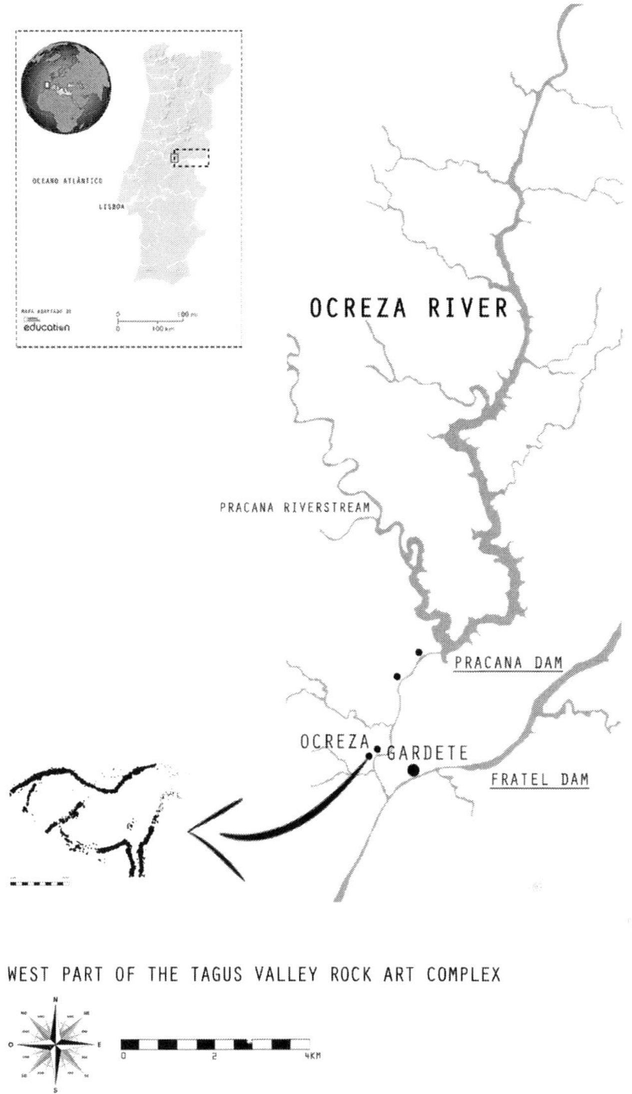

Fig. 1.1: Location map of the rock carvings in Ocreza River (Sara Garcês)

were believed to be very similar to those that are usually found in the deepest recesses of European caves. Soon after the Mazouco discovery, there were other discoveries that hinted of the importance of open-air Palaeolithic rock art such as those found at the rock of Fornols-Haut (in Campôme, French Pyrenees). Accompanying horses were many Upper Palaeolithic filiform engravings (Sacchi, 1993). The much larger site of Domingo Garcia (in Segovia, Spain) contained 155 figures that included horse, deer and wild goats (ibex) that dated from the late Solutrean (*c*. 18,000 BP) until the Magdalenian periods (17,000–12,000 BP) (Lucas Pellicer, 1974; Ripoll López & Municio

Fig. 1.2: The Przewalski horse in present day Mongolia (Image: G. H. Nash)

Gonzalez, 1992). From the same region is the Piedras Blancas Palaeolithic horse from Andalusia, Spain. This engraving was chronologically characterised as belonging to the late Gravettian or Solutrean (date range: 20,000–17,000 BP) (Martínez-García, 1986–1987; 1992).

Probably one of the most important discoveries was made in 1989 at the Upper Palaeolithic open-air site of Siega Vierde (in Ciudad Rodrigo, Spain) (Balbín Behrmann *et al.* 1991). This site, along with other open-air panels within the Iberian Peninsula, is located close to the foreshore of the River Águeda (rather than inside a cave or rock shelter).

During the Upper Palaeolithic, the horse was an essential economic resource and, based on parietal cave art, there is clear evidence of the horse being incorporated into a number of hunting scenes. Horses painted on several frescos at Lascaux for instance show clear evidence of arrows embedded into the rear and underbelly of each animal. In terms of identifying specific species, Bahn and Vertut (1988, 120) suggest that only physiological evidence, i.e. studying the faunal remains is the only reliable technique. For many years scholars attempted to classify different breeds of horse using rock art. The anatomical structure of the Ocreza horse (and Mazouco horse) is similar to other engraved horses within this region of Europe; having similar anatomical attributes to the endangered Przewalski horses (*Equus ferus prizewalski*) that currently roam the steppes of Central Asia, albeit in limited numbers (Fig. 1.2). Plaquettes from Gönnerdorf in Germany and the recent plaquette discoveries in the Sabor Valley in northern Portugal suggest that the horse, along with cervids and bovines was one of the dominant species within portable art. The horse representations in the Côa Valley in north-east Portugal account for around 30% of the total number of engraved figures present and a small number of them may possess simple harnesses suggesting some form of limited control or even domestication; however, the presence of harness gear may also imply a later date (Bednarik pers. comm.). The form [shape], proportions and size of the horses from the Côa Valley vary considerably though, suggesting that many different artists were applying their own style (and maybe over a long period of time). Unique to this area of Portugal is the probable stylistic expression of movement associated with horse figures, whereby the artist has engraved two heads onto one torso (Baptista 2009). Movement is one of the most intriguing characteristics of the Côa Palaeolithic rock art, which was also noticed on the first discoveries (Baptista & Gomes 1995; Zilhão *et al.* 1997; Zilhão 1997).

The Ocreza Horse

Similar to other engraved horses in an open-air context, the Ocreza figure is a small equine, engraved on a smooth angled-surface that forms part of a large schist outcrop. The outcrop continues along many hundreds of metres, towering over the banks of the river. The figure is considered headless by several researchers (e.g., Baptista 2001); however Gomes (2010) and the authors of this paper suggest that there are very faint pecked lines that form the upper and lower extremes of the head. The figure is oriented northwards towards the upper section of the river. Determining sex is problematic, although Baptista (2001) considers the figure to be female. The figure is engraved in profile, displaying at least two upper leg sections that are engaged in a running stance. As well as missing sections of the head, only one hoof is displayed; the rear lower section of a leg is missing, probably damaged via natural erosion. The line of the underbelly is very pronounced, being semi-circular in form and representing a possibly pregnant female. The cervical-dorsal line and tail form a single continuous line, typical of many horse depictions within the Upper Palaeolithic world such as those in the Côa Valley. In essence, the morphology of the Ocreza horse is not untypical of horses found elsewhere (Baptista 2001).

History of the Discovery

The Ocreza horse engraving [OCR04], along with four other panels of later prehistoric date stand approximately 1.1 km north of the Tagus River. The first rock art discoveries were made in 1973, with the Ocreza horse being finally discovered in September 2000 by António Martinho Baptista and the CNART[2] team who officially referred to it as Rock No. 21 (Baptista 2001).

Other panels within this section of the Ocreza Valley included a single engraved spiral [OCR02] (Fig. 1.3), a complete and part-cervid, probably red deer [OCR03][3] (Fig. 1.4), a herd of cervids, probably red deer [OCR05] (Fig. 1.5) and two stylised

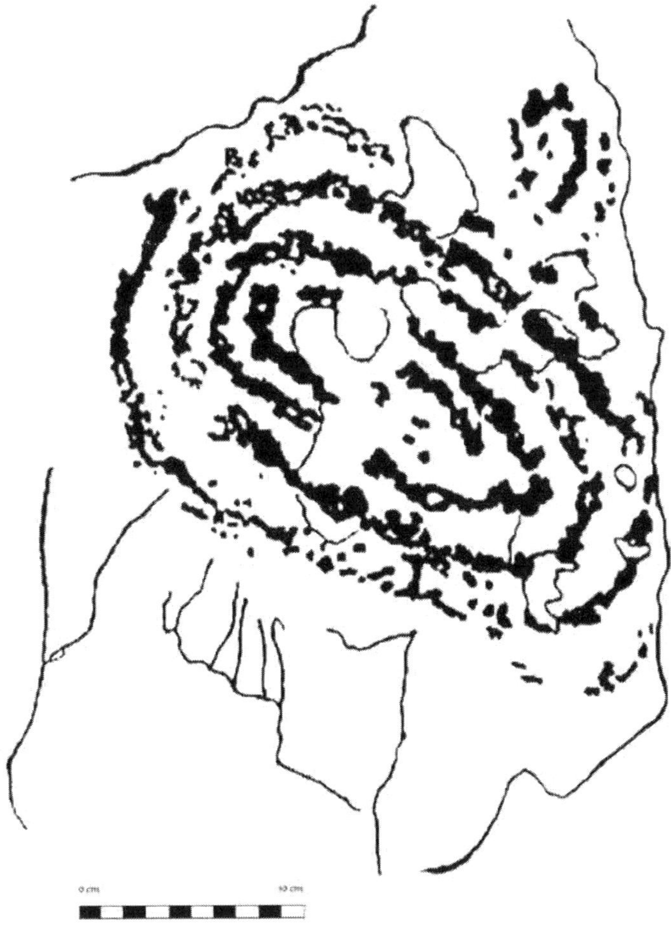

Fig. 1.3: Rock of the spiral (Mação Museum)

anthropomorphic figures [OCR01] (Fig. 1.6), (Garcês 2009; Garcês & Oosterbeek 2009). The engravings were discovered in advance of a road scheme, which included the construction of a bridge that spanned over the Ocreza River, although these may have been known of previously by locals, but were never reported. At this time, the discovery of the Ocreza horse was regarded as the first Upper Palaeolithic pecked figure to be found within this region (Bahn 2000, 753). Since the initial discoveries, student teams from the Prehistoric Rock Art Museum in Mação have investigated the area.

Conception and Method

Based on previously published material, the Ocreza horse has been recorded a number of times using a variety of methods (Baptista 2001; Oosterbeek 2003; Nash

Fig. 1.4: Rock of red-deer (Mação Museum)

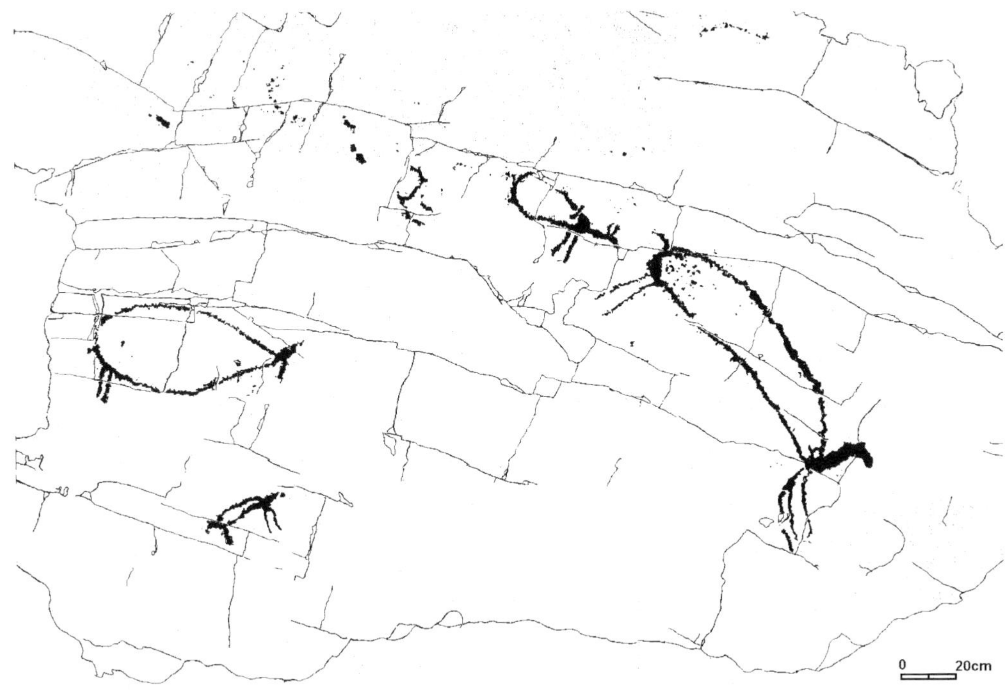

Fig. 1.5: Rock of the cervid (Mação Museum)

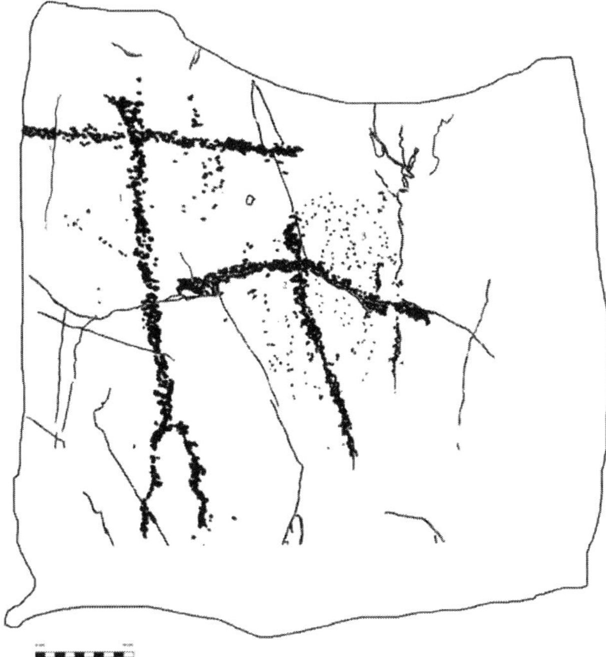

Fig. 1.6: Rock of the anthropomorphic figures (Mação Museum)

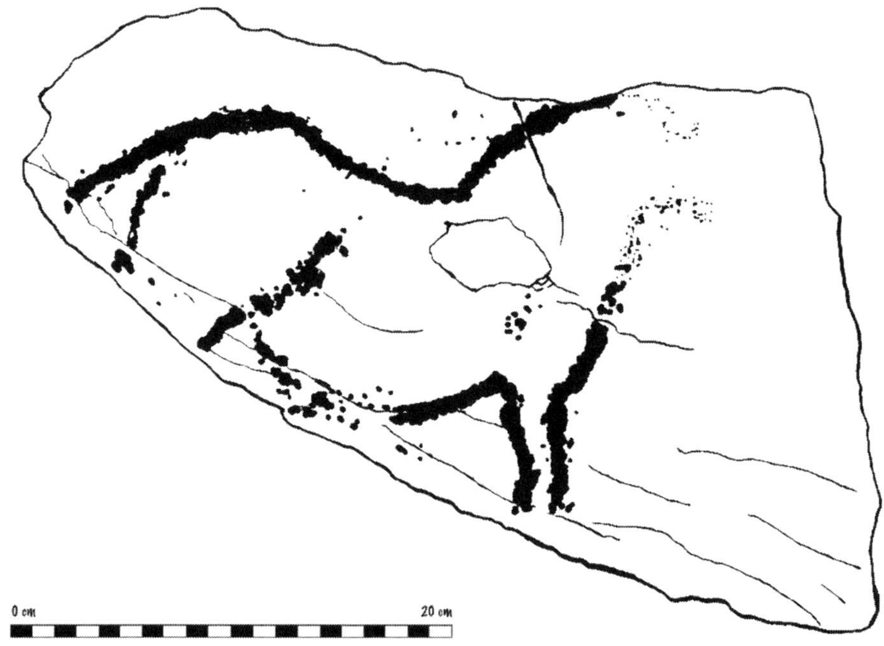

Fig. 1.7: The Ocreza horse engraving recorded by Nash & Garcês in 2013 (Mação Museum)

& Garcês – this volume).[4] For this exercise we decided to trace the image using both oblique and natural lighting in order to tease-out the ephemeral sections of the engraving, especially the area around the head and neck (Figs 1.7 and 1.8). In order to accurately trace the horse we assessed the canvas surface (the panel); scholars working within this narrow field will be aware that several other single horses exist within central and northern Portugal and there could be similarities in the way these figures are applied. Based on the body language of these individuals, we could make reasonably accurate assumptions on the body parts either missing from the panel or too faint to record (such as the head and neck areas). In addition to understanding panel behaviour, we also considered the landscape position of the Ocreza horse and realised that this has similarities with other other engraved Upper Palaeolithic horse sites.

The engraved horse panel at Mazouco, located 280 km north of Ocreza, is probably the nearest parallel to the Ocreza horse. The panel comprises a single horse which is within a few metres from water – the Douro River and the confluence of a tributary (Ribeira da Albagueira).[5] The horse, which is engraved onto a vertical schist panel was discovered in 1981 (Jorge *et al.* 1981) and was, at that time, the first verified Upper Palaeolithic open-air rock art in Portugal. Above and to the side of the horse, are the faint engravings of several incomplete zoomorphic figures, probably horses too. The Mazouco horse, measuring *c.* 0.62 m in length is similar to others found within the Franco-Cantabrian region and can thus be described as cartoonesque with its

Fig. 1.8: Digital image of the Ocreza horse engraving and the landscape beyond (Nash & Garcês 2013)

Fig. 1.9: The Mazouco horse located on the Douro River (Baptista 2009)

disproportionate bulky body, thick mane and short legs (Fig. 1.9). Although this horse has been clearly pecked during archaic times, probably Gravettian or Solutrean in date, a large section of the horse's outline has been enhanced in recent times using a metal instrument; however, this enhancement should not detract from the importance of the original engraving.

The Ocreza image and the Mazouco horse are located in similar landscape positions – i.e. standing close to water and within the zone of jagged rocks in a steep-sided V-shaped valley. Due to the construction of a number of dams along the Douro during the 20th century, the current water level is considerably higher than during Upper Palaeolithic times. Likewise, a similar scenario exists for the Ocreza horse whereby damming upstream on the Ocreza River has radically altered the water levels in recent times.

Significance of Location

Anthropologist Christopher Tilley, among other scholars, has applied geographic and philosophical approaches to understanding prehistoric landscapes. In *A Phenomenology of Landscape* (1994) and, later, *The Materiality of Stone* (2005), Tilley deconstructs landscape using phenomenological perspectives developed by Husserl and Merleau-Ponty. Using prehistoric monuments, Tilley experiences grammar classification and uses (his) knowledge to deconstruct landscape. This knowledge may be accumulated as Tilley (or anyone else) moves through a landscape and experiences the way monuments are distributed. Familiarisation with a landscape inevitably creates a pattern of behaviour, especially when processing to and from, and viewing monuments/sites. Predictability arises partly from the manner in which people understand and perceive the world and the things that operate within it. Within this world, phenomenology assists in describing the conceptual processes and structures that control and manipulate our world. However, these processes are governed by experience and intentionality. The intentionality involved in replicating place location and in deciding whether it should be intervisible with another, is unclear. Of course, we cannot replicate the ancient mindset with any degree of certainty, although, in structuralist and post-structuralist terms, the same universal rules can apply to both the ancient and modern mindset. Within the factional world of semiotics, different schools apply different approaches when trying to make sense of the world in which we live. Arguably, semiotics analyses the process of communication; the conveying of meaning in one form or another to different social agencies. Language is generally taken to be the foremost of all human semiotic systems (Jakobson 1990, 455) but semiotics is broadly concerned with 'everything that can be taken as a sign' (Eco 1976, 7). Indeed, most communication is non-verbal and although primarily based on sight and hearing can involve all the senses. Architecture, furniture, the wearing of clothes, cooking, music, gesture, indeed all non-verbal dimensions of social culture incorporate encoded information in a manner analogous to verbal language (Leach 1976, 10). Sign systems are fundamental to the way in which we live our daily lives: when dealing with neighbours, for example, or working with groups of people, the rhetoric of signs is paramount in order to access where one stands within the world.

Theoretically, turning a space into a place involves a number of elements and the schist panel on which the Ocreza horse is engraved is no exception to this rule. Although we can never fully understand the reasons why such an engraving should be located where it is, one can surmise a number of possibilities that include:

- Engravings become an important focal point through an event or multiple events;
- Engravings are used as mechanisms to evoke memory (i.e. using a place over many occasions);
- Engravings act as a device for transmitting a story and story-telling (i.e. creating a narrative for the site); and
- Engravings becoming engrained into ancestry as a myth and memory that were retold and elaborated upon through shamanistic practices.

Through these factors *place* becomes special and its attributes embedded in time and memory (Clottes 2013). Sometimes the original story becomes diluted and even forgotten, resulting in new additions to the original narrative. The Ocreza horse, however, is the only motif present on the panel and therefore one must assume that its physical presence and meaning must have remained over many generations of community.[6] When initially commissioned and executed, the Ocreza horse would have created a new focal point within an otherwise busy and chaotic landscape. The jagged rock outcropping, extending along the length of the valley would have been a continuous geological form; one rock resembling another. Following the choosing of a suitable surface to engrave a horse, the rock, the site and the place would have created new experiences and scenarios. Over time, the engraved horse may have become embedded into local history, used as a mnemonic device for folklore/story-telling and relayed by story-tellers to an engrossed audience.

The ruggedness of the landscape and the sometimes harsh nature of the seasonal climate may have provided a temperamental backdrop for early communities to revere this enclosed and sometimes dangerous landscape. Within this pastiche of rock art and rock outcropping, hunter-gatherers may have used the Ocreza horse over many generations as a known marker with this landscape. Each of these generations would have told stories about the horse, often elaborating on certain elements of the story. Over time, the story would have probably changed considerably. However, according to Lévi-Strauss (1964; 1973) the formulaic would have remained the same (e.g. good against evil; weak and helpless individuals triumphing over the strong and powerful etc.). This progressive set of predictable histories could have been both personal and collective; each event becoming a focus for memory and being transmitted through a number of authoritative media including poetry, chanting and oral tradition; each time the story would have constituted a memorable event. Events (or the memories of events) may also have been relayed through ideological or physical change such as changes to the form of the river, including flood and drought events, each event gaining a mnemonic momentum over time, eventually evoking a power of place for the horse.

Lévi-Strauss's *From Honey to Ashes* (1973) emphasises the intricate web of plots and sub-plots within a series of myths and narratives that show animals, humans and things transforming and metamorphosing. Many of the South American myths recognised by Lévi-Strauss involve human figures that become supernatural beings and in the same stories animals transform into other animals, humans and objects. The audience, listening to these stories, would have needed knowledge of how the mundane and supernatural worlds interacted and behaved. Usually, this knowledge would be organised through a universal set of rules, or what Lévi-Strauss would term as structures. Many of these structures which are arguably present within the modern world and as yet uncorrupted within contemporary non-western tribal societies, are entrenched and rely on a rich ancestral past (Nash 2008; Nash *et al.* 2016).

Shamanistic Concepts to Landscape

A landscape composed of physical features such as mountains, rivers, streams, spurs and woodland can be perceived in different ways by different people; no two individuals can completely agree on what a landscape represents or means (Children & Nash 1997, 1). Landscape is thus constructed, controlled and manipulated by the individual rather than as a bilateral state of mind, although in general terms encoding at a base-level is universally recognised. The grammar of landscape is reliant on human interaction, in particular the ancestral geography and the experience that landscape brings to the individual. According to Lévi-Strauss (1963), the natural environment, as interpreted by the human mind, is bound-up in memory and myth. Depending on the shape and texture, rock outcropping can metamorphose into beasts, humans and inanimate objects and create intricate stories of a world before the present. This recipe of myths, story-telling and landscape would have been a fertile ground for shamanistic practices whereby the artist performing as a shaman would have relayed the stories from the rocks to the audience; he or she being the mediator between the rock on which the engraving is made and the audience (Clottes pers. comm.).

In many stories of the Australian Aboriginal 'dreamtime', such features have a direct relationship with the artist/story-teller. The pictorial narratives, which have been told over many generations and elaborated upon, would have involved animals, many spaces, landscapes and landscape forms; such as the dreamtime stories that involve, say, the crocodile and its living space and ancestral home, the river or the kangaroo and the *bush* (e.g. Morphy 1989; Reed 1965). The division of landscape establishes conceptual maps that specify areas that are public, private and taboo space; with the latter that should not be entered. The anthropological and ethnographic evidence for such categorisation is abundant but identifying this process in the archaeological record is far more problematic, what Taçon and Chippindale (1998) term as formal methods (i.e. the relationship lost between artist/story-teller and chronicler). One can therefore consider a possible link between the panel, the artistic endeavour, the artist/story-teller, the location of the panel and the surrounding landscape; all appear to be inextricably linked.

In terms of landscape position, the Ocreza horse is the only Upper Palaeolithic engraving to be recorded so far within the Ocreza Valley. The site is located between two significant 90° bends in the river. Located close to the eastern bend is OCR01 (two stylised anthropomorphic figures), whilst on the northern bank on the western bend is panel OCR05 (a herd of cervids); both panels are considered to be late prehistoric in date (probably Bronze Age) (Oosterbeek *et al.* 2012). This portion of the Ocreza Valley and the short section that connects the Ocreza with Tagus River comprise steep-sided slopes; the lower section of which is constructed of smooth rock outcropping that form the bed and banks of the river. Above this are three further zones of topography, several relating to direct and visible human agency. Immediately above river-line are a series of jagged rocks, generically described as schist outcropping; it is within this zone that all rock art is located. The rock outcropping extends the length of the Ocreza River, from the recently-constructed bridge to the confluence with the Tagus River. Intermittently dispersed between the smooth water-eroded rocks and the jagged schist are a number of small pebble-beaches, the result of water-lain transport deposition. These beaches are usually located on the bends and meanders of the river and are active and dynamic; depositing and redepositing material usually during seasonal water flow. During the summer months, the river dries up and the water flow is restricted between semi-stagnant rock pools. It is during this time that the river bed is fully exposed and is prone to algae infestation; from the banks one witnesses a green film extending across the river bed and banks along the course of the river. Above the jagged rocks are a further two topographical zones, natural earthen slopes that are intermittently interrupted with extensive rock outcropping and above this are the remnants of agricultural terracing, the result of human agency. The terracing was constructed probably during medieval and recent historical times and is used for the cultivation of olive trees and viticulture (very common within this region of Portugal). The lower terracing appears around *c.* 30 m above the course of the river. Based on limited archaeological prospection, no rock art has been found within this zone, even though it extends the entire length of the valley.

Although the summer months restrict the continuous flow of water to the Tagus River, the winter months witness a very different scenario where great quantities of water flow through the valley; sometimes the water levels exceed average seasonal water levels, rising to within a few metres of the Ocreza horse engraving (Figs 1.10 & 1.11). During normal seasonal winter water flow, a number of rapids are formed, usually the result of water velocity in relation to the underlying river bed and the rock outcropping and those boulders that sit within the middle of the river. Visually, the rapids create white [oxygenated] water. The water flow and the soundscape it creates form a dramatic backdrop for the rock art.

Interestingly, the rock art sites appear to be located where the rapids are formed. Based on this simple observation, one can make a number of poignant statements for both the horse and the water rapids that are philosophically similar. For example, both the horse and the rapids arguably represent potency and wildness; attributes that have already been identified by Hodder (1990) and Tilley (1994). In terms of the concepts of potency and wildness, Hodder considers these to be linked to maleness, whilst Tilley, in discussing the location of certain Neolithic stone chambered monuments, argues that the soundscape of the rapids was an important factor in monument location. Although the two examples are used for different chronologies and geographical contexts, the general themes expressed by Hodder and Tilley do hold validity; however, we must be cautious – what we witness through the mindset of 21st century archaeologists may not in fact be representative of the mindset of a prehistoric artist/story-teller.

The Horse as a Symbol of Sacred Geography

One can consider that 'things' derived of human agency constitute a place (however large or small). Place can be represented in a number of ways, sometimes as a physical entity or sometimes as a cognitive [mnemonic] process based on an event or series of events. When considering rock art – the place may have acted as a marker, creating a series of signatures across an otherwise wild and inaccessible landscape. The concept is not new and has been widely applied to rock art and other prehistoric sites elsewhere (Bradley 1998; 2000; 2009; Devereux & Wozencroft 2014). It is probable that the prehistoric mindset had fixed within the Ocreza landscape a series of markers

Figs 1.10 and 1.11: Two moods of Ocreza: one passive, the other angry (Images: Nash & Garcês)

that related to prominent visual features such as certain rock outcropping and/or noticeable audible points within the valley where the seasonal rapids emerge. One can consider therefore that the narrative of the art contains a number of metaphors that associated the image with the surrounding landscape.

In terms of a semiotic grammar, both the horse and the river can be considered as one entity, bound by the notion of untamed wildness and uncontrollable energy. This concept can arguably be tamed and controlled if the artist engraves; the panel, the place itself being the focus and not the chaos of the surrounding landscape. Lévi-Strauss (1963) promoted this concept using structuralist principles that included binary association and opposition as an inherent force within society. Simple associations/oppositions can include left/right, light/dark and so on. Using these principles for the Ocreza horse, one can consider the following binary associations:

- The natural river – the natural horse
- The untamed river – the untamed horse
- Potency – the velocity of the river – potency of the horse
- The movement of the river – the movement of the horse

The Ocreza horse, similar to many other engraved wild animals is static, even though it and others are engraved in a running stance. However, the horse's running stance may have an association with the water flow of the Ocreza; this is despite the fact that the Ocreza water flows west and the horse appears to be running in the opposite direction. The potency of both is lost when one considers the seasonal flow of the river, especially during the summer months. Although the Ocreza River is now controlled upstream by damming, during Palaeolithic times the river would have seasonally ebbed and flowed; its seasonality and accessibility may have drawn individuals and communities to visit this site and witness the animation of a horse running against the seasonal flow of the river.

Concluding Remarks

The Ocreza horse can be considered a significant Upper Palaeolithic engraving that has, and will contribute widely to the debate of the spread of hunter-gatherer communities within this part of the Iberian Peninsula. Since its discovery, significant Upper Palaeolithic rock art has been found along many of the major river systems and tributaries of central and eastern Portugal (usually as a result of geo-prospection in advance of hydro-electric schemes such as the recent dam project within the Sabor Valley).

Based on our long-term research programme, the Ocreza horse figure and other panels within the Ocreza Valley probably represent a small percentage of what was originally engraved. The horse, one of the four dominant species within central and northern Portugal would have been a potent symbol for hunter-gatherer communities using the Ocreza Valley. Its stance (pose) and style appears to be an indicative design used throughout many regions of Western Europe during this time. However, despite the generic style of horse engravings *per se* the Ocreza horse does possess certain idiosyncratic differences suggesting a personalisation of the image, indicating individual/group identity (and ownership). Part of this personalisation is the missing attributes of the horse including arguably the lower leg sections and the head.[7] Based on the anthropological and ethnographic records (e.g. Keyser 2013; Loubser 2013) and according to Clottes (2013) there may have been a direct spiritual link between the rock, the image and the artist; the artist being the mediator between the spiritual entities of the rock and the audience, a practice widely used, according to ethnographers by shamans (Keyser 1992; Price 2001).

The survival of such an important engraving, even during historical times when the valley was intensely used for viticulture, suggests that the Ocreza horse was a mnemonic device, which would have been revered and respected by generations of community; its image probably evoking many stories among the prehistoric and historic settlers within this secluded valley.

Acknowledgements

First, the authors would like to thank Dr Fernando Coimbra for invaluable comments on this paper. All mistakes are of course our responsibility. Sara Garcês benefited from a FCT PhD. individual scholarship under QREN – POPH – Typology 4.1. – Advanced Training, subsidized by the European Social Fund and by national MEC funds (SFRH/BD/69625/2010). Professor George Nash benefited from a travel grant awarded from the Tilley Foundation.

Notes

1 The Ocreza River is dammed further up stream and waterflow can vary during the summer months as well.
2 Centro Nacional de Arte Rupestre, Portugal
3 Rear section only
4 The horse was traced by the Mação Museum team in 2007, along with several other panels within this section of the valley.
5 Located in Mazouco parish, within the Municipality of Freixo de Espada-à-Cinta
6 There are several sections of the Ocreza panel missing, presumably the result of natural weathering.
7 The head may have eroded away.

References

Bahn, P. G. 2000. New rock-art find in Portugal. *Antiquity* 74, 753–754.

Bahn, P. G. & Vertut, J. 1988. *Images of the Ice Age*. London: Winwood Press.

Balbín Behrmann, R., Alcolea González, J., Santonja, M. & Pérez Martín, R. 1991. Yacimiento artístico paleolítico al aire libre. In *Del Paleolítico a la Historia*. Salamanca: Museo De Salamanca, 33–48.

Baptista, A. M. 2001. Ocreza (Envendos, Mação, Portugal Central): Um novo sítio com arte Paleolítica de ar Livre. In A. R. Cruz & L. Oosterbeek (eds), *Territórios, Mobilidade E Povoamento No Alto-Ribatejo.*

II: Santa Cita E O Quaternário da Região, Tomar. Perspectivas Em Diálogo. Arkeos 11. Tomar: Ceiphar, 163–192.

Baptista, A. M. 2009. *O Paradigma Perdido. O Vale Do Côa E A Arte Paleolítica de Ar Livre Em Portugal.* Parque Arqueológico Do Côa: Edições Afrontamento.

Baptista, A. M. & Gomes, M. V. 1995. Arte rupestre do Vale Do Côa. 1. Canada Do Inferno. Primeiras Impressões. In: *1º Congresso De Arqueologia Peninsular, Porto, Faculdade de Letras do Porto.* Trabalhos De Antropologia e Etnologia 35, 349–385.

Bradley, R. 1998. *The Significance of Monuments: on the Shaping of Human Experience in Neolithic and Bronze Age Europe.* London: Routledge.

Bradley, R. 2000. *An Archaeology of Natural Places.* London: Routledge.

Bradley, R. 2009. *Art and Audience: Rethinking Prehistoric Art.* Oxford: Oxford University Press.

Children, G. & Nash, G. H., 1997. Establishing a discourse: The language of landscape. In G. H. Nash (ed.), *Semiotics of Landscape: Archaeology of Mind.* Oxford: Archaeopress. British Archaeological Report S661, , 1–4.

Clottes, J. 2013. Why did they draw in those caves? *Time & Mind* 6(1), 7–14.

Devereux, P. & Wozencroft, J. 2014. Stone Age eyes and ears: a visual and acoustic pilot study of Carn Menyn and the environs of Preseli, Wales. *Time & Mind* 7(1), 47–70.

Eco, U. 1976. *A Theory of Semiotics.* Bloomington IN: Indiana University Press/London: Macmillan.

Garcês, S. 2009. *Cervídeos. Na Arte Rupestre do Vale do Tejo: Contributo Para O Estudo Da Pré-História Recente.* Dissertação De Mestrado Em Arqueologia Pré-Histórica E Arte Rupestre [Policopiado]. Instituto Politécnico de Tomar/Universidade de Trás-os-Montes e Alto Douro.

Garcês, S. & Oosterbeek, L. 2009. Cervídeos Na Arte Rupestre Do Vale Do Tejo. Contributo Para O Estudo da Pré-História Recente. *Zahara* 14, 90–94.

Gomes, M. V. 2010. *Arte Rupestre Vale Do Tejo. Um Ciclo Artístico-Cultural Pré E Proto Histórico. Dissertação De Doutoramento Em História, Especialidade Em Arqueologia.* Faculdade De Ciências Sociais E Humanas: Universidade Nova De Lisboa.

Hodder, I. 1990. *The Domestication of Europe.* London: Blackwell.

Jakobson, R. 1990. Linguistics in relation to other sciences. In L. R. Waugh & M. Monville-Burston (eds), *On Language.* Cambridge MA: Harvard University Press, 451–488.

Jorge, S. O., Jorge, V. O., Almeida, C. A. F., Sanches, M. J. & Soeiro, T. 1981. Gravuras rupestres de Mazouco (Freixo De Espada À Cinta). *Arqueologia* 3, 3–12.

Kaagan, L. M. 2000. The Horse in Late Pleistocene and Holocene Britain. Unpublished Ph.D. London: Department of Biology, University College.

Keyser, J. D. 1992. *Indian Rock Art of the Columbia Plateau.* Seattle, WA: Douglas & McIntyre.

Keyser, J. D. 2013. Giving voice to the past: Developing the Plains Biographic Rock Art Lexicon. *Time & Mind* 6(1), 97–104.

Leach, E. 1976. *Culture and Communication: an Introduction to the Use of Structuralist Analysis in Social Anthropology.* Cambridge: Cambridge University Press.

Leroi-Gourhan, A. 1965. *Préhistoire de L'art Occidental.* Paris: Mazenod.

Lévi-Strauss, C. 1963. *Structural Anthropology.* London: Nicholson.

Lévi-Strauss, C. 1964. *Mythologiques.* Paris: Plon.

Lévi-Strauss, C. 1973. *From Honey to Ashes: Introduction to a Science of Mythology* Volume 2. London: Jonathan Cape.

Loubser, J. 2013. A holistic and comparative approach to rock art. *Time & Mind* 6(1), 29–36.

Lucas Pellicer, M. R. 1974. *El Arte Rupestre en la Provincia De Segovia.* Madrid: Cuadernos de Prehistoria y Arqueología de la Universidad Autónoma I, 57–69.

Martínez García, J. 1986–1987. Un grabado Paleolítico al aire libre en Piedras Blancas (Escullar, Almería). *Ars Praehistorica* V–VI, 49–58.

Martínez García, J. 1992. Arte Paleolítico en Almería. Los primeros documentos. *Revista De Arqueología* 130, 24–33.

Morphy, H. (ed.). 1989. *Animals into Art*. One World Archaeology 7. London: Unwin Hyman.
Nash, G. H. 2008. *Northern European Hunter/Fisher/Gatherer and Spanish Levantine Rock-Art: A Study in Performance, Cosmology and Belief*. Trondheim: NTNU.
Nash, G. H., Farmer, R. & Rowlands, M. 2016. A rare occurrence of a bas-relief engraved horse at Old Oswestry hillfort, Oswestry, Shropshire. *Shropshire Archaeological & Historical Society* 91, 103–108.
Oosterbeek, L. (ed.). 2003. Vale do Ocreza – Campanha 2001. *Techné* 8, 41–70.
Oosterbeek, L., Collado-Giraldo, H., Garcês, S., Coimbra, F., Delfino, D. & Cura, P. 2012. Arqueologia rupestre da Bacia do Tejo: Ruptejo. In L. Oosterbeek, J. Cerezer, J. Campos & J. Zocche (eds) *Arqueologia Ibero-Americana e Arte Rupestre*. Tomar: Arkeos 32, 133–172.
Price, N. 2001. *The Archaeology of Shamanism*. London: Routledge.
Rebanda, N. 1995. *Os Trabalhos Arqueológicos E O Complexo De Arte Rupestre do Côa*. Lisbon: Instituto Português Do Património Arquitectónico E Arqueológico.
Reed, A. W. 1965. *Aboriginal Fables and Legendary Tales*. Sydney: Reed.
Ripoll López, S. & Municio Gonzalez, L. J. 1992. *Las representaciones de estilo Paleolítico en El Conjunto De Domingo García (Segovia)*. Espacio, Tiempo Y Forma, Serie I, Madrid: Prehistoria y Arqueología V, 107–138.
Sacchi, D. 1993. A rock with Palaeolithic engravings in the French Pyrenees. *International Newsletter on Rock Art* (Inora) 4, 14–15.
Stuart, A. J. 1977. The vertebrates of the last cold stage in Britain and Ireland. *Philosophical Transactions of the Royal Society of London* B 280, 295–312.
Stuart, A. J. 1982. *Pleistocene Vertebrates in the British Isles*. London: Longman.
Taçon, P. & Chippindale, C. 1998. An Archaeology of rock-art through informed methods and formal methods. In C. Chippindale & P. Taçon (eds), *The Archaeology of Rock-Art*. Cambridge: Cambridge University Press.
Tilley, C. 1994. *A Phenomenology of Landscape: Places, Paths and Monuments*. Oxford: Berg.
Tilley, C. 2005. *Materiality of Stone*. London: Berg.
Whitley, D. S. 2000. *The Art of the Shaman: Rock art of California*. Salt Lake City UT: University of Utah Press.
Zilhão, J. 1997. Súmula dos resultados científicos. In J. Zilhão (ed.) *Arte Rupestre E Pré-Histórica do Vale do Côa. Trabalhos De 1995-1996*. Lisboa: Ministério Da Cultura, 12–39.
Zilhão, J., Aubry, T., Carvalho, A. F., Baptista, A. M., Gomes, M. V. & Meireles, J. 1997. The rock art of Côa Valley (Portugal) and its archaeological context: First results of current research. *Journal of European Archaeology* 5, 7–49.

Chapter 2

Göbekli Tepe – A Shamanic Landscape

Dragoş Gheorghiu

Abstract *The pre-pottery Neolithic was a period of many cultural changes; although the world-view of the hunter-gatherer still preserved Mesolithic and Palaeolithic traits related to shamanism. At this time a monumental architecture, sometimes decorated, was employed for new forms of shamanistic performance. One intriguing example is Enclosure D from the Göbekli Tepe architectural complex. Here the iconography could be interpreted as promoting shamanistic practices in relation with the local landscape.*

Introduction

During the last decades in the vast ethnographic literature[1] one could witness increasing levels of archaeological interest in shamanism, to cite only a few of the scholars that approached it (Clottes & Lewis-Williams 1998; Frankfort & Hamayon 2001; Price 2001; Lewis-Williams & Pearce 2005; Otte 2008; Clottes 2011; Pásztor 2011; Peatfield & Morris 2012).

Despite a reticence in the generalization of the concept of 'shamanism' in prehistory (see Bahn 2001), the idea 'that most, if not all people from the Palaeolithic to the Neolithic had a religion akin to what we know ethnographically from around the world as shamanism' (Wason 2010, 283, n.6). This subject, bridging many disciplines started to be accepted by specialists, together with the increasing awareness that it could be 'the source ... of all religions' (La Barre 1980, 83; see also Anttonen 2007).

The subject of shamanism was and remains a challenge for archaeology, in that it is forever searching for 'methods for determining practices of shamanism in archaeological cultures' (Séfériades 2010; 2011; Hasanov 2016), altered states of consciousness (ASC) (Price 2001; Nash 2001; Gheorghiu 2011), or attempts to demonstrate 'the extension in time and space of the phenomenon, as well as its diversity' in both the archaeological and anthropological records (Gheorghiu *et al.* 2017).

It is the opinion of the present author that, at some point in the development of the spiritual life in prehistory, the 'shamanic' activity as mediation 'between members of his/her social group (in some cases with members of another social group) and the supernatural powers' (Hultkrantz 2007, 8), or as a construction of a cosmos (Lewis-Williams & Pearce 2005, 60ff; Lewis-Williams & Challis 2011, 159, 186) was more widespread in society, as a cognitive and social experience (as for example the today vanished shamanism of technologies, see Gheorghiu 2011), than what the ethnography of the last centuries presents. Consequently, the aim of the chapter is to discover new areas of the use of shamanism as a methodological tool for prehistory, by approaching the iconography of the Pre-Pottery Neolithic (PPN) in the Near East, where recognised shamanistic traits were intermingled with new ideologies. These traits were probably related to the landscape and assisted in defining the shamanic world-view (see Pentikäinen 1998, 61; Jordan 2001, 88), in the moment of cultural transition.

Landscape and Method

Apparently a product of modernity (Barrett 1999, 22), with few examples in the art of antiquity, landscape was employed to symbolically situate a scene (Daniels & Cosgrove 1988). But, beside these iconic representations of the natural forms, there were also other visual methods for approaching it. For example, one can speak about landscape from an indirect viewpoint, as indexical. According to Peirce (1998), one image could at the same time support an iconic, indexical and symbolical interpretation. Therefore, an image could offer simultaneously different sets of information. Such examples are scenes depicted on the Roman mosaics where the zoo-botanical data situate and explain the scenes in a landscape, thus applying an indexical mode (Gheorghiu 2015, 71).

The purpose of the chapter is to analyse the singular indexical PPN's iconography from the Göbekli Tepe site, using a semiotic approach, and to present its images as making reference to landscape and shamanism, a relationship identifiable in historical cultures (see Espinosa Arango & Andoque 1999). The iconography of the site will be discussed in broad environmental and cultural contexts of the PPN communities and in relationship with the ethnographic data that focuses on shamanism.

The Pre-Pottery Neolithic

For the hunter-gatherers from the Near East, the PPN represented a period of cultural change (Cauvin 2000; Kuijt & Goring-Morris 2002; Matthews 2003), of 'new ways of engaging with the material world' (Herva *et al.* 2014). The slow approach to sedentism (Watkins 2010; Belfer-Cohen & Goring-Morris 2011), was preceded by, and continued with the building of public edifices (also named 'cult buildings') that necessitated a complex social coordination (Dietrich *et al.* 2017, 113 ff.). In time, a new geometry (that of the right angle) would create a new spatial perception and a new architecture, different from the old ideas involving circular building plans (Özdoğan 2010).

This new concept of public monumental architecture represented, not only a 'controlled organization' (Bar-Josef 2014, 306), but an activity of [complex] socialisation (Twiss 2008, 419–426; Dietrich *et al.* 2017, 117) as well.

Göbekli Tepe is situated in the northern part of the Fertile Crescent in Upper Mesopotamia, in south-eastern Anatolia, on the plain of Haran, within the Urfa region. In terms of climate and environment, the site is in a semi-arid region bordered to the east by the Balikh/Jallab river, a tributary of the Euphrates River, and to the west by the Euphrates River. Together with Karahan Tepe and Ayanlar Höyük it represents one of the largest early PPN sites in the region (Çelik 2016, 361), situated near the Euphrates River tributaries.

The construction phases of the Göbekli Tepe site belonged to the monumental architecture of the PPN period, the site being considered to have been a centre with high cultic value (Dietrich & Notroff 2015, 87), whose formation was the result of acts of socialisation through feasting (Dietler & Herbich 1995; Hayden 2009; Dietrich *et al.* 2017, 119), and whose 'shamanic background,' as interpreted by Harald Hauptmann (2011, 98) and Klaus Schmidt (2012, 205); the views of which will be argued later in this chapter.

Due to snow melting in the spring, the volume of melt water that flows into the local rivers reaches its peak between March and May[2] (see also Ur 2009, 4). Memories about 'the unpredictability of the Tigris-Euphrates river system' floods occurring in springtime are to be found in the mythology of Mesopotamia (Fiala 2005, 431) under the form of conflicts between tribal groups mentioned in *The Epic of Ghilgamesh* (Sandars 1972, 108).

Compared with the Euphrates River (Maisels 1993, 111), the Balikh River flow is smaller. In the proximity of the Balikh Valley, in a zone rich in springs, lies the city of Urfa (or Shanliurfa), described as 'an oasis town' (Schmidt 2012, 22). In this region of hydrologic contrasts, Göbekli Tepe is situated, to cite Klaus Schmidt its excavator, 'within eyeshot' (Schmidt 2012, 19), 'at the horizon from the city of Urfa (Schmidt 2012, 22), and acted as a sort of de central ritual place (Hauptmann 2011, 105).

Iconography

The site is composed of a number of round and elliptical enclosures, many of them not yet excavated. Their walls are built from ashlar stones and T-shaped pillars, with simple and complex zoomorphic figures in bas-relief, fixed on their perimeters. In the centre of enclosures B, C and D two larger T-shaped pillars were erected (Schmidt 2012, 160, fig. 76). There appears to be craft specialisations devoted of these spaces. These may be due to: '[i]n Enclosure A snakes are the dominating species, in Enclosure B foxes are frequent, in Enclosure C boars take over this role, while Enclosure D is more varied, with birds playing an important role (Dietrich *et al.* 2017, 115). In enclosure H one pillar displays a complex scene with many terrestrial and aquatic animals (see Dietrich *et al.* 2017, 115, fig. 5.19).

The Shamanic Hypothesis: The Archaeological Evidence

As already stated, a 'shamanic background' for the ceremonies performed in the spaces mentioned was 'assumed with some certainty' by Hauptmann (2011, 98) and Schmidt (2012, 205; see also Peters & Schmidt 2004, 211–212; Kolankaya-Bostanici 2014), but without any evidence.

The existence of a PPN shamanism is supported by some archaeological data from other sites located within the neighbouring geographical region. Excavations in the southern Levant revealed a shaman presence in the Natufian (15,000–11,500 cal BP); a shaman grave discovered at Hilazon Tachtit (Grosman *et al.* 2008) exposed the 12,000 year-old skeleton of an old woman in relationship with osteological parts from a series of animals including an auroch's tail (*Bos primigenius*), two marten (*Martes foina*) skulls, tortoise (*Testudo graeca*) carapace and plastron fragments, a carpometacarpus and first phalanx of digit II of a golden eagle (*Aquila chrysaetos*), as well as the radius and ulna of a wild boar (*Sus scrofa*) (Grosman *et al.* 2008, 17667, fig. 5). It is worth noting here the rhetorical manner of the presentation of the animals' symbolic attributes as metonymies of the whole (i.e. the wing, the limb, the head, or the scale). For example, the tail of the aurochs could be a symbol of the aggressiveness of the animal, as one can see from the prehistoric iconography or from contemporary images of bison or African bulls fighting, with raised tails.

An additional piece of evidence for the presence of shamanism in PPN is offered by the art; life-size masks from the Southern Levant (Kuijt & Goring-Morris 2002, 411 ff.), and the Göbekli Tepe miniature mask made of limestone (Schmidt 2011, 53), infer the existence of shamanic practices (see also Kolankaya-Bostanici 2014). Sculpture too show possible shamanic features, to cite the dynamic compositions from Nevali Çori (see Hauptmann 2011, 134, fig. 24a/b), representing human characters positioned back-to-back and with a bird of prey on the top, or from Göbekli Tepe the anthropic-theriomorphic collage under the shape of a stone pole (see Schmidt 2012, 83, fig. 35), both of which are evidence of a dynamic art, with morphological transformations and inter-species interactions, that demonstrate a world-view tributary to the Palaeolithic (see Hauptmann 2011, 106), and could be ascribed to shamanism.

Enclosure D: The Iconography[3]

Enclosure D (Fig. 2.1), with its rounded architecture 'suggests a PPNA age' (Peters & Schmidt 2004, 183), dated *c.* 9163–8744 cal. BC (Kromer & Schmidt 1998); it contains eleven T-shaped pillars decorated with alto-reliefs, fixed in the ashlar wall, and two larger ones, positioned in the centre of the space.

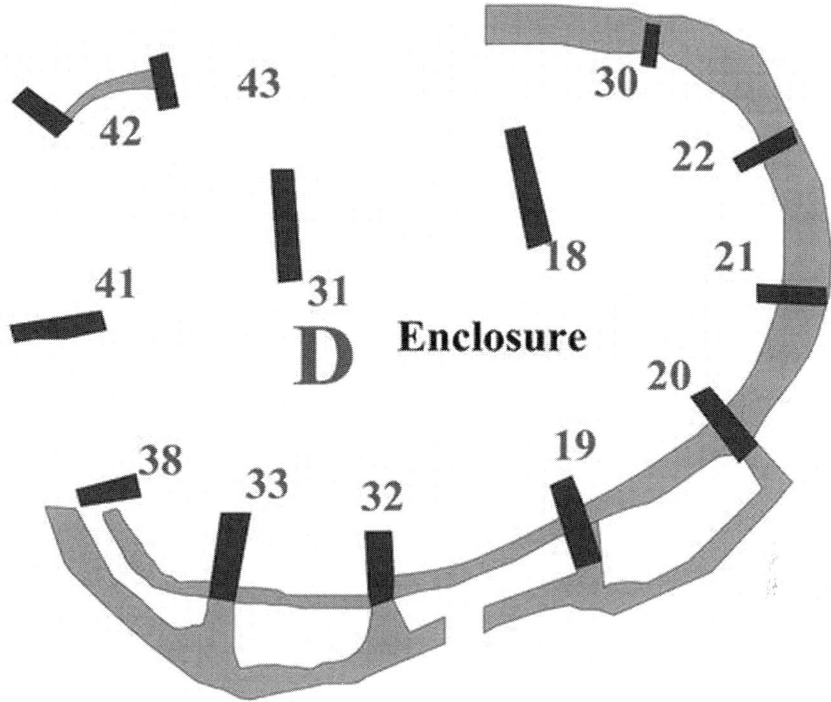

Fig. 2.1: Enclosure D (Gheorghiu 2016, 13)

All animals carved on the stone pillars can be identified from the osteological record (Peters & Schmidt 2004), and the ethnographic descriptions of the Euphrates region, to cite only Wilfred Thesiger's (2007) accounts about the life in the Tigris-Euphrates marshes. Therefore one can identify in the iconography the local terrestrial and aquatic animals of those biotopes; for example: the fox (*Vulpes vulpes*) or the jackal (*Canis aureus*), the leopard (*Panthera pardus*), the equids (*Equus hemionus*), the wild boar (*Sus scrofa*), the aurochs (*Bos primigenius*), the goitred gazelle (*Gazella subgutturosa*), and the mouflon (*Ovis orientalis*), the common crane (*Grus grus*), and demoiselle crane (*Anthropoides virgo*) (Peters & Schmidt 2004, 207; Hodder & Meskell 2010). From the mammals described, the jackal, the boar and the aurochs were and still are the animals specific to the marshlands of the Euphrates (see also Thesiger 2007).[4]

By relating the animals mentioned to their specific ecosystem, one can interpret Göbekli Tepe's iconography as an indexical visual strategy to present the local landscape (Gheorghiu 2015). A semiotic decoding of part of the iconography as representing landscapes was also suggested by Peters & Schmidt (2004, 211–212), who stressed that: '[w]hile the combination of gazelle and Asiatic wild ass on P[illar]21 is indicative for dry, open landscapes, other species such as aurochs, wild boar and cranes are partial to moist, riparian habitats. Such a mixture of biotopes is found at the ecotone of steppe and river valley vegetation, and this must have been the case along

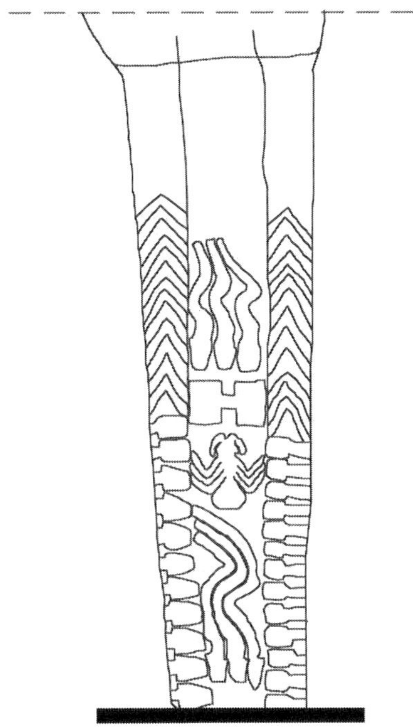

Fig. 2.2: Fishes swimming in group (Gheorghiu 2016, 14)

most water courses in both the Euphrates and Tigris drainage regions.' Bestowing this interpretation 'we shall not see the decontextualized image of an animal, but rather the animal in its relationship with a specific place, which is its habitat, and consequently the iconography would not be zoomorphic, but topomorphic' (Gheorghiu, 2015, 67).

According to this interpretation the snake-like creatures identified by Peters & Schmidt (2004, 183) as being vipers, which are represented individually or as compact groups swimming in a wave-like style, and in close connection with waterfowl, could represent fishes (Fig. 2.2), due to the positioning in dense groups, which is specific to fish congregations during spring spawning, rather than to snakes (Gheorghiu 2015; 2016). These animals could belong to the family *Anguillidae*, such as the Mesopotamian spiny eel *Mastacembelus mastacembelus* (common names: Marmahi = snake fish, marmahi-ye khardar = snake fish with spines or spiny snakefish; Coad 2015, 2), which lives in south-eastern Anatolia (Gumuş *et al.* 2010; Dağli & Erdemli 2009; Çakmak & Alp 2010; Olgunoğlu 2011) and could reach almost one meter length (Coad 2015, 4). Other 'snake' images with different body proportions could also signify fishes of different species. For instance, the animals with a short body and large triangular heads could represent the cat fish *Silurus triostegus* (whose osteological remains were found on the site, see Peters & Schmidt 2004, 206), with the cranium triangular in shape (Ünlü *et al.* 2012, 121), which lives only in the Euphrates and Tigris basins) (Ünlü and Bozkurt 1996; Coad & Holcik 2000), and whose dimensions could reach up to 1 m length, too.

Within the iconography of Enclosure D there are two different ways to present the mammals: horizontally, with animals depicted in movement and jumps (as on Pillar 21), and vertically, in a static attitude. The close association of the vertical animals with the two species of fish that are necrophagic could infer they are drowned animals, and, relating the iconography with local geography, a group of fish swimming along a small mammal lying [floating?] on one side on the north-eastern part on Pillar 30 could evoke a flooded landscape. (Fig. 2.3) It is worth noting that the presence of these two species in the iconography is closely related to a special representation of mammals (i.e. in a lateral-vertical position) as shown for example on Pillars 20 and 30.

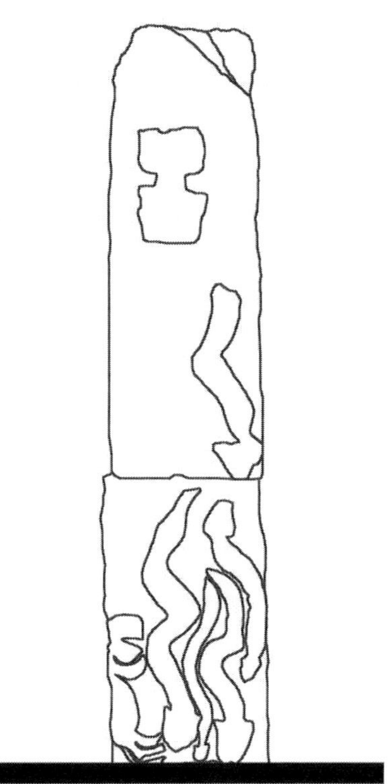

Fig. 2.3: Fish swimming along a small drowned mammal (Gheorghiu 2016, 15)

Another animal in relationship with the *Anguillidae* is an arthropod with a short thorax, bent feet turned upward in a V-shape form, and with bowed antennae positioned along the body, walking in the opposite direction to the fish. (Fig. 2.2) The connection with the aquatic fish feeding on detritus could indicate another necrophagic creature, possibly a crayfish. The one represented on Pillar 33 could be the narrow-clawed crayfish (*Astacus leptodactylus*), a native species in Turkey (Harlıoğlu & Güner 2006; see also Gheorghiu 2015, 69). The undifferentiated length of the chelae and feet could indicate a female *Astacus* (Romaire *et al.* 1977), or a young crayfish with no developed chelae (Balik *et al.* 2005, 298), which is an indication of warmer temperatures.

Positioned together with the representation of fishes, the chevron patterns on Pillar 33, from the south-western part of the enclosure, could signify mud or sand ripples (Ball 2009, 80–1) (Fig. 2.4 a, b), or the waves created by the ebb and flow of water passing by reeds,[5] (Fig. 2.5 a, b) or produced by a congregation of fish swimming near the surface (Gheorghiu 2015, 67), as suggested by the wave-like image of the compact groups of anguilliform fishes positioned on the lateral parts of the pillar. It is well known that on the Euphrates River huge fish mass migrations occur in late spring (Charvát 2005); large schools of fish are forming during the late spring ready for spawning (see Sahinöz *et al.* 2007).

Pillar 33 could therefore evoke a riverine landscape, with flowing water, populated by waterfowl, fish and crayfish. In the south-western part of the enclosure is Pillar 38 which displays a canid [a jackal?], a wild boar and a crane. This set of creatures could evoke a swampy landscape. Flooded landscapes with floating drowned mammals consumed by water-necrophagic animals could be inferred in the south-eastern part of the enclosure in the iconography of Pillar 20 (a cat-fish in front of a bovid lying on one side) (Fig. 2.6) and in the Northern part on the 'capitol' of Pillar 43 (a crayfish in front of a felid lying on one side, positioned on a vertical axis). This scene is bordered on the lateral side of the pillar by a complex image of a possible landscape; the scene includes the upper part of three round roofed forms positioned in a marshy landscape with a reed bed. This interpretation is supported by the presence of an anguilliform fish and a wading ibis, and at the centre and bottom of this landscape scene are birds of prey and a decapitated human body.

a

b

Fig. 2.4: a. Mud and b. sand ripples (Photo: author)

a

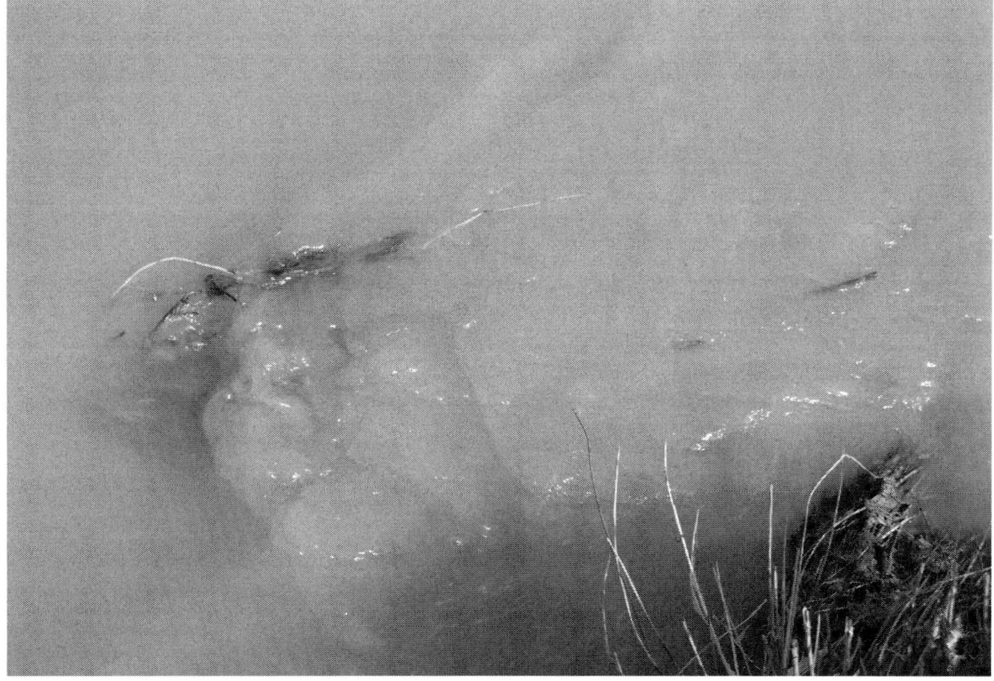

b

Fig. 2.5: a. Waves on a river surface; b. a flow of water passing by reeds (Photo: author)

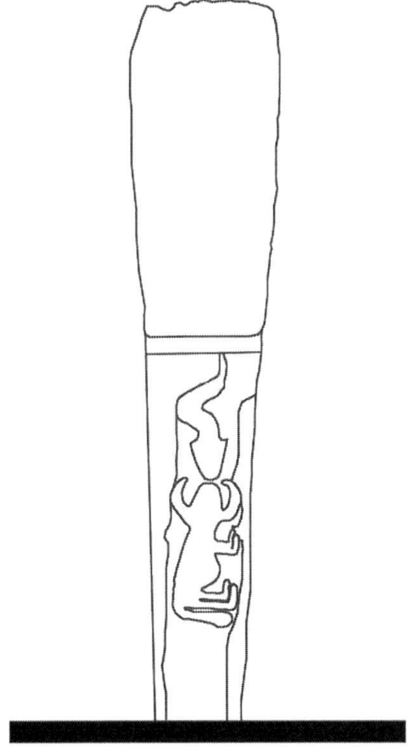

Fig. 2.6: Cat-fish in front of a drowned bovid (after Gheorghiu 2016, 14)

The bald ibis (*Geronticus eremita*) is a migratory bird specific to the Mesopotamian region, 'typical cliff-nesting species' that prefer 'cliffs with natural ledges and holes, ensuring protection from terrestrial predators' (Serra *et al.* 2009, 770), and living in colonies (Kasparek 2016), in the proximity of birds of prey (Serra *et al.* 2009, 773). Consequently, the round forms below and over the reed bed on Pillar 43 could indicate the hollowed ibis nest inside, a terrace bordered by wetland.

Enclosure D: The Shamanic Traits

Space

The semi-covered space of the enclosures (Hauptmann 1999, 79; see also Banning 2011, 629) seems to have been a place of [nightly?] performance for connecting animal-spirits, a 'fundamental to shamanism' (Dobkin de Rios & Winkelman 1989), and to generate the spirit possession (Bourguinon 1978). Here, the geometry of the space offers information about the ritual within: the circular movements of the performer inside the enclosures around the two central pillars are rhythmic by the perimeter pillars. Another structuring of the space is generated by the two central anthropomorphic pillars that suggest a rite of passage performed between them.

Analogies with such spatial organisation could be found at 'round the structures of Nemrik and Qermez Dere which displayed a special configuration with two pillars' (Kozlowski & Kempisty 1990, 352–358, figs 4–6), and later, around the rectangular cult buildings at Çayönü and Nevali Çori (Hauptmann 1999, 75), where the iconography of the T-shaped pillars disappeared.

Acoustics

Some of the images discussed in this text (for example, the flow-pattern of the fish and the flow of the river) are analogous to the entoptic images perceived during altered states of consciousness (ASC) (see 'Entoptic phenomena,' Lewis-Williams & Dowson 1988, 206, fig. 1), produced during hallucinogenic experiences (Helvenston & Bahn 2002, 23). These aquatic images could be related to the sound of water that allowed the shamans to attain ASC states (Goldhahn 2002; Oestigaard 2011). A relationship between Palaeolithic iconography and the sound of running water was already attested in the Tagus Rock Art Complex (Garcês & Nash 2017).

To produce an efficient ASC experience images could have been supported by sounds; it is known that a rhythm-induced trance could have been produced by repetitive chanting, drumming and dancing (Winkelman 1989, 166 ff.; Vaitl *et al.* 2005, 107). In shamanism acoustics played a major role; for example the natural sounds produced by the percussion of stones were considered to represent the 'spirits in the rocks' (Devereux 2001, 20ff.).

As one can see at the Göbekli Tepe site, the upper part of the T-shaped pillars is covered with cupules, represented mainly as parallel rows. It is suggested that cupules could be associated with the intentional production of sound (Devereux 2001, 119; Bednarik 2008), in 'rituals at which the production of percussive sound such as hammering or drumming was required' (Ouzman 1998, 38; see also Devereux 2001, 139; Bednarik 2008, 75). In this perspective the T-shaped pillars fixed in the floor bedrock could have been functioned as lithophones (Dams 1985; Devereux 2001, 124ff.) or rock gongs (Montage 1965), due to their shape that favoured an ideal and desired resonance, like the thin flake lithophone from Jhiri Nala (Bednarik 2008, 75).

Lithophones: 'can be of many different rock types ... It is important to note that the crucial characteristics are not those of the material, but those of shape and contact with the supporting mass. Irrespective of rock type, the best lithophonic sound results are always obtained from rocks that are thin, discoid or elongate, and only supported at very limited contact surfaces. Ideally, they are long and slender, and supported only at one end, which is why stalactites make excellent candidates. To function best, the stone must be as free as possible to resonate unhindered when struck, which allows it to increase the intensity and prolongation of sound by sympathetic vibration' (Bednarik 2008, 73).

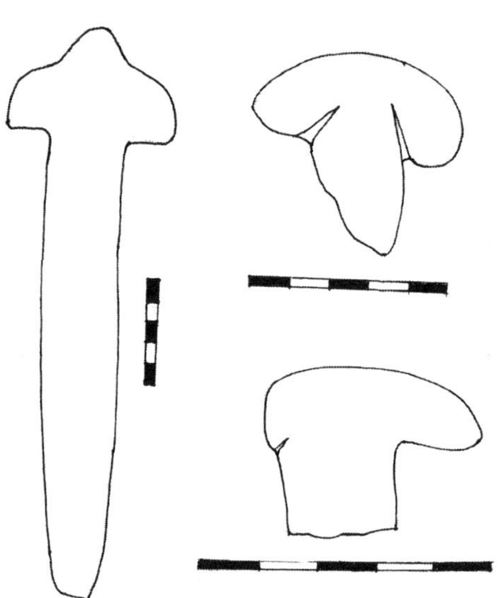

Fig. 2.7: Eel-shaped pestles (after Dietrich et al. *2017, 122, fig. 5.24)*

A complementary set of objects to the cupules could have been the eel-shaped pestles (Fig. 2.7) or 'sceptres' of the Nemrik type (Dietrich *et al.* 2017, 121, fig. 5.24), whose shapes and hard materials, together with the high state of fragmentation of some of them, infer they could have been used as percussion tools for the T-shaped lithophones.

A T-shaped lithophone could produce sounds even during lighter percussion events like the knock with the fist; for example the central pillar No. 18, hit with the fist 'generates a very distinct resonance frequency as powerful as a drum. The main resonance frequency looks to be around 68–69 Hz with harmonics of 91 Hz and 138 Hz' (Debertolis *et al.* 2017, 112). Lithophones' sounds, drumming and chanting performed in the relatively close space of the enclosure could have produced, like in other prehistoric round stone enclosures, an 'echo ricocheting around the inside of the circle' (Watson 2006, 12), which is an acoustic phenomenon perceived only in the centre of the enclosure.

Similar types of sounds, like the resonance in the closed spaces of the caves (see Reznikoff 1995; 2002; 2006; 2009; Reznikoff & Dauvois 1988; Iannace & Trematerra 2014; Fazenda *et al.* 2017), or in funerary megalithic stone monuments (see Devereux & Jahn 1996; Watson & Keating 1999), were possibly exploited in shamanic ceremonies. It is plausible that the semi-covered space of the Enclosure D would have permitted a good aural experience of the sounds of water and animals during shamanistic performances that bound together sounds, places and spaces (Scarre 2006).

A local animal whose sounds would have been reproduced within the shamanic ceremonies is the jackal. Tristram (1868, 111) remarks its acoustic presence during nighttime when 'their sudden howl would break the deadly stillness of the night' and 'caught up from pack to pack ... till the air seemed filled as if with the wailing of a thousand infants.' Such a dominant acoustic landscape (see Devereux & Nash 2014) could have influenced the shamans' rituals.

Colour and light

Colour could have played an important role in the perception of the engraved bas-reliefs images on the pillars (see Lynch 1998) at Göbekli Tepe. These images highlighted with colour resemble the murals at Çatal Hüyük (Mellaart 1967), producing a dramatic effect upon the viewer, and allowing a more coherent understanding of each of the scenes (Fig. 2.8).

A dramatic highlight of the coloured images could have been produced by nocturnal and high-shadow illumination (a 'nightly use of the enclosure' was proposed by Schmidt 2012, 153), with probable dynamic effects. For example, a tangential and sequential illumination of the scenes with entoptic patterns (like the V-shaped patterns or the flow-like pattern of the fish) could animate the scene, generating a movement of flow that evoked the movement of fishes in water and of the water flowing in a river bed.

Colour was also used on human skulls, as revealed by the ochre on a cranial bone fragment (Gresky *et al.* 2017, 1, 5), a practice common in PPN Anatolia and the Levant (Gresky *et al.* 2017, 5; see also Kenyon 1981; Bonogofsky 2001; Erdal 2015).

Dynamic images of the flow

As already mentioned, the iconography suggests movements of water flow. As we see on Pillar 33 the V-shaped patterns of the water running and the swimming of the *Anguillidae* illustrates the undulating kinematics (Gillis 1996) specific to this species

Fig. 2.8: Coloured bas-reliefs

that allows the eel to swim backwards, a peculiarity that confers the animal a special symbolic status. The eel as a symbol of undulating movement and of time (its spawning is an indicator that the beginning of spring has arrived) is to be found in the Palaeolithic iconography, in the Magdalenian engravings at Montgaudier (Charente) (see David & Lugol 1950), where the most explicit on the perforated stick that depicts seals and eels (identifiable by the dorsal wing). At Göbekli Tepe the eel is also present on a stone plaque (see Dietrich *et al.* 2017, 116, Fig. 5.20; Schmidt 2012, 255, fig. 114) as serpent-like lines positioned on either side of a V-shaped pattern (Fig. 2.9), like the iconography of Pillar 33, where there is a suggestion of a water flow.[6]

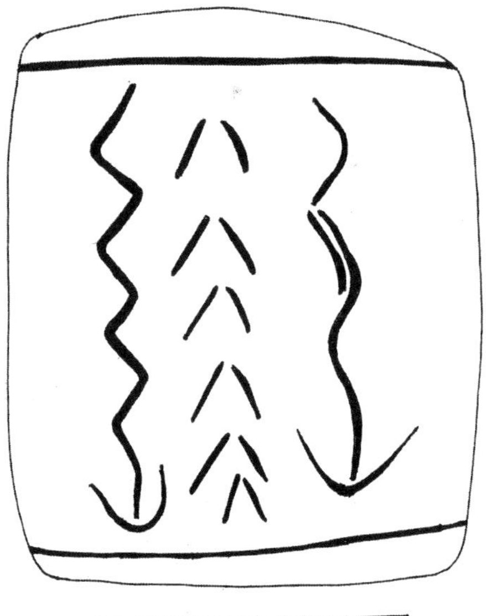

Fig. 2.9: Two eels and water flow (after Dietrich et al. *2017, 116, fig. 5.20)*

Death as a rebirth experience

Besides evoking the flow of water, the images of the eels could have carried another meaning, related to the death-and-rebirth experience which is specific to shamanism (see Winkelman 2002, 1880). The eel might have been a symbol of death-and-rebirth because of its ability to survive, as postulated by Coad: '[t]hey may burrow in mud and even survive some drying in ponds through their air-breathing ability,' and 'may be able to survive desiccation by burying themselves in mud. They are not commonly caught with nets and may be mostly nocturnal in habits' (Coad 2015, 2; 6). One could also remark that eels migrate and return annually to their spawning grounds, from the sea to the rivers and streams. Once the males have fertilised the eggs, they die; this could be seen as a metaphor of life rising from death.

Severed heads and excarnation

Despite the fact that human crania were not discovered in the enclosures, fragments of human bones (691 pieces, of which 408 are skull fragments; Gresky *et al.* 2017, 1), some with intentional defleshed cut marks (Schmidt 2010, 243), of which 40 skull fragments with one drilled perforation, three pieces with deep incisions, ochre colouring and fine cut-marks (Gresky *et al.* 2017, 1) infer the existence of a ritual of excarnation of the bodies and decapitation (as suggested by the cut-marks on two cervical vertebrae). 'Excarnation and the severing of heads from bodies is a brutal enactment of the "death" and "rebirth" of a shaman' (Lewis-Williamms & Pearce 2005, 117), and here the iconography could complete the data missing in the archaeological record.

Fig. 2.10: Selection from the iconography of Pillar 43: headless ithyphallic character, two birds of prey, a jackal (?) and a detached skull (?) (after Schmidt 2011, 78, fig. 29)

Detachable human heads (like the perforations on top of the cranium, to be hanged by a cord, see Gresky *et al.* 2017, 6), could infer severing and manipulation of the skull (suggested also by the headless ithyphallic character and a round shape that could be the detached head, carved on Pillar 43) (Fig. 2.10), therefore the life size human head made of limestone found near Pillar 31 (Schmidt 2010, 249), could have been a skeuomorph used in shamanic rituals, suggesting the materiality of bone.

In Göbekli Tepe the excarnation of the human bodies could have been undertaken metaphorically by necrophagic animals as shown by the iconography at Çatal Hűyűk. All the water animals depicted in Enclosure D are necrophagic. Catfish and crayfish feed on dead fish and animals, and eels are also necrophagic, feeding on drowned animals. One of the most eloquent examples supporting this assertion could be found in Gunter Grass's (2004) *The Tin Drum*', where the author describes the capture of eels using the head of a dead horse, a scene comparable with the one on Pillar 30, where a group of anguilliform animals is positioned along a small quadruped, presented in the vertical position. I correlate this image with that from Pillar 1 from Enclosure A. Here, represented are a group of anguilliform animals, positioned in a reticular pattern, with heads at both ends (which could symbolise the backward swimming of the eels), positioned near a ram. The excarnation of a human skull by eels could have been symbolised by the sculpture of a human head with an anguilliform shape on the brow (see Schmidt 2010, 245, fig. 15), found at the Nevali Çori site. Many of the birds depicted in Enclosure D are considered necrophagic as well, being avian scavengers, like the Griffon vulture (*Gyps fulvus*)[7] from the scene with a headless human character (for similarities with the Çatal Hüyük iconography, see Mellaart 1967).

A mammal most frequently depicted at Göbekli Tepe is the jackal. The frequency of this image and the importance of its positioning infer this scavenger had a special importance with communities using this site. Being a scavenger (Van de Ven *et al.* 2013) the jackal was probably implied in the process of de-fleshing of the deceased. In the Near East it is present in the Egyptian mythology, under the form of the god Anubis. Another mammalian scavenger sculpted on a fragmented bas-relief in Enclosure D is a hyena (see Schmidt 2010, 254, fig. 11), positioned near a vulture.

The 'brown hyena and black-backed jackal can be considered as either meso-carnivores or apex depending on the presence or absence of larger carnivores' (Mondal *et al.* 2012, 106–107). A possible growth of big felid population in the area changed the ecosystem dynamics (Yarnell *et al.* 2013, 156), and diminished the importance of the two species of scavengers, as one can see from the iconography of Layer II, where the images of large felids (Peters & Schmidt 2004, 184) are doubled compared with Enclosure D. A sculpted head of a felid dated between the early PPNB and middle PPNB was found at Ayanlar Höyük (Çelik 2016, 363–364).

Anthropomorphism

In enclosure D anthropomorphism is limited to the representation of human hands on the central pillars of Nos 18 and 31. Pillar 18 displays a canid (that I identify as jackal) near the right arm and is fixed in a stone support decorated with a row of ducks that infer the presence of water. Both anthropomorphic entity wearing decorated belts possibly made of the fur of canids were identified as being shamanic figures, or of some spirit-world trickster (see Hodder & Meskell 2010, 63), or of some form of supernatural beings (Peters & Schmidt 2004, 210). They could also be the anthropomorphic symbols of natural elements, as rivers or geomorphs, due to their relationship with the whole iconography and the enclosure.

Enclosure D as a Ritualised Map

All the iconography of Enclosure D supports an interpretation of this space as a cartography of the shamanic practices in the landscape, using animals as strategic references. An analogy to this world view could be the shaman's drum decorated with diagrams and animals and functioning as a 'cognitive map' (Pentikäinen 1998) whereby the imagery of drum works in harmony with the percussionist. In this perspective Enclosure D could be perceived as a shamanic cognitive map, due to the following plausible reasons:

- it identifies the biotopes after the indexical animals;
- it identifies the animals' soundscape that could have been copied in shamanic performances;
- it identifies the temporal sequences in the landscape after the period of spawning of the indexical animals;
- it identifies catastrophic events occurring in the landscape, like floods; and
- it identifies natural cycles of life and death.

Discussion

Göbekli Tepe's iconography reveals two aspects worthy of comment: a continuation of the Natufian shamanic symbolism (see the inventory of the cave from the Hilazon Tachtit site in Grosman *et al.* 2008), and the emergence of a novel art form concerned with human figures (due to the increasing number of anthropomorphic sculptures) (Schmidt 2010, 247).

Arguably, the landscape is represented in the Enclosure D as being in a direct association with water. It is known there was a relationship between water and shamanism (Oestigaard 2011) and that 'both underground and underwater travel is widely reported as shamanistic experiences' (Lewis-Williams 2004, 145; n.29; but see also Eliade 1972). One example is the Shoshone world view, structured on a vertical axis, starting from the water which is seen as an entrance to the underworld (Lewis-Williams & Chalis 2011, 186).

At Göbekli Tepe landscapes are temporarily determined, and are in flow due to nature's rhythms that control and manipulate the *life* of water and the animals it harbours. Here water, land, life and death are interwoven into the landscape, and the necrophagic aquatic and terrestrial animals contribute to this continuous flow. The ebb and flow of life and death has an acoustic counterpart as well, which is the watery and animal soundscapes. The water running and the jackals howling are only two of many sounds with which the shamans would operate when describing the imagery of the pillars.

Göbekli Tepe chronologically belongs to a time when ancient Anatolia was about to embrace the Neolithic world (Herva *et al.* 2014), and the Palaeolithic imagery (Hauptmann 2011, 106), is structured according to the rigours of the built space and geometry that divides the landscape and visualises various times of the year. Additionally, architecture reveals a shamanic group experience (Turner 2005) due to the energy consumed for building the enclosures. The architecture of the 'communal houses' (Hodder & Meskell 2010, 62) with benches between pillars suggests the presence of a large audience (see Bradley 2009) and a community shamanism of 'vertical' type (Hugh-Jones 1996), where 'esoteric knowledge is revealed to and transmitted to a small elite' (Lewis-Williams & Pearce 2005, 86). At the same time such an enclosure with benches could have functioned as a 'house of the dead,' with the corpses being deposited to be consumed by necrophagic animals.

Enclosure D also confirms the emergence of a new religious order (see also Anttonen 2007) issued from the hunter-gatherers' shamanism, where 'the dimension of religious belief becomes prominent' (Lewis-Williams & Pearce 2005, 86; see also La Barre 1980, 83). The architecture though indicates a transition in ideological views of the world; between the realms of the hunter-gather to the agriculturalist.

Concluding Remarks: A Shamanic Story about the Flood

As a conclusion, the dynamic visual narrative of Enclosure D could be decoded as being a story of a complex landscape, even an image of the world, revealing the cosmos at a singular moment. The shamanic cosmos (Gulløv & Appelt 2001, 157–158; Lewis-Williams 2004; Lewis-Williams & Pearce 2005, 148; Wason 2010, 283 ff.) in Enclosure D is structured by time. The role of the animal representations was to show a distinct moment in time, a characteristic of Palaeolithic art (Dubourg 1994), because 'the construction of time' (Guilaine 2015, 10) is a trait specific to hunter-gatherers' communities, determined by the 'seasonal rhythms of societies' (Guilaine 2015, 58).

The images that create the various compositions are dynamic and indicate a directional flow of the engraved narrative. The narrative would have probably been enhanced with how the artificial light interacted with each section of the engraved panel; the light illuminating various sections of the panel, whilst the succeeding shadow closing the storey. (Figs 2.11–2.13)

In concluding this chapter I propose an exercise of archaeological imagination, by visualising the shamanic story inside Enclosure D, through the meaning of the iconography: a story about the flooding occurring at the end of winter, when vast landscapes were covered by the floodwaters of Euphrates and its tributaries'. From this flooded landscape the carcasses of drowned animals are floating on its surface. The narrative could also be about a riverine landscape at the beginning of spring with

Fig. 2.11: Illuminating the capital of Pillar 33 (3D reconstruction)

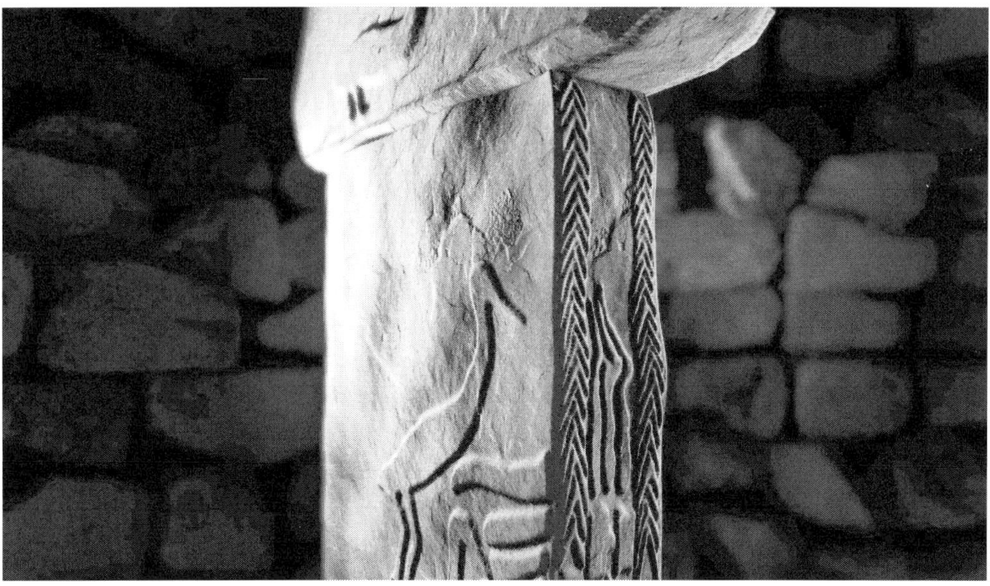

Fig. 2.12: Illuminating the middle part of Pillar 33 (3D reconstruction)

quiet running waters filled with different species of fish and waterfowl, and whose muddy riverbanks hid jackals, boars and aurochs.

We can imagine this prehistoric sanctuary as a shamanic story in stone involving a world of water, about the gentle Balikh and fearful Euphrates rivers, which could relate to most ancient of stories about the (Biblical) Flood.[8]

Fig. 2.13: Illuminating the lower part of Pillar 33 (3D reconstruction)

Acknowledgements

The author thanks Mrs. Cornelia Cătuna, M. Bogdan Căpruciu, Professor George Nash, Dr. Herman Bender and Dr. Emilia Pásztor for their useful comments. Many thanks also to the students who helped with the 2D and 3D illustrations: Smaranda Laiu, Alina Corciu and Marius Hodea.

Notes

1. For an extended bibliography see Siikala & Hoppál 1992; Price 2001, 3–16; Hamayon 2004; Hoppál 2006; Witzel 2011.
2. http://www.oocities.org/timessquare/labyrinth/2398/bginfo/geo/euphrates.html [accessed 17.10.2017]
3. In the present chapter the discussion on art (i.e. the alto-reliefs on the T-shaped pillars) is restricted to the iconography of the well preserved enclosure D.
4. http://www.oocities.org/timessquare/labyrinth/2398/bginfo/geo/euphrates.html
5. https://www.shutterstock.com/video/clip-8388478-stock-footage-water-stream-flowing-in-the-autumn-forest-among-dry-grass-and-reeds.html [accessed 13.11.17]
6. An additional visualisation of the water flow could be via the vertical positioning of fishes and drowned animals, positioned on the course of the water flow.
7. http://www.thewonderofbirds.com/griffon-vulture/ [accessed 23.11.2017]
8. I would like to illustrate the perception of such an event by those people using this site in ancient times, with a quote from *The Epic of Ghilgamesh* (Sandars 1972, 108), that can be visualised as a shamanic performance with dance, sounds and light, inside the Enclosure D: 'With the first light of dawn a black cloud came from the horizon; it thundered within where Adad, lord of the storm was riding. In front over hill and plain Shullat and Hanish, heralds of the storm, led on. Then the gods of the abyss rose up; Nergal pulled out the dams of the nether waters,

Ninurta the war-lord threw down the dykes, and the seven judges of hell, the Annunaki, raised their torches, lighting the land with their livid flame. A stupor of despair went up to heaven when the god of the storm turned daylight to darkness, when he smashed the land like a cup. One whole day the tempest raged, gathering fury as it went, it poured over the people like the tides of battle; an imam could not see his brother nor the people be seen from heaven. Even the gods were terrified at the flood, they fled to the highest heaven, the firmament of Ann; they crouched against the walls, cowering like curs... For six days and six nights the winds blew, torrent and tempest and flood overwhelmed the world, tempest and flood raged together like warring hosts. When the seventh day dawned the storm from the south subsided, the sea grew calm, the flood was stilled; I looked at the face of the world and there was silence, all mankind was turned to clay.'

References

Anttonen, V. 2007. Transcending bodily and territorial boundaries. Reconceptualizing shamanism as a form of religion. *Shaman* 2(1–2), 5–22.

Bahn, P. 2001. Save the last trance for me: An assessment of the misuse of shamanism in rock art studies. In H-P. Frankfort & R. N. Hamayon (eds) *The Concept of Shamanism: Uses and Abuses.* Bibliotheca Shamanistica 10. Budapest: Akademiai Kyadó, 31–93.

Balik, Ü., Çubuk, H., Özök, R. & Uysal, R. 2005. Some biological characteristics of crayfish (*Astacus leptodactylus* Eschscholtz, 1823) in Lake Eüirdir. *Turkish Journal of Zoology* 29, 295–300.

Ball, P. 2009. *Nature's Patterns. A Tapestry in Three Parts.* Oxford: Oxford University Press.

Banning, E. B. 2011. So fair a house: Göbekli Tepe and the identification of temples in the Pre-Pottery Neolithic of the Near East. *Current Anthropology* 52(5), 619–660.

Bar-Josef, O. 2014. Southeast Turkish Neolithic: A view from the Southern Levant. In M. Özdoğan, N. Başgelen & P. Kuniholm (eds) *The Neolithic in Turkey. 10500–5200 BC: Environment, Settlement, Flora, Fauna, Dating, Symbols of Belief, with Views from North, South, East, and West.* Istanbul: Archaeology and Art Publications, 293–320.

Barrett, J. C. 1999. Chronologies of landscape. In P. J. Ucko & R. Layton (eds) *The Archaeology and Anthropology of Landscape. Shaping your landscape.* London and New York: Routledge, 21–30.

Bednarik, R. G. 2008. Cupules, *Rock Art Research* 25(1), 61–100.

Belfer-Cohen, A. & Goring-Morris, A. N. 2011. Reflections on Neolithisation processes. Jacques Cauvin: The right man for the right season. *Paléorient* 37(1), 89–99.

Bonogofsky, M. 2001. Cranial modeling and Neolithic bone modification at 'Ain Ghazal: New interpretations. *Paléorient* 27, 141–146.

Bourguinon, E., 1978. Spirit possession and altered states of consciousness: The evolution of an enquiry. In G. D. Spindler (ed.) *The Making of Psychological Anthropology*, Berkley CA: University of California Press, 479–515.

Bradley, R. 2009. *Image and Audience: Rethinking Prehistoric Art.* Oxford: Oxford University Press.

Çakmak, E. & Alp, A. 2010. Morphological differences among the Mesopotamian spiny eel, *Mastacembelus mastacembelus* (Banks & Solander 1794), populations. *Turkish Journal of Fisheries & Aquatic Sciences* 10, 87–92.

Cauvin, J. 2000. *The Birth of the Gods and the Origins of Agriculture*, Cambridge: Cambridge University Press.

Çelik, B. 2016. A new Pre-Pottery Neolithic site in Southeastern Turkey: Ayanlar Höyük (Gre Hut). *Documenta Praehistorica* XLIV, 360–367.

Charvát, P. 2005. *Mesopotamia Before History,* London: Routledge.

Clottes, J. 2011. *Pourquoi l'art préhistorique?* Paris: Gallimard.

Clottes, J. & Lewis-Williams, J. D. 1998. *The Shamans of Prehistory: Trance and Magic in the Painted Caves.* New York: Abrams Press.

Coad, B. W. 2015. Review of the spiny eels of Iran (Family Mastacembelidae), *Iranian Journal of Ichthyology* 2(1), 1–12.
Coad, B. W. & Holcik, J., 2000. On *Silurus* species from Iran (*Actinoptrygii: Siluridae*). *Folia Zoologica* 49, 139–148.
Dağli, M. & Erdemli, A. U. 2009. An investigation on the fish fauna of Balıksuyu Stream (Kilis, Turkey). *International Journal of Natural & Engineering Sciences* 3(1), 19–24.
Dams, L. 1985. Palaeolithic lithophones: descriptions and comparisons. *Oxford Journal of Archaeology* 4(1), 31–46.
Daniels, S. & Cosgrove, D. 1988. Introduction: iconography and landscape. In D. Cosgrove & S. Daniels (eds) *The Iconography of Landscape*. Cambridge: Cambridge University Press, 1–10.
David, P. & Lugol, M. 1950. Gravures magdaléniennes inédites de Montgaudier (Charente). *Bulletin de la Société Préhistorique de France* 47(6–8), 376–378.
Debertolis, P., Gullà, D. & Savolainen, H. 2017. Archaeoacoustic analysis in Enclosure D at Göbekli Tepe in South Anatolia, Turkey, the 5th Human and Social Sciences at the Common Conference September, 25–29, 2017. *History and Archaeology*, 107–114. DOI:10.18638/hassacc.2017.5.1.240
Devereux, P. 2001. *Stone Age Soundtracks. The Acoustic Archaeology of Ancient Sites*. London: Vega.
Devereux, P. & Jahn, R. G. 1996. Preliminary investigations and cognitive considerations of the acoustical resonances of selected archaeological sites. *Antiquity* 70, 665–666.
Devereux, P. & Nash, G. H. 2014. Indications of an acoustic landscape at Bryn Celli Ddu, Anglesey, North Wales. *Time and Mind* 7(4), 385–390.
Dietler, M. & Herbich, I. 1995. Feasts and labor mobilization: Dissecting a fundamental economic practice. In M. Dietler & B. Hayden (eds) *Feasts. Archaeological and Ethnographic Perspectives on Food, Politics, and Power.* Washington, DC & London: Smithsonian Institution Press, 260–264.
Dietrich, O. & Notroff, J. 2015. A sanctuary, or so fair a house? In defense of an archaeology of cult at Pre-Pottery Neolithic Göbekli Tepe. In N. Laneri (ed.) *Defining the Sacred. Approaches to the Archaeology of Religion on the Near East.* Oxford: Oxbow Books, 75–89.
Dietrich, O., Notroff, J. & Schmidt, K. 2017. Feasting, social complexity, and the emergence of the Early Neolithic of Upper Mesopotamia: A view from Göbekli Tepe. In R. J. Chacon & R. G. Mendoza (eds) *Feast, Famine or Fighting?* Studies in Human Ecology and Adaptation 8. Cham: Springer International, 91–132.
Dobkin de Rios, M. & Winkelman, M. 1989. Shamanism and the alteration of consciousness: An introduction. *Journal of Psychoactive Drugs* 21(1), 159–180.
Dubourg, C. 1994. Les expressions de la saisonnalité dans les arts paléolithiques – les arts sur support lithique – du bassin d'Aquitaine. *Préhistoire ariégeoise* XLIX, 145–189.
Eliade, M. 1972. *Shamanism: Archaic Techniques of Ecstasy*. Princeton, NJ: Princeton University Press.
Erdal, Y. S. 2015. Bone or flesh: Defleshing and post-depositional treatments at Körtik Tepe (Southeastern Anatolia, PPNA Period). *European Journal of Archaeology* 18, 4–32.
Espinosa Arango, M. & Andoque, F. 1999. Managing the world: Territorial negotiations among the andoque people of the Colombian Amazon. In P. J., Ucko & R. Layton (eds) *The Archaeology and Anthropology of Landscape. Shaping your Landscape*. London and New York: Routledge, 242–255.
Fazenda, B., Scarre, C., Till, R., Jiménez Pasalodos, R., Rojo Guerra, M., Tejedor, C., Ontañón Peredo, R., Watson, A., Wyatt, S., García Benito, C., Drinkall, H. & Foulds, F. 2017. Cave acoustics in prehistory: Exploring the association of Palaeolithic visual motifs and acoustic response. *Journal of the Acoustical Society of America* 142, 1332–1349.
Fiala, A. 2005. Creation myths of the Ancient World. In B. Taylor & J. Kaplan (eds) *Encyclopaedia of Religion and Nature,* London: Continuum.
Frankfort, H-P. & Hamayon, R. N. (eds) 2001. *The Concept of Shamanism: Uses and Abuses*. Budapest: Akadémiai Kiadó.
Garcês, S. & Nash, G. 2017. The relevance of watery soundscapes in a ritual context. *Time and Mind* 10(1), 69–80.

Gheorghiu, D. 2011. Working with Agni: The phenomenological experience of a technical ritual, In D. Gheorghiu (ed.) *Archaeology Experiences Spirituality?* Newcastle upon Tyne: Cambridge Scholars Publishing, 71–88.

Gheorghiu, D. 2015. A river runs through it: The semiotics of Göbekli Tepe's map (an exercise of archaeological imagination). In A. Vianello (ed.) *Rivers in Prehistory.* Oxford: Archaeopress, 65–76.

Gheorghiu, D. 2016. Göbekli Tepe: A hunter-gatherers' architectural world map. *Pleistocene Coalition Newsletter* 8(3), 13–15.

Gheorghiu, D., Pasztor, E, Bender, H. & Nash, G. H. (eds). 2017. *Archaeological Approaches to Shamanism. Mind-Body, Nature, and Culture.* Newcastle-upon-Tyne: Cambridge Scholars Publishers.

Gillis, G. B. 1996. Undulatory locomotion in elongate aquatic vertebrates: anguilliform swimming since Sir James Gray. *American Zoologist* 36(6), 656–665.

Goldhahn, J. 2002. Roaring rocks: An audio-visual perspective on hunter-gatherer engravings in northern Sweden and Scandinavia. *Norwegian Archaeological Review* 35(1), 29–61.

Grass, G. 2004. *The Tin Drum*, London: Vintage Books.

Gresky, J., Haelm, J. & Clare, L. 2017. Modified human crania from Göbekli Tepe provide evidence for a new form of Neolithic skull cult. *Science Advances* 3(6), 3–10.

Grosman, L., Munro, N. D. & Belfer-Cohen, A. 2008. A 12,000-year-old Shaman burial from the southern Levant (Israel). *Proceedings of the National Academy of Sciences* 105(46), 17665–17669.

Guilaine, J. 2015. *La seconde naissance de l'homme: le Néolithique.* Paris: Odille Jacob.

Gulløv, H. C. & Appelt, M. 2001. Social bonding and shamanism among Late Dorset groups in High Arctic Greenland. In N. Price (ed.) *The Archaeology of Shamanism.* London: Routledge, 146–164.

Gumuş, A., Şahinoz, E., Doğu, Z. & Polat, N. 2010. Age and growth of the Mesopotamian spiny eel, *Mastacembelus mastacembelus* (Banks and Solender 1794), from southeastern Anatolia. *Turkish Journal of Zoology* 34, 399–407.

Hamayon, R. 2004. Siberian Shamanism. In M. Namba Walter & E. J. Neumann Fridman (eds) *Shamanism. An Encyclopaedia of World Beliefs, Practices, and Culture* II. Santa Barbara, CA/Oxford: ABC CLIO, 619–627.

Harlıoğlu, M. M. & Güner, U. 2006, Studies on the recently discovered crayfish, *Austropotamobius torrentium* (Shrank, 1803), in Turkey: morphological analysis and meat yield. *Aquaculture Research* 37, 538–542.

Hasanov, Z. 2016, A method for determining the practice of shamanism in archeological cultures, *Anthropology & Archeology of Eurasia* 55(3–4), 188–231.

Hauptmann, H. 1999. The Urfa region. In M. Özdoğan & N. Başgelen (eds) *Neolithic in Turkey. The Craddle of Civilization,* Istanbul: Arkeoloji ve sanat yayilnari, 65–86.

Hauptmann, H. 2011. The Urfa region. In M. Özdoğan, N. Başgelen, & P. Kuniholm (eds) *The Neolithic in Turkey. New Excavations and New Research.* Istanbul: Archaeology and Art Publications, 85–138.

Hayden, B. 2009. The proof is in the pudding: feasting and the origins of domestication. *Current Anthropology* 50(5), 597–601.

Helvenston, P. A. & Bahn, P. G. 2002. *Desperately Seeking Trance Plants: Testing the 'Three Stages of Trance' Model.* New York: R. J. Communications.

Herva, V-P., Nordqvist, K., Lahelma, A. & Ikäheimo, J. 2014. Cultivation of perception and the emergence of the Neolithic world. *Norwegian Archaeological Review* 47(2), 141–160.

Hodder, I. & Meskell, L. 2010. The symbolism of Çatalhöyük in its regional context. In I. Hodder (ed.) *Religion in the Emergence of Civilization:* Çatalhöyük *as a Case Study.* Cambridge: Cambridge University Press, 32–72.

Hoppál, M. 2006. Sámánok, kultúrák és kutatók az ezredfordulón [Shamans, cultures and researchers in the millenary]. In M. Hoppál, B., Szathmári & A. Takács (eds) *Sámánok* és *Kultúrák* [*Shamans and Cultures*]. Budapest: Gondolat, 9–25.

Hugh-Jones, S. 1996. Shamans, prophets, priests, and pastors. In N. Thomas & C. Humphrey (eds) *Shamanism, History, and the State*. Ann-Arbor, MI: University of Michigan Press, 32–75.
Hultkrantz, Å. 2007. Introductory remarks in the study of shamanism. *Shaman* 1(1–2), 5–16.
Jordan, P. 2001. The materiality of shamanism as a 'world-view': Praxis, artefacts and landscape. In N. Price (ed.) *The Archaeology of Shamanism*. London: Routledge, 87–104.
Iannace, G. & Trematerra, A. 2014. The acoustics of the caves. *Applied Acoustics* 86, 42–46. DOI:10.1016/j.apacoust.2014.05.004.
Kasparek, M. 2016. On the age of the colony of the bald ibis, *Geronticus eremita*, at Birecik, Turkey. *Zoology in the Middle East* 1(1), 42–43.
Kenyon, K. 1981. *Excavations at Jericho 3. The Architecture and Stratigraphy of the Tell*. London: British School of Archaeology in Jerusalem.
Kolankaya-Bostanici, N. 2014. The evidence of shamanism rituals in early prehistoric periods of Europe and Anatolia. In M. Alparslan, B. Hürmüzlü-Kortholt, N. Karul & E. Kortanoğlu (eds) *Colloquium Anatolicum* XIII, Istanbul: Institutum Turcicum Scientiae Antiquitatis, 185–204.
Kozlowski, S. K. & Kempisty, A. 1990. Architecture of the Pre-Pottery Neolithic settlement in Nemrik, Iraq. *World Archaeology* 21, 348–362.
Kromer, B. & Schmidt, K. 1998. Two radiocarbon dates from Göbekli Tepe, South Eastern Turkey. *Neo-Lithics* 3(98), 8–9.
Kuijt I. & Goring-Morris, N. 2002, Foraging, farming, and social complexity in the Pre-Pottery Neolithic of the Southern Levant: A review and synthesis. *Journal of World Prehistory* 16(4), 361–440.
La Barre, W. 1980. *Culture in Context*, Durham, NC: Duke University Press.
Lewis-Williams, D. 2004. *The Mind in the Cave. Consciousness and the Origin of Art*. London: Thames and Hudson.
Lewis-Williams, D. & Challis, S. 2011. *Deciphering Ancient Minds. The Mystery of San Bushman Rock Art*. London: Thames and Hudson.
Lewis-Williams, D. J. & Dowson, T. A. 1988. The signs of all times: entoptic phenomena in Upper Palaeolithic art. *Current Anthropology* 29(2), 201–245.
Lewis-Williams, D. & Pearce, D. 2005. *Inside the Neolithic Mind*. London: Thames and Hudson.
Lynch, F. 1998. Colour in prehistoric architecture. In A. Gibson & D. D. A. Simpson (eds) *Prehistoric Ritual and Religion: Essays in Honour of Aubrey Burl*. Stroud: Sutton, 62–67.
Maisels, C. K. 1993. *The Near East: Archaeology in the 'Cradle of Civilization'*. London: Routledge.
Matthews, R. 2003. *The Archaeology of Mesopotamia. Theories and Approaches*, London/New York: Routledge.
Mellaart, J. 1967. Çatal *Hüyük. A Neolithic Town in Anatolia*. London: Wheeler.
Mondal, P. C. K., Sankar, K. & Qureshi, Q. 2012. Food habits of golden jackal (*Canis aureus*) and striped hyena (*Hyaena hyaena*) in Sariska Tiger Reserve, Western India. *World Journal of Zoology* 7(2), 106–112.
Montage, J. 1965. What is a gong? *Man* 5, 18–21.
Nash, G. H. 2001. Altered states of consciousness and the afterlife: A reappraisal of a decorated bone piece from Ryemarksgaard, Central Zealand, Denmark. In A. M. Choyke & L. Bartosiewicz (eds) *Crafting Bone: Skeletal Technologies through Time and Space*. British Archaeological Report S937. Oxford: Archaeopress, 231–240.
Oestigaard, T. 2011. Water. In T. Insoll (ed.) *The Oxford Handbook of the Archaeology of Ritual and Religion*. Oxford: Oxford University Press, 38–50.
Olgunoğlu, I. A. 2011. Determination of the fundamental nutritional components in fresh and hot smoked spiny eel (*Mastacembelus mastacembelus*, Bank and Solander, 1794). *Scientific Research and Essays* 6(31), 6448–6453.
Otte, M. 2008. *Cro Magnon. Aux origins de notre humanité*. Paris: Éditions Perrin.
Ouzman, S. 1998. Towards a mindscape of landscape: rock art as expression of world-understanding. In C. Chippindale & P. S. C. Taçon (eds) *The Archaeology of Rock Art*. Cambridge: Cambridge University Press, 30–41.

Özdoğan, M. 2010. Transition from the round plan to rectangular. Reconsidering the evidence of Çayönü. In D. Gheorghiu (ed.) *Neolithic and Chalcolithic Architecture from Eurasia: Building Techniques and Social Implications of Technology.* British Archaeological Report S2097. Oxford: Archaeopress, 29–34.

Pásztor, E. 2011. Prehistoric sky lore and spirituality. In D. Gheorghiu (ed.) *Archaeology Experiences Spirituality?* Newcastle-upon-Tyne: Cambridge Scholars Publishing, 89–116.

Peatfield, A. D. & Morris, C. 2012. Dynamic spirituality on Minoan peak sanctuaries. In K. Roundtree, A. D. Peatfield, & C. Morris (eds) *Archaeology of Spiritualities.* New York/Heidelberg/Dordrecht/London: Springer, 227–245.

Pentikäinen, J. 1998. *Shamanism and Culture.* Helsinki: Etnika.

Peters, J. & Schmidt, K. 2004. Animals in the symbolic world of Pre-Pottery Neolithic Göbekli Tepe, south-eastern Turkey: a preliminary assessment. *Anthropozoologica* 39(1), 179–218.

Peirce, C. S. 1998. *The Essential Peirce* 2. Peirce Edition Project. Bloomington, IN: Indiana University Press.

Price, N. (ed.). 2001. *The Archaeology of Shamanism.* London: Routledge.

Reznikoff, I. 1995. On the sound dimension of prehistoric painted caves and rocks. In E. Taratsi (ed.) *Musical Signification: Essays on the Semiotic Theory and Analysis of Music.* New York: Mouton de Gruyter, 541–557.

Reznikoff, I. 2002. Prehistoric paintings, sound and rocks, In A. D. Kilmer & R. Eichmann (eds) *Studien zur Musikarchaologie III. The Archaeology of Sound: Origin and Organisation, Papers from the 2nd Symposium of the International Study Group on Music Archaeology at Monastery Michaelstein (September 17-23).* Rahden/Westfahlen: Marie Leidorf.

Reznikoff, I. 2006. The evidence of the use of sound resonance from Palaeolithic to Medieval times. In C. Scarre & G. Lawson (eds) *Archaeoacoustics.* Cambridge: McDonald Institute for Archaeological Research, 77–84.

Reznikoff, I. 2009. The sound dimension of the painted Palaeolithic caves. *Cognitive Processing* 10, 138.

Reznikoff, I. & Dauvois, M. 1988. La dimension sonore des grottes ornees. *Bulletin de la Societe Prehistorique Francaise* 85(8), 238–246.

Romaire, R. P., Forester, J. S. & Avault, J. W. 1977. Length-weight relationships of two commercially important crayfishes of the genus *Procambarus. Freshwater Crayfish* 3, 463–470.

Sahinöz, E., Faruk, A. & Zafer, D. 2007. Changes in Mesopotamian spiny eel, *Mastacembelus mastacembelus* (Bank & Solender in Russell, 1794) (*Mastacembelidae*) milt quality during a spawning period. *Theriogenology* 67, 848–854.

Scarre, C. 2006. Sound, place and space: towards an archaeology of acoustics. In C. Scarre, & G. Lawson (eds) *Archaeoacoustics.* Cambridge: McDonald Institute for Archaeological Research, 1–10.

Schmidt, K. 2010. Göbekli Tepe – the Stone Age sanctuaries. New results of ongoing excavations with a special focus on sculptures and high reliefs. *Documenta Praehistorica* XXXVII, 239–256.

Schmidt, K., 2011. Göbekli Tepe. In M. Özdoğan, N. Başgelen, & P. Kuniholm (eds) *The Neolithic in Turkey. New Excavations and New Research.* Istanbul: Archaeology and Art Publications, 41–83.

Schmidt, K. 2012. *Göbekli Tepe. A Stone Age Sanctuary in South-Eastern Anatolia.* Berlin: ex-Oriente.

Séfériades, M. 2010. A propos d'un spondyle de Nitra (fouilles J. Pavuk). Shamanisme protohistorique en Europe centrale et sud-orientale. In *Panta Rhei. Studies on the Chronology and Cultural Development of South-Eastern and Central Europe in Earlier Prehistory Presented to Juraj Pavuk on the Occasion of his 75th Birthday.* Bratislava: Comenius University in Bratislava and Archaeological Centre, Olomouc, 593–599.

Séfériades. M. 2011. Protohistoric *Spondylus gaederopus L.* shell: some considerations on the earliest European long-distance exchanges related to shamanism. In A. Vianello (ed.) *Exotica in the Prehistoric Mediterranean.* Oxford: Oxbow Books, 3–12.

Serra, G., Peske, L., Scheisch Abdallah, M., al Qaim, G. & Kanani, A. 2009. Breeding ecology and behaviour of the last wild oriental northern bald ibises (*Geronticus eremita*) in Syria. *Journal of Ornithology* 150, 769–782.

Siikala, A-L. & Hoppál, M, (eds). 1992. *Studies on Shamanism*. Ethnologica Uralica 2. Helsinki/Budapest: Finnish Anthropological Society – Akadémiai Kiadó.

Thesiger, W. 2007. *The Marsh Arabs*. London/New York/Toronto/Sydney: Harper Perrennal.

Tristram, H. B. 1868. *The Natural History of the Bible*, 2nd edition. London: Society for Promoting Christian Knowledge.

Turner, E. 2005. Shamanic power and the collective unconscious: An exploration of group experience. *Shaman* 13(1–2), 115–132.

Twiss, K. C. 2008. Transformations in an early agricultural society: Feasting in the southern Levantine pre-pottery Neolithic. *Journal of Anthropological Archaeology* 27, 418–442.

Ünlü, E. & Bozkurt, R. 1996. Notes on the catfish, *Silurustriostegus* (*Siluridae*) from the Euphrates River in Turkey. *Cybinum* 20, 315–317.

Ünlü, E., Değer, D. & Çiçek, T. 2012. Comparison of morphological and anatomical characters in two catfish species, *Silurus triostegus* Heckel, 1843 and *Silurus glanis L.*, 1758 (*Siluridae, Siluriformes*). *North-Western Journal of Zoology* 8(1), 119–124.

Ur, J. 2009. Cycles of civilization in northern Mesopotamia, 4400–2000 BC. *Journal of Archaeological Research*, http://www.springerlink.com/content/u423066748kl93v5/? p=74dff5d53bd648b9a263eb810fd1370d&pi=1 [accesses 09.11.2017]

Vaitl, D., Birbaumer, N., Gruzelier, J., Jamieson, G. A., Kotchoubey, B., Kübler, A., Lehmann, D., Miltner, W. H. R., Ott, U., Pütz, P., Sammer, G., Strauch, I., Strehl, U., Wackermann, J. & Weiss, T. 2005. Psychobiology of altered states of consciousness. *Psychological Bulletin of the American Psychological Association* 131(1), 98–127.

Van de Ven, T. M. F. N., Tambling, C. J. & Kerley, G. I. H. 2013. Seasonal diet of black-backed jackal in the Eastern Karoo, South Africa. *Journal of Arid Environments* 99, 23–27.

Wason, P. K. 2010. The Neolithic cosmos at Çatalhöyük, In I. Hodder (ed.) *Religion in the Emergence of Civilization:* Çatalhöyük *as a Case Study*. Cambridge: Cambridge University Press, 208–299.

Watkins, T. 2010. Changing people, changing environments: How hunter-gatherers became communities that changed the world. In B. Finlayson & G. Warren (eds) *Landscapes in Transition*. Oxford: Oxbow Books, 106–114.

Watson, A. 2006. (Un) intentional sound? Acoustics and Neolithic monuments. In C. Scarre & G. Lawson (eds) *Archaeoacoustics*. Cambridge: McDonald Institute Monographs, 11–22.

Watson, A. & Keating, D. 1999. Architecture and sound: an acoustic analysis of megalithic monuments in prehistoric Britain. *Antiquity* 73, 325–336.

Winkelman, M., 1989. Shamanism and altered states of consciousness: An introduction. *Journal of Psychoactive Drugs* 21(1), 159–180. DOI: 10.1080/02791072.1989.10472137

Winkelman, M. 2002. Shamanism as neurotheology and evolutionary psychology. *American Behavioral Scientist* 45(12), 1873–1885.

Witzel, M. E. J. 2011. Shamanism in northern and southern Eurasia: Their distinctive methods of change of consciousness. *Social Science Information* 50(1), 39–61.

Yarnell, R. W., Louis Phipps W., Burgess, L. P., Ellis, J. A., Harrison, S. W. R., Dell, S., MacTavish, D., MacTavish, L. M. & Scott, D. M. 2013. The influence of large predators on the feeding ecology of two African mesocarnivores: the black-backed jackal and the brown hyena. *South African Journal of Wildlife Research* 43(2), 155–166.

The Epic of Gilgamesh, English version by N. K. Sandars, 1972. Penguin Classics.

Chapter 3

Caves and the Sacral Landscape: A Case Study on the Neolithic and Early Aeneolithic Periods in South-east Central Europe

Vladimír Peša

Abstract *Interpretive models of the function and significance of caves in prehistoric society are closely related to developments in the field of archaeology and changes in thinking during the 19th and early 20th centuries, which in Central and South-east Europe continues to have a strong influence on these models to this day. Looking at the proto-Neolithic to the Early Aeneolithic, the periods of shamanic religion in central Europe, this chapter tests the relationship between archaeological finds, cave characteristics (morphology), and basic functional models of their use (habitation, pastoralism, social-ritual behaviour and cult practices). The most important archaeological sites in Czech Republic, Slovakia, Hungary, Romania and Bulgaria (i.e., working regions) are associated primarily with the recesses of dark or semi-dark caves, and for the most part show evidence of cult activity and shaman rituals. At this same time, the main phases of cave use correspond to periods of significant climatic change with periods of drought and instability (about 5300, 5000/4900 and 4000 cal. BCE). It would appear that cult activity during these periods of climatic disruption occurred only in traditional societies, whereas caves were not used by cultures that were more advanced from a civilisation viewpoint. From a general cosmological viewpoint, the underworld is part of the nonhuman realm and, like the heavens, is reserved for the deities and gods. As a natural archetype in human society, the cave was a space for communicating with the gods and, along with archaeological sites from hilltops, may express a knowledge of the mythological Cosmic Axis as early as during the Neolithic and Aeneolithic. Cave sites were probably important cult or religious centres that fall within the concept of the sacral shamanic landscape, whose universality is documented by geographically remote analogies (Mezoamerica, Siberia, etc.). Such a concept of the landscape is closer to the traditional view of the Central European landscape of the Middle Ages and the early modern era, and has only been relatively recently forgotten by the modern world.*

Introduction

From the beginning of archaeological excavations in the 19th century up to the present day, caves as archaeological sites have most often been interpreted as longer- or shorter-term habitation sites, hideaways or shelters for herdsmen; other interpretations that have been considered for caves are centres for cult activity and their use as shelters for social outcasts. Based on these ideas, I see the beginnings of these notions of caves' universal functions in two contexts (Peša 2011). Firstly, until the second half of the 20th century there was a predominant interest throughout most of Palaeolithic Europe, and an interpretive model of Palaeolithic cave settlement was subsequently applied to what were often less distinct or even different artefact situations dating to post-Mesolithic periods. Secondly, at the close of the 19th century most of the scientific community (i.e., including archaeologists) considered caves as shelters from warfare or as cover from inclement weather while engaged in agricultural activities away from the main settlement. Any speculation on the greater importance of cult activities and the symbolism of caves does not appear with greater regularity in the literature until the 1980s, and yet the general impression of central European caves as settlements persists. Using the Neolithic period as an example, this chapter attempts to describe the phenomenon of cave-use both within the broader chronological context and as a functional interpretation of archaeological evidence in relation to the natural character of caves. Cult rituals and practices in the Neolithic world can be considered as shaman religion because of the hierarchy of this society and redistribution of wealth (comparison with Nicholson 1993).

Methodology

This chapter looks at the Neolithic and early Aeneolithic periods in an attempt at describing the phenomenon of cave-use within a broader chronological context and as a functional interpretation of archaeological evidence with a view towards the natural character of caves and the landscape in general. The chronological section is limited to the beginning of agriculture in the Near East and the end of the Lengyel complex in central Europe (Fig. 3.1). Particular attention is paid to the diverse nature of the periods of interest and the lack of interest in caves from the viewpoint of archaeological cultures and their potential spatial and temporal relationships. Also discussed is the question of whether cave sites reflect local socio-cultural expressions or whether they are a more universal phenomenon across culturally diverse regions – for instance in relation to climate change. The second point to consider is interpretation. Part of this study focuses on evaluating the arguments for the currently popular theory of caves' as possessing multifunctional use as described above.

The author considers caves as a specific type of archaeological site whose natural character combines the world of nature (represented by the form and character of the underground spaces) with the cultural world in cases where human agency has left

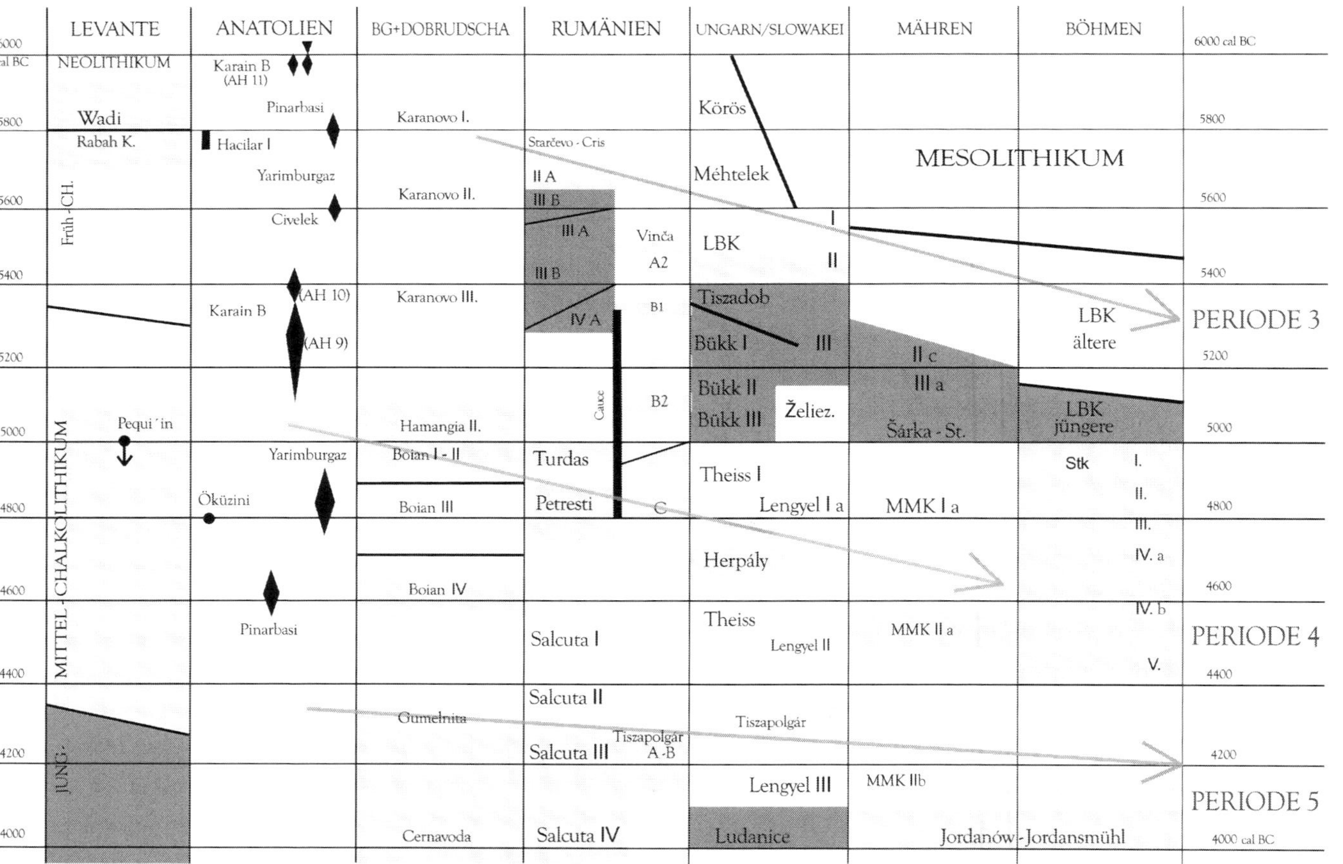

Fig. 3.1: A chronological and geographical overview of the use of caves in the region stretching from the Near East to Central Europe, showing the hypothetical waves of the spread of the cave phenomenon (arrows). Cultures with an especially strong relationship to caves are marked in red (drawing by author)

surviving archaeological evidence (such as cave art). This interrelationship is found not only in archaeology (specifically, the sub-discipline of *speleoarchaeology*), but also in other areas of human culture that are studied by ethnology, history, psychology, and other disciplines. Unlike other form of human activity, caves are natural sites that remain essentially unchanged over time which I consider other 'non-archaeological' viewpoints to be potentially important, for they may allow for a better understanding of caves as archaeological sites. I include these complex and mutual interrelationships under the term *speleoanthropology* (Peša 2013c).

Source Material

Essentially, speleoarchaeology as a specific sub-discipline of archaeology as we know it in central Europe does not exist in south-eastern Europe, Anatolia, or further east. This affects not only the manner in which cave sites are published (there are no monographs of cave regions, nor summary overviews or similar works), but also the interpretation of the sites themselves. By working overwhelmingly with primary publications, the source material has attempted to provide a systematic overview of most of the published cave sites and to collect information of finds in caves from the studied transect stretching from the Levant to central Europe. Re-evaluations of sites and new interpretational studies have already been presented for the Levant and Anatolia (Peša 2011), the Western Carpathian region (Slovakia, Hungary: Peša 2013a), and the Bohemian Karst (Peša 2013b). In the Balkans, important information on an interpretational level in general and more specifically for the situation further to the northwest in and around the Carpathian Basin is provided by Romanian caves, whose partial interpretation (including several new findings and observations) is summarised in Case Study 1. More detailed attention is also paid to Moravian caves (Case Study 2), which form the main foundation for speleoarchaeological research in the Czech Republic.

Case Study 1: Romanian Caves

With its thousands of caves and several hundred known speleoarchaeological sites, Romania represents a significant potential region for cave archaeology. In Romanian caves, the Mesolithic has been documented (or rather, identified) practically only in the greater environs of the Iron Gates on the Danube River. Both the open Mesolithic settlement at Schela Cladovei and two other studied cave sites (the Cuina Turcului rockshelter and the terrace in front of the Veterani/Maovaţ cave) show complex settlement horizons with diverse groups of finds pointing towards both profane and sacral activities by these hunter-fisher-gatherer communities. In the Iron Gates region, this observation can also be applied to the subsequent Early Neolithic period, when the Starčevo-Criş culture (phase IIA/IIB) adopted Late Mesolithic traditions probably more or less fluidly (Boroneanţ 1970a; Bolomey 1973, 199; Păunescu 1970 and 1979). In my view, the comprehensive artefact spectrum, combined with numerous scattered hearths lacking any further settlement features, paints an image of a long-term, intensively and frequently visited places where semi-sedentary or sedentary Mesolithic and to some extent also Neolithic populations engaged in everyday activities (Fig. 3.2). The latest studies of the transition between the Mesolithic and the Early Neolithic in the Iron Gates area also indicate a local continuity tending more towards the adoption of new ideas and objects instead of the penetration of more numerous agricultural groups (Radovanović 1996). If we call these sites *temporary settlements* in terms of habitation, then the other Neolithic and Proto-Aeneolithic cave sites paint a different picture of cave use. In its middle and later phases (II B–IV A, i.e., an interval of roughly 250 years, Mantu 1998), the Early Neolithic period of the Starčevo-Criş culture is the first post-Mesolithic horizon of cave use in Romania. Until the Late Aeneolithic, however, it is important to bear in mind that the number of caves per culture is relatively small and is statistically of a limited informational value. Despite this issue, however, one can at least sketch a working hypothesis as to the general outlines of cave use in Romania. Only a few isolated sites are known from the Vinča culture (A2–C), and the only larger known groupings of sites from this period are from Dobruja during the late Hamangia culture, or even more noticeably from the Cluj-Cheile Turzii cultural complex (CCTLNI). This may have been a precursor to the subsequent Late Neolithic and Proto-Aeneolithic between *c.* 4700 and 4400 cal. BCE (Mantu 1998), which represents the second horizon of cave use in Romania (the Herpály, Petreşti, and older Gumelniţa cultures). Interest in caves continues during the Early Aeneolithic, although its geographic distribution changes. New cave sites appear in the Banat and western Transylvania as part of the Sălcuţa II–III, Herculane I and Tiszapolgár A–B cultures, with these sites used by the subsequent Middle Aeneolithic cultures without any more significant hiatuses until the conspicuous increase in interest during the transition to the Early Bronze Age. By comparison, during the subsequent Tiszapolgár period, the Herpály cultural space shows a decline in utilised sites until their complete absence in the Middle Aeneolithic. In Dobruja the transition from the Early to Middle Aeneolithic (late Gumelniţa – Cernavoda I) marks the definitive end of the prehistoric use of karst caves in the region.

A general look at the changing interest in caves in Romania thus leads to the following conclusions:

- Late Neolithic: following a 'preparatory' period during the Middle and perhaps also Early (?) Neolithic, most regions with caves witness the beginning of long-term (though more or less interrupted) cave use, reaching its climax in the Late Aeneolithic both in terms of the number of sites and the complicated structure of several find situations.
- This long-term and only locally influenced relationship between human communities and caves must have emerged from a continuous awareness of the importance or social value of these specific places, or for other socio-economic reasons that were of repeated importance for several centuries of development of Aeneolithic society.

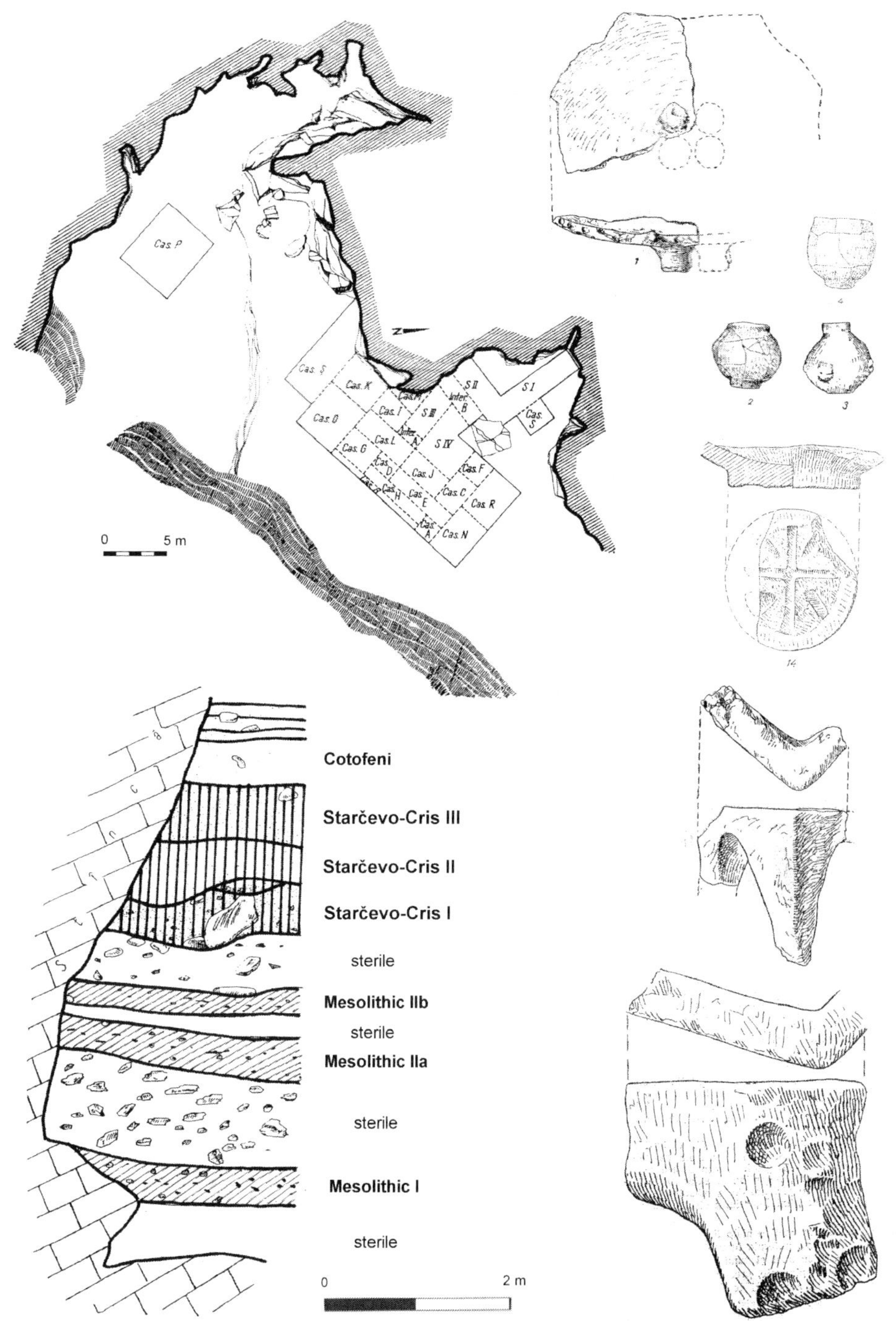

Fig. 3.2: Cuina Turcului rockshelter in the Iron Gates (Romania). Plan and a cross-section with the crosshatched Neolithic sequence, and uncommon ceramic shapes of the Starčevo-Criş IIA – III culture (after Păunescu 1970; 1979)

Deposition and Interpretation

The typical Romanian cave site consists predominantly of a thin cultural layer from the period under review with surviving or scattered hearths and no other features. The find assemblages contain varying numbers of pottery shards, with only rare occurrences of stone or bone tools or small decorative items present. Where we have data from the literature, there is a relatively frequent incidence of fine ceramic tableware but practically no storage vessels. There are only rare examples of exceptional find situations from Romanian caves. Besides the Iron Gates region, thicker cultural layers with a larger number of finds are found in Dobruja, where the dominant assemblage is pottery. As compared to the Iron Gates, other categories are represented very weakly or not at all. This also applies to bone from domesticated animals, which are often used to hypothesise a site's use by pastoralists. For Dobruja, the only sites evidenced in the literature are from the settlement area of the La Adam Cave and the nearby rock-shelters (Radulesco & Samson 1962; Vencl 1968, 44). Surprisingly, animal bone is very scarce in many cave sites, and a similar shortage of food waste speaks against the caves' more intensive or long-term settlement in the sense of habitation. Nor were the caves generally used for productive or everyday artisan activities, because there is practically no production waste of bone or polished stone tools; the only exception are the Devenţ and Cauce Caves. Two caves (Climente I and Spurcată) contain unusual features – pits with a large volume of pottery lacking a corresponding cultural layer. During the Neolithic and Early Aeneolithic, there are still no signs of any burial caves in the sense of special underground mortuary areas with surface burials of the kind found in Romania during later prehistory. Again, there is an exception to this rule – the small shallow cavity known as Piatra Jurcoaiei with one crouched burial accompanied by several typical grave goods (Ignat 1973; Ignat Sava 1974). Exceptional find situations that in my opinion allow us to consider the possibility of cult activities have been documented in the Hoţilor Cave near Băile Herculane (Roman 1971) (Fig. 3.3) and the 'Water Cave' (*Peştera cu apă*) near Româneşti (D. B. 1949; Mogoşanu & Stratan 1966). Most local activities, however, are focused around the Middle and Late Aeneolithic – i.e., the period during which in all likelihood the earliest post-Palaeolithic wall paintings appeared in Romanian caves (cf. Cârciumaru 1987).

One point demanding further consideration is the concept of caves as a natural feature and their suitability for human activities. With a view towards the find situations, only two sites from the Mesolithic or Early Neolithic (the Cuina Turcului rock-shelter and the terrace in front of Veterani Cave by the Iron Gates – Boroneanţ 1970a; 1970b; Bolomey 1973; Păunescu 1979). These examples can be called settlement sites in the sense of them being intensive or long-term inhabitation sites. The Early Neolithic Starčevo-Criş culture already shows a tendency towards the utilisation of various forms of underground spaces – i.e., not only light and dry caves suitable for settlement, but also the entryways of more extensive karst systems (e.g. Liliecilor Cave: Cădariu & Petrovszky 1975, Caves Ponicova and Muierilor: Gheorghiu *et al.*

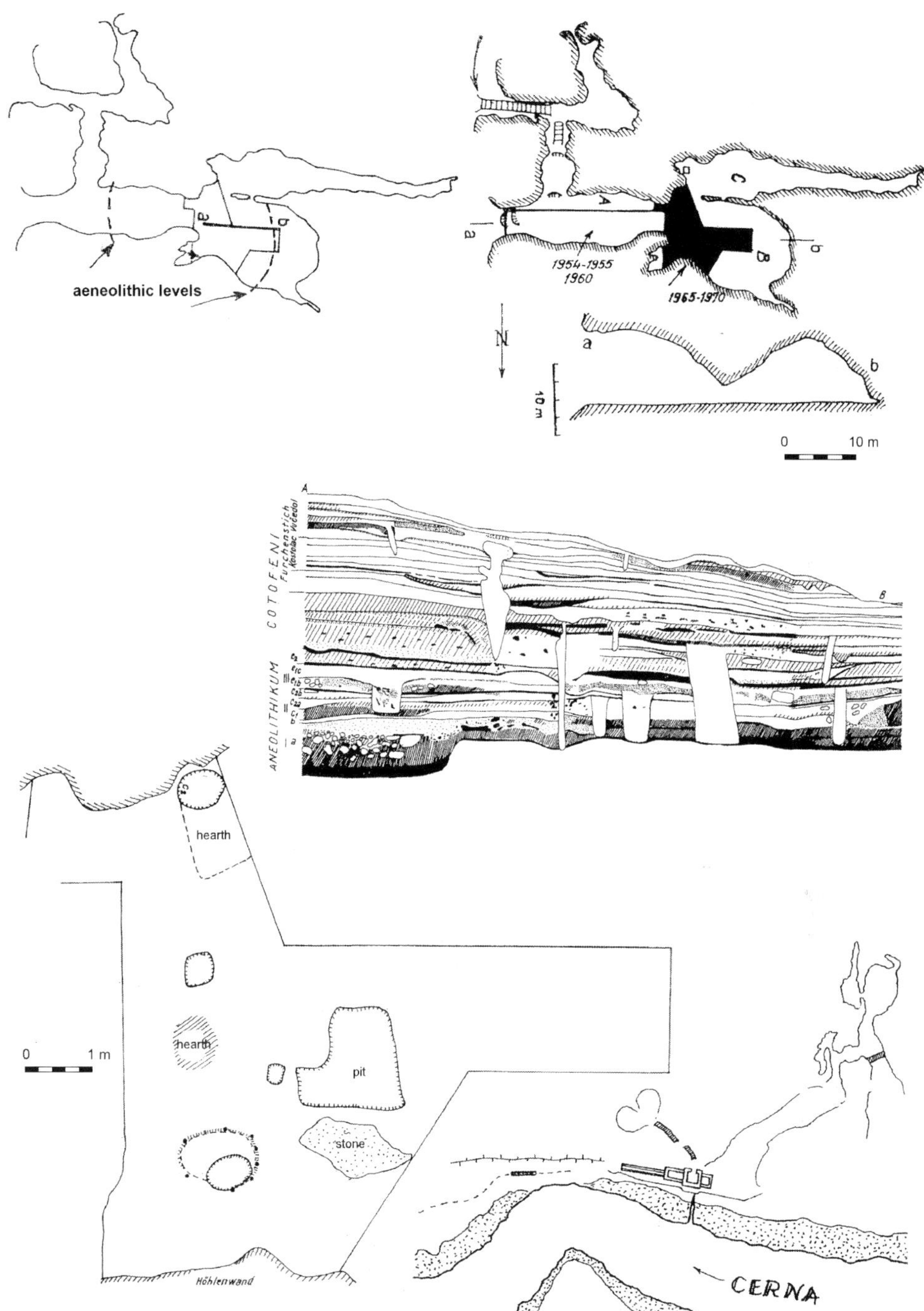

Fig. 3.3: Peştera Hoţilor (Băile Herculane, Romania). Plans and find situation of the Early Aeneolithic horizon (after Roman 1971), below cave position in areal of the antique spa (Lalescu-Benea 1997–98)

1954; Nicolăescu-Plopşor *et al.* 1957a). Other cave sites are marked by the presence of underground water systems, such as subterranean streams (Dumbrava), speleothems (Ponicova, Cioclovina, Mereşti?), large, centrally located phallus-shaped stalagmites (Bordu Mare: Nicolăescu-Plopşor *et al.* 1957b, fig. 5), or the preference of dark spaces over light spaces within one and the same cave (Dîmbul Colibii II: Vlassa 1961, 1976). These characteristics are reminiscent of the situation during late prehistory, when similar sites are associated with cult activities, with the accentuated presence of metal artefacts in the form of sacrifices. The deposition of Vinča A culture vessels in the shallow cleft cave known as the 'Cave with Vessel' (*Peştera cu vas*: Luca *et al.* 1997; 2000, 10) may also point to another cult practice from later periods, when vessels – presumably containing sacrifices. These items were often placed into difficult-to-reach caves (cf. Peša 2006; 2008). If we consider the number of natural caves and thus also the large range of suitable rock hollows, in all of Romania's karst regions under discussion the prehistoric population shows a striking tradition of use and continued awareness of certain caves' existence (Devenţ, Peştera cu apă near Devenţ, Peştera Mare de la Cerişor, Ungurească, with the last two examples showing exceptional ritualised activity: Roman *et al.* 2000, Lazarovici *et al.* 2004; 2006). 'Uninhabitable' caves of the Late Neolithic/Proto-Aeneolithic include the Meziad, Igriţa and Ungurului cave systems, the finds from the dark parts of the caves in Dîmbul Colibii II, and the Calului stalactite cave near Mereşti.

Case Study 2: Caves in the Moravian Karst, Czech Republic: General Chronology

I now wish to turn my attentions to the caves of Moravia. There are currently 18 sites that allow for a closer chronological determination and that hint at having some common signs of utilisation. Most of these sites, 16 in title, show activities during the Linear Pottery Culture (Linienbandkeramik, LBK). Caves remained entirely outside of human attention during the subsequent Stroke-Ornamented Ware Culture (the only unpublished exception so far is Býčí Skála (Martin Golec pers. comm.), and people did not begin to visit caves until during the Moravian Painted Ware Culture (MMK), for which up to ten cave sites are known. So far, the sporadic finds for the Jordanów Culture (2–3 caves) and for the subsequent period of the Early and Middle Aeneolithic (Neruda *et al.* 2007; Svoboda & van der Plicht 2007) point only towards occasional activities, and this situation remains unchanged until the next large wave of interest in caves during the Early Bronze Age (Stuchlík 1981).

During the Neolithic, it was thus not common for people to look for and utilise cave sites; cave use was not a typical characteristic of LBK society, nor did it satisfy their everyday needs during this 600 to 700-year period. Based on available evidence, the earliest agriculturalists appear to have not been drawn to cave sites. This situation only changed 400 years later with the development of phase II, when the cave sites were utilised for the first time.

Caves in the Middle Neolithic (LBK)

The current interpretation of the presence of LBK in Moravian caves is based on the discovery of a vessel fragment that has an anthropomorphic face relief in the Koňská Jáma cave (see Fig. 3.13) and on alleged evidence of anthropophagy in Barová Cave, which has been ascribed to cult practices or periods of famine (Podborský 1993, 81, 99). These theories date back to the time of Josef Skutil during the 20th century, who explored Koňská Jáma and personally experienced its atmosphere on the boundary between light and dark, an experience coloured by the exceptional find situation. As a knowledgeable expert of other cave sites in the Moravian Karst, he assumed a cult significance for other caves as well – e.g., Výpustek (Skutil 1962; 1970, 323). M. Oliva (1995; 2013) has studied the general use of Moravian caves since the 1990s, and assumes a cult significance for numerous sites as well.

What do the presumed Neolithic cult caves look like? Before being devastated by military in the first third of the 20th century, the Výpustek Cave (Fig. 3.4) was the most extensive cave labyrinth in Moravia. Because of its several vertical shafts, starting in the

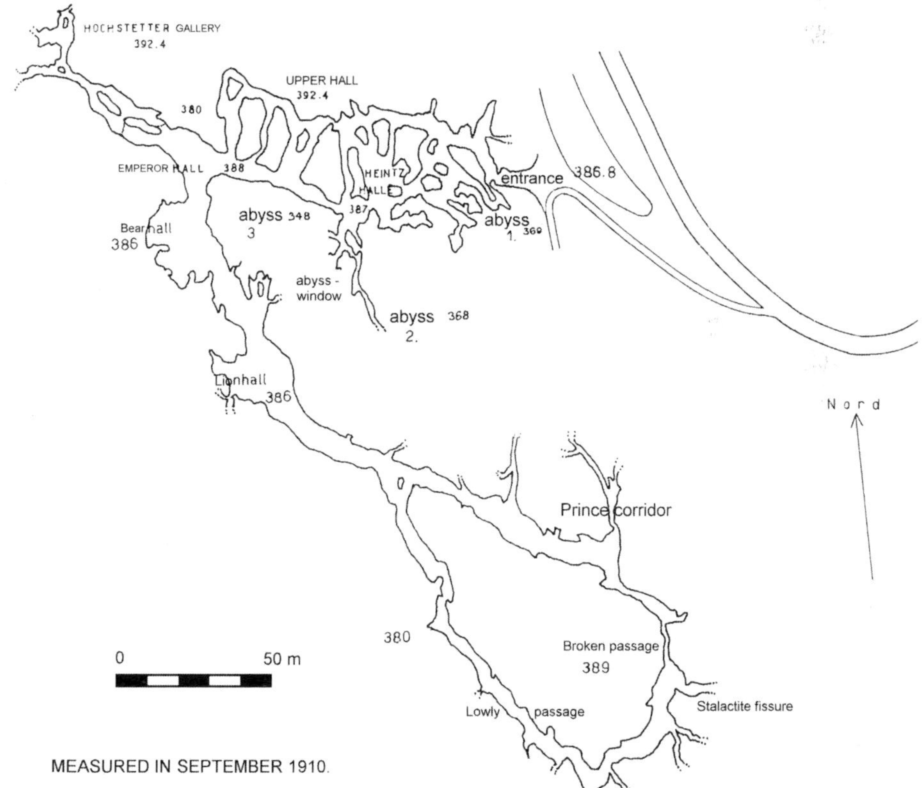

Fig. 3.4: Výpustek Cave (Moravian Karst, Czech Republic). Plan (1910) after copy by Norbert Havlíček in 1942 (archive of the Czech speleological society, Prague)

early modern era it was also considered one of the most dangerous caves for visitors. Its Neolithic cultural layer, which reached into the ancillary crawlspace corridors, yielded numerous finds, including around 60 bone tools, 12 polished stone and 30 chipped stone artefacts, 6 grinding stones, and small decorative items (Musil 2010). Szombathy discovered a find resembling an urn grave that is still awaiting analysis (Hochstetter 1883; Měchurová 1992, no. 7). The draught in the cave provided excellent conditions for the existence of fires, whose smoke reached all the way into the rear reaches of the entryways and, together with waste from torches, created a carbon layer on the sinter-covered cave floor. The inhospitable nature of cave system and their effect on the human psyche is documented by the testimony of people who worked in the local underground factory during World War II, who described long-term feelings of confinement from the cave atmosphere (Skutil 1947). Another site – Koňská jáma – is an example of a mid-sized cave. Because of its narrow entrances, its dome-shaped upper level is for the most part without daylight. The low stalactite corridor on the lower level is accessible via a shallow chasm. The larger portion of Neolithic finds was spread out near the entrances, but partially reached deeper into the cave and in isolated instances (including one hearth) was located on the bottom of the completely dark rear dome. The famous fragment of a vessel with a face relief was found in the zone of transition between light and dark, although it could of course have been thrown there from the entrance area (Skutil 1962; 1963b; Jarošová 2002, 255). Excavations performed using modern archaeological techniques have confirmed observations from other Neolithic cave sites regarding the conspicuous absence of chipped stone industry, represented at most by isolated tools (Štrof & Štrofová 1988, 23). The cave's inclined stone floor and permanent darkness do not combine to create inhabitable conditions.

The third cult site, Barová Cave, is located more than 100 m above the valley floor. From its dark first chamber, corridors drop steeply into the abyss of the active karst system of Býčí skála (Bull Rock Cave). Some authors have described a draught in the cave that blows from the abyss, and in the past one could hear the murmur of the underground Jedovnický Creek. There are minor LBK and MMK finds (fragments of vessels, stone hatchets, bones of game animals, traces of fire), and the cave's utilisation was probably limited solely to the dark entry hallway (Sobol 1949; Strnad 1949; Horáček *et al.* 2002, 316–318). The human skeletal remains found in connection with the 'Neolithic' hearth in front of the cave were associated with the Neolithic era by mistake, for the site's oldest horizon dates to the Aeneolithic, as confirmed by archaeologist Jiří Svoboda (Sobol 1968; Skutil 1970, 319; Svoboda 1987 and oral information from 2009). By comparison, there is no record of any post-Neolithic finds from the cave itself – a fact I consider particularly interesting. It seems likely that at some point between the Late Neolithic and Middle Aeneolithic, the low entryway (which is below today's ground level) was made inaccessible by a natural sedimentary layer in front of the cave, meaning that any further use of the cave was limited to the small terrace beneath the slightly overhanging rock wall, which provides only limited shelter from the elements and is mostly covered by snow in the winter. So why was this place (which was uninteresting in terms of utilisation) repeatedly visited by Aeneolithic, Bronze-Age and Hallstatt peoples, if they had more easily accessible and spacious caves such as Jáchymka and Kostelík nearby? The location may have possessed some specific significance based on ancient tradition or on a perception of the landscape that continued even after the cave had become inaccessible. During the Neolithic, the cave *per se* may thus have been a means for achieving higher (religious?) objectives, and not the main reason for the visits. In this context, we should mention the dominant rock wall above the entrance to the famed Býčí Skála, on whose upper reaches Barová Cave is located and which may also have been of symbolic significance within the landscape. The last cave more generally considered to have been a cult site is the crevice known as Kapustovka in Babická Skalka, which despite its limited size yielded a relatively abundant and diverse range of items (fragments of ceramic tableware and containers, a bone pin, a flint knife, and a drilled white-stone disc – Blatný 1962) that contrast markedly with the cave's presumed functional use during the modern era, when it acted merely as a shelter for a military deserter who left no surviving traces. Non-ceramic artefacts, however, could also come from later use dated to the time of the Jordanów Culture.

Additional caves with a remarkable morphology of spaces are concentrated, in particular, within the northern part of the Moravian Karst, but these have yielded no exceptional finds. Kateřinská Cave near Koňská Jáma contains a large natural dome – during the 19th century it was still one of the largest in central Europe – that may have been accessible by a low crawlspace as early as during prehistoric times. Besides speleothems (later destroyed), the dome also yielded surface finds of Pleistocene bones that occasionally fell down from one of the lateral chimneys. However, only experienced explorers who could find their way through the maze of rocks back to the entrance corridor dared to visit. The randomly preserved Neolithic cultural layer, found only in the spacious antechamber below the cave's entrance portal, yielded fragments of fine LBK pottery, one fragment of a container, and the scorched bones of a bovine (Svoboda & Seitl 1985; Geislerová *et al.* 1986). Similarly, the moist and cool Pod Hradem Cave yielded only a few fragments of LBK vessels in a thin cultural layer near the corridor's entrance (Ondruš 1965). Pod Hradem is a typical bear cave from the Pleistocene, and so it is possible that during prehistory it was home to surface remains of cave bears that did not go unnoticed by Neolithic visitors. Studies of Michalka Cave described exceptionally abundant speleothems with various forms of white sinter shapes including a phallus-shaped (?) stalagmite (Soukop 1859, 81; Absolon 1970/1, 159). The cave's corridor is easily accessible and passable, suggesting that Neolithic visitors surely witnessed the sinter formations. Michalka's entryway yielded a relatively thick cultural layer with numerous LBK fragments, horse and cow bones, and possibly also two chipped stone artefacts (Knies 1922, 68 et seq.; Trampler 1900; Skutil 1961, 31).

Contrasting sharply with caves with problematic or expressly inauspicious conditions for settlement or habitation are spacious and light-filled sites that are

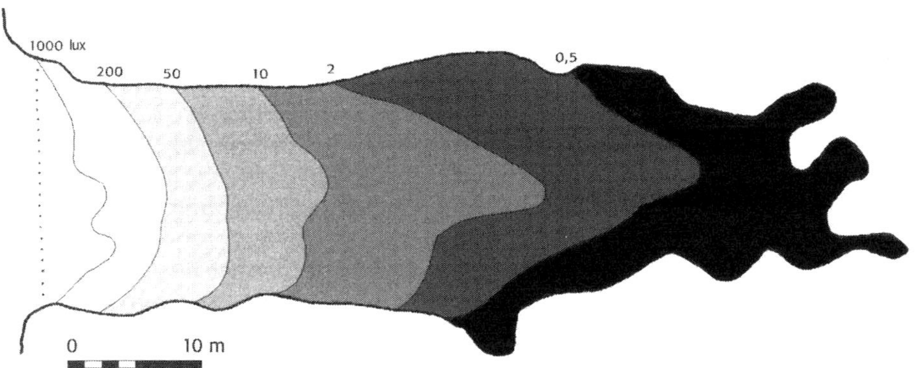

Fig. 3.5: Pekárna Cave (Moravian Karst, Czech Republic). Light conditions in the cave (mesured in lux by Peša & Majer) (image: V. Peša 1999)

usually associated with settlement. Of these, the first that should be discussed here is the best-known such site – Pekárna Cave (Fig. 3.5), a centrally-located site in the southern part of the Moravian Karst to whose settlement interpretation I add the following exceptions:

- Certain indications allow us to consider a different picture of the cave at the beginning of its Neolithic use: Most archaeologists who have studied Pekárna are consistent in describing a layer of sinter or travertine that separated the Neolithic horizon from the Palaeolithic horizon, probably in the entire front part of the cave. In addition, excavations from the late 19th century, which only rarely reached down into the Pleistocene sediments, are described as possessing isolated fragments of speleothems (Krasser 1882; Kříž 1898; Absolon & Czižek 1926, 1927–28; 1932). A follow-up study by J. Svoboda identified a microclimate conducive to the formation of sinter for the period from 500 to 3300 years ago (Svoboda *et al.* 2000, 64). At the beginning of its Neolithic use during the Younger Atlantic, should we thus imagine Pekárna as a partial 'stalactite' cave with sinter covering the floor all the way to the entryway, plus perhaps the limited existence of speleothems? Such a type of cave, however, would be far less attractive for settlement than one in the state as we know it today.
- Early reports and the data from Absolon's excavation describe a small amount of Neolithic chipped stone industry, limited exclusively to single pieces from various excavations – i.e., a situation similar to the one in Koňská Jáma Cave (Geislerová *et al.* 1986). This observation speaks against activities associated with the production or working of chipped stone industry, which was one of the most common work activities at sedentary sites.
- Despite their unclear association with the Neolithic layers of the caves' prehistoric sediments, animal bones are also worthy of attention. Pekárna's prehistoric (and

thus partially also Neolithic) layers would appear to be dominated by red deer and roe deer, which are mentioned by all authors. Domesticated animals are more frequently mentioned by the authors of 19th-century studies, whereas the findings of Absolon's excavations generally describe them in second place or even at the end of the list of animal species. The fragmentary data from the other caves of the Moravian Karst might support the greater significance of members of the deer family (sp. *Cervidae*). The picture of a cave with a shelter for domesticated animals (and their associated death or consumption) would thus appear to be erroneous.

- Standing out from the find situation of Absolon's excavation in Pekárna is the Neolithic fire pit at the cave entrance with several noteworthy findings that are unusual for a hearth's inventory – clay weights, spindle whorls, and a bone tool in the shape of a 'dagger' (Absolon & Czižek 1927–28, 120).
- M. Kříž (1892; 1897) describes the incidence of bones from black and brown rats in the uppermost cultural layer. These rodents, which are considered important indicators of more permanent settlement, have been documented among other places at large settlements of the proto-Neolithic Natufian Culture, which is assumed to have been inhabited for several months out of the year or even year-round (Bar-Yosef & Tchernov 1966). Although the research method prevents us from knowing the age of the black and brown rat bones at Pekárna, their location in the uppermost layer allows a dating to the historic era or at least the late prehistoric era – i.e., not the Neolithic, for which Kříž provides a separate list of microfauna.

To summarise these qualifications, it would seem that there was no long-term or more permanent settlement at Pekárna during the Neolithic. This finding is in agreement with the lack of evidence of chipped stone industry and with the small number of domesticated animals at the site. If the cave's oldest image is of a cave with a thick layer of sinter and at least some speleothems, at the beginning of its Neolithic use Pekárna would be placed alongside other sites with speleothems or sinter that have been described as possessing a cult context (caves Výpustek, Michalka, Kateřinská). The cave's tradition as a cult site could have endured for a long time afterwards, even if the sinter layer was later covered by a cultural layer and the speleothems were covered in soot or destroyed.

The second large and light-filled cave is Kůlna, located within the northern part of the Moravian Karst, on the margins of the LBK settlement area. Its location probably accounts for the limited finds from this otherwise comprehensively studied site (Kříž 1889, 53 et seq.; 1909, 9). A follow-up study by Valoch determined a find-poor layer of LBK, preserved solely in front of the cave. It also showed a minimal incidence of chipped stone industry (Valoch 1967, 570; 1988, 16). Despite the cave's large size, microclimatic observations show poor conditions for normal inhabitation – a strong draught sometimes blows through the entire cave, and a large volume of water leaks through the cave's ceiling during year-round rain showers (Knies 1910; 1911, 137).

The other sites lack both more distinctive finds or find situations, as well as, any information on climatic conditions or unusual cave interiors. Some are quite small (Hadí Cave – Klíma 1961; Liščí Díra – Klíma 2002; Stuchlík 2002; Žitný Cave – Valoch 1957) and if necessary could offer barely enough shelter for one family. There basically remains just four caves that support the possibility of serving in a settlement capacity: the large, light-filled, and dry Rytířská jeskyně (Absolon jun. 1939–40; Absolon 1970/1, 233 et seq.; Skutil 1961; 1963a; 1970, 323; Jarošová 2002; Tichý 2002), the partially collapsed Švédův Stůl Cave (Klíma 1962) with a sunny disposition and good view of various parts of the Říčka Valley, the passage-like Křížova Jeskyně/Kříž's Cave (Klíma 1951), and possibly also the strongly damaged and changed hall-like Stará Drátenická Cave, most of whose finds were probably destroyed without ever being noticed (Skutil 1970, 320). Apparently only Rytířská jeskyně and Švédův Stůl Caves yielded a larger set of pottery fragments that allow us to theorise as to their repeated or more frequent use.

Caves in the Late Neolithic (MMK)

People's interest in karst regions during the Late Neolithic appear to have begun during MMK Phase IIa and was focused primarily in the southern part of the Moravian Karst. The most visited cave appears to have been Pekárna, which by all indications was part of a greater regional complex that included other features and structures on the karst plain of Mokerský Les/Mokrá Forest above the cave (Kos 1997; 1999; Škrdla & Šebela 1999). The interpretation of the entire site on the plain remains ambiguous, but artefact deposition is linked to sinkholes which themselves are associated with possible cult activities. Within the framework of Phase IIa, the artefact assemblage from Pekárna is contemporaneous with the site in Mokrá Forest and show a similar artefact spectrum containing several stone hatchets, bone tools, and fragments of clay animal sculptures. MMK finds were described only by Absolon's excavations and were not stratigraphically separated from the LBK horizon (Červinka 1926; 1927–28; 1932; Šebela 2001). Other possible evidence of intensive activities within the cave is a large pottery assemblage, including one complete [reconstructed] vessel. For now, the circumstances do not allow us to theorise as to the function of Pekárna or the entire complex, which undoubtedly also included the small Hadí Cave below Pekárna's terrace. Considering the natural surroundings (a water-less plain and a narrow karst valley), the site quite certainly was not an agricultural settlement.

Compared to LBK, the MMK finds from other caves in the Moravian Karst are less numerous or consist of little more than isolated pottery fragments. As a rule, they are not that further set apart from the rest of the Neolithic stratigraphy. The rare occurrences of non-ceramic artefacts are all categorically included into the Neolithic, and only the characteristic flat axes can be dated to the Late Neolithic horizons from Pekárna, Barová Cave (Skutil 1970, 319), and also in Hadí and Švédův Stůl caves. As mentioned previously, in all cases the MMK finds derive from caves that had been previously used by LBK communities – this include presumed cult sites such as Barová

Cave (Horáček *et al.* 2002, 316 et seq.), Kateřinská Cave (Geislerová *et al.* 1986), Pekárna Cave, and Výpustek (cf. Měchurová 1992). Other sites include distinctly small caves such as Hadí Cave (Klíma 1961), Žitný Cave (Valoch 1957, 575), and caves suitable for settlement that include Švédův Stůl Cave (Klíma 1962), Drátenická Cave (Skutil 1970, 320), Pekárna (Šebela 2001). Did the representatives of MMK follow in the footsteps of an 800-year-old tradition that was revived for reasons unknown to us, or is it mere coincidence that their requirements for suitable caves (nevertheless of a highly diverse nature) were the same as those of people from the Middle Neolithic?

Caves in the Early Aeneolithic – The Jordanów Culture

Cave artefact assemblages tell us very little about the subsequent Proto-Aeneolithic period. Jordanów-style pottery has been described in only two caves (Babická Skalka/ Kapustovka – Blatný 1962; Kůlnička – Stuchlík 2002), its dating in Žitný Cave remains ambiguous (Valoch 1957, 575), and the Pod Hradem Cave yielded only a Proto-Aeneolithic hatchet located several meters deeper in the cave corridor than the linear pottery (Ondruš 1965). Based on the contrast between the limited usable space and the diverse range of LBK finds, I have included the Kapustovka cleft cave among cult sites. The Kůlnička Cave is also highly interesting in this regard. The natural shape of its entryway is probably the most faithful depiction of the female genitalia within the Moravian Karst, as also reflected in the cave's symbolic nature as the personification of the feminine principle. This is convincingly documented by the more recent child grave from the Early Bronze Age, placed within the cave entrance much as into a mother's womb (on the symbolism of child burials, see Čermáková 2002 and 2007, 238). I believe that people viewed caves similarly during the Proto-Aeneolithic, meaning that what we see at Kůlnička is a cult symbol. This interpretation raises an interesting question: Why does a cave with such a conspicuous expression of the female or maternal essence of life lack finds from not only LBK but apparently also the Late Neolithic – periods during which society was presumably matrilinear? And why are such items instead found with the emergence of an Aeneolithic society emphasising the masculine principle?[1] At the same time, Kůlnička Cave is located a mere 250 m from the most important Neolithic cave, Pekárna, from where it is easily accessible!

A Near and Distant Perspective

Cave use in the Moravian Karst can be studied from two perspectives. The 'near' perspective looks at individual cave sites, the local natural conditions, the preconditions for use, and the resultant possible interpretations. Twelve of the 17 Neolithic caves in the Moravian Karst can be directly described as cult sites. This assumption is based on their size or the microclimate of each. These constraints would have made it difficult to engage in everyday settlement activities. Also worth emphasising is the absence of evidence of the production or working of chipped stone industry, the presence of a larger set of polished stone industry and grinding stones only in the dark and moist Výpustek Cave, and the conspicuous prevalence of red and roe deer bones over traces of domesticated animals.

Previous reports from the excavations at Pekárna and Výpustek mention finds of speleothems in the prehistoric cultural layers. Both Pekárna, with its hypothesised sinter decoration, and the easily accessible Michalka Cave with its formerly abundant white cave formations of various shapes were frequently visited during the LBK – as shown by the thick cultural layers with evidence of fire pits at both sites. Community interest during the Neolithic in stalactite caves and cave decorations is confirmed primarily by Výpustek, which also offers a possible path towards explaining the frequent visits to these types of karst caves. One key piece of information is Wankel's two mentions of several worked stalactites found among other artefacts in the Neolithic cultural layer (Wankel 1871, 280, 313). Sinter and speleothems as unusual natural phenomena – i.e., growing stone formations or permanently soft white stone (also known as *moonmilk*) – have probably been known to ancient communities since they took their first steps underground, and since then they have apparently belonged to their spiritual perception of the underground world. In Anatolia, speleothems from distant karst caves were used to decorate homes and temples at the Neolithic settlement at Çatal Hüyük (Erdoğu *et al.* 2013). In Bronze-Age Mediterranean civilisations and to some extent in central Europe as well, unusual sinter formations and visually interesting stalagmites were worshipped in cave shrines. From the High Middle Ages until the 18th and in some cases the 19th/20th centuries, speleothems were used as a medicine against a diverse range of ailments, and were therefore extensively mined and sold.[2] In fact, the extensive karst labyrinth of Výpustek, with its formerly abundant sinter decorations, may have been a central site in the Moravian Karst during the Neolithic for the ritualised mining of speleothems. The numerous stone and bone tools found as final deposits in cold and dark spaces dangerous for random visitors would go well with this image of a ritual site, as would the sinter-covered charcoal layer resulting from the long-term use of torches, which reaches all the way into the lower side tunnels with their abundant speleothem decoration. Although I am not aware of a similar situation in Europe, besides the aforementioned settlement at Çatal Hüyük, sinter formations were also used by the Mesoamerican Maya civilisation and its successors (Brady & Prufer 2005). In addition, actual cave sites for the extraction of valuable minerals that were later used for religious and medicinal purposes existed deep inside caves belonging to certain Native American cultures in the eastern United States (Watson 1997; Munson *et al.* 1997).

I now turn to what I term the 'distant' perspective. This considers the broader chronological continuity of interest in and use of caves as natural objects. The significant hiatus between the two Neolithic periods of cave use would appear to be independent from cultural changes both within the individual cultural phases as well as during changes in entire cultural units, as was the case with Stroke-Ornament Ware and Moravian Painted Ware (Fig. 3.1). This global perspective makes it difficult to consider the use of Moravian caves as shelters or refuges during social upheaval, for such considerations would assume an 800-year period of social 'calm' from the late LBK to the late MMK. It is also difficult to find reasons for the use of caves for everyday life, subsistence and related domestic needs – in such a case, the hiatus would point towards more fundamental changes in socio-economic habits that have not been observed in the Neolithic. One possible connection exists between the search for caves and the settlement of the surrounding landscape: the moment the colonisation of the landscape reached the cave area, caves were also included into the cultural landscape. Nevertheless, the question of why this happened and what caves were used for remains unanswered. When I consider their possible ritual function as part of Neolithic cult practices, I am basing such considerations not only on the specific natural character of certain cave sites, but also on their tradition or rather their *genius loci*, which resulted in the sites' revival by MMK people after a long period of 'oblivion.' This phenomenon is typical for important cult sites or natural shrines that were massively visited and worshipped as needed and were forgotten again when this need subsided. It probably was not until the Proto-Aeneolithic that there was a change in how caves were perceived. Depending on the choice of site, this change apparently took place in the cult sphere and also involved a preference of sites suitable for personal or family needs instead of sites serving the greater society. With a view towards the small number of Proto-Aeneolithic sites (2–3), this observation must, however, be understood as just a working hypothesis.

That people in the past understood the landscape differently than we are used to today is documented by the Javoříčko Karst in central Moravia. The clearly visible change in the local perception of the karst landscape and its natural formations over the past several centuries follows a path from the old world of personified natural forces and beings, accompanied by a deeply-felt sense of place within folk traditions, to the modern rational viewpoint and a conscious admiration of these natural phenomena (Blekta 1932, 26; Peša 2013c). Local people of the 19th century still viewed the Javoříčko Karst, where today we focus on its *visible* natural beauty, as a potentially dangerous landscape ruled by *invisible*, often negative natural forces. From this perspective, within ancient folk tradition, did the mouth of Suchý Žleb canyon in the Moravian Karst – with its prominent concentration of rock formations bearing 'diabolical' names such as the Devil's Bridge, Devil's Window, Devil's Gate and the Neolithic cult caves of Koňská Jáma, Kateřinská Cave ('Catherine Cave,' named after a shepherdess who is said to have become lost inside and perished), and Umrlčí Jeskyně ('Dead Man's Cave,' with undated human bones) belong to a similarly hostile space? This tradition also demonised the surroundings of Býčí Skála (cf. discussion of Barová Cave) and the outlet of the Punkva underground river across from the prehistorical site at Pod Hradem cave.

A Connection with Nature or With Human Culture?

A chronological overview (Fig. 3.1) clearly shows periods of interest in caves alternating with other periods (often just as long) of non-interest both on the level of the overall chronology of the period under review and for individual contemporaneous archaeological cultures. These clearly-visible dynamic rules cancel out the element of chance. Instead, a more universal approach to the relationship between community and cave may also reveal the relationship between culture and nature, as is further discussed below.

Caves and Climate Change

The closely-related subject of climate change has been repeatedly considered in connection with cave use with greater (Ložek 1973a; 1973b; Bouzek 1993) or lesser emphasis, or even with scepticism (Matoušek 1996; 1999). A rough outline of changes in climate during the Holocene has already been reconstructed, with the first observations on this subject appearing on the boundary between the Natufian and Pre-Pottery Neolithic (PPN). Despite the presumed improvement in caves' inhabitability (less moisture in the entrance areas), the advent of a cooler climatic fluctuation during the Younger Dryas in the Late Natufian period led to a decline in the number of sites and only their sporadic use. This fact apparently reflects a change in lifestyle among late hunter-gatherer-cultivator communities that were transitioning to a more mobile way of life, meaning that within the larger settlement structure only the most important settlements remained inhabited. In the Near East, another highly probable change in climate with a dry fluctuation (fluctuations) is associated with the key turning period of the Pre-Pottery and Pottery Neolithic. Here, too, we see a decline in cave sites as compared to their intensive and apparently primarily economic use during the PPNB. There is a new phenomenon, however: the search for larger (and thus generally moister) karst caves with dark spaces, speleothem decorations or the presence of groundwater, although archaeologically-speaking these sites are relatively finds-poor and any traces of human presence are usually concentrated in the cave's open and light entry areas (there are exceptions, however, such as Nahal Qanah in Israel) (Peša 2011). Another fluctuation towards a warm and dry climate has been considered in connection with the Neolithisation of the Aegean around 6200 cal. BCE, but the absence of speleoarchaeological sites in the southern Balkans means that it has only been identified in Greek caves.

With a view towards climatic conditions during the Atlantic period, caves in central Europe have been reconstructed as moist spaces with significant sinter production – i.e., spaces unsuitable for settlement. In fact, the Middle Neolithic – which is characterised by an increased interest in caves in many regions of central Europe and the Balkans – is associated with the advent of the new climatic period known as the Epi-Atlantic, which Vojen Ložek defines as a warm and moist climate with short dry fluctuations and large variations in temperature (Ložek 1973b). Changes in settlement structure related to elevation above sea level and soil quality have been observed during the Middle Neolithic in the northern parts of the Carpathian Basin, for instance within the classical Želiezovce culture, and is a prominent horizon for the 'demise' of cultures at the end of this period (e.g., Pavúk & Bátora 1995, 126 et seq.). Palaeoclimatological studies have also identified an unstable climate phase with increased erosion processes in the area between the Bükk Mountains and the Aggtelék

Karst – i.e., the era's most important cave region in central Europe. Two climatically unstable periods have been observed for this region, with the first around 5300 cal, BCE, notably correlating with the great increase in interest in caves among the late Linear Pottery Culture and its Tiszadob group, and the second, around 5000/4900 cal, BCE, corresponding with the presumed demise of the Bükk Culture. Climatic conditions reached equilibrium with the onset of the Late Neolithic (Juhász in Gál *et al.* 2005, 43 and 50); again, in this context there is a lack of finds in caves.

Based on the example of the Bohemian Karst, during the Middle Neolithic the settlement area is presumed to have expanded to include a karst region with caves in a similar manner as occurred in other areas of the late Linear Pottery Culture in Bohemia, which, together with social and natural factors, was presumed to result in the later local degradation of the landscape (Sklenář & Matoušek 1994, 128 et seq.; Matoušek 1996, 25–26). Palaeoenvironmental research in the Carpathian Basin has documented fundamental changes in climate that might have had a more widespread impact on the surrounding regions of Moravia and Bohemia as well. What is more, dry fluctuations in climate were surely first felt in the ecologically most sensitive types of landscape such as karst regions with their limited surface waters and low water retention. If the karst region had begun to dry out (including moist caves that were not connected to the karst's lower active level), it could hardly have become the target of economic interest. Instead, environmental degradation reduced the landscape's potential – for instance, pastoralism would be clearly easier in more abundant river valleys than in the desiccating limestone steppe.

In summary, one could postulate that in some archaeological cultural periods where climate change had a significant impact, may have led to situations that resulted in greater cave use. This happened in proto-agricultural societies in the Near East on the boundary between the Pre-Pottery and Pottery Neolithic, and during several phases of the south-central European Neolithic and early Aeneolithic. While climate fluctuations tend towards dry periods, the most distinctive archaeological situations are in moist caves or in those areas with sources of water. At the same time, during dry periods the karst landscape (and thus its economic and settlement potential) degraded more rapidly than surrounding ecosystems.

Caves and Their Place in Society

During the Pre-Pottery Neolithic in the Levant and apparently in Anatolia as well, there was no interest at all in caves located near the main cultural centres (for example the agglomeration in the Jordan Valley near Jericho). Where they are located farther away, such as in the Judean Highlands, the Dead Sea region, Antalya, it is not clear whether they were related to the proto-urban inhabitants and their extra-settlement activities, or to the surrounding semi-nomadic or nomadic populations (Peša 2011). This model would seem to be at least partially applicable to the Carpathian Basin. Local archaeological cultures with well-developed socio-economic and cultural structures ignored caves and other natural sites – examples include the Tisza Culture (Fig. 3.6),

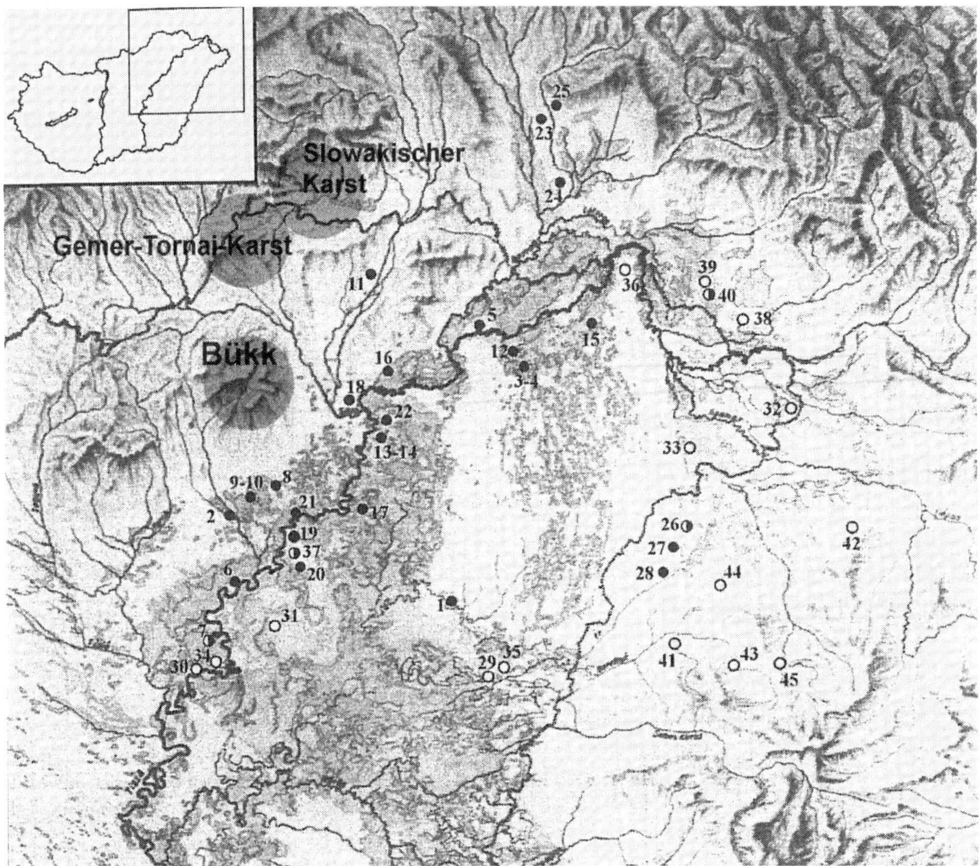

Fig. 3.6: Upper Tisza region in the Early Neolithic: Alföld-LBK, Köros-Criş (after Kovács 2006–7, adapted). Caves not far off settlements were out of interest of the Early Neolithic people

Lengyel I-III, the Tiszapolgár culture in the Tisza River region, Bodrogkéresztúr, the central regions of the Vinča Culture and perhaps also the Starčevo Culture from the Starčevo-Criş complex. Advanced cultural societies seem to exist in opposition to nature, of which the cave is a typical representative. Such a culture may feel confident in its cultural norms and models, meaning that it has gradually lost a sense of belonging to the natural environment even during crisis periods of climatic instability. This would be evidenced by the tell settlements of the Tisza Culture along the upper reaches of the Tisza River (Makkay 1991, 325–326). Tells were abandoned and the population scattered across the surrounding agricultural landscape, however, and based on the archaeological evidence, the nearby caves of the Bükk Mountains remained completely unaffected by these events.

Many of these archaeological cultures with a long history of existence across time and space possess another common feature – the need to visit caves does not appear until during their later stages of each cultural period. In the Starčevo-Criş complex, cave use begins during Phase II B, in the Hamangia Culture during Phase III, in the eastern Linear Pottery Culture during the middle period and massively with the beginning of its late period, and in the western Linear Pottery Culture during the transition from its middle to late period. What is more, interest in caves sometimes survived a period of transition between cultures (from eastern Linear Pottery to Bükk, from western Linear Pottery via the Šárka phase to Stroke-Ornamented Pottery). For this phenomenon, I offer a hypothetical culturological explanation: Every archaeological culture or society in general (for examples, see Bárta & Kovář 2011, for the Vinča culture, Brukner 2002) undergoes a certain regular evolution: it is born and develops until the peak of its possibilities – by which it becomes (usually economically) exhausted – and then it gradually declines and disappears or is transformed into a different social unit. Starting in the Middle Neolithic at the latest, the life of archaeological cultures appears to have been affected by climate fluctuations of a more or less hemispheric nature that, combined with the extensive use of the landscape and increased demands for raw materials that began to influence the local environment, led to social problems and unrest. Such a situation demands a search for solutions in order to save and preserve society. As indicated by the case of advanced Neolithic cultures in the studied region, these 'rescue mechanisms' probably made use of local cultural resources or were at least sought out in the local cultural world. By comparison, archaeological cultures with a 'poorer' agricultural population or with a traditional lifestyle marked by closer ties to nature may have chosen different rescue mechanisms that were closer to the natural environment. If they lacked sufficient cultural self-confidence for resolving the crisis using the socio-economic and cultural means at their disposal, attention had to be focused back on nature. Thus it was time to rediscover semi-forgotten caves as symbols of nature with its god-hoods and natural forces and to incorporate them into the cultural landscape. From this perspective, caves would appear to be the archetype of nature within human society. As can be seen from the following sections, this interpretation is supported by actual archaeological situations and finds.

A Discussion of the Function and Significance of Caves: Long-Term and Short-Term Cave Settlement

Actual cave settlements appear in the Near East (Levant) among the cultural environment of late hunter-gatherers, cultivators and early agriculturalists – i.e., during the Late Upper Palaeolithic (LUP) and Natufian periods, and in some areas still during the Pre-Pottery Neolithic (Peša 2011). Their most characteristic feature is, especially in the Natufian culture, the dwelling foundations that have been uncovered. The Natufian settlement structure consists of larger central settlements and smaller satellite sites that are either open to the countryside or associated with caves. Where they are located in caves, the main settlements are in spacious entryways or on terraces in front of the cave (Hayonim, Nahal Oren, El-Wad, El-Khiam). Smaller sites make use of spacious shallow cavities or overhangs (Kebara, Shuqba, Hilazon Tachtit, Erq el-Ahmar, Jabrud, Baaz). All of these caves or their utilised parts are dry and well-illuminated by daylight. If a cave also includes dark rear sections, these usually remain free of archaeological evidence, but the transition zones between light and dark are home to burial sites (Hayonim, Raqefet; in El-Wad, burials were done in the entrance area as well) or were used for various unspecified activities with the unusual creation of waste (El-Wad – hall III). A source of water was apparently not a priority in the cave, for it appears only rarely (Antelias, El-Wad?). Natufian cave sites are characterised by thick cultural layers that, combined with radiocarbon dating and other scientific analyses, provide evidence for their long-term inhabitation – for some of the central settlements (Hayonim), practically year-round (Bar-Yosef & Tchernov 1966; Pichon 1991). The cultural layers generally contain various settlement structures corresponding to the find situations at open settlements (e.g., Ain Mallaha). The archaeological finds, which are numerous, come from various areas of everyday life. Besides the most common finds – chipped stone and stone industry, bone items, and food remains – sites with burials contain a larger number of small jewellery (personal decoration or amulets and talismans) or other decorative or artistic objects (sculptures) that come from other, no longer extant, graves. These items are a complete rarity at sites without burial activity (Peša 2011).

A very similar form of cave habitation continues in both phases of the Pre-Pottery Neolithic. Thick cultural layers containing numerous artefacts of everyday life, including ritual life, are also found in the Epi-Palaeolithic environment of Mediterranean Anatolia (Öküzini, Beldibi, Belbaşı), in the Mesolithic caves of Greece (Franchthi, Theopetra), and in the Iron Gates region on the lower Danube (Cuina Turcului – Fig. 3.2, Veterani/Maovaţ).

As is the case for the Balkans at the start of the Early Neolithic, the cave sites that appear in the Near East with the onset of the Pottery Neolithic offer a different image as compared to the previous period. Any caves with thick cultural layers in the Levant and Anatolia in the Neolithic and Chalcolithic do not contain clear settlement features, and except for the dominant pottery fragments all other find groups are represented unevenly or only selectively. Instead, many sites show evidence of cult activities and burials (in the sense of independent graves with burials on the surface of the cave interior). The character of the visited caves changes as well, with larger and predominantly dark cave systems gaining in popularity, in isolated cases even with sources of water or speleothem decorations; these are sites that were not used during the preceding period stretching from the Epi-Palaeolithic to the Pre-Pottery Neolithic. Archaeological evidence from these typically karst caves are concentrated predominantly at the caves' entryways, although they sometimes penetrate into their darker portions as well.

A similar picture of the change in perceived preferences for visited caves is found in the Balkan interior and the Carpathian Basin. Besides a highly variable morphology of cave interiors, we also frequently encounter uneven find assemblages that, with just a few exceptions, lack evidence of the on-site working of chipped or polished stone industry, or in which food remnants are significantly under-represented (cf. Romania, the Moravian Karst).

From the above findings, it is clear that caves gained a new meaning and function at the beginning of agricultural civilisation. Generally speaking, their role within the cultural landscape was no longer as regular inhabited places or sites of shelter during times of need. This claim attempts to describe a widespread phenomenon, meaning that we cannot rule out individual, regional, or socially contingent cases of cave inhabitation during the late prehistoric era.

Pastoralism and Caves

Pastoralism has been one of the subjects most commonly associated with the use of central European caves since they were first studied towards the end of the 19th century, but only in rare cases has this connection been based on more concrete evidence. By comparison, Near Eastern sites offer an abundant volume of study material (Henrickson 1985; Tellenbach 1983, 122). The existence of a pastoral or nomadic lifestyle for a part of the subsistence-economy population was first discussed for the late PPNB in the Levant (Cauvin *et al.* 1997; Verhoeven 2002), but such lifestyles have yet to be associated with cave use. The oldest known sites with preserved layers of ash, an abundance of sheet/goat coprolites, and limited artefacts without any more exceptional objects are not found until the Pottery Neolithic in the southern Levant, where they are associated with rock shelters in the Negev Desert (abri Ramon I is dated to 6203–5934 cal. BCE – Rosen *et al.* 2005). In similar traditional Near Eastern landscapes with a nomadic way of life, rock shelters, shallow cavities, and light-filled caves were used as shelter for pastoralists or their herds practically without interruption from the Chalcolithic until the historical era, and sometimes even until the present day. The sites contain characteristic light-coloured layers of ash from the burning of excrement and only a limited range of finds related to a mobile way of life – i.e., no large-scale sets of pottery or other unusual groups of artefacts (e.g. Anati 1963, 182 et seq.; Simms 1988; Kuijt & Russell 1993; Weinstein-Evron 1998, 48 et seq.; Solecki 1998). In the other studied regions of central and southeastern Europe, we encounter essentially no cave sites with the above-described characteristics found in the Levant.

Cult and Shamanic Ritual Activities in Caves

The preceding discussion showed that the most abundant find situations and assemblages of artefacts are frequently found in caves that are more or less unsuited for inhabitation. Although at some central European sites these situations hint at the presence of cult activities, only a small part of the cave interior tends to be set aside for such activities (e.g. Domica and Ardovo in Slovakia – Fig. 3.7) or only certain cult activities were held in the cave (e.g., Istállóskö in Hungary), and only rarely are these activities extended to the site as a whole (Koňská Jáma in the Moravian Karst or Jungfernhöhle in Bavaria).

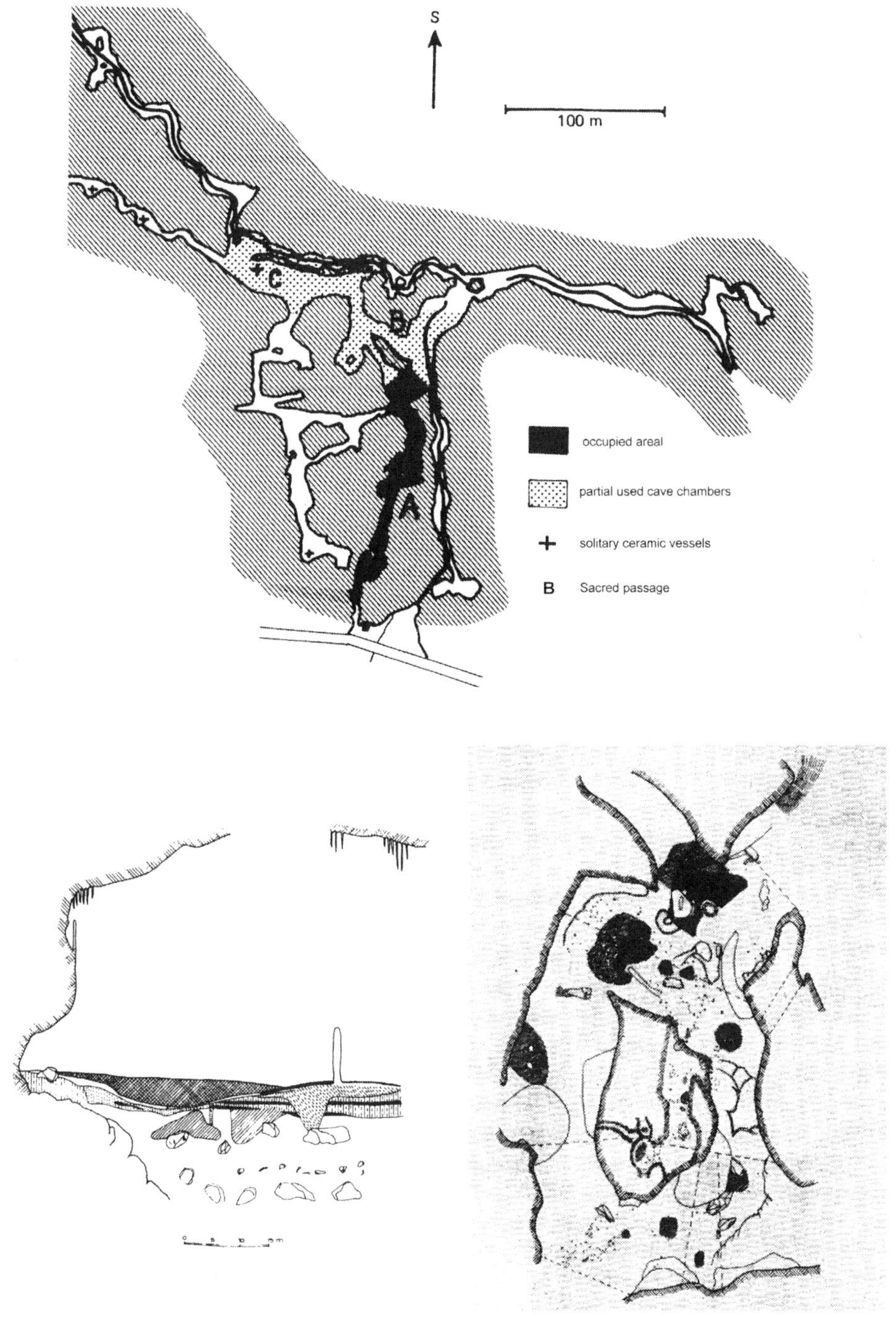

Fig. 3.7: Domica cave (Slovakia) – an extent of the archaeological finds in the all cave plan, and a cut without location, below right: the Hall of eleven flames with find situation (after Lichardus 1968; 1974)

The habitation of spacious, light-filled caves by Epi-Palaeolithic, Mesolithic or Early Neolithic communities did not differ from contemporaneous settlements in the open landscape. Cult activities probably took place only on the level of daily personal and family/clan rituals. In addition, especially in Anatolia there exists a type of site containing cave paintings that is associated both with smaller rock hollows (in the studied region, these are predominantly light-filled) as well as rocky terrains located outside of caves. These sites are relatively poor in archaeological terms, so the paintings and carvings are dated more by style than by context. Recently, the prevalent opinion has been that cave art possesses a specific symbolic meaning that places it among distinctive expressions of cult beliefs often in context of shamanism (Anati 1963; 1968; Whitehouse 1992; Svoboda 2002; Lewis-Williams 2002). In the studied region, we encounter wall carvings or wall paintings primarily in the Balkans – southwestern Romania, Albania (Lepenicë), and Bulgaria (Magurata) – most probably from the Aeneolithic, as is the case for the Alpine regions (Valcamonica, Mont Bégo, Dachstein). Based on radiometric dating, the charcoal drawings in Domica Cave's Holy Corridor probably predate the Neolithic activities at this site and is of the Palaeolithic origin (Gradziński *et al.* 2001; Svoboda & van der Plicht 2007).

The changing significance of caves in agricultural societies during the Pottery Neolithic across the studied transect was expressed primarily in the choice of new types of caves that had not been sought out before and that were less suited or entirely unsuited for settlement purposes. It would seem that the reason for visiting such sites may have been their specific natural characteristics such as speleothem decorations with a diverse range of (often anthropomorphic or zoomorphic) sinter formations, the presence of underground water, the general nature of dark spaces free from any sensory stimuli that were well-suited for meditation or evoking altered states of mind as shamanic characteristics, and perhaps even the presence of the bones of large Pleistocene animals (*giants*). Other indirect evidence includes the worked speleothems found in Anatolia's Çatal Hüyük. Perhaps the archaeologically most distinctive function of caves is their use as a place for the final, apparently votive, deposit of various items, of which vessels (both filled and empty) later clearly predominate. The oldest evidence of the deposit of used ritual items is from the Pre-Pottery Neolithic at Nahal Hemar Cave in the southern Levant (Bar-Yosef & Alon 1988). The conscious deposit of vessels seems to have been relatively common during the Chalcolithic (Epstein 2001), although in view of the fragile nature of pottery undoubtedly only a small percentage of such items have been preserved (Civelek Cave in Anatolia, caves Nahal Zalzal, Umm Qala´a and Murabba´at 2 in the Levant). Another group of votive gifts are items made of precious materials, in particular metal and ivory but also minerals (in Israel and Syria for instance at caves Magharat el-Jai, Netifim, Beit al-Wadi, Nahal Badir 49, Har Yishai, and Nahal David; the unique deposits from the Cave of the Treasure in Nahal Mishmar may also be included; Peša 2011).

In many ways, the situation in South-eastern Europe during the Neolithic is very similar to that in the Near East. While the Neolithic find situations are not too

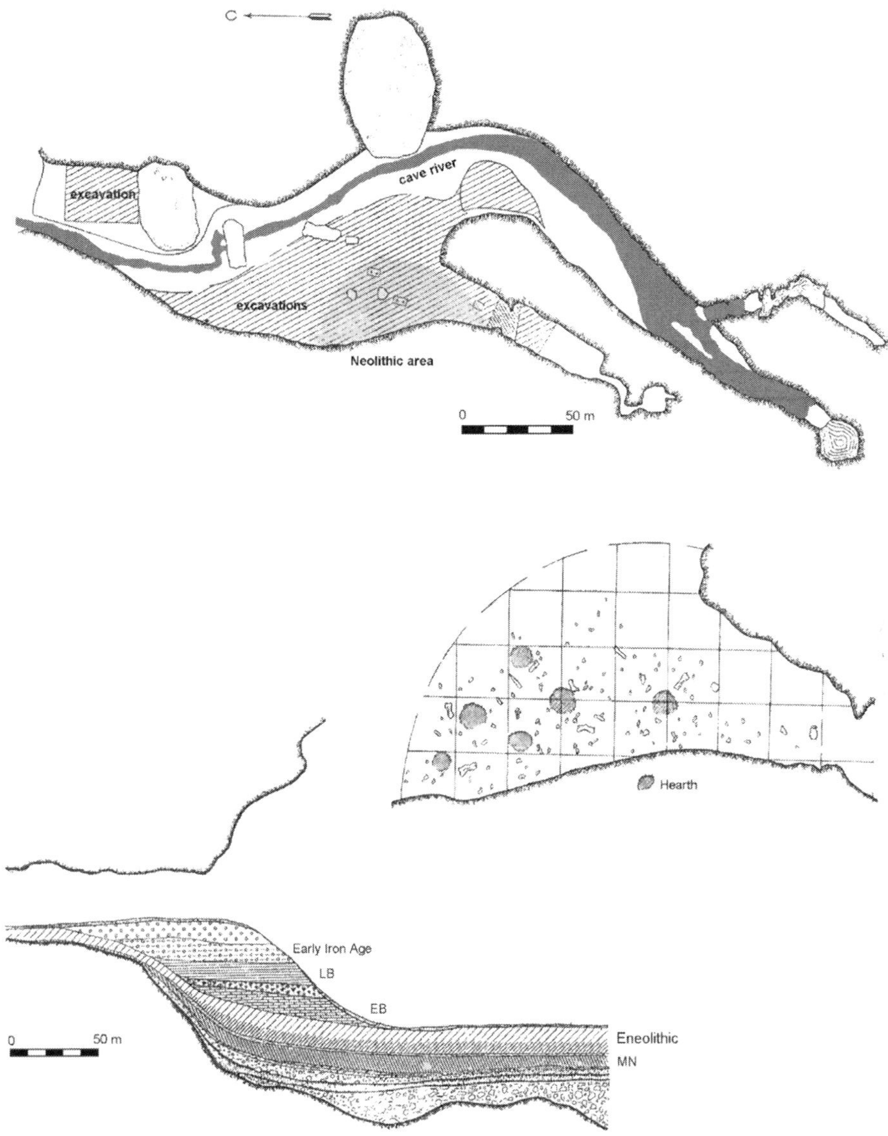

Fig. 3.8: Devetaškata peštera cave (Bulgaria) – multilevel prehistoric site. A 'Neolithic' shift before the portal of the side corridor is emphasised. Middle image: the 'Neolithic' find complex with hearths (grey) (adapted after Mikov & Džambazov 1960)

distinctive, with the onset of the Balkan Aeneolithic they become more so, the cultural layers become deeper, and the number of finds, especially of pottery, increases as well (e.g., caves Devetashkata – Fig. 3.8, Hoţilor, Peştera cu apă near Româneşti). The finds also include preserved vessels, of which some – by their placement or through the character of the underground spaces – again hint at cult activities in the form of votive deposits: e.g., Kjuljuk Cave in Bulgaria (Karanovo I culture), caves Peştera cu vas (Vinča A) and Meziad (Late Neolithic) in Romania. In the karst regions of the western Carpathians, the most important caves (Domica, Baradla, Ardovo) are part of an extensive active karst system that is traversed by many underground streams and rivers. Neolithic finds from these caves are exclusively from their dark parts, located as much as several hundred meters from the entrance (Figs 3.6 & 3.9). In fact, this type of cave possesses the most abundant archaeological situations and finds, and some circumstances – Domica's Holy Corridor with a giant gynecomorphic portal (Fig. 3.10), or the cult platform in Baradla Cave's 'Ossuary chamber' (Fig. 3.11) – have previously led researchers to theorise as to the importance of cult beliefs at these sites, even if only as a basis for cult activities at hypothetical cave settlements (Tompa 1934/1935; Böhm 1933; Lichardus 1968, 85 et seq.).

The specific importance of these caves or the activities performed therein is attested by archaeological finds with a high incidence of anthropomorphic decorations of vessels (nearly half of all known items: Kalicz & Makkay 1977, 63; Kalicz & Koós 2000), as well as the more frequent incidence of fine ceramic tableware as compared to plains settlements (Šiška 1989, 260). In the Bükk Mountains, the preferred type of cave to be chosen was more spacious with both light and dark parts, which could indicate the presence of larger groups than just families or individuals (Fig. 3.12). The cult layers contain human bones associated not only with isolated burials (Büdöspest), but possibly also with ritual activities (alleged anthropophagy in Istállóskö). One example of a site used for the final deposit of vessels is in the narrow cleft passages of Csengö Cave in Ordöggát. It is generally true that objects from other non-pottery categories or otherwise exceptional artefacts are predominantly associated with caves that are rather unsuited for habitation and that also contain the richest cultural layers. The same can be said of the second wave of interest in west Carpathian caves by the Ludanice culture at the beginning of the Aeneolithic. Here, too, the find situations include cult items (Liskovská Cave, Dzeravá skala?), the oldest central European cave burial site (Dúpna diera, Liskovská Cave?), and possible ritual activities (Čertova Pec Cave). It is conceivable that the items found could be associated with forms of cult or shamanistic practices.

We encounter cult activities in Czech caves as well. In the Moravian Karst, these include Koňská Jáma, which contained a fragment of an anthropomorphous vessel (Fig. 3.13), and the Výpustek cave labyrinth (see Fig. 3.4) with its exceptionally rich and diverse assemblage of finds from the late Linear Pottery Culture. Here, too, caves with speleothem decoration seem to be popular (Výpustek, Michalka, and perhaps also Kateřinská and Pekárna?). In the Bohemian Karst, there are more frequent examples of entire vessels being deposited (caves Hlohová, Malá, and perhaps Galerie), and Nová Jeskyně/New Cave possesses exceptional find situations for both the late Linear Pottery Culture and for the Stroke-Ornamented Ware Culture – probably in connection with winter solstice rituals (Fig. 3.14). Generally speaking, the local caves are small and more suited for individual or family/clan use (Peša 2013b).

As sizeable as the evidence of cult or ritual activities in Neolithic and Proto-Aeneolithic caves is when compared with previous sedentary or pastoralist models,

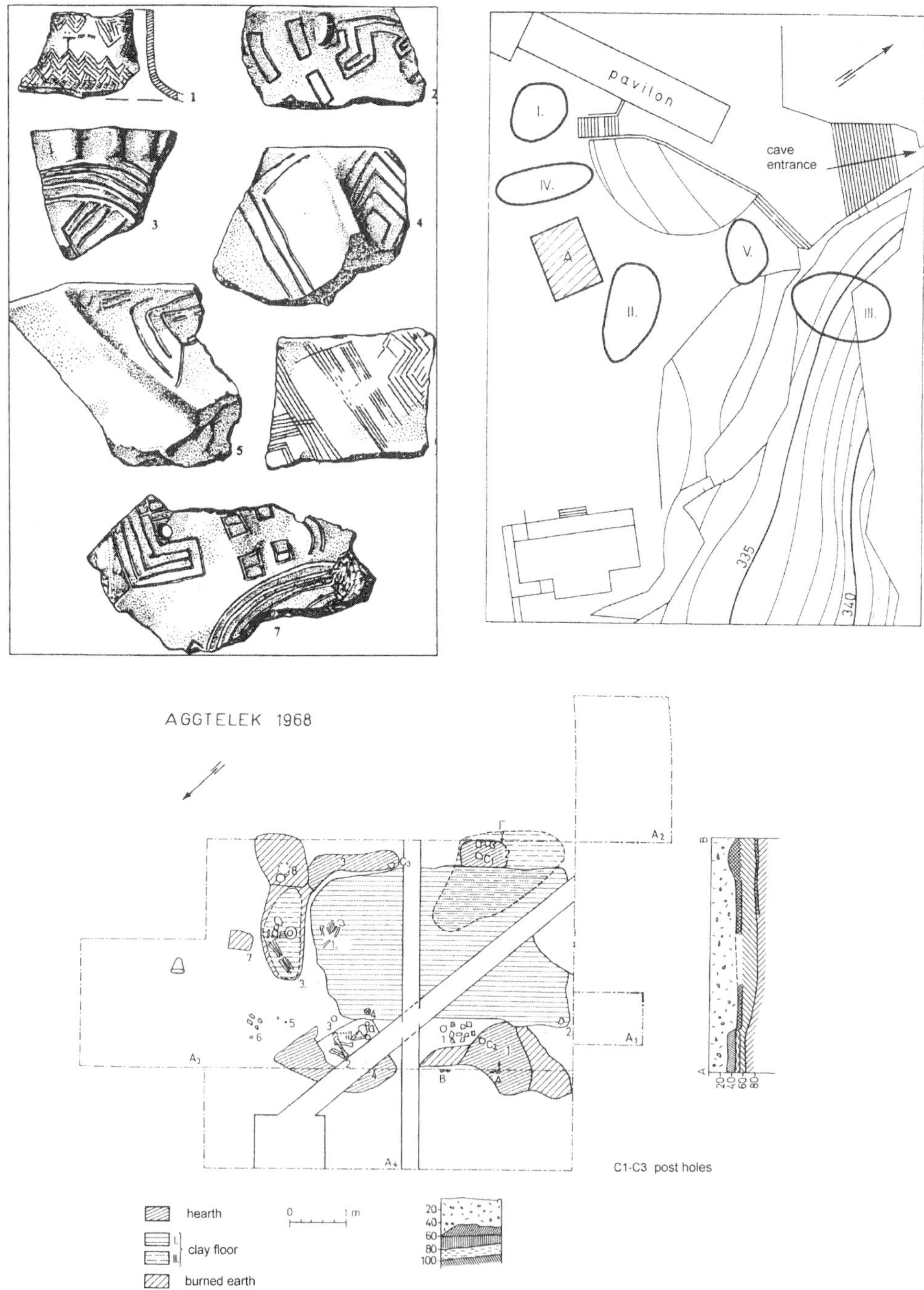

Fig. 3.9: Aggtelek (Hungary) – the area before the cave entrance of Baradla with Neolithic structures, and one researched structure of them (after Korek 1970). Vessel fragments with symbolic decoration of the Baradla cave (after Kalicz & Koós 2000, fig. 10)

Fig. 3.10: Domica cave (Slovakia) – the Sacred corridor with the vulva-shaped formation far from the cave entrance (image: V. Peša 2004)

and although it has been documented in all the studied regions, it nevertheless consists of only a small portion of the total number of cave sites that were visited and used in the period under review. These other caves can be interpreted only on a general level – either as functionally universal and potentially diverse sites whose use corresponds remarkably with overall changes in the palaeoclimate, or as less distinctive entities of one single system that placed caves – as an archetypal representation of nature within human society – into the cult sphere with its corresponding sacral attributes of the shamanic world.

Concluding Remarks: Caves within the Human Consciousness and the Sacral Landscape

Based on archaeological sources, I can say that for the studied area of the Near East, the Balkans, and the SE part of Central Europe there is clearly more information on various forms of cult activities starting in the Neolithic than the mostly unclear evidence of a habitational, economic, or pastoralist character. If we take into account the period of the past 400 years, practically every generation has experienced some war or period of unrest, but archaeologically speaking these events have left only very imperceptible traces in caves (Peša 2013c). A similar situation can be found in Central Europe and further to the east in relation to modern pastoralism, which has left very different and less conspicuous traces than the majority of important Neolithic cave sites. This theory is supported by the above-described findings on Neolithic sites and their unsuitability for habitation by humans or domesticated animals, and also by the incomplete evidence of everyday activities.

The conspicuous alternation of periods of intensive cave use with periods containing no archaeologically documented interest has been repeatedly discussed by researchers (e.g., Matoušek 1996), albeit with uncertain or pessimistic conclusions. The alternation of several centuries of hiatus with another several centuries of more or less continuous usage (Fig. 3.1) tends to indicate regional causes that go beyond the specific local problems of society. Should the majority of important Neolithic caves yield evidence of cult or ritual use, then this would mean that periods of interest in

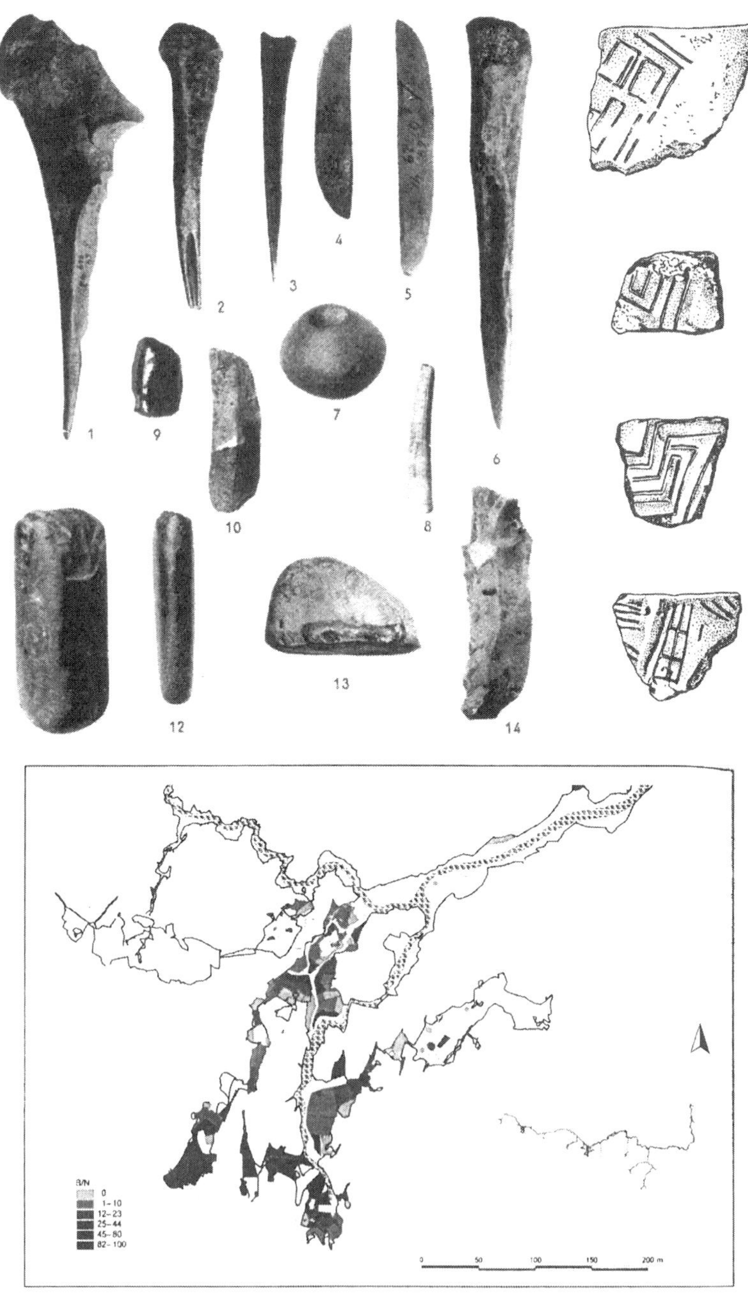

Fig. 3.11: Aggtelek – Baradla cave, a Hungarian part of the cave complex Baradla-Domica. Artefacts of bone and stone and pottery (after Tompa 1934/1935, Kalicz & Koós 2000, fig. 12). Below: map of the find density from the Neolithic to Bronze Age (after Holl 2007)

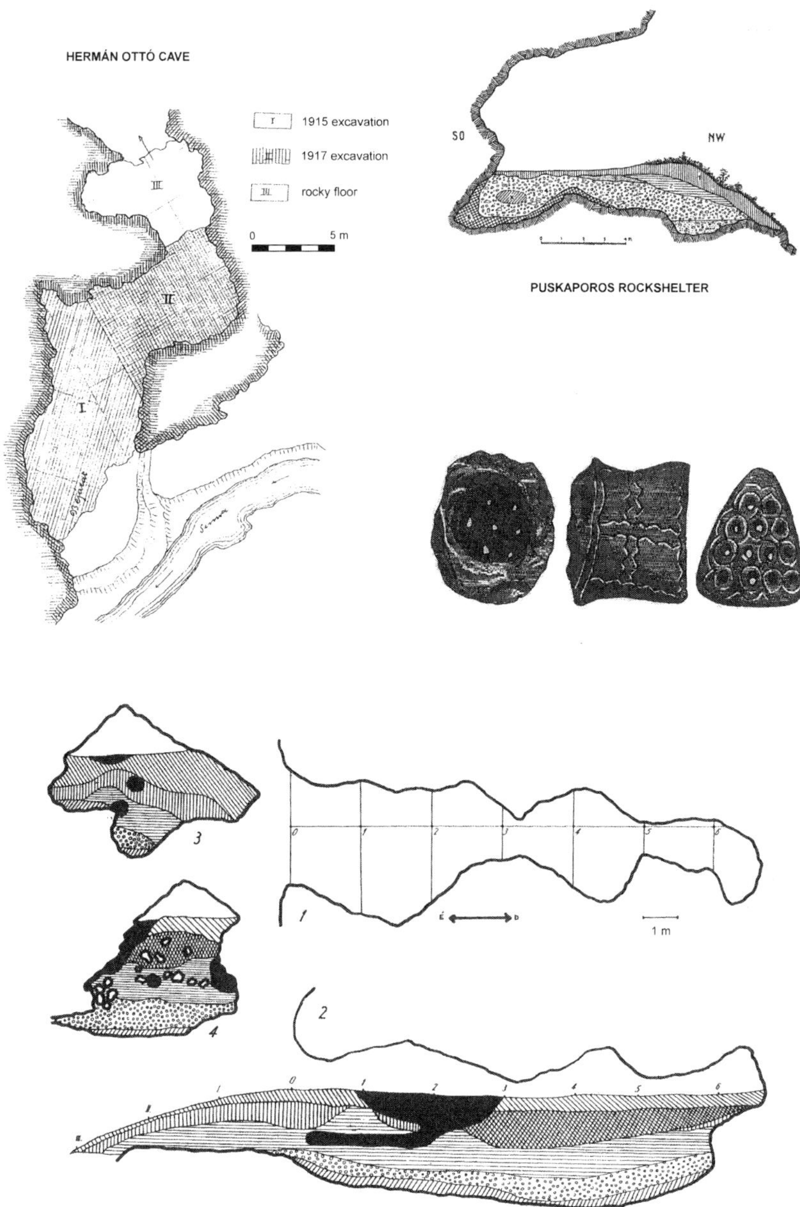

Fig. 3.12: Different types of caves in Bükk Mountains (Hungary). Above left: rock tunnel (so-called Felsnische) above the entrence of Herman-Ottó cave (after Ringer et al. 2006), and a decorated ceramic nozzle from that lower cave (after Bela 1916). Above right: Puskaporos cave in the cut (after Kadić 1934), below: Lambrecht-Kalmánov cave (after Vértes 1953)

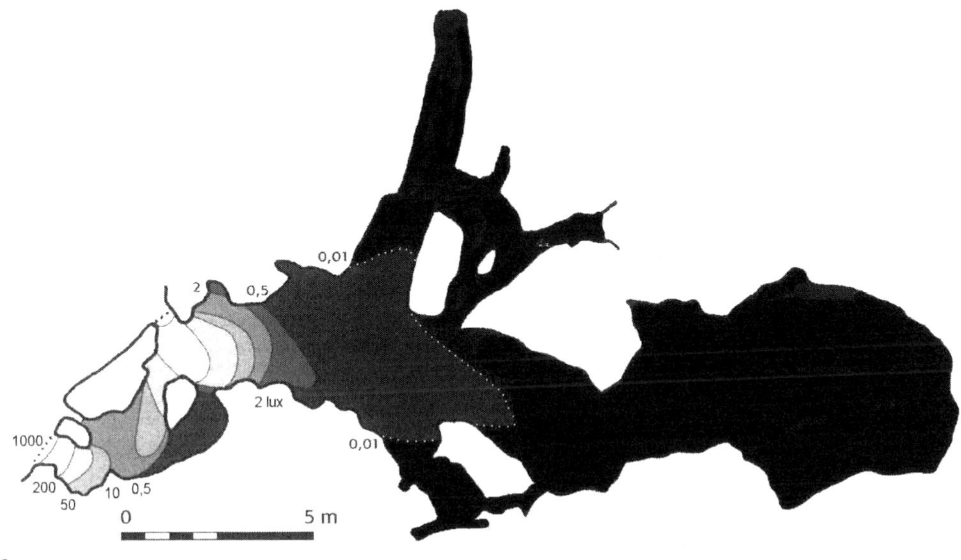

a

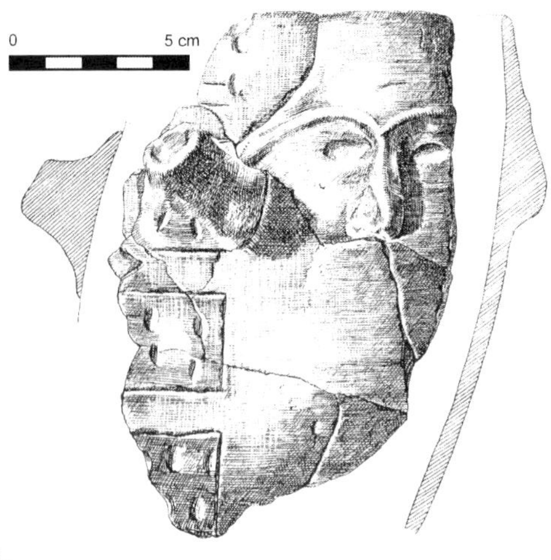

b

Fig. 3.13: Koňská jáma Cave (Moravian Karst, Czech Republic): a. plan of the light conditions in lux (after Peša & Majer 2003); b. the most important Neolithic find of anthropomorphic vessel from the twilight zone (after Skutil 1962).

caves are related to the religious topics of the era and the long-term needs of communicating with the spiritual realm. Human culture can be threatened by extensive military conflicts or regional changes in climate. Both causes have been felt in the past and continue to have a catastrophic impact primarily on a society's economic and agricultural potential. As compared to conflicts, climatic change is reflected either indirectly through changes in settlement structure and topography, or are increasingly documented and thrown into a clearer light by palaeoclimatological research. The strong correlation between unstable climatic fluctuations of the Sub-Boreal period and an increase in cult practices (not just in caves but also at other natural features) serves to corroborate events from the Late and Final Bronze Age and may offer an explanation for the situation in the Neolithic and Aeneolithic as well (cf. fluctuations between 5200 and 5000 cal. BCE – Gál *et al.* 2005; Gronenborn 2012), for this time interval possesses a demonstrable connection with climatic events and interest in caves

Fig. 3.14a: Nová cave (Bohemian Karst, Czech Republic) with finds of LBK and SBK cultures. The unique find complex provided ritual hearths, fragmented human bones and well-preserved artefacts (image: V. Peša 1999)

Fig. 3.14b: Nová cave (Bohemian Karst, Czech Republic) – the morning sun rays in the time of winter solstice leak through the narrow entrance in the rear cave wall generating a vulva-shaped form above one of the ritual hearths (image: V. Peša 1997)

In response to the question, 'If all the cultures from this period were under the same environmental pressures, why didn't they all use caves during this same period?' I offer the following hypothesis: Cultural societies express their identity via cultural norms, through which they define their relationship to extra-cultural phenomena – which, according to cultural definitions, include all that is biological and natural. The stronger a society's socio-cultural sensibilities and the deeper its faith in its mechanisms of cultural development, the lower its need to turn to culturally indefinable and incomprehensible nature and its forces. As is clearly visible from an overview of the cave phenomenon from the Neolithic to the Early Aeneolithic (Peša 2011), the most civilised societies in terms of the most advanced expressions of material culture and social (power) hierarchies – i.e., the inhabitants of large settlements, tells or agglomerations – show only an imperceptible or often no interest in caves – as compared to the agricultural populations of less fertile regions with a lower social and power hierarchy. For these traditional societies, caves may have represented an unchanging archetype of the natural forces that were more than tangible during times of environmental change.

Global climate changes with periods of drought affected first and foremost landscapes with a sensitive ecosystem – of which karst regions and their caves are a perfect example. As the landscapes economic potential declined, the region's underground cave system with its wet spaces (and, in rare instances, underground streams of water) must have appeared all the more attractive and promising. According to the shamanic cosmological division of the world into three planes (the sky and the underworld as the seat of the gods and the earth's surface as the realm of people), caves were part of the non-human realm. This is confirmed among other things by observations from various parts of the world made by cultural anthropologists (e.g. Eliade 1965; 1971; Nicholson 1993; Brady & Prufer 2005). The underground, with its typical attributes of permanent darkness and the absence of stimuli, differs significantly from the natural environment. In the mythologies of non-European nations, it is inhabited solely by gods or demigods that rule the forces of nature associated in particular with rainfall and harvests. In mythology, the main significance of the underworld is as the potential source of all rivers and streams that spring from the ground, as well as all plants that grow out of it. Similarly, on the basis of ethnoarchaeological analogies, caves contain a multitude of meanings as sacral symbols or as diverse parts of comprehensive ideological systems, and when associated with the vagina or the womb of the earth and fertility, they may represent places of transition between different states of existence used often by shamans (Lewis-Williams 2002; Sandstrom 2005, 47). What is more, caves' frequent location on mountains or hillsides forms a figurative Cosmic Axis – *Axis Mundi* – connecting the underworld with the heavenly realm (Satari 1981; Nicholson 1993; Matoušek 1999). This connection may in fact be why caves are ascribed the ability to influence the weather and why people have sought the source of winds in the underground, i.e., in the draughts coming from caves (for Mesoamerica, see Heyden 2005; for Central Europe Peša 2013c). Even in the recent past, this vertical view of the world was still a natural, universally valid and respected part of the human awareness of existence (e.g. Eliade 1971). In fact, the concurrent existence of cult activities in caves as well as on hilltops and mountain peaks – which is well-documented for the end of the Bronze Age and can perhaps also be related to older periods such as the Middle Aeneolithic and Middle Neolithic (hill sites in eastern Slovakia, Šiška 1999) – may represent an archaeologically tangible testament to this Cosmic Axis and to the shamanic practices of these communities.

It is probable that because they were accessible natural features from the underground realm of the universal cosmological model of the world, caves represented primarily a place for communities to communicate with the relevant deities that according to the various cultural mythologies ruled over the natural elements. Thus, during times of climatic pressure, not only actual sources of underground water but perhaps also most other caves in general became places of worship and cult rituals. Of course, this return to natural values as the result of global events could take place in those cultures and societies that retained at least a partial awareness of humans being a part of nature. According to our picture of caves, in most cases this therefore did not include highly developed societies with significant social hierarchies and advanced levels of organisation – at least not in the studied territory from the Neolithic to the Early Aeneolithic. Also, despite the presumed universality of this interpretation, this does not mean that all caves were necessarily and unconditionally used merely as places of cult activity or sacrifice. In many cases, specific regional or societal customs or cultural traditions surely played a role as well. Although from a comprehensive perspective caves generally fulfil their religious function and do not oppose it in any of the discussed factors, in view of the ambiguous nature of archaeological sites, any retroactive application to specific cave sites is uncertain and in many cases impossible.

Caves as important cult or religious sites fall within the concept of the sacral landscape, whose universality is documented by geographically distant analogies. Such a concept of the landscape:

> ... in which indigenous people attached special significance to geographic features appears to have been of central importance to Mesoamerican cultures from the earliest times. Mountains, large rocks, caves, springs, rivers, trees, roads, features along the seashore, or landmarks with strange or unique forms were identified with mythological events in the remote past, the creation of the world, the origin of human groups, the deeds of ancestral heroes, or places inhabited by powerful spirits or deities. (Aguilar *et al.* 2005, 69) (Fig. 3.15)

Such a reconstruction of the shamanic sacral landscape, which in the Americas is based on numerous reliable ethnological findings from diverse regions, comes surprisingly close to the traditional view of the central European landscape during the Middle Ages and modern era, which has emerged from a *mosaic* formed by the historical record, place names, folklore, or folk customs. The universal view of human development as an integral part of the landscape seems to have been generally forgotten only recently.

Fig. 3.15: Jáchymka cave in front with the famous Býčí skála cave (Moravian Karst, Czech Republic) is an example of the site with very conspicuous forms (e.g. a vulva-shaped rock window) (image: V. Peša 2005)

Notes

1. The Aeneolithic as a new era with the emergence of the *Männerbund* and male culture and related archaeological finds (drinking sets, weapons, evidence of metalworking, etc.) – were presented by, e.g., Neustupný (2008).
2. On antiquity, see Rutkowski 1986; summary for Czech Republic and Germany in Peša (2013c), for Italy with possible traditions dating back to prehistory in Whitehouse (1992), other isolated caves in Romania and Hungary in author´s unpublished thesis.

References

Absolon, K. 1970. *Moravský kras*. Vols 1 & 2. Prague: Academia.

Absolon, K. & Czižek, R. 1926. Palaeolithický výzkum jeskyně Pekárny na Moravě (I). Die palaeolithische Erforschung der Pekárna-Höhle in Mähren (I). *Časopis Moravského zemského muzea*, 24, 1–59.

Absolon, K. & Czižek, R. 1927–28. Palaeolithický výzkum jeskyně Pekárny na Moravě (II). Die palaeolithische Erforschung der Pekárna-Höhle in Mähren (II). *Časopis Moravského zemského muzea*, 25, 112–201.

Absolon, K. & Czižek, R. 1932. Palaeolithický výzkum jeskyně Pekárny na Moravě (III). Die palaeolithische Erforschung der Pekárna-Höhle in Mähren (III). *Časopis Moravského zemského muzea*, 26–27 (1929–1930), 479–532.

Absolon, K. jun. 1939–40. Výzkum nové diluviální stanice Jeskyně Rytířské v Moravském krasu. *Vesmír* 18, 231–233.

Aguilar, M., Jaen, M. M., Tucker, T. M. & Brady, J. E., 2005. Constructing mythic space: the significance of a Chicomoztoc complex at Acatzingo Viejo. In J. Brady & K. Prufer (eds) *In the Maw of the Earth Monster. Mesoamerican Ritual Cave Use.* Austin: University of Texas Press, 69–87.

Anati, E. 1963. *Palestine Before the Hebrews.* New York: Alfred A. Knopf.

Anati, E. 1968. Anatolia's Earliest Art. *Archaeology*, 21, 22–35.

Bar-Yosef, O. & Alon, D. 1988. Nahal Hemar Cave – the excavations. *Atiqot* 18, 1–30.

Bar-Yosef, O. & Tchernov, E. 1966. Archaeological finds and the fossil faunas of the Natufian and microlithic industries at Hayonim Cave (Western Galilee, Israel). *Israel Journal of Zoology*, 15, 104–140.

Bárta, M. & Kovář, M. (eds). 2011. *Kolaps a regenerace: Cesty civilizací a kultur.* Prague: Academia.

Bella, L. 1916. A Herman Ottó-barlang holocaenkori régiségei. Alluvialzeitliche Funde aus der Herman Ottó-Höhle. *Barlangkutatás* 4, 17–24, 44–46.

Blatný, L. 1962. Neolitické osídlení v Babicích n/Svit. *Vlastivědné zprávy z Adamova a okolí*, 6(1), 9–12.

Blekta, J. 1932. Kras mezi Konicí a Litovlí. *Věstník Klubu přírodovědeckého v Prostějově*, 22 (1930–31), 1–48.

Böhm, J. 1933. Slovenský kras v pravěku. *Sborník Československé společnosti zeměpisné* 39, 90–95.

Bolomey, A. 1973. The present stage of knowledge of mammal exploitation during the Epipalaeolithic and the earliest Neolithic on the territory of Romania. In J. Matolcsi (ed.) *Domestikationsforschung und Geschichte der Haustiere.* Budapest: Akadémiai Kiadó, 197–203.

Boroneanţ, V. 1970a. La période épipaléolithique sur la rive roumaine des Portes de Fer du Danube. *Praehistorische Zeitschrift* 45, 1–25.

Boroneanţ, V. 1970b. La civilisation Criş de Cuina Turcului. In *Actes du VIIe Congrès International des Sciences Préhistoriques et Protohistoriques, Prague 1966* I, Prague: Státní archeologický ústav, 407–410.

Bouzek, J. 1993. Climatic changes: new archaeological evidence from the Bohemian Karst and other areas. *Antiquity* 67, 386–393.

Brady, J. & Prufer, K. (eds), 2005. *In the Maw of the Earth Monster. Mesoamerican Ritual Cave Use.* Austin TX: University of Texas Press.

Brukner, B. 2002. Die Vinča-Kultur im Raum und Zeit. *Godišnjak Sarajevo* 30, 61–103.

Cădariu, Ş. & Petrovszky, R. 1975. Cercetări arheologice în valea Caraşovei. *Tibiscus* 4, 147–154.

Cârciumaru, M. 1987. *Mărturii ale artei rupestre preistorice în România (Témoignages de l'art rupestre préhistorique en Roumanie).* Bucureşti: Editura Sport-Turism.

Cauvin, J., Cauvin, M.-C., Helmer, D. & Willcox, G. 1997. L'homme et son environnement au Levant nord entre 30 000 et 7 500 BP. *Paléorient* 23(2), 51–69.

Čermáková, E. 2002. Problémy dětství v neolitu střední Evropy. *Pravěk* 12, 7–45.

Čermáková, E. 2007. Postavení ženy, muže a dítěte ve společnosti tvůrců lengyelské kultury. In E. Kazdová & V. Podborský (eds) *Studium sociálních a duchovních struktur pravěku.* Brno: Masarykova univerzita, 207–254.

Červinka, I. 1926; 1927–28; 1932. Předvěké vrstvy v Pekárně. *Časopis Moravského zemského muzea* 24, 30–34; 25, 152–154 and 26–27, 533–535.

D. B. 1949. Cercetări archeologice in două localităţi din Banat. *Studii - revistă de ştiinţă şi filosofie* 2/I, 95–97.

Eliade, M. 1965. *Le Sacré et le Profan.* Paris: Gallimard.

Eliade, M. 1971. *The Myth of the Eternal Return: Cosmos and History.* Princeton NJ: Princeton University Press.

Epstein, C. 2001. The significance of ceramic assemblages in Chalkolithic burial contexts in Israel and neighboring regions in the Southern Levant. *Levant* 33, 81–94.

Erdoğu, B., Uysal, I. T., Özbek, O. & Ulusoy, Ü. 2013. Speleothems of Çatalhöyük, Turkey. *Mediterranean Archaeology and Archaeometry* 13(1), 21–30.

Gál, E., Juhász, I. & Sümegi, P. (eds). 2005. *Environmental Archaeology in North-Eastern Hungary.* Varia archaeologica hungarica XIX. Budapest: Archaeological Institute of the Hungarian Academy of Sciences.

Geislerová, K., Seitl, L., Svoboda, J. & Svobodová, H, 1986. Záchranný výzkum před Kateřinskou jeskyní. *Regionální sborník okresu Blansko '86*, 64–73.

Gheorghiu, A., Nicolăescu-Plopşor, C., Haas, N., Comşa, E., Preda, C., Bombiţă, Gh., Enea, Gh., Gheorghiu, F., Iofcea, S., Nicolăescu-Plopşor, D., Neagoe, Al., Silveanu, R. & Surdu, I. 1954. Raport preliminar asupra cercetărilor de paleontologie umană dela Baia de Fier (reg. Craiova) din 1951. *Probleme de antropologie* 1, 73–86.

Gradziński, M., Hercman, H., Nowicki, T., Bella, P., 2001. Dark coloured laminae within speleothems as an indicator of the prehistoric man activity: Case study from Domica Cave (Slovakia), preliminary results. In *Speleo Brasil 2001, vol. 1, Proceedings of the 13th International Congress of Speleology*. Campinas: Brazilien Society of Speleology, 208–212.

Gronenborn, D. 2012. Das Ende von IRD 5b: Abrupte Klimafluktuationen um 5100 den BC und der Übergang vom Alt- zum Mittelneolithikum im westlichen Mitteleuropa. In Smolnik, R. (ed.) *Siedlungsstruktur und Kulturwandel in der Bandkeramik*, AFD – Beiheft 25. Dresden: Landesamt für Archäologie, 241–250.

Henrickson, E. 1985. The early development of pastoralism in the central Zagros highlands (Luristan). *Iraniqa Antiqua* 20, 1–42.

Heyden, D. 2005. Rites of passage and other ceremonies in caves. In J. Brady & K. Prufer (eds) *In the Maw of the Earth Monster. Mesoamerican Ritual Cave Use*. Austin TX: University of Texas Press, 21–34.

Hochstetter, F. von. 1883. Höhlenforschungen (Sechster Bericht). *Sitzungsberichte der mathematisch-naturwissenschaftlichen Classe der kaiserlichen Akademie der Wissenschaften* 87, Abt. I, 168–170.

Holl, B., 2007. Archaeological survey of the Baradla Cave (Res.). *Archaeologiai Értésitö* 132, 267–288.

Horáček, I., Ložek, V., Svoboda, J. & Šajnerová, A. 2002. Přírodní prostředí a osídlení krasu v pozdním paleolitu a mezolitu. In J. Svoboda (ed.) *Prehistorické jeskyně*. Dolní Věstonice studies 7. Brno: Archeologický ústav AVČR, 313–343.

Ignat, D. 1973. Contribuţii la cunoaşterea neoliticului din Bihor. *Acta Musei Napocensis* 10, 477–492.

Ignat Sava, D. 1974. Ceramica neolitică pictată de pe valea Crişului Repede. *Crisia* 4, 121–134.

Jarošová, L. 2002. Výzkumy Josefa Skutila v severní části Moravského krasu. In J. Svoboda (ed.) *Prehistorické jeskyně*. Dolní Věstonice studies 7. Brno: Archeologický ústav AVČR, 255–287.

Kadić, O. 1934. *Der Mensch zur Eiszeit in Ungarn. Mitteilungen aus dem Jahrbuch der kgl. ungar. geolog. Anstalt* (A Magyar királyi földtani intézet évkönyve) 30, Heft 1. Budapest: Franklin Verein.

Kalicz, N. & Koós, J. S. 2000. Újkőkori arcos edények a kárpát-medence északkeleti részéböl (Neolithische Gesichtsgefäße im Nordosten des Karpatenbeckens, Auszug). *A Herman Ottó Múzeum Évkönyve* 39, 15–44.

Kalicz, N. & Makkay, J. 1977. *Die Linienbandkeramik in der Großen ungarischen Tiefebene*. Studia archaeologica VII, Budapest: Akadémiai Kiadó.

Klíma, B. 1951. Křížova jeskyně v Moravském krasu. *Archeologické rozhledy* 3, 109–112, 123, 129–130.

Klíma, B. 1961. Archeologický výzkum jeskyně Hadí (Mokrá u Brna). *Anthropozoikum* 9 (1959), 277–289.

Klíma, B. 1962. Die archäologische Erforschung der Höhle „Švédův stůl' in Mähren. In *Die Erforschung der Höhle Švédův stůl 1953-1955*, Anthropos 13 (N.S. 5). Brno: Krajské nakladatelství, 7–96.

Klíma, B. 2002. Jeskyně v údolí Říčky: Kůlnička, Liščí a Klímova. In J. Svoboda (ed.) *Prehistorické jeskyně*. Dolní Věstonice studies 7. Brno: Archeologický ústav AVČR, 158–172.

Knies, J. 1910. Jeskyně Kůlna. *Pravěk* 6, 26–28.

Knies, J. 1911. Nové nálezy ze sídliště diluviál. člověka v Kůlně u Sloupu. Časopis Vlasteneckého spolku muzejního v Olomouci, 28, 132–143.

Knies, J. 1922. Údolí Holštýnské na Moravě, jeho vznik a palaentologický výzkum. *Věstník Klubu přírodovědeckého v Prostějově* 18 (1920–21), 51–78.

Korek, J. 1970. Eine Freilandsiedlung und Gräber der Bükk-Kultur in Aggtelek (Auszug). *Archaeologiai Értesitő* 97, 3–22.

Kos, P. 1997. Otevřená sídliště z mladého paleolitu a neolitu v jižní části Moravského krasu. *Přehled výzkumů* (1993–94). Brno: Archeologický ústav AV ČR, 27–44.

Kos, P. 1999. Mokrá-Horákov (kat. úz. Mokrá, okr. Brno-venkov). *Přehled výzkumů* 40 (1997–98). Brno: Archeologický ústav AV ČR, 193–194.

Kovács, K. 2006–2007. A tiszaszölös-aszóparti középsö neolitikus település legkorábbi idöszakának viszgálata a kronológiai és a kulturális kapcsolatok tükrében. *Ösrégézeti Levelek* 8–9, 19–38.

Krasser, F. A. 1882. Die Mokrauer Höhle bei Brünn. *Mitteilungen der Anthropologischen Gesellschaft in Wien* 11 (N.F. 1), 98–99.

Kříž, M. 1889. *Kůlna a Kostelík*. Brno: publisher.

Kříž, M. 1892. Die Höhlen in den mährischen Devonkalken und ihre Vorzeit II, IV. *Jahrbuch der k. k. geologischen Reichsanstalt in Wien* 42, 463–513, 564–625.

Kříž, M. 1897 and 1898. O jeskyni Kostelíku na Moravě. *Časopis Vlasteneckého spolku muzejního v Olomouci* 14, 49–61 and 15, 19–41.

Kříž, M. 1909. O důležitosti archeologických nálezů z jeskyně Kůlny u Sloupa na Moravě. *Pravěk* 5, 7–19.

Kuijt, I. & Russell, K. W. 1993. Tur Imdai Rockshelter, Jordan: Debitage analysis and historic Bedouin lithic technology. *Journal of Archaeological Science* 20, 667–680.

Lalescu, I. & Benea, D. 1997–98. Contribuţii la istoria aşezării de la ad mediam (Băile Herculane). *Sargetia* 27(1), 267–301.

Lazarovici, G., Băltean, I., Biagi, P., Spataro, M., Lazarovici, M., Colesniuc, S. & Vrâncean, P. 2004. Petreştii de Jos, com. Petreştii de Jos, jud. Cluj, no. 139. Cronica cercetărilor arheologice 2003. Available from: www.archweb.cimec.ro/arheologie/CronicaCA2004 [Accessed 14 Februay 2018].

Lazarovici, G., Biagi, P., Spataro, M., Lazarovici, M., Colesniuc, S., Suciu, C., Roman, C., Chitic, O., Sote, A. & Arpad, T. 2006. Petreştii de Jos, com. Petreştii de Jos, jud. Cluj, no. 137. Cronica cercetărilor arheologice 2005. Available from: www.archweb.cimec.ro/arheologie/CronicaCA2006 [Accessed 14 February 2018].

Lewis-Williams, D. 2002. *The Mind in the Cave. Consciousness and the Origin of Art*. London: Thames and Hudson.

Lichardus, J. 1968. *Jaskyňa Domica - nejvýznačnejšie sídlisko l'udu bukovohorskej kultúry*. Bratislava: Slovenská akadémia vied.

Lichardus, J. 1974. *Studien zur Bükker Kultur*. Bonn: Saarbrücker Beiträge zu Altertumskunde 12.

Ložek, V. 1973a. *Příroda ve čtvrtohorách*. Praha: Academia.

Ložek, V. 1973b. Význam krasu pro poznání přírodní historické krajiny. *Československý* kras 24 (1972), 19–36.

Luca, S. A., Ciugudean, H. & Roman, C. 2000. Die Frühphase der Vinča-Kultur in Siebenbürgen. *Apulum* 37(1), 1–49.

Luca, S. A., Roman, C. & Baicoană, M. 1997. Materiale arheologice din peşteri ale judeţului Hunedoara (I). *Corviniana* 3, 17–32.

Makkay, J. 1991. Entstehung, Blüte und Ende der Theiß-Kultur. In J. Lichardus (ed.) *Die Kupferzeit als historische Epoche*, Bd. I. Bonn: Rudolf Habelt, 319–328.

Mantu, C.-M. 1998. Absolute chronology of Neolithic cultures in Romania and relations with the Aegeo-Anatolian world. In M. Otte (ed.) *Préhistoire d'Anatolie*. ERAUL 85. Liège: Université de Liège, 159–173.

Matoušek, V. 1996. Archeologické nálezy z jeskyní Českého krasu 3x jinak. *Archeologické rozhledy* 48, 16–28.

Matoušek, V, 1999. Hora a jeskyně. Příspěvek ke studiu vývoje vztahu člověka a jeho přírodního prostředí ve střední Evropě od neolitu do raného středověku. *Archeologické rozhledy* 51, 441–456.

Měchurová, Z. 1992. *Archeologické nálezy z Moravy ve sbírkách Prehistorického oddělení Přírodovědeckého muzea ve Vídni (Archäologische Funde aus Mähren in den Sammlungen der Prähistorischen Abteilung des Naturhistorischen Museums in Wien)*. Prague: Zprávy České archeologické společnosti při ČSAV, Supplement 13.

Mikov, V. & Dzhambasov, N. 1960. *Devetaškata pestera*. Sofia: Izdatelstvo na Balg. Akad. na naukite.

Mogoşanu, F. & Stratan, I. 1966. Noi descoperiri paleolitice în Banat. *SCIV* 17(2), 335–344.

Munson, Ch. A., Munson, P., Tankersley, K. & Rogers, B. 1997. Prehistoric uses of caves in North America: A regional synthesis. In *Proceedings of the 12th International Congress of Speleology, La Chaux-de-Fonds, Switzerland, 1997.* Basel: Speleo Projects vol. 3, 45–48.

Musil, R. 2010. Výpustek – bájná jeskyně u Křtin. Její 400letá historie a význam. *Acta speleologica* 1, Prague: Česká speleologická společnost.

Neruda, P., Nerudová, Z. & Valoch, K. 2007. Zpráva o revizním výzkumu jeskyně Puklinové v údolí Říčky (Moravský kras). *Acta Musei Moraviae - Sciences sociales* 92, 79–102.

Neustupný, E. (ed.). 2008. *Archeologie pravěkých Čech, 4 - Eneolit*. Praha: Archeologický ústav AVČR.

Nicholson, Sh. (ed.). 1993. *Shamanism. An Expanded View of Reality*. Wheaton: Theosophical Publishing House.

Nicolăescu-Plopşor, C. S., Comşa, E., Nicolăescu-Plopşor, D. C. & Bolomey, A. 1957a. Şantierul arheologic Baia de Fier. *Materiale şi cercetări arheologice* 3, 13–27.

Nicolăescu-Plopşor, C. S., Haas, N. & Păunescu, A. 1957b. Şantierul arheologic Ohaba-Ponor. *Materiale şi cercetări arheologice* 3, 41–49.

Oliva, M. 1995. Pravěké osídlení jeskyň Moravského krasu. *Veronica* 9(4), xxvii-xxix.

Oliva, M. 2013. The Moravian karst in the anthropological perspective. In M. Filippi & P. Bosák (eds) *Proceedings of the 16th International Congress of speleology, Brno 2013.* Prague: Czech Speleological Society, vol. 1, 18–21.

Ondruš, V. 1965. Die vorgeschichtlichen Funde aus der Höhle Pod hradem. In R. Musil (ed.) *Die Erforschung der Höhle Pod hradem 1956-1958.* Brno: Anthropos 18 (N. S. 10), 107–108.

Păunescu, A. 1970. Epipaleoliticul de la Cuina Turcului - Dubova. *SCIV* 21, 3–47.

Păunescu, A. 1979. Cercetările arheologice de la Cuina Turcului - Dubova (jud. Mehedinţi). *Tibiscus* 5, 11–56.

Pavúk, J. & Bátora, J. 1995. *Siedlung und Gräber der Ludanice-Gruppe in Jelšovce*. Nitra: Archeologický ústav SAV.

Peša, V. 2006. Využívání jeskyní v mladší době bronzové až halštatské ve vybraných oblastech střední Evropy (Höhlennutzung in der Jungbronzezeit bis Hallstattzeit in ausgewählten Gebieten Mitteleuropas). *Památky archeologické* 97, 47–132.

Peša, V. 2008. Cult caves and settlement patterns in the rocky landscape of the Elbsandstone Mts. (Saxony/Bohemia). In *Proceedings of the 10th International Symposium on Pseudokarst, Gorizia 2008*, Gorizia: Centro Ricerche Carsiche 'Carlo Seppenhofer,' 71–74.

Peša, V. 2011. Jeskyně v neolitu a časném eneolitu: pohled z Předního východu. *Praehistorica* 29, 275–296.

Peša, V. 2013a. Jeskyně, člověk a krajina na příkladu neolitu a staršího eneolitu západních Karpat. *Slovenský kras* 50(2), 225–242.

Peša, V. 2013b. Archaeology and the winter solstice in the caves of the Bohemian Karst, Czech Republic. In M. Filippi & P. Bosák (eds) *Proceedings of the 16th International Congress of speleology, Brno 2013.* Praha: Czech Speleological Society, vol. 1, 189–191.

Peša, V. 2013c. Der neuzeitliche Mensch in der Höhle: Die Speläoanthropologie als archäologische Quelle. *Památky archeologické* 104, 231–316.

Peša, V. & Majer, A. 2003. Světelné podmínky v jeskyních z pohledu speleoarcheologie (Res.: Light conditions in caves: the archaeological approach). *Speleofórum* 22, 22–28.

Pichon, J. 1991. Les Oiseaux au Natoufien, avifaune et sédentarité. In O. Bar-Yosef & F. Valla (eds) *The Natufian Culture in the Levant*. Ann Arbor MI: International Monographs in Prehistory - Archaeological Series 1, 371–380.

Podborský, V. (ed.), 1993. *Pravěké dějiny Moravy*. Brno: Muzejní a vlastivědná společnost.

Radovanović, I., 1996. Mesolithic/Neolithic contacts: a case of the Iron Gates region. Mezolitsko/neolitski stiki: primer področja Džerdapa. *Poročilo o raziskovanju paleolitika, neolitika in eneolitika v Sloveniji*, 23, 39–48.

Radulesco, C. & Samson, P. 1962. Sur un centre de domestication du Mouton dans le Mésolithique de la grotte „La Adam'en Dobrogea. *Zeitschrift für Tierzüchtung und Züchtungsbiologie* 76, 282–320.

Ringer, A., Szolyák, P., Kordos, L., Regös, J. & Heinzlmann, K., 2006. Revision possibilities of the Palaeolithic assemblages of the Herman Ottó Cave and the Herman Ottó Rock-shelter (abstract). *A Herman Ottó Múzeum Évkönyve* 45, 5–23.

Roman, P. 1971. Strukturänderungen des Endäneolithikums im Donau-Karpaten-Raum. *Dacia* N.S. 15, 31–169.

Roman, C. C., Daiconescu, D. & Luca, S. A. 2000. Săpături arheologice în Peştera nr. 1 (Peştera Mare) de la Cerişor (com. Lelese, jud. Hunedoara). *Corviniana* 6, 7–59.

Rosen, S., Savinetsky, A., Plakht, Y., Kisseleva, N., Khassanov, B., Pereladov, A. & Haiman, M. 2005. Dung in the desert: Preliminary results of the Negev Holocene Ecology Project. *Current Anthropology* 46(2), 317–327.

Rutkowski, B. 1986. *The Cult Places of the Aegean*. New Haven & London: Yale University Press.

Sandstrom, M. 2005. The cave-pyramid complex among the contemporary Nahua of northern Veracruz. In J. Brady & K. Prufer (eds) *In the Maw of the Earth Monster. Mesoamerican Ritual Cave Use*. Austin TX: University of Texas Press, 35–68.

Satari, S. 1981. Mountains and caves in art: new finds of terracotta miniatures in Kudus, Central Java. *Bulletin of the Research Center of Archaeology of Indonesia* 15, 1–17.

Simms, S. R. 1988. The archaeological structure of a Bedouin camp. *Journal of Archaeological Science* 15, 197–211.

Sklenář, K. & Matoušek, V. 1994. *Die Höhensiedlung des Böhmischen Karstes vom Neolithikum bis zum Mittelalter*. Prague: Fontes archaeologici pragenses 20.

Skutil, J. 1947. Válečný osud křtinského Výpustku v Moravském krasu. *Časopis turistů* 59, 119–120.

Skutil, J. 1961. Předběžná zpráva o výzkumu Verunčiny díry a některých jiných přilehlých jeskyní v Suchém žlebu v Mor. Krasu. *Přehledy výzkumů* (1960), 29–35.

Skutil, J. 1962. Nález figurální plastiky na volutové keramice z jeskyně Koňské jámy v Moravském krase. *Přehledy výzkumů* (1961), 33–37.

Skutil, J. 1963a. Předběžná zpráva o hlavních výsledcích výzkumu Rytířské jeskyně (Lažánky, okr. Blansko) v Mor. krase. *Přehledy výzkumů* (1962), 12–14.

Skutil, J. 1963b. Výsledky výzkumu jeskyně Koňské jámy (Suchdol, okr. Blansko). *Přehledy výzkumů* (1962), 10–11.

Skutil, J. 1970. Pravěk a časná doba dějinná Moravského krasu a středověké osídlení našich jeskyň. In K. Absolon (ed.) *Moravský kras* 2. Prague: Academia, 315–329.

Sobol, A. 1949. Barová jeskyně u Býčí skály, nová jeskynní lokalita s nálezy volutové keramiky. *Československý kras* 2, 137–138.

Sobol, A. 1968. Pravěké lidojedství v jeskyni Barové a Býčí skále u Adamova. *Vlastivědné zprávy z Adamova a okolí* 12(1), 1–5.

Solecki, R. S. 1998. Archaeological survey of caves in northern Iraq. *International Journal of Kurdish Studies* 12, 1–70.

Soukop, J. 1859. Macocha a její okolí. *Moravan* 8, 52–82.

Strnad, V. 1949. Fauna Barové jeskyně pod Krkavčí skálou u Adamova. *Československý kras* 2, 123–127.

Stuchlík, S. 1981. *Osídlení jeskyň ve starší a střední době bronzové na Moravě*. Studie Archeologického ústavu ČSAV v Brně 9, sv. 2. Prague: Academia.

Stuchlík, S. 2002. Postpaleolitické osídlení jeskyně Kůlničky a Liščí jeskyně. In J. Svoboda (ed.) *Prehistorické jeskyně*. Dolní Věstonice studie 7, Brno: Archeologický ústav AV ČR, 173–176.

Svoboda, J. 1987. Výzkumy v Moravském krasu v roce 1984 (okr. Blansko). *Přehledy výzkumů* (1984), 12–13.

Svoboda, J. 2002. Aktuální trendy ve výzkumu paleolitického parietálního umění. In J. Svoboda (ed.) *Prehistorické jeskyně*. Dolní Věstonice studies 7, Brno: Archeologický ústav AV ČR, 394–407.

Svoboda, J., Horáček, I., Ložek, V., Svobodová, H. & Šilar, J. 2000. The Pekárna Cave. Magdalenian stratigraphy, environment, and the termination of the loess formation in Moravian Karst. *Anthropozoikum* 24, 61–79.

Svoboda, J. & van der Plicht, J. 2007. Býčí skála and other caves in the Middle Danube region: Dating rock art. In *Rock Art in the Frame of the Cultural Heritige of Humankind. XXII Valcamonica Symposium 2007*. Capo di Ponte: Edizioni del centro, 467–472.
Svoboda, J. & Seitl, L. 1985. Výzkum v Moravském krasu. *Přehled výzkumů* (1983), 8–9.
Šebela, L. 2001. Nález zoomorfní plastiky z jeskyně Pekárna, k. ú. Mokrá/okr. Brno-venkov/. *Pravěk - Supplementum* 8, 191–196.
Šiška, S. 1989. *Kultúra s východnou lineárnou keramikou na Slovensku*. Bratislava: Veda.
Šiška, S. 1999. Výšinná sídliská bukovohorskej kultúry na Slovensku. *Sborník prací Filozofické fakulty Brněnské univerzity (SPFFBU)* M 4, 47–60.
Škrdla, P. & Šebela, L. 1999. Mokrá (okr. Brno-venkov). *Přehled výzkumů* 39 (1995–96), 281–284.
Štrof, M. & Štrofová, A. 1988. Archeologický výzkum jeskyně Koňská jáma v Suchém žlebu. *Regionální sborník okresu Blansko ´88*, 10–25.
Tellenbach, M. 1983. Materialien zum Präkeramischen Neolithikum in Süd-Ost-Europa. Typologisch-stratigraphische Untersuchungen zu lithischen Gerätschaften. *Bericht der Römisch-Germanischen Kommission* 64, 23–123.
Tichý, R., 2002. Kultura s lineární keramikou v jeskyních Rytířská a Koňská jáma. In J. Svoboda (ed.) *Prehistorické jeskyně*. Dolní Věstonice Studies 7. Brno: Archeologický ústav AVČR, 288–292.
Tompa, F. 1934/35. 25 Jahre Urgeschichtsforschung in Ungarn 1912–1936. *Bericht der Römisch-germanischen Kommission* 24/25, 27–127.
Trampler, R. 1900. Die Michaelsgrotte bei Holstein im mährischen Karst. *Mittheilungen der Section für Naturkunde des Österreichischen Touristen Clubs* 12, 2–7.
Valoch, K. 1957. Paleolitické osídlení Žitného jeskyně. *Práce brněnské základny Československé akademie věd* 29(12/364), 573–600.
Valoch, K. 1967. Paleolitické osídlení jeskyně Kůlny u Sloupu v Moravském krasu. *Archeologické rozhledy* 19, 566–575.
Valoch, K. 1988. *Die Erforschung der Kůlna-Höhle 1961-1976*. Brno: Anthropos 24 (N. S. 16).
Vencl, S. 1968. Zur Frage des Bestehens eines präkeramischen Neolithikums in der Slowakei. *Acta Archaeologica Carpathica* 10, 39–61.
Verhoeven, M. 2002. Transformations of society: The changing role of ritual and symbolism in the PPNB and the PN in the Levant, Syria and South-east Anatolia. *Paléorient* 28(1), 5–14.
Vértes, L. 1953. Az alsópaleolitikum emberének elsö biztos eszközlelete Magyarországon (Rez.: Pervyi dostovernyi ekzempliar orudia iz nižnego paleolita v Vengrii). *Archaeologiai Értesitö* 80, 17–26.
Vlassa, N. 1961. O contribuţie la problema legăturilor culturii Tisa cu alte culturi neolitice din Transilvania. *SCIV* 12, 17–24.
Vlassa, N. 1976. Asupra unor probleme ale neoliticului final şi ale începutului epocii bronzului în Transilvania. In N. Vlassa (ed.). *Neoliticul Transilvaniei*. Cluj-Napoca: Bibliotheca Musei Napocensis III, 90–99.
Wankel, H. 1871. Prähistorische Alterthümer in der mährischen Höhlen. *Mitteilungen der Anthropologischen Gesellschaft in Wien* 2 (Czech in Sborník Okresního vlastivědného musea v Blansku 5, 1973, 147–171).
Watson, P. J. 1997. The prehistory of Salts Cave & Mammoth Cave, Mammoth Cave National Park, Kentucky, USA. In *Proceedings of the 12th International Congress of Speleology, La Chaux-de-Fonds, Switzerland, 1997*. Basel: Speleo Projects, vol. 3, 29–30.
Weinstein-Evron, M. 1998. *Early Natufian el-Wad Revisited*. ERAUL 77. Liège: Université de Liège.
Whitehouse, R. D. 1992. *Underground Religion. Cult and Culture in Prehistoric Italy*. Specialist Studies on Italy 1. London: University of London.

Chapter 4

As Above, So Below: St Melangell and the Celestial Journey

Caroline Malim

Abstract *The church of St Melangell which stands within a remote valley in the foothills of the Berwyn Range in Powys, Wales is one of a number of early churches in Britain identified as having been built within a later prehistoric sacred enclosure. A number of such churches have early legends linking them with their founding saints and St Melangell's is no exception. The sacred nature of these sites remains, but the belief systems have changed over time. Likewise, it is possible that some of these 'founding' legends originated in prehistory and were adapted over time with changing belief systems. This paper describes and contextualises St Melangell's prehistoric site and explores the extraordinary legend within the context of the monument's surrounding land and skyscape to determine, not what it purports to tell us about a pious female saint in this peaceful Welsh valley, but more about what it can tell us about a wider ritual/shamanic belief system in the region as a whole.*

Introduction: The Site of St Melangell

St Melangell's is a charming stone church nestled in a steep-sided valley known as Cwm Pennant in the foothills of the Berwyn range in Powys, Wales (Fig. 4.1). The valley is orientated approximately north-west–south-east, with the source of the River Tanat rising near the valley head at the north-west. The church is situated within a large sub-circular enclosure and is located on the north side of the River Tanat, near its confluence with the smaller stream Nant Ewyn ('foam'), the head of which is known as a healing spring. St Melangell's is accessed via a single track road from the nearest settlement Llangynog 3.3 km away, the valley itself being populated by only a handful of scattered farmsteads. The stone church, elements of which date to the 12th century, is unique in its dedication to Saint Melangell.

It was and continues to be, a place of pilgrimage, with people coming from all over the world to visit the reconstructed shrine, reputed to be one of the oldest examples of Romanesque architecture in Europe (Britnell & Watson 1994) (Fig. 4.2).

Fig. 4.1: St Melangell's Church from the south-west. The lychgate is just visible in the background, to the right of the image

After years of neglect, restoration work at the church underwent archaeological excavation and recording in 1958, and intermittently from 1989 to 1994 during works to the Cell y Bedd (shrine of the grave), where the shrine was originally situated (Britnell & Watson 1994). In the small area available for excavation, it was found that beneath the Cell y Bedd walls and floor were the remains of at least 29 cremation burials with further cremations continuing underneath the walls beyond the confines of the excavation area (Fig. 4.3). Further cremations were identified when two small areas were excavated under part of the tower floor and nave.

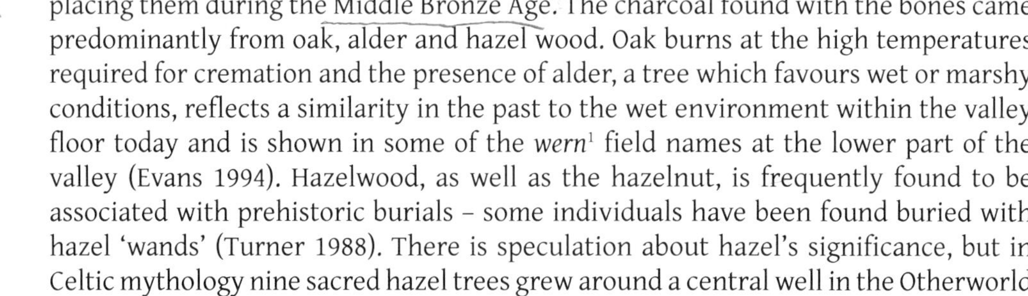

Analysis of the fragmentary bones identified them to be human and radiocarbon dating promoted a date range between *c.* 1500–1000 years BCE (Britnell 1994a), placing them during the Middle Bronze Age. The charcoal found with the bones came predominantly from oak, alder and hazel wood. Oak burns at the high temperatures required for cremation and the presence of alder, a tree which favours wet or marshy conditions, reflects a similarity in the past to the wet environment within the valley floor today and is shown in some of the *wern*[1] field names at the lower part of the valley (Evans 1994). Hazelwood, as well as the hazelnut, is frequently found to be associated with prehistoric burials – some individuals have been found buried with hazel 'wands' (Turner 1988). There is speculation about hazel's significance, but in Celtic mythology nine sacred hazel trees grew around a central well in the Otherworld (Paice MacLeod 2011). Although the remit of the excavation was not to determine the full extent of the prehistoric cemetery, comparison with other local Bronze Age cremation cemeteries would suggest there could have been a burial mound at the spot where the church now stands.

Fig. 4.2: The reconstructed Romanesque shrine dedicated to St Melangell

The churchyard measures approximately 80 m across from north to south and 95 m east to west, enclosing an area of *c.* 0.52 ha. There are six mature yew trees within the boundary of the enclosure and in 2008 the Ancient Yew Group classified two of them as 'Veteran' – giving them a minimum age range from 500 to 1200 years; two further yews were classified as 'Ancient' giving them a range from at least 800 years old (Ancient Yew Group 2017)[2] (there is no upper age limit in this category). Some of the older yews are growing out of what appear to be circular mounds 0.5–1.0 m high (Fig. 4.4). One theory suggests that they were created as a result of piling loose soil dug from graves, however they could be the vestiges of further Bronze Age burial mounds. Another mound in the north-west sector of the enclosure suggests the location of another burial mound or perhaps the location of another long-standing yew tree now gone. A parallel to this can be seen 15 km (as the crow flies) to the north-east at St Garmon's Church at Llanarmon Dyffryn Ceriog where, situated in the churchyard are two ancient yews as well as a Bronze Age Barrow.

Although deadly poisonous, the yew was associated with everlasting life, due in no small part to the way in which it grows. Some branches grow down into the ground to form new stems which rise up around the old central growth. They develop as separate but linked trunks until no longer distinguishable from the original, thus the tree constantly regenerates itself. Some yews appear to die-off completely only to be replaced by a shoot which can develop into a new tree. Britain has the highest concentration of ancient yews in Europe (Bevan-Jones 2002) and, as yet, no upper age limit has been established for the species.

It is possible that seeds from the yew berry were used in prehistory for their entheogenic properties. In the Irish Celtic legend The Dream of Angus, the heroine Cáer Ibormeith (yew berry) is a female magician who wears a swan cloak. Robert Wallis (2003) speculates that her wearing of the cloak and transformation into a bird could be a metaphor for entering into a trance and shape-shifting into a spirit helper, induced by the entheogenic properties of the highly toxic yew seed.

Robert Wallis

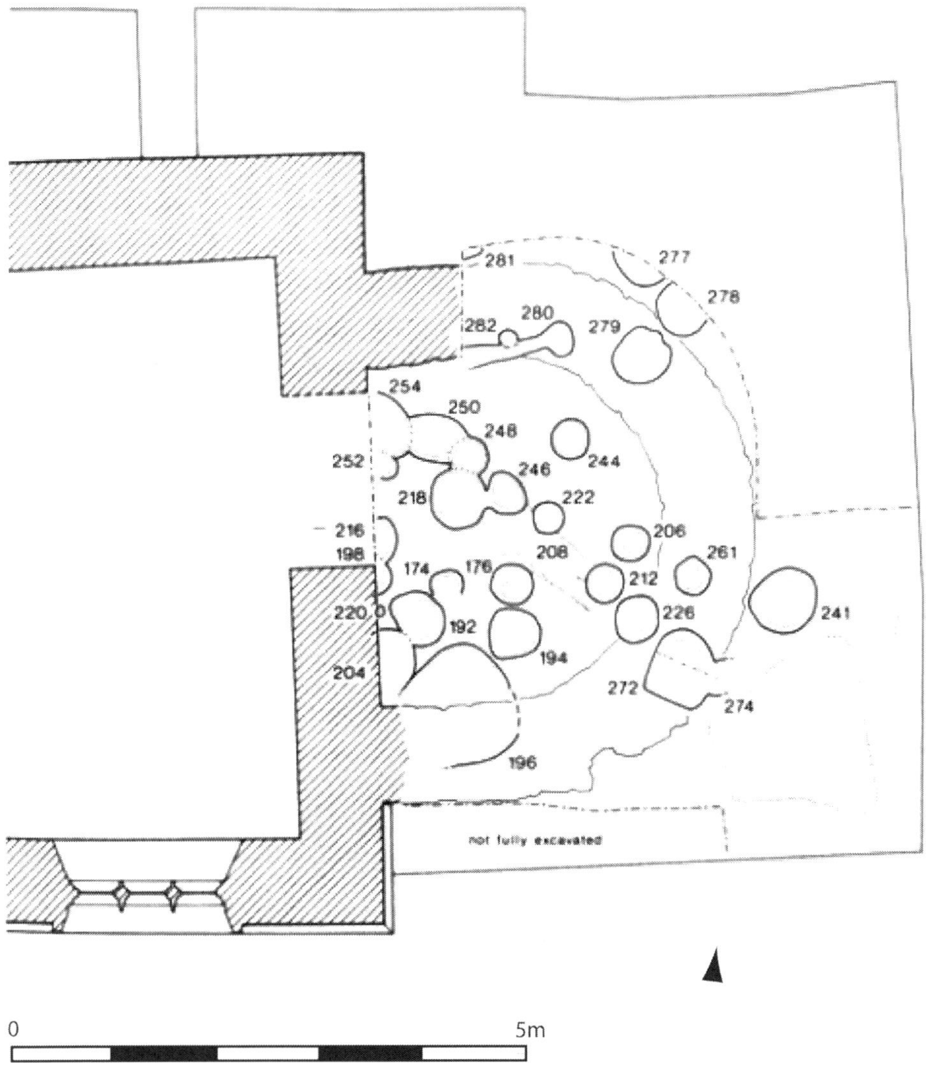

Fig. 4.3: Bronze Age cremation burials identified during excavation in the subsoil under the floor of the Cell y Bedd (after Britnell 1994a). With permission from the editor of the Montgomeryshire Collections

Yggdrasil, the world tree or *Axis Mundi* of Norse mythology, is believed by some to be not an ash but a yew (Bevan-Jones 2002), supported by the fact that it was described as an evergreen. Etymology may also support the yew theory: according to Franz Schröder (Simek 1996) Yggdrasil could mean 'Yew Pillar', deriving *yggia* from *igwja* ('yew-tree'), and *drasill* from *dher* ('support').

Yggdrasil was said to rise through a number of worlds – a concept of shamanic lore, shared by many peoples in northern Eurasia and, as noted by Ellis Davidson (1993),

Fig. 4.4: Female yew tree on a mound adjacent to the lychgate at St Melangell

'[t]his seems to be a very ancient concept, perhaps based on the Pole Star, the centre of the heavens' and furthermore 'among Siberian shamans, a central tree may be used as a ladder to ascend the heavens.' The yew seed's entheogenic properties, potential links with shamanic trance and shape-shifting, as well as its life cycle of growth, apparent death and regeneration (Yggdrasil was said to continually grow and die), would suggest that there is a good case for yew's place as the world tree.

Within the Christian graveyard at St Melangell's, over 1000 burials have been recorded since records began, the majority of which are unmarked. The earliest burial records date to 1680 and suggest an average of 3.7 burials per year occurred between the late 17th and late 18th centuries. It is assumed that a further 1–2000 unmarked burials took place in the centuries stretching back to the 12th century (Britnell 1994b).

Until the mid-19th century the parish of Pennant Melangell was extensive, containing a number of widely scattered townships – several remote (Britnell 1994a). A reorganisation of parishes was made in 1878 by means of an Order of Council, with new parishes being formed from areas that had originally fallen under the patrimony of St Melangell (Allchin 1994). Clement Davies, a leading member of Churchill's war cabinet, had grown up in an outlying district of the old parish and noted in the 1950s that, despite the distance: 'it was to this sacred spot that the families bore their dead .... Orders in Council can and do accomplish much, but they cannot alter or affect the traditions of the people.'

Parishioners have long felt passionate about St Melangell, considering it a place of healing and a liminal place where one can step from one world into another. Between 1788 and 1812, the vicar of Melangell, Ezekiel Hamer wrote:

You see Cwm Pennant shining; a high valley,
To ward off hardship,
A healing valley; for you there is not
More than one step between our valley and heaven.

The church undoubtedly served as an important focal point for the scattered community. There was, for example, an interesting custom of playing ball games to the north of the church, explaining perhaps why there are so few windows in the north wall. Ball games continued well into the 19th century and were played on Sundays as well as weekdays but by the late 19th century 'had generally been suppressed within the diocese, strict injunctions having been given to the church wardens in the neighbouring deanery of Mechain for instance to 'break off that evil custom" (Britnell 1994a). The term 'Evil custom' suggests that this tradition was considered to be non-Christian, and potentially ancient. Indeed evidence of such practice can be found in other early churches and is found in the English fairy tale *Childe Rowland* (Steel 2016). The story starts off with a ball game in a churchyard, but the narrative quickly moves to the taboo of moving 'widdershins' (anti-clockwise) around churches and Childe Rowland's journey to rescue his sister and brothers, all of whom had been playing with the ball but were taken to the Otherworld after having moved widdershins around the 'church'. Here his trials involve the taking of heads, the abstinence from food and drink (fasting) and single combat with the king of the Otherword. Of particular interest is the anointing of the dead brothers' bodies:

> The Elfin King[...] took a phial that was filled with a blood-red liquor. And with this liquor he anointed the ears and the eyelids, the nostrils, the lip, and the finger-tips of the bodies ... And immediately they sprang to life and declared that their souls only had been away, but had now returned. (Steel 2016, 246)

The ears, eyes, nose and mouth represent the senses for hearing, sight, smell and taste (and are also 'thresholds' associated with the head), the fingertips represent touch. The act of anointing areas linked to all five senses indicates a belief in their combined importance to the living and the 'dead'. The 'evil' ball games at St Melangell's may therefore be linked to an earlier belief system linked to rituals associated with death and resurrection or shamanic journeying to the otherworld and back, emphasised by the fact that 'widdershins' is the direction the stars revolve around the north star (now Polaris) and, in shamanic tradition, represents the *Axis Mundi* by which shamans can travel between worlds or realms (Herman Bender pers. comm.).

Another custom in the valley and the wider parish regarded the protection of hares known locally as 'Melangell's lambs'. Until the 17th century, nobody would kill a hare and according to N. W. Thomas, writing in 1900 (Alchin 1994): '[t]he hare is also noted as the animal with local sanctity, that must not be killed in Cwm Pennant'. As we shall discover, this custom may have pagan roots originating in ancient times which persisted to relatively modern times.

At the end of the 19th century, the Reverend Owen made note of another custom that had fallen out of use:

> The people in these parts were much given to observing the saints' days. They say their church was dedicated to two saints, and for miles around the people congregated to the church to keep the saints' festivals, and amused themselves on the occasion with many rustic games and with cock fights – and other fights – and with interludes ... The festivals lasted, I am told, for a fortnight (Britnell 1994b, 51)

It is interesting to note that the congregation understood the church to be dedicated to two saints but clearly only recognised and remembered St Melangell. Her feast day is 27 May but the feast day of the other saint is not recorded. Although locally recognised, none of the Welsh Saints, with the exception of Saint David, were officially recognised by the Church. In order to understand the feast day of St Melangell, and explore a potential date for the other saint, it is necessary to look to the formation of the early Christian church.

Christian Background

Christianity was legalised as a religion by the Emperor Constantine the Great with the Edict of Milan in AD 313, from that point until AD 391 both paganism and Christianity were legal forms of worship. This changed in AD 392 when Emperor Theodosius I (a devout Christian) passed legislation prohibiting all pagan worship, which in turn led to a gradual but increasing tide of pagan persecutions. The Roman Empire recalled its legions from Britain in AD 410. In AD 416 under Theodosius II a law was passed banning pagans from public employment in a further effort to force conversions to Christianity.

Nearly 200 years later, in AD 596, Pope Gregory the Great sent a group of 40 missionaries (known as the Gregorian or Augustinian Mission) to Britain to convert the Anglo Saxons. Pope Gregory made Augustine the first Archbishop of Canterbury, giving him control over the southern part of the British Isles and over the clergy of the native Britons (although long established Celtic bishops refused to accept his authority). Of particular interest however is the *Epistola ad Mellitatum*, a letter he gave to one of the missionaries called Mellitus (first Bishop of London and third Archbishop of Canterbury), instructing Augustine to consecrate pagan temples for Christian use and move or convert pagan feast days to Christian ones – all in order to ease the transition to Christianity.

This practice had already been adopted by the early Celtic Christian church in Ireland where the pagan solar goddess Britannia was Christianised around AD 470 to become St Brigid. A monastery was built over Britannia's fire temple at Kildare and the eternal flame associated with her worship at the pagan shrine was thereafter tended by nuns and continued to burn without interruption until the Reformation in the 16th century. Her importance throughout Ireland was such that her pagan feast day was kept but Christianised and dedicated to The Purification of the Virgin Mary and Presentation of Jesus at the Temple of Jerusalem, better known as Candlemas. It runs from sundown on the 1 February to sundown on 2 February – the Eve of St Bride and St Bride's Day respectively, also known as the Celtic festival of Imbolc. Although most often linked to lambing and the first signs of Spring in Europe, it is more specifically linked to astronomy, being one of the four cross quarter dates in the solar calendar, in this instance the halfway point between the Winter Solstice and the Spring Equinox in the northern hemisphere.

The small scale archaeological excavations at St Melangell's identified the presence of a Bronze Age cremation cemetery beneath the church, but was this still a sacred burial site and place of worship when the first Christians came to sanctify it?

This is the only church dedicated to St Melangell and her feast day lies on 27 May, about the same time as the feast day of St Augustine which (depending upon different sources) takes place on 26 or 28 May (St Augustine being the same archbishop who consecrated pagan temples and altered feast days to ease transition to Christianity). If the convergence of the feast days of these two saints was deliberate it might suggest that, prior to its consecration, the site at Cwm Pennant was not a redundant pagan sacred burial ground, but rather one that was still in use. St Augustine may therefore have been the second saint to whom the church was dedicated. But this raises several further questions. According to Pryce (1994), written records provide no reliable evidence for when Melangell lived, was Melangell an early Christian saint or was she, like St Brigid, a much loved and highly respected pagan deity already worshipped at the prehistoric site? If so, who was she? When was her original feast day? How was she worshipped and what was the religious significance of the site?

Legend and Sacred Significance

Without the extraordinary legend of St Melangell, which is also depicted on the rood screen (Fig. 4.5), it would have been virtually impossible to unravel the origins of her importance and the significance of this ancient site within its wider landscape. The following is a translation of a 17th century manuscript, by Professor Oliver Davies of St David's University College, Lampeter:

> The Life of Melangell
>
> In Powys there was once a certain most illustrious prince by the name of Brychwel Ysgithrog, who was the Earl of Chester and who at that time lived in the town of Pengwern Powys, which means in Latin the head of Powys marsh (now known as Salop), and whose home or abode stood in that place where the college of St Chad is situated today. Now that very same noble prince gave his aforesaid home or mansion for the use of God as an act of almsgiving both by his own free will and from a sense of religious duty, making a perpetual grant of it for his own sake and for the sake of his heirs. When one day in the year of our Lord 604 (the

Fig. 4.5: Detail of the carved rood screen showing the hunting scene from the legend of St Melangell

year St Augustine died), the said prince had gone hunting to a certain place in Britain called Pennant, in the said principality of Powys, and when the hunting dogs of the same prince had started a hare, the dogs pursued the hare and he too gave chase until he came to a certain thicket of brambles, which was large and full of thorns. In this thicket he found a girl of beautiful appearance who, given up to divine contemplation, was praying with the greatest devotion, with the said hare lying boldly and fearlessly under the hem of her or fold of her garments, its face towards the dogs.

Then the prince cried 'Get it, hounds, get it!,' but the more he shouted, urging them on, the further the dogs retreated and fled, howling, from the little animal. Finally, the prince, altogether astonished, asked the girl how long she had lived on her own on his lands, in such a lonely spot. In reply the girl said that she had not seen a human face for these fifteen years. Then he asked the girl who she was, her place of birth and origins, and in all humility she answered she was the daughter of King Jowchel of Ireland and that 'because my father had intended me to be the wife of a certain great and generous Irishman, I fled from my native soil and under the guidance of God came here in order that I might serve God and the immaculate Virgin with my heart and pure body until my dying day'. Then the prince asked the girl her name. She replied that her name was Melangell. 'I find that you are a hand-maid of the true God and a most sincere follower of Christ. Therefore, because it has pleased the highest and all powerful God to give refuge, for your merits, to this little wild hare with safe conduct and protection from the attack and pursuit of these savage and violent dogs, I give and present to you most willingly these my lands for the service of God, that they may be a perpetual asylum, refuge and defence, in honour of your name, excellent girl. Let neither king nor prince seek to be so rash or bold towards God that they presume to drag away any man or woman who has escaped here, desiring to enjoy protection in these your lands, as long as they in no way contaminate or pollute your sanctuary or asylum. But, on the other hand, if any wrongdoer who enjoys the protection of your sanctuary shall set out in any direction to do harm, then the independent abbots of your sanctuary, who alone know of their crimes, shall, if they find them in that place, ensure that the culprits be released and handed over to the Powys authorities in order to be punished'.

This virgin Melangell, who was so very pleasing to God, led her solitary life, as stated above, for thirty-seven years in this very same place. And the hares, which are little wild creatures, surrounded her every day of her life just as if they had been tame or domesticated animals. Nor, by the aid of divine mercy, were miracles and various other signs lacking for those who called upon her help and the grace of her favour with an inner motion of the heart.

After the death of the said most illustrious prince Brochwel, his son Tyssilio held the principality of Powys, followed by Conan, the brother of Tyssilio, Tambryd, Gurmylk and Durres the Lame, all of whom sanctioned the said place of Pennant Melangell to be a perpetual sanctuary, refuge or safe haven for the oppressed (thereby confirming the acts of the said prince). The same virgin Melangell applied herself to establish and instruct certain virgins with all concern and care in the same

> region in order that they might persevere and live in a holy and modest manner in the love of God, and should dedicate their lives to divine duties, doing nothing else by day or night. After this, as soon as Melangell herself had departed this life, a certain man called Elissa came to Pennant Melangell and wishing to debauch, violate and dishonour the same virgins, suddenly perished and died there in the most pitiful manner. Whoever has violated the above mentioned liberty and sanctity of the said virgin has rarely been seen to escape divine vengeance on this account, as may be witnessed every day. Praises be to the most high God and to Melangell, his virgin. (Allchin 1994, 45–47)

In another version of the legend, the hunter attempted to blow his hunting horn to rally the hunting dogs, but the horn stuck to his lips and it made no sound (Allchin 1994).

From my analysis of this narrative, I believe the legend describes the founding of this site as a holy place and how the valley became a sacred sanctuary. It also states that Melangell's work was carried out by women who dedicated their lives to her cause, and how anyone violating the valley or the women could expect to be punished by death. The most significant part of the legend, for the benefit of this paper, concerns the hunter and his dogs who chased a hare into the folds of Melangell's skirt; a charming story which has an element of the fairy tale about it, particularly the fierce hounds fleeing and howling from the little hare.

The hare is the first significant clue in the legend regarding the nature of worship at the prehistoric burial site. Hares are predominantly nocturnal and closely linked to the moon goddess in legends around the world. Sometimes the hare is the goddess herself in disguise, and sometimes it is her messenger and this connection would suggest that the pre-Christian burial ground was linked to lunar worship.

Hares are remarkably fecund, mating when scarcely a year old. The female nests in a depression on the surface of the ground rather than in a burrow, and the young are active as soon as they are born. Litters may consist of three or four young and a female can bear three litters a year, with hares living for up to 12 years, as such they are symbols of fertility in many cultures. They are also among the top ten fastest animals in the world, reaching speeds of up to 75 km per hour (Jennings 2017).

The eating of hare meat was taboo in some cultural traditions, due in no small part to the belief that women, witches and the moon goddess would shape shift into the form of a hare (as can some shamans). For example, in Kerry, Ireland, the eating of hare meat was likened to eating one's own grandmother. In 1663 a woman, Julian Cox, was formally accused of witchcraft in Somerset, England for being able to turn herself into a hare. The witness, a certain Joseph Glanville, went hare hunting with his dogs who chased one in full view into a 'great bush, the dogs refused to go any further and Glanville discovered Julian Cox on the ground exhausted and out of breath from running (O'Donnell 1994). The story bears a strong resemblance to Melangell's legend. Clearly Julian Cox was a scapegoat, but the trial shows us that folk memory of lunar worship in the region from the distant past, was still alive in 17th century Somerset. The Northumberland legend of the Acklington Hare (Green

2015) is another example of a hare being hunted by a local lord and his dogs. The lord, who was passionate about hunting, succeeded in wounding a white hare and chased it to the house of a certain Nancy Scott. No hare could be found but Nancy was nursing a wound on her leg.

In Iron Age Britain Boudicca used the hare as a form of divination through which the moon goddess Andraste (a war goddess) could communicate. According to Dio Cassius (1925), before battle with the Romans Boudicca: 'employed a species of divination, letting a hare escape from the folds of her dress; and since it ran on what they considered the auspicious side, the whole multitude shouted with pleasure, and Boudicca raising her hand toward heaven, said, I thank thee Andraste ...'.

The Luyi of Zambia and the KhoiKhoi of South Africa believed the hare was responsible for the origin of death (Barnard 1992), according to their mythology, the moon sent the hare to humans with the message that just as the moon dies and is reborn, so humans would also be reborn after they died. Unfortunately the hare became confused and inserted the word *not* in the message and told humans they would not be reborn. The moon hit the hare when she found out – splitting its lip (Lynch 2010).

In the Egyptian *Book of the Dead* and the *Coffin Texts*, the hare goddess Wenet was a guardian of the Otherworld who swiftly guided and protected the newly dead soul from the forces of darkness and helped it rejuvenate and live for ever (Wallis Budge 1989; Faulkner 2004). In China the Moon Hare is also associated with immortality because it mixes the elixir of eternal life (Chen 2011).

The association of the hare with the moon, the otherworld, rebirth and everlasting life, would therefore suggest that the hare in the Melangell legend could be part of a much older story linked to the prehistoric burial sanctuary, with Melangell as a moon goddess, the hare as her messenger and the concept of the rebirth of the dead featuring heavily.

In Latin Melangell was referred to as *Monacella* meaning Our Lady's Shrine, but the name Melangell incorporates the Welsh *Mel* (Honey) suggesting 'Honey Angel' or a honey/bee deity. In Bronze Age Greece, priestesses to another moon goddess, Artemis at Ephesus, were referred to as Melissa (bees) and Potnia was the Minoan-Mycenaean Mistress referred to as 'The Pure Mother Bee' whose priestesses were also 'bees'. The Delphic priestess of the oracle was also frequently referred to as 'the Delphic bee'. In the ancient Near-East and Aegean cultures the bee just like the hare, acted as messenger between this world and the next. Similarly, bees may have represented shapeshifters or spirit guides: a Mycenaean gem dating to *c.* 1500 BC (within the date range of the Bronze Age cremations at Melangell) was found at Vapheio, and was decorated with two anthropomorphic lion figures wearing bee coverings, holding jugs (of honey or mead?) over a plant growing between a pair of bull's horns (Baring & Cashford 1993) (Fig. 4.6).

The presence of 'bees' suggests the presence of honey, which has long been regarded as an immortal food owing to its healing, regenerative and long lasting properties.

Fig. 4.6: The Vapeio gem showing 2 anthropomorphic lion figures wearing bee coverings

Venerated as the nectar of the gods, it is hardly surprising that the Egyptians used it in their funerary rites. According to the *Book of the Dead*, honey was offered at various points throughout the Opening of the Mouth Ceremony, and when the ritual was complete, the ability to see, breath, eat, drink and speak had been transferred to the deceased in the afterlife. One incantation referred to the dead person as a bee – which is thought to have been a reference to the person's Ka or life force (Heller 2010). The ceremony imitated the resurrection of Osiris (god of the Otherworld). It is also similar in concept to the anointing of the five senses in the Childe Roland legend mentioned earlier.

Residues of what has been interpreted as mead have been found in Bronze Age beaker burials. At Ashgrove in Scotland (Dickson 1978) large amounts of small leaved lime, meadowsweet and heather pollens were analysed from the contents of a beaker in the burial. It is plausible to conclude that honey or mead may also have been used for ritual purposes by Melangell's 'bees'. It is also interesting to consider that the old British custom of 'telling the bees' of a death, birth or marriage in the community may have originated from the belief that bees where (like hares) messengers between this and the otherworld, if not shapeshifters or 'bee' priestesses who practised divination (Baring & Cashford 1993).

The most significant annual lunar festival falls during the first full moon on or after the Spring Equinox on 20/21 March, which marks the astronomical start of spring half way between the winter and summer solstices. At this time the Romans celebrated the fact that their moon goddess Magna Mater (great mother) conceived, and the Saxon goddess Ostara (who gives her name to Easter) is remembered for transforming a bird into a hare that lay eggs only at this time. Being a lunar event the festival is not a fixed date in the calendar and might fall any time from 20–22 March to 22 April, it is possible that this marked St Melangell's original Feast Day and would have had some significance for the burial site.

The Valley

Cwm Pennant is a deep, narrow glacial valley-cut into the eastern side of the Berwyn Range. Thomas Pennant, a well-known travel writer in Wales during the 18th century (Allchin 1994) enthusiastically wrote that '[t]his valley is exceedingly picturesque, enclosed by hills on all sides except at its entrance; watered by the Tanat which

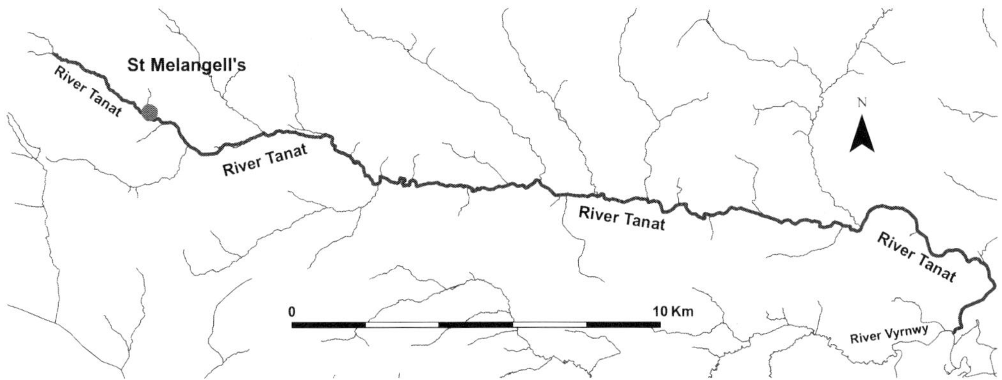

Fig. 4.7: Diagram showing the full length of the River Tanat and location of St Melangell's

springs not far off. The upper end is bounded by two vast precipices, down which at times fall two great cataracts ...' At the mouth of the valley it opens up and the River Tanat flows in a roughly south-easterly direction until it joins the River Vyrnwy 30 km away (Fig. 4.7). Cwm Pennant lies within what was a medieval Welsh administrative region or cantref called Mochnant. The region was renowned for its trees and the name Mochnant itself suggests a wooded environment (Evans 1994), and as late as the mid-19th century the tithe apportionments for parishes in the Tanat Valley are full of place name and field name elements denoting woodland which is now lost. The late medieval poet Llywarch ab Llywelyn who spoke of the beautifully wooded environs of Mochnant and the legend of Melangell, also tells how the hunter came across her in a large thicket. One might imagine therefore that the prehistoric cemetery site lay within an enclosure – similar if not the same as the sub-circular enclosure present today, that was ringed with yew trees and set within a wooded landscape, through which the River Tanat flowed. Today the site is remote and peaceful and the landscape around is open and light. In antiquity it would have been equally remote but also hidden by the wooded landscape.

If St Melangell's was once a sacred site dedicated to the moon, the night sky would have been of particular importance and as well as noting the phases and positions of the moon, the apparent movement of the stars and planets would also have been observed. Cwm Pennant, situated at the head of the Tanat River valley, is orientated on a north-west to south-east axis, with the remaining valley meandering in an approximately east-south-easterly direction (Fig. 4.7). Today the constellation of Orion 'the Hunter' rises in the east, near the autumn equinox but *c.* 1500 BC, due to the precession of the equinoxes, Orion rose heliacally in the south-east on 1 August (Herman Bender pers. comm.) (Fig. 4.8).

Orion appeared near the entrance of Cwm Pennant valley, like the hunter in the legend, and in the sky with Orion are the constellations of Canis Major and Canis Minor, with the dog stars Sirius and Procyon and at Orion's feet, almost within reach of Canis Major is the constellation of Lepus – the hare (Fig. 4.9). This group

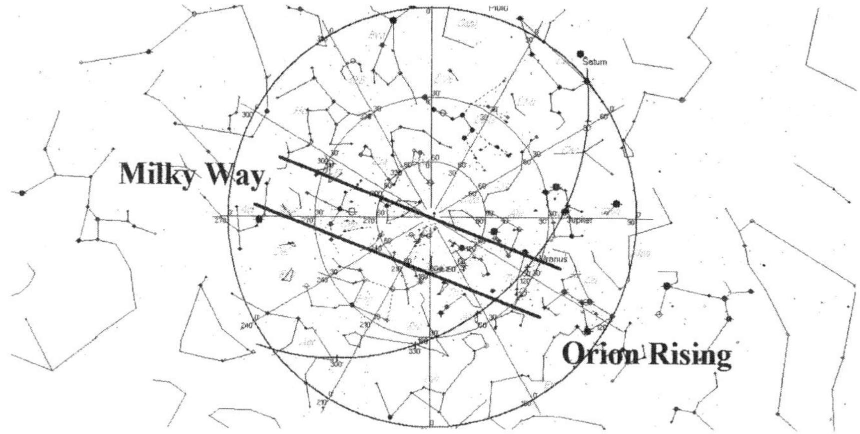

Fig. 4.8: Orion and the Milky Way 1 August 1500 BC (courtesy Herman Bender)

of constellations mirrors the beginning of the Melangell legend and it is possible to surmise that this stellar 'event' provided the catalyst for the story. The hunting horn, which miraculously stuck to the hunter's mouth and made no sound, may have been inspired by the sighting of a crescent moon at the apparent position of Orion's head which is near the ecliptic (Fig. 4.10).

It has already been seen that the hare is closely associated with the moon, the Otherworld and rebirth and as such, has some relevance to the Bronze Age cemetery but what, if any, is the relevance of Orion the hunter? Orion's heliacal rising on 1 August may be significant. It is one of the four cross-quarter days of the year, lying half-way between the summer solstice and the autumn equinox, today it is known as Lammas, named after the bread made from the flour of the first harvest of the year. In the Celtic calendar it is known as *Lughnasadh*, named after the god Lugh of Irish mythology (Gregory 1994). Lugh, like Orion, was a great warrior with a fearsome hunting dog, and was accredited with bringing the harvest to humankind after defeating the spirits of the Otherworld, and as such was a god of regeneration and agriculture, he was also a 'magician'.

Orion was visible in the night sky for approximately 5 months *c.* 1500 BC rising late in the evening about the time of Samhain (Fig. 4.10) and set in the early evening shortly after sunset (and twilight) about the time of the Vernal or spring equinox (Fig. 4.11). In between these two dates, it came to culmination after sunset transiting the meridian and reaching its highest altitude above the horizon (Fig. 4.12) around the February cross quarter day, known to the Celts as Imbolc (Groundhog Day), which celebrates the birth of the Celtic solar goddess Brigid (Britannia).

Fig. 4.9: Photograph of the night sky showing the positions of Orion, Lepus, and Sirius (Canis Major) in relation to each other. (Courtesy Herman Bender)

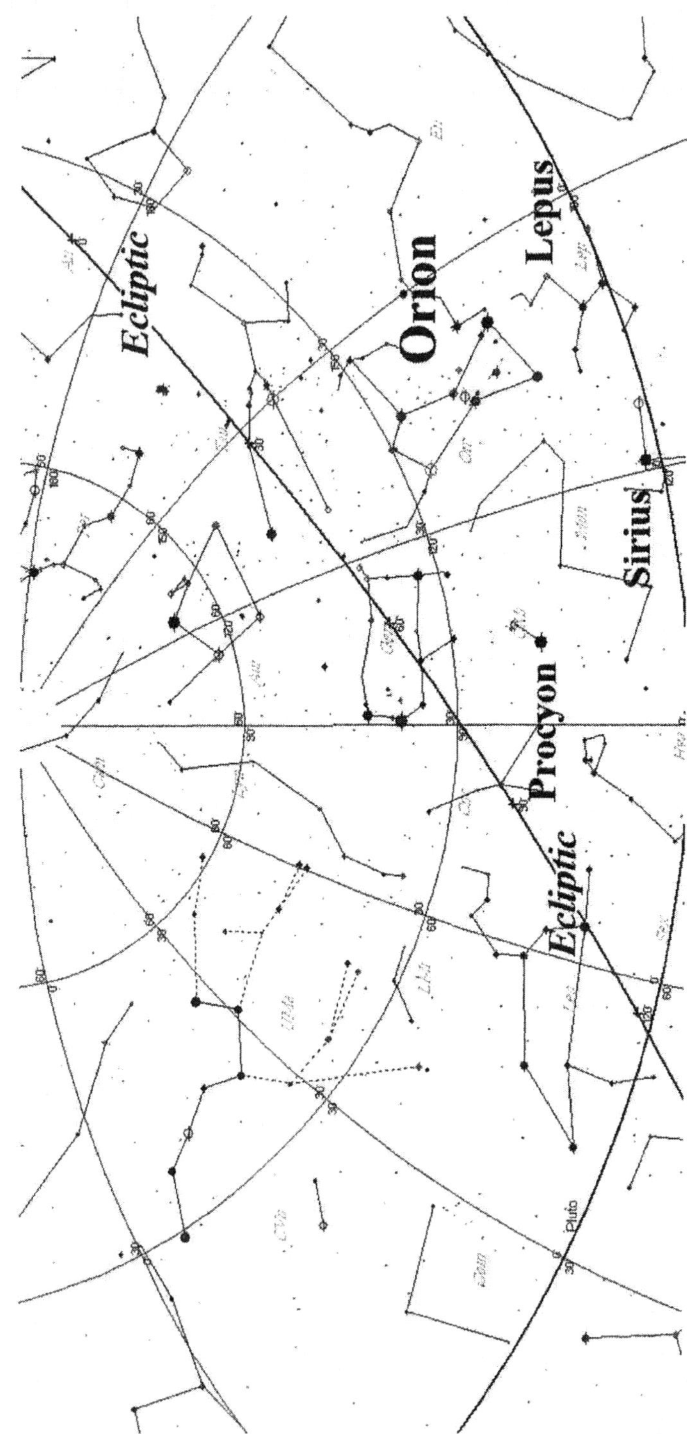

Fig. 4.10: Orion, Lepus, Procyon and Sirius rising late in the evening near midnight on 31 October, c. 1500 BC. View is looking east (courtesy Herman Bender)

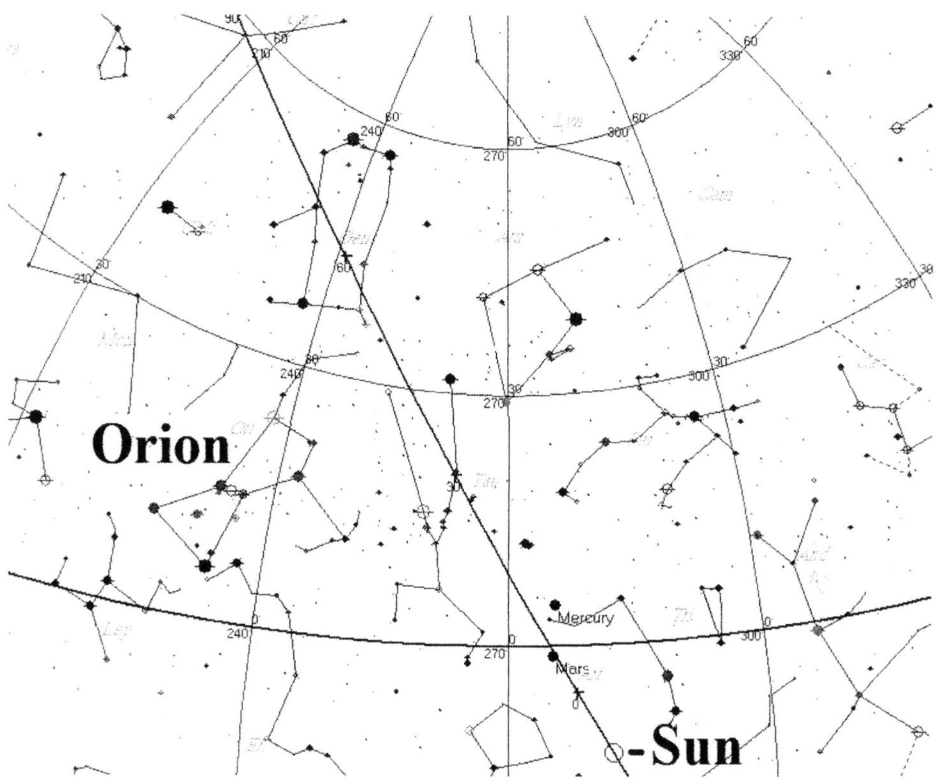

Fig. 4.11: Orion setting after sunset on 21 March, c. 1500 BC. View is looking west (courtesy Herman Bender)

Children born at this time were believed to have been conceived during the Celtic fertility festival of Beltane – the May cross-quarter day, 9 months previously. Imbolc is associated with birth, and although apparently still in winter, it traditionally presents the earliest signs of spring, so may be another date of significance to the Melangell site given the association with Orion or Lugh as a god of agriculture and regeneration. At this time Lugh would have gone to the Otherworld to fight for the harvest which he brought 6 months later, Brigid in the meantime heralded the warmth of the sun needed for the onset of spring and summer.

Orion was identified by the ancient Egyptians as Osiris, god of the Otherworld who, like Lugh, was associated with the afterlife, regeneration and agriculture. Osiris was credited with bringing the knowledge of agriculture and thus the harvest to his people, his Otherworld assistant was Anubis the jackal. Below Osiris' feet is not a hare but a ship which transports him to the otherworld – Lugh possessed a magical coracle. The connections and similarities between Orion, Osiris and Lugh suggest they are the same person. Lugh's rising on the August cross-quarter day 1500 BC (about the time of the first harvest of the year) would indicate that this day was not only associated

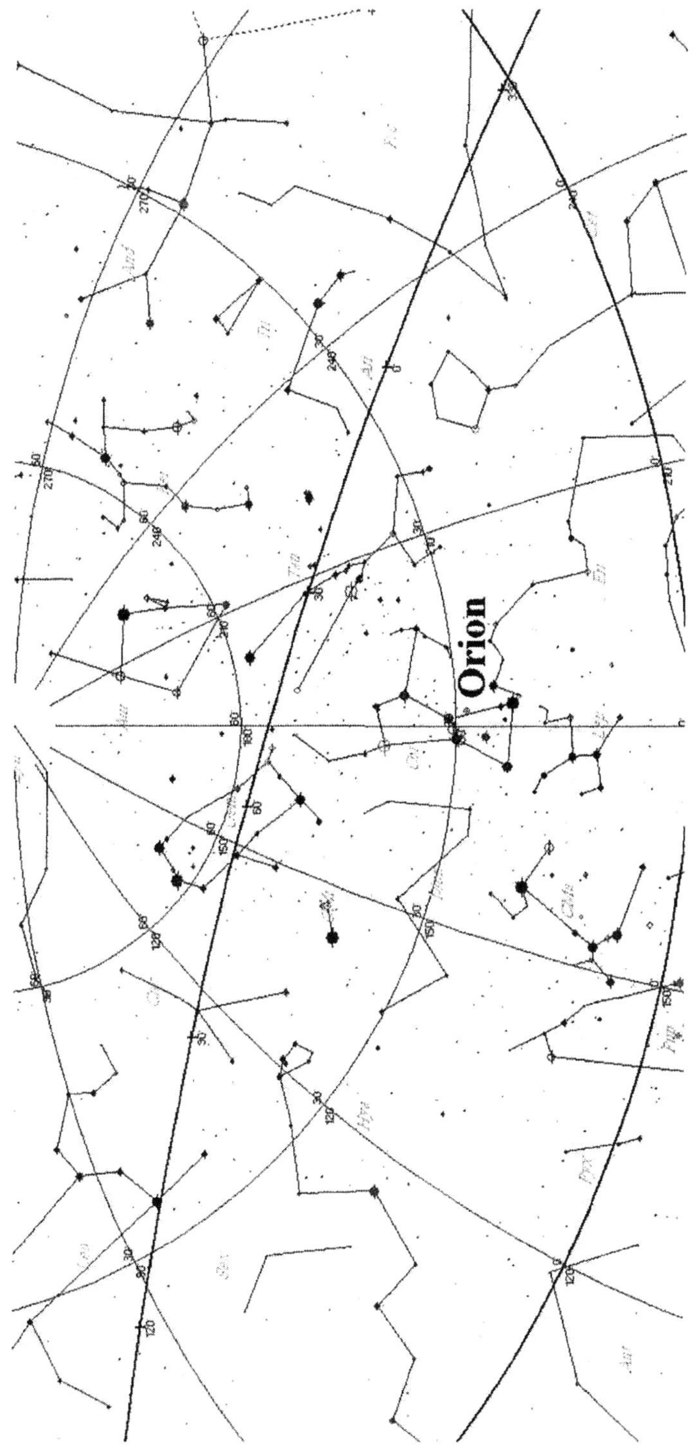

Fig. 4.12: Orion at culmination after sunset on 1 February, c. 1500 BC. View is looking south (courtesy Herman Bender)

with the harvest but through his association may also have had connections with the Otherworld and rebirth. The constellation's connection with rebirth can be found in the Welsh legend of Owain llaw Goch, a giant buried in a hidden underground cave (burial chamber?) somewhere near the Brecon Beacons National Park. He sleeps until the 'correct time' comes for him to reawaken and become the rightful king of Britain, until then he is watched over by his counterpart 'Orion' in the sky (Griffiths 2017). Lugh corresponds to the Welsh god Lleu Llaw Gyffes a warrior and magician who journeyed to the Otherworld and came back to become the rightful king of Gwynedd, more of whom will be discussed below.

Orion lies partly in the Milky Way which, in many cultures, is predominantly likened to a sky river. The southern Australian Kaurna Aboriginal people see it as a river in the *skyworld* and believe a number of dwellings are positioned along it (Clark 2015). In eastern Asia it is the 'Silver River' or 'Heavenly River' (Romain 2017) and in the Hindu Bhagavata Purana it is the Akasaganga or Ganges of the sky (Menon 2007). To North American Indians it is a pathway that souls follow on their way to the Otherworld (see Bender, this volume). In other cultures The Milky Way is also, as its name suggests, a milky road – either from the milk of a divine cow or cow goddess, such as the Egyptian Goddess Hathor. In Irish legend the River Boyne is named after the cow goddess Boanne who is credited with creating it (Gwynn) by walking anticlockwise around the well at the centre of the Otherworld, and thus causing the waters to create the river. The Boyne's connection with a cow goddess and the Otherworld, would suggest that it was an earthly representation of the Milky Way's sky river to the Otherworld.

The base of the name Tanat is *tân* (fire) describing the river as fiery or bright! This does not make sense when describing a river, but is logical when describing the Milky Way as it appears in the sky – perhaps the River Tanat was another earthly manifestation of the Milky Way. This is re-enforced by the fact that Welsh legend did not equate the Milky Way with milk or water – but with fire. It is known as 'Sarn Gwydion' and depicts the hot, fire embers scattered by Gwydion, whilst journeying in the sky, to enable Lleu Llaw Gyffes (the Welsh equivalent of Lugh) to find his way home (Griffiths 2017). The mythological events leading to this can be interpreted as a folk memory based on a shamanic belief system: Blodeuwedd, the wife of Lleu Llaw Gyffes was created for him by two 'magicians', Math and Gwydion – using the flowers of the oak, meadowsweet and broom. Through her influence Lleu died, transformed into an eagle and flew to the otherworld. Gwydion journeyed after him, scattering the glowing embers as he went to create a sky path for Lleu to find his way home. Once returned Gwydion transformed Lleu back into his human form. Bloedeuwedd was then transformed into an owl (Bloedeuwedd means 'owl' in Welsh). Bloedeuwedd bears the resemblance of a spirit helper induced by the ingestion of a concoction which required the properties of the named flowers. What followed can be interpreted as shapeshifting and journeying, with Lleu guided or assisted by more experienced shamans. It is worth mentioning that the 'hot, glowing, ashen path' is also used by the Bushmen of Africa to describe the Milky Way (Hinckley Allen 2010), suggesting a very early date for this concept.

The Neolithic passage graves of Knowth, Dowth and Newgrange were built near the River Boyne and the complex has lunar as well as solar associations (Taylor 2012). At Newgrange, the inner chamber is lit up by the sun during the winter solstice sunrise – a time which arguably signifies the rebirth of the sun – and perhaps the rebirth of those buried within the chamber. Newgrange was designed to 'work' at a specified time of year. The Bronze Age cremation cemetery at St Melangell's may also have been designed to 'work' at a set time, possibly with the appearance of Orion/Lugh/Leu/Osiris in the summer on his ship on the sky river. Themes of conception, rebirth and journeying to the Otherworld via the Milky Way would suggest a cemetery designed to enable the journey of a fertilised egg (or launch of a ship with many souls), which must journey along a birth canal, sky river or (at some point in the distant past) a path of coals, to everlasting life. Each year the 'egg' or vessel might set sail at Lughnasadh, after the moon goddess had conceived during the spring equinox.

The archaeological excavations at St Melangell's were too small to determine if the Bronze Age cemetery served a select few or a much wider community. It is reasonable to imagine however that not many locations fitted the required criteria needed to achieve the physical manifestation of the celestial journey necessary to take the dead to their new life. As such it is reasonable to assume that the cemetery served an area at least as extensive as its original Christian parish. Historical records and physical evidence demonstrate that this site has remained a very popular destination for burials, and as a place of pilgrimage is growing in popularity as increasing numbers come to St Melangell's shrine to ask for her help and guidance.

Final Thoughts

To recapitulate, the legend of Melangell started with a hunter, or Orion who appeared near the entrance of Cwm Pennant to the south-east on the August cross quarter day *c.* 2000–1000 BC. The moon goddess's conception and messages, via her hare, of eternal life for humankind and the arrival of the god of the Otherworld on the sky river at an auspicious date, goes some way to explaining when and why the Bronze Age cemetery was situated here.

The rising of Orion *c.* 2000–1000 BC on the August cross-quarter day, indicates a much earlier origin for the legend, whilst placing the Bronze Age site squarely within the dating range of the sampled Bronze Age cremations excavated to date (and potentially up to 500 years earlier for the Bronze Age burial site). It is unlikely that further archaeological work will be carried out in the near future, but it has the potential to clarify any earlier dating for the prehistoric cemetery put forward here. Although archaeological work may have to wait, analysis of the seasonal movements of the sun, moon and the Milky Way will be carried out to provide a fuller understanding of the significance of this site.

It is anticipated that further work will increase our knowledge of this extraordinary burial site which, thanks to the survival of Melangell's legend, would appear to have incorporated a complex mix of complimentary early belief systems over time, influenced by the movement of peoples and ideas of different cultures near and far. This was however primarily a belief system which incorporated landscape, animals, plants, divination, shapeshifting and astronomical alignments (the domains of shamans) uniting the material with the non-material world and using a combination of sacred time and sacred place. This created a liminal environment, a gateway through which one could pass from one state to another. As so aptly put by Ezekiel Hamer, vicar of St Melangell's between 1788 and 1812 '... there is not more than one step between our valley and heaven'.

Acknowledgements

My thanks to Herman Bender for his very helpful comments and advice on this chapter, for running his precessional software programme identifying Orion's rising during the August cross-quarter day and for producing the star maps and the photograph of Orion for this chapter.

Notes

1 'Wern' in Welsh = alder, but also came to be used as a name for the kind of wet terrain in which alder grows

2 http://www.ancient-yew.org/s.php/welsh-churchyard-yews/13/65/ Site Updated May 2017

References

Allchin, A. 1994. *Pennant Melangell Place of Pilgrimage.* Oswestry: Border Business Centre Oswestry.

Baring, A. & Cashford, J. 1993. *The Myth of the Goddess, Evolution of an Image.* London: Arkana.

Barnard, A. 1992. *Hunters and Herders of Southern Africa: A Comparative Ethnography of the Khoisan Peoples.* Cambridge: Cambridge University Press.

Bevan-Jones, R. 2002. *The Ancient Yew: A History of* Taxus Baccata. Macclesfield: Windgather Press.

Britnell, W. 1994a. The boundaries of the parish of Pennant Melangell. National Library of Wales Aberystwyth: *Montgomeryshire Collections* 82, 1–8.

Britnell, W. 1994b. Excavations and recording at Pennant Melangell Church. National Library of Wales Aberystwyth: *Montgomeryshire Collections* 82, 41–102.

Britnell, W. & Watson, K. 1994. St Melangell's shrine, Pennant Melangell. National Library of Wales Aberystwyth: *Montgomeryshire Collections* 82, 147–166..

Chen, L. 2011. *Chinese Myths and Legends.* Cambridge: Cambridge University Press.

Clark, P. 2015. The Aboriginal Australian cosmic landscape. Pt2 plant connections with the Skyworld. *Journal of Astronomical History and Heritage* 18(1), 23–37.

CPAT Historic Landscape Characterisation of the Tanat Valley http://www.cpat.org.uk/projects/longer/histland/tanat/tnnatura.htm

Dickson, J. H. 1978. Bronze Age mead. *Antiquity* 52, 108–113.

Dio, Cassius, 1925. *Roman History* Vol. 8, 62, 6. Cambridge MA: Harvard University Press.

Ellis Davidson, H, 1993. *The Lost Beliefs of Northern Europe.* London: Routledge.

Evans, G. 1994. Place names and field names of Pennant Melangell. National Library of Wales Aberystwyth: *Montgomery Collections* 82, 9–22.
Faulkner, R. 2004. *The Ancient Egyptian Coffin Texts.* Liverpool: Liverpool University Press.
Green, M. 2015. *Northumberland Folk Tales.* Stroud: History Press.
Gregory, I. 1994. *Lady Gregory's Complete Irish Mythology.* London: Octopus.
Griffiths, M. 2017. *Dark Land, Dark Skies: The Mabinogion in the Night Sky.* Bridgend: Seren Books.
Gwynn, E., (ed.) *Metrical Dindshenchas, Vol 3, poem 2: 'Boand I' at CELT.* (corpus of electronic texts) http://celt.ucc.ie/ (accessed January 2018)
Heller, J. (ed.) 2010. *Collins Beekeepers Bible.* London: HarperCollins.
Hinckley Allen, R. 2010. *Star Names and Their Meanings.* Glastonbury: Lost Library.
Jennings, N. 2017. *Hares. RSPB Spotlight.* London: Bloomsbury.
Lynch, P. 2010. *African Mythology A-Z.* New York: Chelsea House.
Menon, R. 2007. *Bhagavata Purana.* New Delhi, India: Rupa.
O'Donnell, W. (ed.) 1994. *W. B. Yeats Later Essays.* New York: Charles Scribner's Sons.
Paice MacLeod, S. 2011. *Celtic Myth and Religion: A Study of Traditional Belief.* Jefferson, NC: McFarland and Company.
Pryce, H. 1994. A new edition of the Historia Divae Monacellae. National Library of Wales Aberystwyth: *Montgomeryshire Collections* 82, 23–40.
Romain, W., 2017. The archaeoastronomy and feng shui of Xanadu: Kublai Khan's imperial Mongolian capital. *Time and Mind* 10(2), 145–174.
Simek, R. 1996. *Dictionary of Northern Mythology.* Translated by Angela Hall. Cambridge: D. S. Brewer.
Steel, F. A, 2016. *English Fairy Tales.* London: Macmillan.
Taylor, K. 2012. *Celestial Geometry, Understanding the Astronomical Meanings of Ancient Sites.* London: Watkins.
Turner, R. 1988. A Cambrian bog body from Scaleby. *Transactions of the Cumberland & Westmorland Antiquarian & Archaeological Society* 2nd ser. 88, 1–7.
Wallis, R. 2003. *Shamans/neo Shamans: Contested Ecstasies, Alternative Archaeologies, and Contemporary Pagans.* London: Routledge.
Wallis Budge, E., 1989. *The Book of the Dead.* London: Arkana.

Chapter 5

Songs of the Shamans? Acoustical Studies in European Prehistory

Chris Scarre

Abstract *Sound is one of the lost dimensions of the prehistoric and early historic past. In recent years, multisensory approaches have sought new ways of addressing this deficiency, moving beyond those developed by music archaeologists to consider not the sound producers (instruments) but the spaces in which sound and 'music' may have played a particular important role. This has included analyses of Palaeolithic painted caves and Neolithic chambered tombs and stone circles. The otherworldly significance of special sounds is well attested by ethnographic studies. The transfer of such a general perspective onto mute prehistoric structures is however methodologically challenging. This chapter briefly reviews recent work in this field and argues that close attention to the archaeological evidence may sometimes be effective in constraining the range of possible scenarios. Whether music was used to induce altered states of consciousness or heighten awareness among participants within these ceremonial structures, however, remains open to question.*

Introduction

Ancient structures sometimes produce curious acoustic effects. Among the most famous is the sound associated with the Colossi of Memnon, the pair of gigantic seated statues set-up at Thebes in Egypt by pharaoh Amenhotep III in the 14th century BCE. The Greek writer Strabo, towards the end of the 1st century BCE, provided the earliest account, describing how on certain days soon after dawn one of the statues emitted a noise likened by a later writer to the breaking of a lyre string. Strabo suspected that the sound was a trick produced by someone standing close to the base of the statue (Strabo *Geography* 17: 46). On the other hand, Philostratus (*Life of Apollonius of Tyana* 6: 4) was convinced that the statue spoke. This curious phenomenon drew important visitors: inscriptions carved on the base of the statue record that they included the

Roman emperor Hadrian in November AD 130, and his successor Septimius Severus in AD 199, but by the end of the following century repairs had rendered the statue silent (Bowersock 1984). The 'voice' was in fact an accidental phenomenon, resulting from the partial collapse of the monolithic statue shortly before Strabo's visit, and something that no ancient Egyptian or Roman engineer or architect had designed or intended.

The 'singing' Colossus of Memnon serves to introduce some of the difficulties in interpreting the acoustical properties of ancient structures and spaces. There can be little doubt as to the reality of the effect. What is in question is whether human agency may be held responsible for that effect.

This is the dilemma that confronts archaeologists seeking to interpret the acoustics of enclosed spaces. Those spaces include not only what we may loosely call 'buildings' but also natural places such as caves and rock shelters. Barry Blesser and Linda-Ruth Salter have speculated on the meaning and impact of sound for our distant ancestors. Imagine passing by a cave mouth.

> Sound entering a cavern is changed sufficiently that, when it radiates back through the opening, it seems as though it is coming from within. The cavern would not be quiet: as you passed by its opening, you would have heard the cavern speak to you. The voice of a resonant cave is more than a literary metaphor. You would have felt the cave was alive when it acknowledged your presence by responding to your footsteps with a voice of its own. From an experiential perspective, a cave is something that has a voice and sounds alive. Only from a modern, scientific perspective is it simply a natural hollow with sonic reflections and resonances. (Blesser & Salter 2007, 71)

These 'aural architectures', each with its own acoustic, are capable of influencing our moods and associations. An open space can produce feelings of freedom or insecurity, while the aural architecture of a chapel can enhance the privacy of quiet contemplation (Blesser & Salter 2007, 2). Furthermore, Blesser & Salter note the 'native ability of human beings to sense space by listening' illustrated, for example, by the way most people when blindfolded can detect the proximity of a wall through changes in the background noise as they approach it. Striking examples of this ability are provided by blind people who are capable of cycling in unfamiliar places by the simple use of echo-location (Blesser & Salter 2007, 38).

Yet while the biology of hearing is invariant across peoples and cultures, the way we listen is not. Understanding aural architecture requires an acceptance of the cultural variability of human sensory experiences. Since Aristotle, Western societies have generally considered sight to be the primary sense, followed by hearing, smell, taste, and then touch, in that order. Aristotle occasionally declared hearing to be more conducive to knowledge than sight, and Aquinas regarded hearing as the most important, since it was the sense through which the word of God is perceived (Classen 1993, 3). Nevertheless it is visualism that has been dominant in Western culture. That dominance became increasingly pronounced with the spread of literacy, and has been held to be the primary basis of science and the Enlightenment.

Other societies do things differently. The Suya of the Brazilian Mato Grosso consider hearing to be the mark of the fully-socialised individual, and sight to be an anti-social sense, cultivated only by witches and demons. The Tzotzil of Mexico order their world by temperature, the Ongee of the Andaman Islands by smell and the Desana of Colombia by synaesthetic colours (Classen 1993, 9–10). As Classen remarks, '[t]hese sensory cosmologies make us aware of the many different ways in which cultures shape perception, and the inability of standard Western models to comprehend such sensory and symbolic diversity' (Classen 1993, 137). Much is attributed to the environments in which different societies live. Thus the Kaluli of highland Papua New Guinea dwell in dense tropical rainforest where distant views are rare. 'Adaptation to life in a forest environment develops acute spatial skills for audition, and Kaluli use these to advantage over vision' (Feld 1982, 62). Birdsong is especially important within this visually limited environment, and forest birds play a key role in Kaluli myth and symbolism. Sounds structure time and the seasons. For the Kaluli, indeed, 'the environment is like a tuning fork, providing well-known signals that mark and coordinate daily life' (Feld 1984, 394).

This approach to the anthropology of the senses has not been without its critics. Ingold, for example, challenges the contrast that has so frequently been drawn between the dominance of the visual in Western society and the primary place occupied by other senses in other non-Western societies. He accepts that some societies may use metaphors referring mainly to vision, while for others metaphors of hearing are more common. Ingold suggests, however, that the metaphors arise not from social conditioning but through shared bodily experience, by 'people's efforts to make themselves understood ... by drawing comparisons between their own sensory practices and experiences and those attributable to their fellows' (Ingold 2000, 285). He argues that the emphasis should be on the lived experience of individuals rather than on the collective consciousness of societies. Hence individuals even within a single society may have different perceptions of the world. Nonetheless, insofar as members of different societies share common experiences of specific environments and practical engagements, their understanding of the senses may still be very unlike that familiar to modern Western observers.

All this argues caution in interpreting the nature of aural experiences in the past. Twenty-first century technology provides us with an impressive array of equipment through which to examine surviving ancient structures. Modern audio engineers can synthesise the acoustics of those structures, backed up in some cases by the survival of musical instruments and written records describing performance. We cannot, however, re-create the aural experience of the original communities and individuals who used or lived in the structures. However hard we try, we will still hear acoustic environments from our own perspective as modern listeners (Blesser & Salter 2007, 68). This extends to 'naturally' produced sounds, such as the howls of the wolves reintroduced to Yellowstone National Park in 1995. Their reintroduction may be thought to have restored an element of the 'original' environmental soundscape, but as Coates remarks, even if the sound itself is 'materially identical to the howl of a wolf there when the first Euro-American explorer showed up or when the first human of any kind was around to hear it', the way we perceive it today is different to how Native Americans or others would have perceived it in the past (Coates 2005, 657–658).

It is evident, nonetheless, that the natural world creates special or striking sounds that enhance the sensory qualities of particular settings or spaces. These often add to a sense of mystery, with wind and water featuring frequently as the primary agents. The noise of the rushing water over the Nämforsen rapids in northern Sweden conferred on them a special power and may explain the concentration of rock art found on the rock faces and outcrops (Goldhahn 2002). A similar suggestion has been made for the rock art of the Tagus valley (Garcês & Nash 2017). In the Upper Palaeolithic decorated cave of La Garma in northern Spain, a group of five hand stencils marks the only place within the cave where the sound of a river at a lower level of the karst can be heard (Arias 2009, 268). The sounds of ground movement, water, wind and wildlife in caves, waterholes and limestone sinkholes may have been one of the factors that encouraged Mesoamericans to regard them as sacred (Bruchez 2007). Nor are these associations exclusive to pre-modern or non-western societies. Seventeenth-century Englanders considered thunder 'a speech act on the part of God or perhaps demons ... [N]atural sounds – which emanated from the speech acts of the invisible world – could break buildings, judge, and kill' (Rath 2003, 13–14).

Thus acoustic effects are part of the natural world animate and inanimate, and have evoked powerful human responses. They have been incorporated into mythologies and cosmologies, and into frameworks of symbolism and morality. They may also have formed part of prehistoric practices and beliefs sometimes labelled as 'shamanistic'. A shamanistic significance has been proposed for example for decorated Neolithic drums from TRB sites in northern Europe (Wyatt 2009, 2010). Whether 'shamanism' is an appropriate term in this context is open to question, but music or sound is a key feature of most social ceremonies and is likely to have been so in prehistory.

'Art' and Acoustics

Caves and rock shelters illustrate the ability not just of humanly built structures but also of natural places to produce acoustic effects that can be culturally interpreted. The issue is to determine whether they were so interpreted – whether particular echoes or sounds were held significant – by the early societies who experienced them. This is especially challenging in prehistoric contexts that by definition do not offer the supporting evidence of written testimony. The problem is that every such space will have its own acoustic, and enclosed spaces have acoustics that set them apart from the world of outdoor experience. Identifying which of those spaces, and which of these acoustic effects, were culturally significant to prehistoric societies must therefore be argued either from broad ethnographic analogy or from direct archaeological evidence.

The deep caves of south-west France contain some of the earliest symbolic and figurative motifs in western Europe. Some 20 years ago, in a pioneering study, Dauvois and Reznikoff analysed the acoustic properties of two painted caves, Le Portel and Oxocelhaya, paying particular attention to the property of resonance, where the air within the cave amplifies sound owing to the morphology of the enclosing rock walls (Reznikoff & Dauvois 1988; Scarre 1989). In both caves a close locational match was found between simple red dots and places of maximum resonance. Reznikoff argued that since prehistoric people visiting the caves would have done so in conditions of near-darkness, they would have made sounds as a kind of sonar, to determine whether there was space ahead and in which direction to move (Reznikoff 2006, 80). The coincidence of red dots and maximum resonance goes beyond what might be expected by chance alone, and indicates that those who visited and decorated these subterranean locations were aware of their special acoustic properties.

Recent research is adding a new dimension to the analysis of motifs and acoustics in Upper Palaeolithic caves, assessing the acoustics of the caves as a whole. Robust measuring methodologies followed by statistical processing are providing a greater level of reliability in interpretation, and introducing the all-important criterion of repeatability (Till 2014; Fazenda *et al.* 2017). Robust methodologies are being applied to the archaeoacoustics of decorated rock shelters in southern Spain, southern France, and the central Mediterranean (Díaz-Andreu & García Benito 2012; Díaz-Andreu *et al.* 2014; Díaz-Andreu & Mattioli 2016; Mattioli & Díaz-Andreu 2017; Mattioli *et al.* 2017). Soundscape and archaeoacoustics approaches have also been applied to Temple Period Malta (Skeates 2017; Till 2017).

The superpositioning of motifs both in subterranean caves and in open air locations such as the Côa valley of northern Portugal (Blake & Cross 2015) suggest that it may have been production of the motifs as much as (or more than) their final appearance that was important. The act of carving of images on a rock face may have been intended to release powers or properties present in or beneath the surface, and the production of images will have been accompanied by the sound of the stone tools used to create them. The echoes from the pecking would have echoed around the valley. Ethnographer Åke Hultkrantz was told by the Wind River Shoshoni of the rock art they considered to be representations of the spirits. 'According to my informants, the drawings have been steadily augmented in a mysterious way; one can hear the spirits chiselling their pictures if one comes near these places in the winter-time' (Hultkrantz 1986, 54).

Analysing Spaces

For later periods of European prehistory, attention turns from caves and rock shelters to chambered tombs and standing stones. The scarcity of musical instruments from Neolithic contexts in western Europe (Wyatt 2009, 2010) contrasts markedly with the monumentality of the structures raised by early farming societies of the 5th–3rd millennia BCE. These structures, sometimes megalithic in character, include well-known stone circles such as Stonehenge and Avebury, and closed burial chambers beneath cairns or mounds exemplified by Maeshowe on Orkney and Newgrange in Ireland.

The value of these studies is undeniable, and the potential for further work in this area is considerable. They suggest that the architecture of many Neolithic monuments allowed or encouraged the creation of sound effects using voice, hand-claps or simple percussion instruments (Watson & Keating 2000, 262).

Naturally enough, Stonehenge is among the prehistoric monuments that have attracted interest for their acoustical properties. There has long been debate on the nature of the rituals or ceremonies that were conducted at Stonehenge, especially in its latest phase (Stonehenge 3) when the construction of the lintelled circle and trilithons created a striking and impressive setting. Since 1723, when William Stukeley first remarked that the main axis was aligned on midsummer solstice sunrise, attention has focused on seasonal rituals, concerned perhaps with the waxing and waning of the year. More recently, it has been observed that a stronger argument can be made for a midwinter ritual, since the position of midwinter solstice sunset lies at the diametrically opposite horizon position on the same axis, and anyone approaching Stonehenge along its avenue (the paired banks and ditches leading up the site) would have been facing south-west rather than north-east (Chippindale 2004, 236–237). The central space at Stonehenge is very restricted, and would have allowed only a selected few to be directly present at whatever ceremonies were performed there.

Recent reinterpretation, in conjunction with new excavations at the neighbouring henge of Durrington Walls, opens the possibility that Stonehenge was not in fact intended for the living, but was a ceremonial structure associated with the dead and the ancestors (Parker Pearson & Ramilisonina 1998; Parker Pearson 2012). During the first few centuries of its existence it was a place of burial, with cremations inserted in the Aubrey Holes and the encircling ditch (Parker Pearson *et al.* 2009; Willis *et al.* 2016). Ceremonies for the living, including midwinter feasts (for which there is evidence from pig remains: Parker Pearson *et al.* 2006, 234; Craig *et al.* 2015) were (it is argued) performed at Durrington Walls, a place of timber monumental structures. At Stonehenge, the sarsen structures linked to solar and lunar cycles symbolised permanence, eternity and perhaps eternal afterlife (Parker Pearson *et al.* 2006, 257, Parker Pearson 2012).

Watson and Keating led the way by undertaking a pioneering analysis that documented how sounds produced at the centre of the monument are affected by the arrangement of the stones (Watson 2006; Was & Watson 2017). Within the central area, the massive surrounding sarsens create enhanced sounds; while beyond the sarsen ring, higher frequencies are attenuated and only emerge through the gaps between the stones. The effects are heightened by the careful smoothing of the inner surfaces of the stones, as contrasted with their irregular outer faces. Yet, as Watson remarks, the existence of these effects does not in itself demonstrate that the monument was designed with acoustics specifically in mind (Watson 2006, 19).

One concern in such analyses is that Stonehenge today is visibly a degraded and ruinous monument. It has been suggested, indeed, that it was never completed (Ashbee

1998; Tilley *et al.* 2007), although gaps in the outer sarsen ring have left parchmarks, indicating that those sarsen unprights had once been in place (Banton *et al.* 2014). Missing elements may have been removed as building stone or as souvenirs or charms: as many as two-thirds of the original bluestones might have been destroyed in this way (Darvill & Wainwright 2009). At the same time, Stonehenge in its present form is a product of significant 20th century restoration. Of 36 sarsen uprights apparently *in situ*, six have been re-erected, two removed and replaced, and 15 straightened; while of the 19 bluestones standing today, six have been removed and replaced (Lawson in Cleal *et al.* 1995, 345–346).

Rupert Till endeavoured to overcome the limitations of the dilapidated condition of Stonehenge by analysing the acoustics of the concrete replica erected at Maryhill in Washington State (USA) in 1926 (Till 2009). The analysis assumed that Stonehenge was originally completed to a regular or uniform plan, and Till was again successful in demonstrating that the specific design of the monument generated significant acoustical effects. In particular, he noted that the outer sarsen circle created a sonic threshold; the acoustics seemed to focus on the central space bounded by the trilithons and the entrance. Sounds from the centre (including speech) were amplified, and it is easy to imagine how this may have enhanced performance within the monument in prehistory. Till sketches a hypothetical reconstruction of ceremonies involving rhythmic percussion within the circle, and the changing perception of these sounds as a celebrant or participant approached and then entered the circle.

These archaeoacoustical studies at Stonehenge reveal clear acoustical responses, but their relationship to prehistoric practices and activities is inevitably in some degree conjectural. Similar considerations apply in studying the acoustics of Neolithic chambered tombs (Watson & Keating 1999, 2000; Marshall 2016). Chambered tombs vary considerably in size, and the larger examples would lend themselves to practices impossible to perform in the smaller spaces typical of many chambered tombs. Furthermore, these may not have been empty spaces, but would have been littered with corpses or skeletal remains. The character of the burial deposits at many of these chambered tombs indicate that the associated practices involved repeated entry into the tomb, the insertion of new corpses, and (very often) the removal or rearrangement of earlier remains. A primary purpose of the passage may indeed have been to allow the remains of the dead (in the form of isolated skeletal elements taken from decomposed bodies) to circulate among the living, forming a material and symbolic bond between those buried and those still alive. It is entirely plausible that in the course of these activities, individuals (or small groups where space allowed) entered the burial chamber in order to commune with the dead. Voices, flutes and drums or rattles may all have played a part in these rituals, and the acoustical properties will have enhanced any such performance, producing effects that were unexplained and perhaps considered mysterious or even other-worldly (Watson & Keating 1999). The evidence of excavated sites suggests, however, that people entering these spaces will often have had to pick their way among decaying corpses and defleshed skeletons, which (where present in sufficient quantities) may themselves have modified the acoustic response. The remains of the recently dead will certainly have had a powerful impact on the experience of any such musical performance. We should also recall, however, that the most striking aural feature of Neolithic chambered tombs is the exclusion of the ambient noise of the everyday world: the sound of silence itself marks them as special.

The response from many archaeologists to these and other archaeoacoustical studies has been cautious. It is easy to recognise the fundamental importance of sounds and performance to prehistoric societies, but less easy to develop a robust methodology for their investigation. Measuring the acoustical properties of prehistoric structures does not in itself resolve the uncertainty as to whether those properties were intended or whether even they were recognised and exploited (Scarre 2006). As Richard Bradley has observed, the particular acoustic effects at certain passage graves are unlikely to have been part of the design, since that would require a knowledge of theoretical physics (Bradley 2009, 70). The argument that intentionality is a modern Western concept – that seeking to know whether these effects were intended is an anachronistic endeavour – does not in itself resolve the challenge of determining an acceptable methodology that will be found persuasive by the greater part of the archaeological community.

Where open-air sites are concerned, the issue of environmental noise is also to be considered. The acoustic interference of a circle of modest-sized stones some 30m or 50m in diameter is inevitably relatively small and is easily masked by wind or rain. Stonehenge is an exception in this regard, the size and tight spacing of the large sarsens producing a truly enclosed effect. As Rupert Till has observed, Thomas Hardy wrote in *Tess of the D'Urbevilles* of the wind at Stonehenge producing 'a booming tune, like the note of some gigantic one-stringed harp' (Till 2009). The smaller and more dispersed stones of Castlerigg or Callanish in themselves can make only a modest contribution to wind noise, but their exposed locations ensure that wind (and rain) will frequently generate sounds at levels sufficient to mask human voices at any distance (Fig. 5.1). The alternative, that they were built as mute stone monuments, beyond the realm of the living, remains a distinct possibility.

These observations remind us of the importance of archaeological context in applying archaeoacoustical analysis to prehistoric monuments. Beyond Europe, archaeoacoustical research has sometimes had the advantage of other lines of evidence that support the importance of sound and performance within the monumental setting. Chavín de Huántar in Peru, where acoustic effects from subterranean passages built into the structure were first noted in the 1970s (Burger 1992), continues to provide an excellent illustration. The discovery of *Strombus* shell trumpets, showing signs of wear, in one of these galleries, strengthens the case that musical or acoustic effects were an important part of ceremonies conducted here, and that the architecture was designed to enhance them (Rick 2005; Kolar 2017). Elaborate carvings and psychoactive drugs also played a part in the ritual practices at Chavín, acting along with the modified

Fig. 5.1: Castlerigg stone circle (Cumbria), illustrating the relatively exposed upland location and the widely spaced stones (image: Chris Scarre)

landscape and the highly planned ritual context as part of a 'finely tuned manipulation on the part of the site's planners, executors, and orchestrators ... to promote a vision of the world at variance with prior experience, a world of differentiated humans of intrinsically different qualities, among them authority' (Rick 2005, 86–87). The Tello obelisk that was situated at the heart of Chavín, carved perhaps to represent the Giant Cayman of the Amazon, may connect to the roaring sound produced by pouring water down the central subterranean canal, 'a sonic interface for a roaring cayman who inhabits the building, its underground spaces, or another unseen dimension of Chavín's ritualscape' (Kolar 2017, 54). It is tempting to associate the megalithic monuments of western Europe with similar ritual performance. What we need first, however, is to focus our attention on the ceremonial practices and their remains, not just the architectural forms and their inherent acoustic.

Conclusion

The ubiquity of human musical behaviour makes such behaviour an essential concern in any attempt to understand the nature of lived experience in prehistoric societies, as in those of more recent periods. Yet the recoverability of that musical behaviour, in the absence of written records, inevitably poses a challenge. As we have seen, indications are available in the form of surviving musical instruments and in ethnographic testimony that alerts us to the kinds of musical behaviour that may be at issue. The key messages from ethnography are the primary role of the human voice and body in most societies, and the kinds of other sound producers ('instruments') that have been used. Many of these will have been of organic materials that are unlikely to survive in archaeological contexts. Drums are a prominent feature of Siberian shamanistic practices, but will have left little direct trace in the archaeological record. Ceramic drums, on the other hand, or animal bones strung as rattles, may have been more common than is currently apparent (Aiano 2006).

The area of research that has seen most activity in recent years is without doubt the investigation of the acoustics of enclosed spaces, be they natural caves and rock shelters, or built structures. The potential of a multi-sensory approach to the past is beyond question, and consideration of non-material aspects such as taste, smell and sound should be the essential complement to all studies of material remains. We must avoid the temptation, however, of regarding prehistoric structures as we might Classical Greek theatres. All enclosed structures will present associated acoustic properties, but independent lines of evidence or argument are required if we are to determine how those properties were used. Excavation of individual sites may sometimes encourage reappraisal of scenarios that have been proposed, but also reveals evidence of specific activities and ritual practices that can inform archaeoacoustical interpretations. Archaeology already has its rock art; the study of archaeoacoustics may yet be able to reveal the character, if not the notes, of its rock music.

Acknowledgements

I am grateful to Kate Sharpe for comments on an earlier version of this paper.

References

Aiano, L. 2006. Resonators and receptacles: a summary of an acoustic enquiry into Late Neolithic pottery goblet drums from Europe. *Excapades* 1, 96–105.

Arias, P. 2009. Rites in the dark? An evaluation of the current evidence for ritual areas at Magdalenian cave sites. *World Archaeology* 41, 262–294.

Ashbee, P. 1998. Stonehenge: its possible noncompletion, slighting and dilapidation. *Wiltshire Archaeological and Natural History Magazine* 91, 139–151.

Banton, S., M. Bowden, T. Daw, D. Grady & Soutar, S. 2014. Parchmarks at Stonehenge, July 2013. *Antiquity* 88, 733–739.

Blake, E. C. & Cross, I. 2015. The acoustic and auditory contexts of human behavior. *Current Anthropology* 56, 81–103.

Blesser, B. & Salter, L.-R. 2007. *Spaces Speak, Are You Listening? Experiencing Aural Architecture.* Cambridge, MA: MIT Press.

Bowersock, G. W. 1984. The miracle of Memnon. *Bulletin of the American Society of Papyrologists* 21, 21–32.

Bradley, R. 2009. *Image and Audience. Rethinking Prehistoric Art.* Oxford: Oxford University Press.

Bruchez, M. S. 2007. Artifacts that speak for themselves: sounds underfoot in Mesoamerica. *Journal of Anthropological Archaeology* 26, 47–64.

Burger, R. L. 1992. *Chavín and the Origins of Andean Civilization.* London: Thames & Hudson.

Chippindale, C. 2004. *Stonehenge Complete.* London: Thames & Hudson.

Classen, C. 1993. *Worlds of Sense. Exploring the Senses in History and Across Cultures.* London: Routledge.

Cleal, R. M. J., Walker, K. E. & Montague, R. 1995. *Stonehenge in its Landscape. Twentieth-century Excavations.* London: English Heritage.

Coates, P. A. 2005. The strange stillness of the past: towards an environmental history of sound and noise. *Environmental History* 10, 636–665.

Craig, O. E., Shillito, L.-M., Albarella, U., Viner-Daniels, S., Chan, B., Cleal, R., Ixer, R., Jay, M., Marshall, P., Simmons, E., Wright, E. & Parker Pearson, M. 2015. Feeding Stonehenge: cuisine and consumption at the Late Neolithic site of Durrington Walls. *Antiquity* 89, 1096–1109.

Darvill, T. & Wainwright, G. 2009. Stonehenge excavations 2008. *Antiquaries Journal* 89, 1–19.

Díaz-Andreu, M. & García Benito, C. 2012. Acoustics and Levantine rock art: auditory perceptions in La Valltorta Gorge (Spain). *Journal of Archaeological Science* 39, 3591–3599.

Díaz-Andreu, M., García Benito, C. & Lazarich, M. 2014. The sound of rock art. The acoustics of the rock art of southern Andalusia (Spain). *Oxford Journal of Archaeology* 33, 1–18.

Díaz-Andreu, M. & Mattioli, T. 2016. Archaeoacoustics of rock art: quantitative approaches to the acoustics and soundscape of rock art. In S. Campana, R. Scopigno, G. Carpentiero & M. Cirillo (eds) *CAA2015 Keep the Revolution Going. Proceedings of the 43rd Annual Conference on Computer and Quantitative Methods in Archaeology.* Oxford: Archaeopress, 1049–1058.

Fazenda, B., Scarre, C., Till, R. Jiménez Pasalodos, R., Rojo Guerra, M., Tejedor, C., Ontañon, P. R., Watson, A., Wyatt, S., García Benito, C., Drinkall, H. & Frederick, F. 2017. Cave acoustics in prehistory: Exploring the association of Palaeolithic visual motifs and acoustic response. *Journal of the Acoustical Society of America* 142, 1332–1349.

Feld, S. 1982. *Sound and Sentiment. Birds, Weeping, Poetics and Song in Kaluli Expression.* Philadephia, PA: University of Pennsylvania Press.

Feld, S. 1984. Sound structure as social structure. *Ethnomusicology* 28, 383–409.

Garcês, S. & Nash, G. 2017. The relevance of watery soundscapes in a ritual context. *Time and Mind* 10, 69–80.

Goldhahn, J. 2002. Roaring rocks: an audio-visual perspective on hunter-gatherer engravings in northern Sweden and Scandinavia. *Norwegian Archaeological Review* 35, 29–61.

Hultkrantz, Å. 1986. Rock drawings as evidence of religion: some principal points of view. In G. Steinsland (ed.) *Words and Objects. Towards a Dialogue between Archaeology and History of Religion.* Oslo: Norwegian University Press, 42–66.

Ingold, T. 2000. *The Perception of the Environment. Essays in Livelihood, Dwelling and Skill.* London: Routledge.

Kolar, M. A. 2017. Sensing sonically at Andean Formative Chavín de Huántar, Perú. *Time and Mind* 10, 39–59.

Marshall, S. 2016. Acoustics of the West Kennet Long Barrow, Avebury, Wiltshire. *Time and Mind* 9, 43–56.

Mattioli, T. & Díaz-Andreu, M. 2017. Hearing rock art landscapes: a survey of the acoustical perception in the Sierra de San Serván area in Extremadura (Spain). *Time and Mind* 10, 81–96.

Mattioli, T., Farina, A., Hameau, P. & Díaz-Andreu, M. 2017. Echoing landscapes: echolocation and the placement of rock art in the Central Mediterranean. *Journal of Archaeological Science* 83, 12–25.

Parker Pearson, M. 2012. *Stonehenge. Exploring the Greatest Stone Age Mystery.* London: Simon & Schuster.

Parker Pearson, M., Pollard, J., Richards, C., Thomas, J., Tilley, C., Welham, K. & Albarella, U. 2006. Materializing Stonehenge. The Stonehenge Riverside Project and new discoveries. *Journal of Material Culture* 11, 227–261.

Parker Pearson, M., Chamberlain, A., Jay, M., Marshall, P., Pollard, J., Richards, C., Thomas, J., Tilley, C. & Welham, K. 2009. Who was buried at Stonehenge? *Antiquity* 83, 23–39.

Parker Pearson, M. & Ramilisonina, 1998. Stonehenge for the ancestors: the stones pass on the message. *Antiquity* 72, 308–326.

Philostratus [1912] *The Life of Apollonius of Tyana, the Epistles of Apollonius, and the Treatise of Eusebius* (trans. F.C. Conybeare: Loeb Classical Library). London: Heinemann.

Rath, R. C. 2003. *How Early America Sounded.* Ithaca, NY: Cornell University Press.

Reznikoff, I. 2006. The evidence of the use of sound resonance from Palaeolithic to Medieval times. In C. Scarre & G. Lawson (eds) *Archaeoacoustics*. Cambridge: McDonald Institute for Archaeological Research, 77–84.

Reznikoff, I. & Dauvois, M. 1988. La dimension sonore des grottes ornées. *Bulletin de la Société Préhistorique Française* 85, 238–246.

Rick, J. W. 2005. The evolution of authority and power at Chavín de Huántar, Peru. *Archaeological Papers of the American Anthropological Association* 14, 71–89.

Scarre, C. 1989. Painting by resonance. *Nature* 338, 382.

Scarre, C. 2006. Sound, place and space: towards an archaeology of acoustics. In C. Scarre & G. Lawson (eds) *Archaeoacoustics*. Cambridge: McDonald Institute for Archaeological Research, 1–10.

Skeates, R. 2017. Soundscapes of Temple Period Malta. *Time and Mind* 10, 61–67.

Strabo [1932] *The Geography of Strabo* (trans. H.L. Jones: Loeb Classical Library). London: Heinemann.

Till, R. 2009. Songs of the stones: the acoustics of Stonehenge. In S. Banfield (ed.) *The Sounds of Stonehenge*. British Archaeological Report 509. Oxford: Archaeopress, 17–39.

Till, R. 2014. Sound archaeology: terminology, Palaeolithic cave art and the soundscape. *World Archaeology* 46, 292–304.

Till, R. 2017. An archaeoacoustic study of the Ħal Saflieni Hypogeum on Malta. *Antiquity* 91, 74–89.

Tilley, C., Richards, C., Bennett, W. & Field, D. 2007. Stonehenge – its landscape and architecture: a reanalysis. In M. Larsson & M. Parker Pearson (eds) *From Stonehenge to the Baltic. Living with Cultural Diversity in the Third Millennium BC*. British Archaeological Report S1692. Oxford: Archaeopress, 183–204.

Was, J. & Watson, A. 2017. Neolithic monuments: sensory technology. *Time and Mind* 10, 3–22.

Watson, A. 2006. (Un)intentional sound? Acoustics and Neolithic monuments. In C. Scarre & G. Lawson (eds) *Archaeoacoustics*. Cambridge: McDonald Institute for Archaeological Research, 11–22.

Watson, A. & Keating, D. 1999. Architecture and sound: an acoustic analysis of megalithic monuments in prehistoric Britain. *Antiquity* 73, 325–336.

Watson, A. & Keating, D. 2000. The architecture of sound in Neolithic Orkney. In A. Ritchie (ed.) *Neolithic Orkney in its European Context*. Cambridge: McDonald Institute for Archaeological Research, 259–263.

Willis, C., Marshall, C., McKinley, J., Pitts, M., Pollard, J., Richards, C., Richards, J., Thomas, J., Waldron, T., Welham, K. & Parker Pearson, M. 2016. The dead of Stonehenge. *Antiquity* 90, 337–356.

Wyatt, S. 2009. Soul music: instruments in a animistic age In S. Banfield (ed.) *The Sounds of Stonehenge*. British Archaeological Report 509. Oxford: Archaeopress, 11–6.

Wyatt, S. 2010. Psychopomp and circumstance or shamanism in context. An interpretation of the drums of the southern Trichterbecher-Culture. In R. Eichmann, E. Hickmann & L.-C. Koch (eds) *Musical Perceptions – Past and Present. On Ethnographic Analogy in Music Archaeology.* Studien zur Musikarchäologie VI. Rahden: Leidorf, 129–150.

Chapter 6

Sights and Sounds of Selected Sacred and Shamanic Landscapes

Paul Devereux

Abstract *The chapter provides a small selection of surviving examples of visual and, to a lesser degree, acoustic sacred landscapes, some of them specifically shamanic. Cross-cultural evidence will be presented indicating that numerous ancient peoples considered spirits to live inside rocks and behind cliff-faces – a spirit world that shamans believed they could reach during trance. The presentation outlines the rich context of the lithophones, giving examples of how such rocks were used and venerated in many ancient cultures.*

Introduction

> '... we use the country itself, as its own map ...'
>
> Lewis Carroll, *Sylvie and Bruno Concluded*

Sacred geography is where the physical world and the 'otherworlds' of spirit or mind meet. For instance, ancient stone roads built by the Tairona people, the ancestral predecessors of the Kogi of northern Colombia, have special, spiritual meaning – they are intended to be walked as a religious exercise as well as used for mundane purposes (Ereira 1990). These physical roads are considered by today's Kogi, as probably the Tairona before them, to be the material traces of routes in *Aluna*, the spirit otherworld that the tribal shamanic elite, the *Mamas*, claim to be able to see with their inner vision superimposed on the physical terrain. Some of the roads, say the Kogi shamans, continue on in *Aluna* even after they have terminated in the physical world. A tall stone stands at the entrance to one of the old, abandoned Tairona towns, and is incised with criss-crossing lines: this is the Map Stone, which marks both the physical and the otherworldly courses of the roads.

This is just one example of sacred geography. Ancient and traditional peoples have found many different ways to invest their home territories with spiritual or mythic meaning. Such geographies of the soul could be small and intimate or cover large tracts of ground; they could be natural or constructed, or a combination of both. They were cultural mindscapes. Physical and virtual features were superimposed on the physical topography: visible and invisible routes for spirits to travel along; large scale ground markings (geoglyphs), and choreographed routes for pilgrimages to sacred places, whether natural or built. Constructed temples and monuments were on occasion arranged so as to relate to one another in a given landscape, or to acknowledge a natural, revered feature. Sometimes, sacred geographies involved the creation of alignments to the movements of heavenly bodies, especially the sun and moon, so that landscapes merged with skyscapes, bringing heaven down to earth. Even ceremonial gardens, such as the Zen gardens of Japan or the Paradise gardens of Persia, were distilled cultural mindscapes. And a key visual factor was simulacra – the accidental likeness of natural features to anthropomorphic, zoomorphic, or iconic images. A simulacrum could bestow sanctity on a whole area or landscape, or form the destination of a pilgrimage route.

Not all sacred geographies relied on either bodily or mental eyes – some were sensory in other ways. For instance, a beach near Sawaieke is believed by traditional Fijians to be the haunt of ancestral spirits on account of the vanilla-like scent of the sands there (Toren 1999). Even touch could be used as an element in constructing a cultural mindscape, as South Pacific islanders have demonstrated: they could – a few still can – navigate the waters of their archipelagos by combining astronomy, bird flight, knowledge of wind directions, and by plunging their bare arms into the water to feel ocean currents playing on their skin. Sound, too, could be used for sensory mapping of cognised landscapes. Echoes, whispering or burbling waters, musical rocks (lithophones), soughing wind and other natural acoustic phenomena were often considered to signal the presence of gods and spirits of various kinds, and this all helped to delineate the contours or foci of ancient sacred geographies.

Such sensory relationship with the environment was called *participation mystique* by the anthropologist Lucien Lévy-Bruhl, by which he meant a spiritual relationship with the land that went beyond mere utility and subsistence (Lévy Bruhl 1935). This paper will provide brief glimpses of a small selection of surviving examples of visual and, to a lesser degree, acoustic sacred landscapes, some of them specifically shamanic.

Visual Features Marking Sacred Landscapes

Whiteshell Park, Manitoba

Two distinctive sacred landscapes are to be found in Whiteshell Park –Tie Creek and Bannock Point. Of these two, Tie Creek is the best preserved, because it is the remotest and access is only allowed with a guide approved by the local Anishinabe (Ojibway)

Fig. 6.1: Tie Creek. Curvilinear petroform design (author)

people. The sacred landscape there is comprised of a broad area of tablerock scraped clear by glaciers tens thousands of years ago, on which abstract and figurative designs were laid out by an unknown people long ago using small rocks.

These petroform designs include large-scale abstract and geometric patterns (Figs 6.1 and 6.2), such as lines, grids, curved and radial settings, as well as smaller depictions of snakes and even wolf and bear paw marks a metre across made from rocks, as if giant versions of these creatures had padded in out of the surrounding forest (Fig. 6.3). There are also a few lightly marked sinuous lines that wander seemingly aimlessly over the tablerock areas between the main design features. The area is considered so sacred that it is known as *Manito Ahbee*, 'Where the Great Spirit Sits,' and gives its name to the entire Canadian province of Manitoba.

The considerable antiquity of some of the features is indicated by dense lichen growth around the rocks, but their exact age is uncertain. Archaeologists have dated the remnants of a campsite found among the ground markings to *c.* AD 500. Present-day Anishinabe lore states that the designs were laid out by the First People.

There are various claims about the meaning of the petroforms in current First Nation (Indian) lore, especially the idea that they are large-scale versions of the bark scrolls traditionally used by Ojibway peoples for teaching purposes. Others may have been diagrammatic depictions of sweat lodges and culture heroes, particularly Waynaboozhoo, the First Anishinabe. But today's Indians do not claim that their

Fig. 6.2: Tie Creek. Grid-like petroform design (author)

Fig. 6.3: Tie Creek. Petroform paw mark design. (author)

interpretations of the ground patterns are necessarily the only or correct ones.

There is also a simulacrum associated with the Tie Creek sacred landscape that the Ashinanabe Indians call Buffalo Rock, a natural boulder presenting the coincidental likeness of a buffalo at rest (Fig. 6.4). It is situated near the beginning of the trail that leads through the forest to the exposed bedrock of Tie Creek. The boulder would have signified the sanctity of the area, and it is difficult to doubt that the location for the petroform patterns was selected because of its presence. Today's First Nation people still make offerings at Buffalo Rock.

The other area of sanctity in Whiteshell is Bannock Point, which is in effect a vision quest area. Vision quest 'beds' abound, typically shaped as turtle outlines (Fig. 6.5). An

Fig. 6.4: Buffalo Rock (author)

individual would spend days and nights at such places, usually without sleep and food, and with only little water, in order to obtain a vision. This would often take the form of an auditory hallucination, which could sometimes form the basis of a chant that the Indian could use for the rest of his life. The area is still a focus for ritual activity and religious observance as is evidenced by votive cloths tied to trees and nearby timber frames of temporary long houses and sweat lodges.

Death Valley, California

Death Valley is so remote and arid it is hard to believe that it harbours an ancient sacred cartography of ritual pathways, shrines, vision quest beds, and curious patterns of rocks – features that speak of ancient shamanism. The valley is 153 km long and 40 km wide, adjacent to the Nevada state line. People inhabited Death Valley from about nine thousand years ago, when a cool period caused a shallow lake to occupy the valley floor. Eventually warmer, arid conditions developed, and it had dried up by about two thousand years ago. Whereas the region looks inhospitable to modern eyes, the collective territory of the valley, the adjacent Panamint Valley and the nearby Coso Mountains to the west, and the wilderness stretching to Charleston Peak outside Las Vegas to the east, was known to the Shoshone as *tiwiniyarivipi* – 'where the stories begin and end' or 'mythic land, sacred country' (Whitley 1996.) (Fig. 6.6).

The Death Valley geoglyphs are to be found in remote locations across that magic land, and take various forms. They are extremely fragile, and so their precise locations are kept fairly secret, but here we can look at just a few examples of what Death Valley has to offer in terms of shamanic landscape markings.

One ground marking is situated on a low volcanic hillock near the salt flat known as The Devil's Golf Course. It has a cover of small volcanic rocks and pebbles, and cutting across it is a ritual path made by the careful removal of this rock litter (Fig. 6.7). Its course passes through or by the remains of various ritual features on the hill, particularly vision quest beds, and leads up to three stone mounds in a cleared area, representing the remains of a former shrine or sacred enclosure. Where the path enters and exits the cleared area small arrangements of stone are laid out, interpreted by their early archaeological investigator, Jay von Werlhof, as 'spirit breaks' to protect the shrine area from any unwanted supernatural influences passing along the path (Werlhof 1987). Also in the complex are scatters of quartz, which was a vitally important magical stone to the Indians here as much as it was elsewhere.

Fig. 6.5: Bannock Point. Turtle-outline vision quest bed (author)

Fig. 6.6: Death Valley at sunset - 'mythic land, sacred country' (author)

Another kind of Death Valley geoglyph, a petroform, is to be found on a mesa-like fan not far from Nevares Spring. The top of this fan is devoid of vegetation, and is covered by a dark veneer of pebbles lightly cemented in place by the effects of the harsh conditions. There is a complex of markings and features, but the most immediately obvious element is a long, meandering line of small rocks (Fig. 6.8). Intaglios (scraped ground surfaces revealing lighter subsoil) are also to be found in the valley, such as a long curving line inscribed on a mesa top at Mustard Canyon. Alongside it is a small, intricate circular arrangement of stones that has been identified as a ritualistic shaman's hearth. This was never used as an actual fireplace, but probably marked a shaman's vision quest site.

There are dozens of other geoglyphs of these various kinds in the valley, and also in the parallel Panamint Valley and in areas further west and south. They often comprise complexes of alignments, meanders, grids and irregular enclosures, and can extend in length for hundreds of metres. What could have been their purpose? Werlhof thinks that, essentially, they were about weather magic. He suggests (Werlhof 1987) that the long-ago shamans of Indian groups living in the valley tried to put a brake on the encroaching aridity – it was part of a shaman's duties. It may seem strange to us that the laying out of ground markings should be seen as a magical act, but we know from the ethnology of the Yuman Indians in southern Arizona that their shamans, at least, did make marks on the ground as part of their deployment of supernatural power. In war, for example, the shaman might scratch a line in the ground between the contending parties. 'The line represented a mountain, the long Sierra Estrella,' the ethnologist Leslie Spier wrote: 'While the line that was drawn may have been a mark beyond which the enemy were dared to come, it was thought of as a mountain magically raised to give protection' (Spier 1933).

Fig. 6.7: Death Valley. Ritual path formed by clearance of rock litter (author)

The research of a current archaeological investigator of the region, David Whitley, suggests an alternative interpretation of some of the Panamint and Death Valley geoglyphs. He notes that vision questing could involve not only days of fasting and going without sleep, but also 'ritual exertion' such as running (Nabokov 1981), or the

Fig. 6.8: Death Valley. An ancient shamanic linear petroform near Nevares Spring (author)

handling of heavy rocks – as would be involved in the laying out of the stone lines and patterns. If this explanation is correct, then some ground markings in and around Death Valley were a consequence of lonely vision quests conducted by the ancient shamans, as well as magical activity aimed at stopping creeping aridity.

Pony Hills, New Mexico

This apparently undistinguished line of hillocks near Cook's Peak in south-west New Mexico is an untouched shamanic landscape. Although initially unimpressive to the eye, the place had been important to past peoples, for the ridge of little hills harbours spring-fed rock pools – crystal-clear water surrounded by an otherwise unremittingly arid landscape. As in so many ancient cultures around the world, whether Celtic springs in Europe or Mayan subterranean lagoons in the Yucatan, water-sources were perceived as sacred (Fig. 6.9).

Here, the rocks around each pool are decorated with petroglyphs depicting turtles or horned snakes, a few depictions of human figures, representations of spirits (Fig. 6.10), geometric designs, and, especially, spirit tracks (Fig. 6.11), carved bear paw prints and human footprints.

This site was the assembly point of Mimbres Indian shamans a thousand years ago. And they were 'bear shamans', a type of shamanism in which the practitioners

Fig. 6.9: Pony Hills. Rock pool with rock markings around its edges (author)

Fig. 6.10: Pony Hills. An ancient Mimbres shaman's depiction of a spirit, looking like something out of a Ghostbusters movie! (author)

Fig. 6.11: Pony Hills. A 'spirit' footprint compared to a human foot. Tracks of these tiny footprint markings link the waterholes, and are probably what various Indian tribes are known to have called 'water baby' spirits, supposedly seen by shamans in trance (author)

Fig. 6.12: Pony Hills. Incised bear paw markings (at left) 'climb' this vertical rock face (author)

believed they transformed into bears during trance states. (In the Pueblo Indian world of New Mexico even today bear tracks symbolise the curing power of the bear, and it is known that certain Pueblo Indian shamans will put on what are effectively bear-paw gloves and boots so as to 'become bears' during healing rituals.) The bear paw markings at Pony Hills can be seen 'climbing' up vertical rock surfaces indicating their otherworld nature (Fig. 6.12).

One carved image in particular tells the whole story of the place. About a metre in length, it is incised on a horizontal slab of bedrock depicting a human being in an apparently ritual posture holding a tall upright stick with an umbrella-shaped top (Fig. 6.13). Images of these ceremonial staffs, 'prayer sticks' or *pahos*, also appear on Mimbres pottery, and examples have been unearthed by archaeologists. Some researchers have suggested that their shape derives from that of hallucinogenic mushrooms. Looking at the carved figure in the bedrock this seems a reasonable interpretation, especially as the size of the staff is extremely exaggerated.

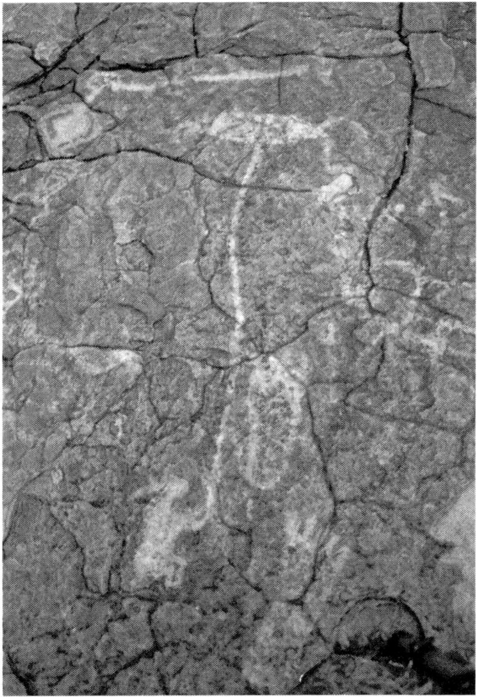

Fig. 6.13: Pony Hills. This horizontal petroglyph, fully a metre long, shows a shaman with his distinctive top knot holding a ritual mushroom-shaped staff. Alongside is a carved human footprint and another carving depicting a bear paw print (author)

Fig. 6.14: One of the Colorado Valley geoglyphs depicting a giant human figure, viewed from the head down (author)

That the figure represents a shaman is indicated by his distinctive top-knot, sign of the Mimbres shaman. Associated with this image are a life-sized carved bear paw print and a human footprint. The footprint would represent that of the shaman, the bear paw that of the transformed, entranced shaman – who knows, perhaps in an altered mind state produced by psychoactive mushrooms.

Colorado River Valley

There is fragmentary ethnology (David Whitley, pers. comm.) and some archaeological evidence telling of a pre-Columbian pilgrimage route used, possibly, by ancestral Yuman Indians. It seems to have started from a point at or near Pilot Knob, a modest peak near Winterhaven in Southern California, close to the border with Mexico. The pilgrimage route went northwards along the Colorado River valley, which forms the state line between Arizona and southern California. Scattered along this north–south corridor there are giant human and animal figures etched into the desert ground (Fig. 6.14). Alongside some of these huge desert geoglyphs researchers have detected circular areas of compacted ground, suggesting that they were dance grounds. It seems highly probable that these points were ritual stations on the route. The destination of that 240 km-long pilgrimage route seems to have been Grapevine Canyon, at the foot of a bare stone peak located just within the southern tip of Nevada, known by several modern names including, aptly, Dead Mountain. Its Indian name is *Avikwa'ame*, 'Spirit Mountain'. Grapevine Canyon is known to have been considered the 'house' of the creator being, Mastamho (Whitley 1996). It was resorted to by

Fig. 6.15: Sears Point. Looking along the line (marked here by a tape) from the vision quest bed end (author)

tribal shamans from hundreds of miles around in order to seek visions there. The record of those visions (at least some of which were instigated by infusions of mind-altering plants such as the datura-containing jimson weed) can be found in hundreds if not thousands of rock engravings that grace the canyon's walls.

Sears Point, Arizona

At Sears Point in the Gila River valley in southern Arizona there are about fifty geoglyphs. One of them, on a low mesa, takes the form of a straight line scored on the ground, and is so old that the once yellow line shining out bright against the dark, oxidised pebbles of the desert pavement has now become darkened itself, so is a subtle feature.

At the eastern end of the line is a rock with a notch in its upper edge; at the other, western, end of the line is a semi-circle of rocks – a vision quest bed. Sitting or kneeling within this arc of stones and looking along the line, the peak of a mountain sacred to the Yuman and Pima Indians is visible through the notch in the rock. At the summer solstice, the sun can be seen to rise up from behind the peak when viewed along the ground line (Hoskinson 1992). In years long past, a Yuman or Pima 'doctor' (shaman) would have settled down overnight in the vision quest bed, drank an infusion of Datura (jimson weed) and 'flown' in trance to the sacred mountain at sunrise on this auspicious day in order to obtain gifts of greater supernatural power from the spirits abiding there. We can reasonably assume that the straight line on the Sears Point mesa was either a record of the trajectory or else the guideline for the shaman's spirit flight to the mountain. (An ethnological account says that Indian shamans or 'doctors' in the region used jimson weed infusions to enter trance 'dreams', in which, they said, they saw the rocks and pebbles on the ground shine in rainbow colours.)

Tempe, Arizona

Other sites provide evidence of associations between altered states of consciousness and straight lines in the Americas. One example was recorded in ethnological archives and examined on the ground by the present writer and colleagues. The account itself was recorded by ethnologist J. Steward and dates to the end of the 19th century, and was given by Papago Foot, a shaman of the Gila River area (Steward 1934). The Indian stated that when he was a young man he went to a sacred cave in a butte

Fig. 6.16: The butte near Tempe, as it appears today. The entrance to the cave is unseen in this picture, on the steep right flank (author)

near Tempe (Fig. 6.16), in modern-day Phoenix, Arizona, and smoked a special 'reed' cigarette that put him into a trance in which he had a powerful vision. A spirit appeared to him in human form, saying he would help Papago Foot become a shaman. 'The spirit tied a cobweb from that butte to Tempe Butte, and thence to Four Peaks, to the San Francisco Mountains ... Papago Foot travelled on that cobweb and had various cures revealed to him at each butte.'

Spier (1933) confirmed that the Indians 'think of the buttes as connected by strings ... The dreamer thinks he is moved along the string through the air ...' Such virtual 'strings' and 'cobwebs' stretched tautly through the air were surely the spectral version of lines marked on the ground elsewhere in the Americas. Papago Foot's out-of-body spirit journey along these strings or web filaments fits neatly into the general idea of the lines being otherworld routes. The cave Papago Foot mentions has been confirmed by this author as still existing, and the linear links between the peaks mentioned can be mapped, forming a virtual sacred geography hovering in the air, so to speak, connecting features of the physical topography.

Himalayan Sacred Geographies

Certain Buddhist pilgrimage routes in the Himalayas are generated by simulacra, and here we can mention two examples, one in India, the other in Tibet.

The area of Kazha, the main town of the Spiti Valley, located in the north-eastern sector of India's Himalayan hill country of Himachal Pradesh, has a distinctive Buddhist culture and is thought to be especially spiritually charged. There is 'a 'sacred' geography which somehow interpenetrates with the mundane geographical features of the landscape,' states Elizabeth Stutchbury (1994). She further explains: 'The yogins of Karzha, through the tantric practices of Tibetan Buddhism ... have transformed ordinary geographical features, such as rivers, caves, rocks and mountains, the macrocosm, into 'sacred' places which constitute a ... geography conceptualised as a mandala.' An 18th-century poem by a local yogin-saint expresses this embrace of topographic simulacra:

The mountain to the right is like a pile of jewels
The mountain to the left like the fierce deity King of Wrath
The mountain in front like the triangle of origin piled up
The mountain behind like a crouching lion.

In the same landscape, a twin-peaked mountain and a glacier facing Kardang temple combine to form the simulacrum of a Buddhist deity that pilgrims come to meditate upon. The face, the eyes, and head of an elephant skin held by the deity are perceivable in the glacier. Another mountain configuration in the region looks like a woman reclining on her back with loose, flowing hair. Indeed, many peaks in the region are perceived as revealing the presence of a sacred being by means of their shapes.

This way of seeing is linked in this and neighbouring Himalayan regions with observations in which the annual progression of the sun is associated with particular skyline features, and is further extended into a tradition called *satalegpa*, a form of landscape divination which, among other things, places attention on the specific geographical location of buildings.

The area of La phyi in south-west Tibet is another important pilgrimage landscape. It is formed by three mountains containing specific pilgrimage venues. One of these peaks is perceived as the body of the deity Vajravarahi, with a rock outcrop known as Ras chen seen as her head, the Seng khyams rock as her belly, and a rock in front of the bDud'dul cave as her knee. Samvara is another deity seen elsewhere at La phyi in the lie of the land. 'When asked to describe the mountain, local residents and pilgrims indicate rock outcrops which represent the deity's head and shoulders, while ridges on either are said to be his legs, the river that flows south from the place is said to be the stream of his urine, and so forth' writes Toni Huber (1994).

Namsan, South Korea

Namsan ('Southern Mountain') in Gyeongju Province is an oval-shaped massif and now a protected National Forest and UNESCO World Heritage site, and is another sacred landscape occasioned primarily by simulacra. Riven by many valleys, it was co-opted by Buddhism in the 6th century AD. but it was sacred before then – shamans conducted rain dances there, and megalithic monuments dating to the 1st millennium BC have been found. There is evidence that certain places on Namsan were used for making offerings to nature spirits, so it is perhaps not surprising that the Buddhists believed that Namsan harboured many buddhas and bodhisəttvas that had descended from heaven to dwell in its rocks and trees. A probable reason that the mountain was such a spiritual focus was the presence of many granite rocks scattered over it resembling animals and objects (Barnes 1999). They are known by such names as Old Man, Python, Fierce Tiger, Lion, Big Bear, Boar, Cat, and even Dung Rock and occur primarily in the Yongjang valley. Namsan is home to over a hundred temples, most of them now archaeological sites, 63 pagodas, nearly 40 statues, and about 90 sculpted rocks.

Soundscapes

While most sacred geography was essentially visually based, in some cases there was the added dimension of sound. For example, when working with indigenous communities in New Guinea, the anthropologist Paul Wirz observed that the people's sacred places had a distinctive acoustic quality to them when not distinguished by some visual peculiarity, especially swamps and areas of gravel deposits where 'curious noises' could be heard. These were places inhabited by the *dema*, the mythical ancestors (Wirz in Levy-Bruhl 1935). Again, on the US-Canadian border, the prominent Rocky Mountain peak known as *Ninaistakis* to the Blackfoot Indians produces sounds in the almost constant winds that circulate around the peak: fissures and hollows in the rocky summit towers form a kind of 'sound system' that produces a singing noise. An individual at one of the numerous vision quest sites near the summit would have heard the mountain spirits singing to him. There are numerous ways in which the land can speak.

Petroglyph Rock, Ontario

This large, sloping slab in Petroglyph Provincial Park near Peterborough is covered with several hundred ancient engravings (Fig. 6.17), while other exposed rock surfaces around are devoid of such carvings. So why was that particular rock surface sought out as such a special place a thousand or more years ago? The answer most probably lies with a fissure about 5 m deep that cuts across the rock's surface. Ground water sporadically flows along the bottom of the fissure causing noises remarkably like

Fig. 6.17: Part of Petroglyph Rock (sometimes known as the 'Teaching Rock'), showing part of the fissure and some of the carvings (© Petroglyph Provincial Park, Ontario)

whispering voices to issue forth. The Indians in this part of the Americas had a belief that spirits, *manitous*, lived inside certain rocks and behind cliff-faces, so voice-like sounds emerging from this rock would readily have been identified as the spirits speaking. It is easy to understand, therefore, why it became a sacred place, perhaps even an oracle centre, thus accounting for the profusion of rock carvings on its surface.

Mazinaw Rock, Ontario

The belief in rock-dwelling spirits probably influenced the choice for locating dozens of ancient rock paintings at another site in Ontario – namely, at Mazinaw Rock, which rises out of Mazinaw Lake and extends for 1.7 km at an average height of 30 m (Fig. 6.18). The approximately 200 panels of rock paintings run along the base of the cliff a little above the waterline (Fig. 6.19); they were painted using red ochre (itself considered a sacred mineral) which is now somewhat faded. The imagery mainly consists of abstract markings but interspersed among these there are some figurative forms, including the large-eared jackrabbit spirit, Nanabush, and human-like beings in a canoe, usually the sign of spirits in American Indian rock art. This site is within Bon Echo Provincial Park, so named because the cliff-face produces remarkable echoes. (In summer, boat trips take place on the lake so visitors can experience the power of the Mazinaw echoes.) The rock panels cluster where the echoes are strongest.

Algonquin shamans in trance considered that they could pass in spirit through rock surfaces to obtain 'rock medicine' or supernatural power from the spirits within the rocks (Dewdney 1962; Rajnovich 1994). Indeed, the belief that a spirit world existed behind rock surfaces and cliff faces was held by many American Indian peoples (Whitley 1998) and probably other peoples around the world – it is known to have existed in southern Africa, for instance (Dowson & Lewis-Williams 1989; Dowson 1992; Lewis-Williams 2002). Echo phenomena surely lie at the heart of these kinds of beliefs. The foot of cliffs that rise out of water, as at Mazinaw, was considered a favourite haunt of the rock *manitous*, which is interesting because such locations are also particularly effective in the propagation of echoes – the water surface acts as a kind of amplifier and transmitter.

Fig. 6.18: Mazinaw Rock rising out of Mazinaw Lake, Bon Echo Park, Ontario (author)

Arapesh Country, Papua New Guinea

Some peoples worked with their sonic environment. Anthropologist Donald Tuzin witnessed a remarkable example of this when living with the Arapesh people of Papua New Guinea. He was particularly

Fig. 6.19: The now faded red ochre rock paintings on Mazinaw Rock are located just above the water line and can only be approached by boat. Here, one panel is being pointed out (author)

studying the men's secret cult known as the Tambaran. They had specially modified musical instruments such as giant amplifying pipes made from hollow, open-ended bamboo tubes up to 4 m in length, bullroarers (objects that make an eerie whistling sound when swung rapidly through the air on the end of a cord), slit drums, whistles, and pan pipes. They are used to create sounds that simulate voices. These sounds are believed by the Arapesh to manifest the utterances of great spirits residing in the forest. When twenty or thirty amplifying tubes are heard in the dark of the forest night, Tuzin confessed that they create the impression of 'a chillingly immense, almost human voice' (Tuzin 1984). The sound was so disturbing and powerful that Tuzin suspected that infrasound (sound vibrating so deeply that it is below the threshold of normal human hearing but can be felt physically, if unconsciously, in some instances) was being produced that helped create the extraordinary supernatural sensation the cult instruments generated. This suspicion was strengthened when he noticed that the Tamabaran men conducted their rituals at times when thunderstorms were active in mountains 19 km away. Thunder produces infrasound that can extend much further than its audible sound, and Tuzin realised that it would wash through Arapesh territory. He concluded that the infrasound produced by the cult instruments unite with and exploit 'the roar of the unheard thunderstorm.'

Fig. 6.20: Part of one of the rock outcrops on Carn Menyn (author/Landscape & Perception Project)

Fig. 6.21: Eliciting the metallic sound of a lithophonic bluestone on Carn Menyn using percussion by a small hand-held hammerstone (author/Landscape & Perception Project)

Mount Nantai, Japan

The basic notion of the land having speech was lodged deeply in early medieval Shingon Esoteric Buddhism, founded by Kūkai. He likened the natural landscape around Chuzenji temple and the lake at the foot of Mount Nantai, near Nikko, to descriptions in the Buddhist scriptures of the Pure Land, the habitation of the Buddhas. Kūkai considered that the landscape not only symbolised but *was of the same essence* as the mind of the Buddha. Like the Buddha mind, the landscape spoke in a natural language, offering supernatural discourse. 'Thus, waves, pebbles, winds, and birds were the elementary and unconscious performers of the cosmic speech of buddhas and bodhisattvas,' explains scholar Allan Grapard (1994).

Carn Menyn, Preseli, Wales

The acoustic properties of the Carn Menyn area manifest in two ways, (i) as lithophones (rocks that produce metallic or musical sounds) and (ii) as exceptional echoes. A significant percentage of the spotted dolerite rocks have been found to issue, variously, pure bell-like tones, tin drum sounds, or deep bass rumbles when struck with a small hammerstone (Fig. 6.21). This property of the Preseli stones had already been signalled by the indefatigable 'rock-gong' hunter, Bernard Fagg, who also noted that the name of a Preseli village, Maenclochog, was Welsh for 'ringing stones' ' or 'bell stones' (Fagg 1956). Did the builders of Stonehenge believe, like the American Indians and the Bushmen of southern Africa, or members of the indigenous Shinto religion in Japan, that spirits dwelled within rocks? Did they believe that spirits within the Preseli rocks produced fairy music? Was that what made the bluestones special? There is no doubt that the Preseli upland as a whole was already highly venerated, as is testified by the numerous megalithic monuments scattered through and around the hill range.

Echoes, the other element of the Carn Menyn soundscape, occur most strongly at the rocky hill known as Carn Alw. The hill is a natural outcrop, but was pressed into service as a fort in Iron Age times, in the final centuries BC. The Welsh name *Alw* can be translated as 'call,' which might allude to the exceptional echoing characteristics of this 'fort of echoes' as it has been called. The Welsh term *carreg ateb* can be used to refer to echoes, and literally translated means 'stone (or rock) replies (or answers).'

Thinking cross-culturally, the possibility arises that the Preseli upland was viewed mythically as an ancestral land of origin by the Stonehenge people. The Huichol Indians in Mexico, as one comparison, make an annual pilgrimage to the Wirikutá plateau, their believed land of origin, and collect the mind-altering peyote cactus for ritual purposes. It so happens that the Preseli hills are rich in 'Liberty Cap' psychoactive psilocybin mushrooms. In ritualised altered states the fairy music from the rocks or the disembodied voices emerging from the flank of Carn Alw would surely have taken on an even more spiritualised significance. We can but speculate.

References

Barnes, G. 1999. Buddhist landscapes of East Asia. In W. Ashmore & A. B. Knapp (eds) *Archaeologies of Landscape*. Oxford: Blackwell.

Bradley, R. 2000. *An Archaeology of Natural Places*. London: Routledge.

Devereux, P. & Wozencroft, J. 2014. Stone Age eyes and ears: A visual and acoustic pilot study of Carn Menyn and environs, Preseli, Wales. *Time & Mind* 7(1), 47–70.

Dewdney, S. 1962. *Indian Rock Paintings of the Great Lakes*. Toronto: University of Toronto Press.

Dowson, T. 1992. *Rock Engravings of Southern Africa*. Johannesburg: Witwatersrand University Press.

Dowson, T. & Lewis-Williams, D. 1989. *Images of Power*. Johannesburg: Southern Book Publishers.

Ereira, A. 1990. *The Heart of the World*. London: Jonathan Cape.

Fagg, B. 1956. The discovery of multiple rock gongs in Nigeria *Man*, 56, 23.

Grapard, A. 1994. Geosophia, geognosis, and geopiety: Orders of significance in Japanese representations of space. In R. Friedland & D. Boden (eds) *NowHere: Space, Time and Modernity*. Berkeley CA: University of California Press.

Hoskinson, T. 1992. Saguero wine, ground figures, and power mountains: Investigations at Sears Point, Arizona. In R. A. Williamson & C. R. Farrer (eds) *Earth and Sky*. Albuquerque NM: University of New Mexico Press, 131–162.

Huber, T. 1994. Putting the *gnas* back into *gnas-kor*: Rethinking Tibetan Buddhist pilgrimage practice. *Tibet Journal* 19(2), 23–60.

Lévy-Bruhl, L. 1935. *Primitive Mythology: The Mythic World of the Australian and Papuan Natives*. St Lucia: University of Queensland Press, 1983 edn.

Lewis-Williams, J. D. 2002. *A Cosmos in Stone*. Walnut Creek CA: Altamira Press.

Nabokov, P. 1981. *Indian Running*. Santa Fe NM: Ancient City Press.

Rajnovich, G. 1994. *Reading Rock Art – Interpreting the Indian Rock Paintings of the Canadian Shield*. Toronto: Natural Heritage/Natural History Inc.

Spier, L. 1933. *Yuman Tribes of the Gila River*. New York: Dover Publications, 1978 edn.

Steward, J. 1934. *Two Paiute Autobiographies*. Berkeley CA: University of California Publications in American Archaeology and Ethnology 33, 5.

Stutchbury, E. 1994. Perceptions of landscape in Karzha: 'Sacred' geography and the Tibetan system of 'geomancy'. *Tibet Journal* 19(4), 59–102.

Toren, C. 1999. *Mind, Materiality and History – Explorations in Fijian Ethnography*. London: Routledge.

Tuzin, D. 1984. Miraculous voices: The auditory experience of numinous objects. *Current Anthropology* 25(5), 579–589.

Werlhof, J. von. 1987. *Spirits of the Earth.* El Centro CA: Imperial Valley College Museum.

Whitley, D. 1996. *A Guide to Rock Art Sites.* Missoula MT: Mountain Press.

Whitley, D. 1998. Finding rain in the desert: landscape, gender and far western North American rock-art. In C. Chippindale & P. Taçon (eds) *The Archaeology of Rock-Art*. Cambridge: Cambridge University Press, 11–29.

Chapter 7

Bronze Age Deposits in the Carpathian Basin – Markers for Spirit-Animated Landscape? The Role of Structured Deposition in Understanding the Worldview of Bronze Age Europe

Emília Pásztor

Abstract *One of the most significant customs of the Bronze Age is that of hoard deposition, one which shares many traits across all of Europe. The sacred function of Bronze Age hoards is argued to be the primary purpose for doing so, especially when deposited in wet places such as marsh, rivers and lakes. The considerable number of hoards hidden in wet places testifies that the act was of frequent ritual activity.In the Carpathian Basin, the arrangement of the artefacts is quite specific and the sites of deposition are often dry places such as on hillsides, hilltops, at the foot of a hill or arable land. The artefacts making up the sacred depots were not mundane or for everyday use; they were unique and/or symbolic with a special meaning. Therefore, the deposition sites must have been viewed as unique spots, places of liminality where those making the sacrifice created a connection with the transcendent. These places are full of transcendental power and represent organic elements of the worldview in the (local) community when creating a sacred landscape. Anthropological records testify that sacred places are mostly unique natural sites with the custom of deposition out in nature and the ethnographical analogies in harmony. Therefore, all the geographical features on the landscape may have held their own spirits whose good will was important and needed to be gained. Anthropological records also indicate how complex the rituals were. The worship/respect of spirits was not unified, even in a cultural group, and this may be the reason for the context and variety of deposits.*

Introduction

Ritual deposition is a much discussed research theme among archaeologists as it was one of the most emblematic activities in world archaeology, especially during the European Bronze Age (Harding 2000, 365). There have been various attempts to define this somewhat enigmatic function. Many interpretations for deposition have been developed from fragmentary evidence associated with private and public collections and times of social and political stress such as war, travelling metallurgist's stock (if there are metalwork tools in it) and merchant hoards (objects that were traded). The intention of collecting or hoarding metalwork may have served ritual and spiritual purposes along with others (Harding 2000, 354).

The choice of place where the artefacts were deposited would have been important to people, even in non-ritual cases. Therefore, investigation can reveal additional information of this significant activity for Bronze Age people. The main issue with studying the location of deposits is the uncertain archaeological context of these hoards as they have been found mainly by non-archaeologists and their original composition may have been questionable. Many times, the discoverers mixed them with other artefacts or did not keep the deposit in its original condition. In particular are the low numbers of Bronze Age assemblages with detailed documentation or reconstructed context and not just in the Carpathian Basin, but also throughout Europe (Tarbay 2014, 224).

Some consider that the rich hoards, buried at settlements or even hilltop fortifications in the middle and eastern regions of the Danube around the end of early Bronze Age, cannot be regarded as ritual offerings to the gods (Vandkilde 2007, 117). Others believe every deposit and hoard can be regarded as sacred and differences can only be interpreted as cultural alternations (Hansen 1994; Kemenczei 1996). In addition, there are researchers who say the main features of votive hoards have a unique composition that includes exotic, valuable objects with many pieces hidden at a special place (Osborn 2004, 6). However, the study of Gábor Váczi shows even small deposits can be the result of ritual deposition say, for example, deposits comprising two to three pieces of metalwork found in marshy areas of the landscape were not likely to be temporarily hidden in such places (Váczi 2007, 135). Therefore, structured deposition can conceivably provide scholars with information on belief systems and the sites that might have been considered sacred during later prehistory (Fontijn 2008, 87–88).

The aim of this chapter is to gain a better understanding about the relationship between Bronze Age society and the natural landscape in which communities lived focusing on buried votive offerings and other forms of deposition. If visible traces of ritual activity exist, then the study of the deposition, ritual or otherwise, can offer scholars new information on how landscapes may have influenced the mindset of Bronze Age people.

I will argue that the concealing of the location of deposits and their various compositions can be interpreted by an animistic – shamanistic – spiritual belief system rather than the idea of divinities, temples and statues which, in many respects, do not characterise the Carpathian Basin (and Central Europe) at this time. Supporting this argument is that Bronze Age communities led a traditional agrarian way of life in the majority of Europe and most likely lived as tribal societies.

Ethnography, anthropology and archaeology are of assistance in understanding the prehistoric past. The examples presented in this chapter were, however, not meant as direct analogies, but primarily as relevant examples for the traditional worldview and relationship to human nature. They offer an insight into the incredible diversity of sacred places and sacrifices in much later times. They also draw attention to just how many differences there are among the ritual behaviours of regional groups, even inside one cultural community, and communities of one language family.

Folklore beliefs may offer significant help for prehistorians working with probable Bronze Age belief systems. As it is argued

> 'folk beliefs are better understood as indications of how people in the past related with the material world. Folk beliefs were not misconceptions about the (working of the) world but embedded in the logic and practice of everyday life ... which means that folk beliefs – or what they have been argued to be about – are potentially relevant to the interpretation of all archaeological data' (Herva & Ylimaunu 2009, 241).

In order to benefit from ethnographic records and employ their attributes to prehistory, we should take Herva and Ylimaunu's stance that the first step is simply to accept that folk beliefs played a deeper role in life in the past than is presently recognised (2009, 241). This short study will also showcase how anthropological-ethnographic research can support archaeological interpretations with numerous examples on the incredibly rich and colourful relationship of human beings with their natural and social surroundings.

Contextual Characteristics of Bronze Age Deposition in Europe

The composition and conditions of funerary deposition and hoards largely differ from each other throughout the Bronze Age. This suggests their social significance could have been different as well (Vandkilde 1998, 247–248). The grave composition contains personal items. Artefacts from deposits may have been owned by the community and used on community occasions. Eventual deposition indicates the purpose could have been essential for the entire community.

Searching for the guiding rules for the practice of deposition, the first problem we face are the details of the significance of diversity. The function of some deposition is not easy to determine and unequivocally enhances the difficulties in interpretation. This chapter presents a short insight focusing on the context into the multicoloured features of the activity.

Research has centred on aquatic finds since they are the most common ones throughout Europe. It is a generally accepted theory that all deposits found in aqueous areas are the result of ritual activities as it was not possible to recover objects from such places. The numerous artefacts from wet places also indicate this ritual was part of a common and regular practice in the Bronze Age Europe. (Fontijn 2008, 87–88).

Based on the best documented Danish deposits, 60% of them axes, are typical of the early bronze artefacts (2700–2350 BCE) found primarily in deposits. The majority of them, 86% are from aqueous areas and only 14% of them are found in dry places (Vandkilde 1998, 243, 248). Even in the far north in places like Norway, assemblages of finds have been discovered predominantly in swamps. The rest of them are found in mountain scree slopes, mainly in east Norway, where there are fewer swamps (Johansen 1993, 156). Danish deposits from the Late Bronze Age show some changes in the average distribution ratio for the country as only 54% are from aqueous areas while 31% came from dry areas. However, considering the chronological periods (IV, V, VI periods), aqueous sites finds are still increasing compared to the dry places as time passed. There was an exceptionally dramatic change in Zealand between period IV and V when the number of aqueous deposits jumped from 48% to 71% (Verlaeckt 1998, 266).

There is a great deal of complexity within aqueous deposition in different parts of Europe. Considering Bavarian sites, for example, assemblages connected to still or running waters can be differentiated based on deposition. Certain types of objects can be found in different ratios in these two types of sites with spearheads only and 85–90% of swords and axes found in rivers and small jewellery, knives and sickles deposited in still waters (Sperber 2006, 200–208). Needles from the BrD period were more common in rivers although during the Ha A1 period they occurred mostly in still waters (Falkenstein 2005, 496–497).

Swords are found in considerable numbers in large rivers in the south of Netherlands as well. There were barely any swords in other hoards even when located near rivers or swamps. Treasures hidden in swamps, marshes or other aqueous areas often consist of objects or jewellery different from those found in graves. Accessories are quite common. 'Inter-regional' accessories primarily come from depositions in wet lands and definitely not from graves. They may have been intentionally removed from social circulation and hoarded in the area specially selected for the purpose (Fontijn 2008, 96–97). In Slovenia, mainly needles and spears were deposited in the river Ljubljanice with axes and swords occurring less frequently (Váczi 2007, 137).

The early Norwegian bronze deposits mainly consisted of weapons, armour and tools, while deposits from the Late Bronze Age (period V) where most finds date, are primarily made up of jewellery and costume accessories (Johansen 1993, 156). In Bavaria in Austria, assemblages are mostly made of swords and needles, while in north Germany axes and spears are the most common objects (Váczi 2007, 137).

Swords were offered as sacrificial gifts throughout the whole of the Bronze Age. This practice ended in Central Europe by the end of 8th century BCE, but continued to exist in northern Germany and southern Scandinavia for another 200 years (Eluère 1999, 250; Jockenhövel & Kubach 1994).

The Danish bronze deposits, in general, are solitary finds like many others in Europe which contradicts the existence of regularly visited, specific open-air shrines

(Randsborg & Christensen 2006, 52). However, a wider area can be also considered as sacred if it attracts regular or many additional deposits. The area around Borgbjerg in Denmark, for example, was possibly such a significant point with unusually rich deposits. There, a large area spanning several square kilometres is covered with sites of hoards akin to a network. (Hansen 2013, 181).

In the Netherlands, zones rather than specific locations for deposition are argued. Therefore, the location (spot?) of a single deposit cannot be regarded as a place of pilgrimage like the majority of other Bronze Age hoard sites in Europe. These zones had similar natural characteristics, for example, where rivers meet, at estuaries of rivers, coastal splits, the edge of swamps or marshes or lakes, near to the high grounds (in rare cases) and so forth. Most bronze deposits were placed at a certain distance from cultivated lands, and the deposits with 'inter-regional' objects were further hidden. However, deposits made of 'local' objects were always placed close to settlements (Fontijn 2008, 96–101).

Deposition practices were also performed in the eastern Mediterranean region. There was even a substantial increase in the number of Cypriot and Aegean hoards during the 13th and 12th centuries BCE. Scholars have also used historical ('crisis' hoards), ritual and/or economic (votive offering or gift-commodity model) approaches to study Late Bronze and Iron Age hoarding activities in eastern Mediterranean sites (Hall 2016, 1).

Mesopotamia had a long cultural connection with the Carpathian Basin. In Mesopotamia, about 200 examples of artefact groups dating *c.* 3300–2000 BCE are known from 25 sites and provisionally identified as hoards and deposits. Unlike in Europe, the majority of these hoards were discovered in houses whilst most deposits had been left in temples. No evidence was found if any of them were 'professional' hoards belonging to merchants, jewellers, founders, or metalworkers (Kingston Bjorkman 1994). The difference between the Carpathian Basin and Near East may be an indication for the difference in the beliefs recorded.

At first glance, the 'selective' or 'structured' deposition of objects is largely the same or very similar throughout Europe. However, they only share a few properties which seem common such as mostly valuable objects being deposited, owners preferring wetlands or close to aqueous spots for deposition and, many times, the artefacts broken into slivers before placing them into the ground or water.

If we investigate the details of depositions (location, composition, arrangement of objects etc.), generally, there are few or hardly any characteristics they share even inside an archaeological group. Common elements can be observed only in small regions. Striking local patterning, however, disappears in a more general summary (Yates & Bradley 2010, 55).

Some Notions about the Interpretations of Deposition Practices

At times, ancient authors mentioned deposition practices. However, in written sources they often describe only the unusual and do not mention the actual practice. The ancient Greek writer Herodotus, who was mainly interested in political history, wrote about the unique offering made by the Lydian king in Delphi, but failed to mention the regular offerings of the Greeks (Osborn 2004, 6).

It is also worth mentioning two other sources because they describe two different practices of sacrificial offering (Randsborg & Christensen 2006, 45):

> 1. 'But if so be I slay him, and Apollo give me glory, I will spoil him of his armour and bear it to sacred Ilios and hang it upon the temple of Apollo.' (Homer: *Iliad*, VII. 81–83, trans. A. T. Murray)
> 2. '... since the country was rich in gold, and also belonged to people who were god-fearing and not extravagant in their ways of living, it came to have treasures in many places in Celtica; but it was the lakes, most of all, that afforded the treasures their inviolability, into which the people let down heavy masses of silver or even of gold. At all events, the Romans, after they mastered the regions, sold the lakes for the public treasury, and many of the buyers found in them hammered mill-stones of silver. And, in Tolosa, the temple too was hallowed, since it was very much revered by the inhabitants of the surrounding country, and on this account the treasures there were excessive, for numerous people had dedicated them and no one dared to lay hands on them.' (Strabo, *Geography* IV. 1. 13, trans. H. Leonard Jones)

The first quote talks about offering the armour and weaponry of the defeated opponent to the gods as a gratitude and proof of victory. Hoards of weapons, especially the ones containing more than two swords, are the signs that Celtic, Germanic or Greek war offerings can also be rooted in the Bronze Age and were generic in the whole of Europe (Kristianssen 2002, 329). However, there are several other reasons for votive offerings such as a victory gift at sport events or in exchange for divine support much like what the second quote refers to (Randsborg & Christensen 2006, 49).

The tradition of deposition practices continued to live on in later eras and can be detected in the early Germanic epics as well. Numerous heroic sagas contain parts revealing the concealment of treasures during the European migration period, their connection to significant communal rituals and how they played a crucial role in solving conflicts within the society. Germanic artefacts ranging in date between the second and the eleventh centuries also indicate that most of the votive artefacts were still being hidden in swamps and other aqueous areas with Viking swords also being discovered in rivers (Tarzia 1989).

Even though deposition can be regarded as communal rituals that reinforced the community's togetherness during the early periods, this may have changed by the second half of the Bronze Age. The group dominance and hierarchy slowly gave way to individual privileges and powerful social elites where the role of the heroic warrior prevails (Vandkilde 1998, 256). The exchange network had already spread significantly during the era of the Urnfield culture (LBA) in Europe. The control over trade and exchange was likely the fundamental basis of power. Important prestige objects were transported through this network system and travelled great distance as commercial goods or personal gifts. Since graves with swords and chariots were, without doubt, the sign of power, the trade of these objects must have played a role in the foundation of power as well. The other manifestation of power could have been with those people who could afford 'spending' fortunes on events like sacrificial offerings in order to establish a connection with the transcendental world or depositing treasures in a sacred wetland (especially during the middle of the Urnfield culture period). It is highly probable the elite class stabilised its social influence by offering valuable objects to the gods or other powerful transcendental beings during special events such as tribute to deceased heroes or celebration of war victories (Soroceanu 1995, 47–9; Kristianssen 2002; Vandkilde 2007, 153–154; Fontijn 2008, 87–88). However, the ritual practice of deposition does not have a simple formula. The offering of lethal weapons to land or water may have been a substitute for humans in ritual depositions (Melheim & Horn 2014). Concealment of precious artefacts due to wars or any danger cannot be excluded either.

There were even attempts to regard the deposition activities as an impact of the spread of Indo-European ideology in Bronze Age Europe since the objects making up the hoards were argued to be classified into Dumézil's three groups: the warriors, the tool users and the religious elite. The last group, though, cannot be unequivocally identified (Lynn 2006, 119–132). Deposits containing two swords may bear some relationship to the cosmological motif of the divine twins as attested to in various parts of Europe from later periods (Brandherm & Horn 2012, 125). The general deposition practices characterising the Bronze Age have even brought up the possible existence of a pan-European belief system as it seems hoards everywhere can be classified into the same categories (Harding 2000, 364).

Eamonn Kelly has developed a remarkable idea regarding the location of the deposits after studying Irish artefacts from the Iron Age. He assumes the locations of human sacrifices (in 40 cases) and other ritual deposits are linked to tribal borders whose remains can be recognised in present-day district borders. Many of the most important metal hoards from that period were found in marshes located near district or parish borders. In many cases, rivers served as borders for cities, parishes, districts, counties or, in still other cases, provincial areas. Deposits can often be found in lakes or on the shore of rivers emphasising the importance of borders, not the water. The deposition of artefacts may indicate borders held a defensive function. In Kelly's opinion, however, deposits discovered at borders were primarily related to coronation rituals, sacred kingdoms or to the inauguration of kings. At medieval inauguration ceremonies harnesses, weapons and costumes used at the coronation were divided among aristocrats, the leading bard and the Church. According to Eamonn Kelly, when a new pagan ruler made a sacred marriage with the local earth goddess, he would bury the coronation objects at the tribal borders to declare his right over the land as part of the ceremony. Saddlery and a wheel-hoard from 400 BCE might indicate that the king marched on horseback or on a ceremonial chariot to the coronation scene. Ornamental vessels were also part of the inauguration banquet (Kelly 2006). Social hierarchy was already clearly visible in the Iron Age, but the tradition might have roots back to the Bronze Age.

Bronze Age Deposition Practices in the Carpathian Basin and Attempts to Interpret Them

A significant number of Bronze Age hoards which made a great influence on the Central European prehistory and also had an impact on the development of the Scandinavian Bronze Age have come to light in the Carpathian Basin. Their most significant classification and attempt to date them was performed by Amália Mozsolics, an internationally recognised Hungarian prehistorian.

The archaeological context is not known or directly collected for most deposits. Like elsewhere in Europe, mostly non-archaeologists found them. They can rarely relate archaeologically to other cultures because of the lack of identifying ceramics and the fact that the same types of bronze objects were used for a long time by many groups. Attempts to interpret them are as diverse as elsewhere in Europe. The characteristics of Bronze Age depositional practices are not uniform either in the Carpathian Basin as they differ in different periods and smaller regions.

Unlike Central Europe, the Carpathian Basin is rich in deposits dating from the Late Early and the Middle Bronze Ages. The significant amount of deposits from the western and eastern part of the Basin bears a noticeable regional difference. While the eastern type, the so-called *Apa-Hajdúsámson*-hoards are mainly composed of whole axes and swords, the western so-called *Kosziderpadlás*-type are marked by an almost entire absence of weaponry (Neumann 2014, 8).

By the end of the Early Bronze Age, quite large hoards with diverse composition were buried in the ground and became the typical deposition model in the middle part of the Danube and the regions to the east. They are mainly connected to normal and fortified settlements. Therefore, the swords and battle axes of high quality of Early Bronze Age *Apa-* and *Hajdúsámson*-type hoards (Amália Mozsolics' classification) and other contemporary deposits were arguably hidden for fighting between big tell settlements and fortifications (Vandkilde 2007, 125).

At the same time Svend Hansen has argued that the Transdanubian (western Hungary) hoards collected by communities are votive deposits while the armed aristocracy in east Hungary, in order to strengthen their position in the community, offered the assemblages containing weapons, ornamental vessels (Hansen 2005, 211–212, 226). The number of deposited weapons and jewellery sharply increased after the Br C period like in other parts of Europe. Similarly, as in Central Europe and in Slovenian regions, most concealments happened during the Urnfield Culture (the Br D and Ha A1 periods). Depositions of two or three objects can mostly be dated to the Br D and Ha A1 periods. While the larger in number, heavier deposits characterise the Ha B period. However the habit of deposition decreased after the Ha A1 period (Váczi 2007, 135–138).

Hoards containing only a few pieces were likely hidden by individuals differing only in numbers from the east Hungarian weapon assemblages. The high numbered, but damaged artefacts which likely became damaged during sacrificial ceremonies, were probably offered by communities. Damage, however, can also signal wealth (Váczi 2007, 137), or a way to disable weapons (Nebelsick 2000). Assemblages containing damaged pieces can also indicate profane function, however, the intact solitary swords from aqueous areas or marshes are witness of votive intention (Teržan 1996). It was only after 1500 BCE that swords in this area were deposited in rivers as elsewhere in Europe.

Low numbers of artefacts are often found in well-defined areas like shallow wading areas, marshes, rocks or caves. Gábor Váczi has argued that the profane nature of burying bronze artefacts can generally be ruled out. Therefore, deposition can mostly be considered as sacrificial offerings from communities or individuals, and treasures containing weapons are sacrificial gifts from the aristocracy (Váczi 2007).

Often the method of deposition strongly indicates it is a sacrificial offering (Soroceanu 1995, 39. figs 11. a, b, e–g). Carefully placed objects following a pattern in arrangement, i.e. structured deposits, are not likely to be valuables or booty from war. Due to a lack of space and few trustworthy descriptions of their discovery, listed below are examples of arrangement from various locations.

From aqueous areas

Many swords (Hampel 1886, CLXXX. t. 11.; Jósa 1893, 168–169. fig. 5; Mozsolics 1972, 188), armour and helmets (Kemenczei 1979, 88–89, figs 1–3; F. Petres 1982, figs 3 a, b) came from the Danube. Near the town of Ercsi on the Danube a clay pot with jewels was found when the riverside collapsed. In a gully near the village of Forró bronze jewels were discovered when hoeing the potato fields (Hampel 1886, XCIII. t. and CLXII. t.).

North of the village Zsujta, six spears, a bird-shaped pole-tip, eight bracelets and eight swords (partly exhibited in the British Museum, Hampel 1892, CI. t. 1–5. CII. t.) were discovered nicely arranged in the ground near a spring. An LBA structured deposit with a well-designed arrangement of broken pieces of weapons, tools and jewels, was also discovered on the foothills near Kesztölc-Bodzás lane (Tarbay 2014, 227), on the steep bank of a wetland area fed by a spring and from a cemetery by a small river.

From dry land

- Three swords standing upright parallel to each other, discovered in the ground at the edge of the forest at the village of Buzica in Slovakia (Hampel 1886, 19);
- six swords found in a 0.5 m area in a mountain forest called Drenova above the village Egereske, Ukraine, after a landslide revealed them (Hampel 1892, 26. CLXXI. t. 1, 5);
- bronze jewellery and two ornamental axes buried 12–15 cm deep revealed during harvest near the village Felsőbalog (now Vyšný Blh, Slovakia), (Hampel 1886, XCIV. t. 8);

- two bronze helmets, six bronze vessels and, below them, 20 swords with alternating tips placed parallel found while digging a fireplace in Szentgyörgy pusta belonging to the town Hajdúböszörmény (Hampel 1886, 49);
- 17 swords with their grips facing north found 30 cm deep during harvest, at Zábráczky lane in the village Krasznokvajda (Mozsolics 1972, figs 2. 3.);
- four golden axes standing upright with their edges parallel to each other found in the sandy ground with gold chains, a solid gold bar, a vessel (later lost) on road between Czófalva (now Ţufalău, Ro) and Barátos (Brateş) (Kállay 1841, 72)'
- nine swords with their blades parallel to each other found at the foot of a steep mountain side, Recsk-Andesite mine (Mozsolics 1972, fig. 6);
- gold jewellery found in the middle of a mountain slope after spring rain washed it out south of the village of Szarvasztó/Sărăsău (Ro) (Rómer 1865);
- 26 bronze vessels, golden hair rings and amber beads found on the top of Szőlőskert mountain, at Temesnagyfalu/Satu Mare (Ro) (Kacsó 1998); and
- 44 sickles found in a rock cavity during quarrying behind a cliff called Devil's Table on the very top of the mountain at the edge of the city Velem-Szentvid (Fekete 2008, hoard no. 1).

As these examples show, in many cases assemblages in the Carpathian Basin were hidden in similar places as in the rest of Europe. Here, the ratio of artefacts hidden in aqueous or dry area seems more balanced, with the possibility of more hoards being buried in dry areas. However, it is hard to know for certain since the landscape has changed tremendously (after the two big river projects, most of the Great Plain was flooded and huge territories were under water for long time) and the archaeological context for most of the deposits has not been recorded.

There is no scholarly consensus on the exact function and reason for the concealment of deposits and hoards. It is possible that there is no exclusive single reason and many of the arguments on different functions are likely correct. Various regions in Europe add colourful details to the overall picture, one of which says the deposition of bronze artefacts became a common practice by the Late Bronze Age and that most deposits can be regarded as sacred assemblages (Melheim & Horn 2014; Neumann 2014, 12; Váczi 2007).

Few researches have analysed the geographical or topographical location of deposits (Fontijn 2008; Kelly 2006; Pásztor 2009; Randsborg & Christensen 2006; Soroceanu 1995). However, it can be clearly stated that deposits and hoards were not buried in random places even if not sacrificial or votive offerings, but were simply buried to preserve them for more peaceful times. Ethnographic records state that European ethnic groups who hid their values next to sacred rocks to entrust them to the protection of gods or spirits during wartime (Krohn 1908, 276). Danish bronze deposits from dry land, for example, can often be found next to graves or boulders (Randsborg & Christensen 2006, 52).

There are interpretations on how and where, but hardly any of them tries to explain the reason for the site selected for deposition.

Sacred Places, Sacrifices – And What Ethnography Tells about Them

Artefacts composing the sacred deposits are not simple objects, but symbols with special meaning. Therefore, a deposit always indicates the location where the ritual took place and was spiritually important since it was where a connection and exchange between gods and those making the offering were made possible (Osborn 2004, 7). It is assumed deposits at sacred places had two functions: partly ritual, connecting with transcendental powers and another partly social, acquiring local support and thus, having influence and power (Vandkilde 2007, 153–154). The fact that swords were often deposited in rivers in certain regions in Europe indicates a special connection between swords and rivers in those areas although many swords were found in the ground in the Carpathian Basin (see the list above). However, it seems these objects were not made exclusively for deposition, as they show signs of usage. This may prove they were likely turned into the object for deposition at a certain point of their life.

According to Richard Bradley, there were already structured deposits of prestige objects dating from the Neolithic that were sacred offerings for the gods and spirits, and different types of locations were for different types of spirits. Historical records about the ritual practices during the Late Iron Age, Celtic and Germanic communities suggest similar meaning (Bradley 2000, 28–32).

Further developing the idea of spirits or non-human beings in the belief system of Bronze Age cultural groups of the Carpathian Basin (that could be extended to most of Europe), I argue the majority (or the whole) of the tradition of deposition and their details can be interpreted by assuming spiritual beings rather than gods and they may have had a significant role in the Bronze Age belief system in the whole of Europe.

The operation of this system may well have been represented by the ethnographic records on spiritual activities performed among traditional societies and described in this chapter. Ancient sacred places around the world are usually sites in nature (mountains, mountain peaks, lakes, rivers, springs, forests, caves or strangely shaped rocks (Figs 7.1).

A sacred area must, in origin, be identified by geography, not buildings. Although the natural features themselves are not enough to become a sacred focus where worship takes place. How then is the focus chosen? Selection needs human thought and interaction which endows the spot with spiritual power (Dowden 2000, 28–30). (Fig. 7.2)

A sacred place is never only a physical part of space nor is it homogeneous and neutral to a religious person. It has parts that are different one from the other in quality (Eliade 1987, 16). It is typical of the belief system of many indigenous nations, traditional societies, or communities that elements of the surrounding world have similar vitality, power as human life force. Therefore, they have to respect them.

a

b

Figs 7.1 a and b: Ritual feeding of a stone with a carved anthropomorphic face possibly created by the Bronze Age Okunev archaeological culture (late 3rd–early 2nd millennia BC). The stone statue, named Ulug Khurtuyakh Tas *(the Great Stone Woman), was locally also called the Mother of Khakassia and was highly honoured as the protector of motherhood. Photographs were taken in the 1930s.*

They do not necessarily regard these forces as evil, but something that can be dangerous if they do not maintain a good relationship with them. Sami people marked the places where they could make connection with the spiritual world (Mulk & Bayliss-Smith 2006, 55). The old Finnish people chose spots where they made offerings partly by chance and where they believed the

Fig. 7.2: Spiritual involvement on the shamans' mountain, Mongolia (author)

spirits were dwelling (Honko 1965, 342–352). For other people, the shamans often selected a place for sacrifice, especially for communal ones, and frequently the spirits help was requested in a ritual activity to help find the right place (Gemuev *et al.* 2008; Kulemzin *et al.* 2006).

A sacred place could have many functions: homes of spirits, places for celebratory/ holy ceremonies, to meet and communicate with spirits or gods, stops for long travellers offering sacrifices to protective spirits, parts of legends or mythologies in relation to gods or ancestor spirits, close to burial sites in order to ask for the protection of ancestor's spirits, sources of spiritual energy and so forth. Sacred places also possessed power and were part of communal rituals and cosmology and were therefore manifestation of the sacred landscape.

In order to show the complexity of the selection process and the religious reverence, the following is a small summary of what the Finno-Ugric nations and the Siberian relatives of their language family regarded as sacred places:

> Norwegian Lapps chose those dangerous points of waterfalls, ice fields as their sacred places which were along their routes or where hunting, fishing was particularly rewarding or terrible. Thus, the Mountain Lapps' sites were on especially high mountains, while the forest Lapps' on nice flat grounds in the forest or at salmon-rich waterfalls. Lapps living at the seaside chose headlands reaching far into the sea for this purpose ... Estonians and Latvians regarded the river south from the

Fig. 7.3: A Sacred tree in Mongolia (author)

> city of Dorpat as sacred. They believed clear sky and sunshine was depending on whether they kept the river clean or not. They erected a triangle shaped plank fence around its spring and thought it to be sacred as well. (Krohn 1908, 46–51)
>
> Finns tell tales of sacred trees, rocks, mountains and springs on which or next to which they made sacred offerings. (Krohn 1908, 274) (Fig. 7.3).

Archaeological artefacts found at springs and swampy areas during excavations are in complete accord with the ethnographic records. This type of artefact is the 'easiest' to find among sacred places and also to help prove its sacredness due to its long, frequent use. For example, organic material and small artefacts played a central role in the Röekillorna spring finds which also proved the place was sacred from the early Neolithic to the Roman Iron Age. The ritual not only involved the sacrifice but also a ceremonial feast. People wanted to communicate with the spirits or gods through the feast as well. The site is considered to be a cultic place for farming people (Stjernquist 1998, 164–165).

Another version of water cult is where the offerings were not organic but jewellery or other items of precious metal work thrown into lakes or rivers although their timing cannot be proved. It is well presented in the whole Europe during the Bronze and Iron Ages. The Celts made a tremendous amount of sacrifices in water bodies or near to aqueous areas. We know many of their gods by name (Green 1986, 1989). Geographical names, Gallic gods and the Irish mythology all prove just how widespread the water cult was in Europe and had specially an important role in German regions. The water cult was especially typical during the classic period in Italy, Greece and in certain areas in Asia (Eliade 1958, 199–202; Stjernquist 1998, 171–173 and its references).

Honouring the water (or water-beings) with deposits roots back at least to the Bronze Age in Europe when there were no or hardly any anthropomorphic divinities as there are too few the number of representations of gods compared to the number of deposits if, indeed, they were actually offerings to gods.

However, artefacts found next to aqueous areas should not be regarded exclusively as votive offerings to the water god or spirit. Ethnographic records prove that on many occasions offerings to other gods (or several gods at the same time) were made on the bank of lakes or the riverside. For example, people made clan sacrifices for *Inmar*, the god of sky and other smaller good spirits in Kachakin village (Ufa regency, district Birszk) every 3 years. The ceremony took place at the steep riverside. Up front, closest to the river, stood the priests and in front of them facing eastwards stood the participants dressed in white. The day of the communal sacrifices was generally picked by the shaman or the elders of the villages (Krohn 1908, 207, fig. 31). Among the Khanty people, the shaman's main responsibility was to perform public sacrifices. Anyone could bring personal sacrifices, but only the shaman could develop relationship with the many divine beings (Kulemzin *et al.* 2006, 64).

Celtic mythology populated not only the lakes and rivers with gods, but also the mountains (Green 1986; 1989). Though few traces of the ancient mountain cult survived in Europe, mountain peaks must have played an important part in beliefs as the meeting point between the sky and the earth (Eliade 1958, 375–378). Crossing through mountains was dangerous. Therefore, it was natural to make offerings at the highest point of the mountain or near to it along ancient routes (Neumann 2014, fig. 8). In Mongolia where animism mixed with Buddhism is still practised, immolation at natural sacred places is a common practise even today. (Fig. 7.4).

Ethnographic records clearly prove how the countless spirits needed sacrifices in order to help or protect people during a large number of occasions. For the Khanty people, for example, each place had its own spirits which acted there. Many spirits protected herds of reindeer, some drove fish into trap and some sent wild animals to the hunters' weapons. There were even specialized ones, for example, who guaranteed success in choosing dogs, etc. There were also local and general spirits, along with personal and family ones. (Kulemzin *et al.* 2006, 107–108)

They all received sacrifices and the small spirits received more than the great ones.

> Though every region has its own powerful spirits, small domestic idols received offerings more frequently than powerful gods. Obi-Ugors believed smaller deities have more time to listen and thus, have more impact on their lives than bigger gods which had more important businesses in the world to take care of. Therefore, even though house spirits have minor reach but their use is the biggest, they are always at hand, and ready to deal with any problem (Vértes 1990, 19. 79).

a

b

Fig. 7.4a: Sacred place on the top of the hill nearby Galt village, Mongolia; b: Sacred rift in the cliff along the river. Note the bull head inside the small cave (author)

Making a sacrifice was the only way to get a spirit's or god's favour. 'Give and you will be given' is the universal principle for communicating with the transcendental world and building a relationship with it in traditional communities. This could also have been the case in prehistory.

Sacrifices were performed regularly and any time the person seeking blessings needed assistance. The Khanty people could ask a shaman or a dream-man for assistance to tell what kind of sacrifice must be done, to which god or spirit, and where in order to comply with the request for health or good luck (Kulemzin *et al.* 2006, 63). Sacrifices were made before and after the hunting season, during the sporadic visits to the master-spirit of a place or river, at child birth, at marriage ceremonies, every spring at the time of ice drifting and on many other occasions (Kulemzin *et al.* 2006, 128–129; Gemuev *et al.* 2008, 118). When strong winds from the neighbouring mountains blew making the Baikal Lake dangerous for navigation, the natives on its shores offered sacrifices to calm its waters (Czaplicka 1914, 10).

Sacrifices can be classified into two categories, blood and bloodless. The most widespread objects of blood sacrifice were domesticated animals as many peoples believed wild animals are the property of spirits or deities and, therefore, the spirits did not need them (Kulemzin *et al.* 2006, 128). Most frequently spirits and gods received food as a bloodless sacrifice, but objects were also seen as significant offerings. Arrows were essential for the Khanty people but they also offered spears, swords, kettles, clay pots and many other things. A special group of sacrifices were small metal objects, mirrors, silver plates and so forth, kept in a small wooden box where the spirits were believed to live (Kulemzin *et al.* 2006, 128). When the Ob-Ugrians were in the formation stage of a state before the 15th and 16th centuries, they had special type of cult places to make sacrifices to the spirit of 'hero ancestors' (known from folklore). The 'heroes' had been military leaders of the local tribal communities who were in charge during wartime and became hero spirits through the ancestor cult. Obi-Ugrian archaeological finds from the first millennium AD prove the earlier existence of heroic cults. Weapons were the obligatory attributes of the warrior spirits. Therefore, arrowheads and other weapons such as spearheads, armours, helmets and swords were offered as sacrifice. Weaponry could even represent the images of guardian spirits (Gemuev *et al.* 2008, 20, 33, 122–123). Weapons were, however, given to other gods or spirits as well. The Mansi people accommodated the Obi Old who lived in the estuary of the Irtis River by offering different weapons and armours as they believed the god of the fish and water animals often fought with each other in the waters and therefore needed their support (Munkácsi 1902, 98).

Discussion

Many people believed in the existence of spirits or non-human beings in Europe in the past. The respect for stones, trees and rivers still existed in medieval Europe. Burchard, bishop of Worms from 1000 to 1025, condemned the 'pagan traditions' of worshiping the sun and the moon in his *Decretum*, and also 'forbade any Christians to participate in rites or observance of performed before stones, trees or crossroads in the manner of pagan' (Bailey 2007, 72).

Folk beliefs concerning non-beings and spiritual powers still flourished in the early modern era and persisted especially in rural areas well into the 20th century (for example Gemuev *et al.* 2008; Herva & Ylimaunu 2009, 234; Kulemzin *et al.* 2006). Folk beliefs describe the world people inhabited along with different non-human beings which, for them, were real and 'this-worldly' entities whom people took seriously in the past (Herva & Ylimaunu 2009, 235). If we assume the existence of beliefs in spiritual or non-beings in the Bronze Age, then ethnographic analogies could be mentioned for all variations of deposits. Every community treating its gods and spirits in a natural way may have followed some local tradition until an organised religion came along which did not demand the adherence of established rules whose compliance was observed by a priest. In human nature, they gave something during sacrifices and expected something in exchange from the spirits.

The hiding places of Bronze Age deposits are in accord with ethnographic analogies and show all geographical formations such as the forest, hunting areas, lakes, marshes or swamps, rivers, mountains and so forth. Each could have its own guardian spirit or offer a dwelling place for spirits with different attributes.

The happiness and welfare of the community depended on the benevolence of the spirits. Often the spirit of the deceased turned into a local guardian spiritual being (Vértes 1990, 50–51). The worship of Water Spirits was more significant since transportation on water was more dangerous than in the forest, but also because of fishing and other symbolic features of the water, e.g. the flowing water of a river or spring bringing life to a substance/material (a basic substrate of genesis) or ritual purification. Traces of these beliefs can be identified in later historical records although we cannot clearly draw a parallel between the location of Bronze Age deposits and the worship of celestial powers. Assemblages hidden on mountain tops or gold treasures may have been meant for the celestial divinities. Ethnographic studies also show that offerings for various gods and other spirits could happen at the same location and rituals without a strong connection to the location were also made, for instance celestial offerings at riversides (Krohn 1908). The worship of gods or spirits was not uniform, even within one nation (Vértes 1990, 32, 37). This can explain the diversity of deposits.

The growing significance of the practice and the similar components of deposits probably relate to social progresses of periods that were similar throughout Europe. When social stratification began, the formation of the elite and their power struggles started (Verlaeckt 1998, 267–268). The similarity of the artefacts was probably connected to the intense development in bronze technology, its spread and exchange with trade becoming general throughout Europe.

Naturally, the economic state of a community or individuals could also affect the frequency or the components of the deposits. Deposits of variable richness could indicate the changing prosperity of communities or the actual welfare, as sacrifices were offered more frequently in hard times. Those with one or two artefacts could have been an individual's sacrifices. Others with a higher number of objects or valuable ornamental weapons, jewels and vessels could have been offerings which served community purpose. Bronze objects were valuable; therefore, they must have been used over a long period of time. Unique objects had a special life story, thus they bore significant social value (Tarbay 2014, 224).

The general assumption, based on the composition of deposits like those made of weapons and tools were probably left by men, while it is most likely women hid the deposits consisting of jewellery and accessories. It is not possible to decide whether the mixed, semi-finished or broken artefacts had a votive or profane function (Fontijn 2008, 102; Teržan 1996). However, male and female objects often occur together in hoards, for example, a sacrificial assemblage found in a swamp in Wierzchowon (Szczecinek, Koszalin, Poland, 11th–10th century BCE) contained a full female costume, accessories and a sword (Eluère 1999, 243). Gábor Váczi (2007, 137), however, argues gender differentiation cannot be solely justified with object types as the most widespread object is the most common.

Composition of the hoards refers first of all to whom they were offered, the spirit or god (who can be male or female) and not to the person making the offer. The sacrifices serve the gods or spirits needs. Therefore, the weapons were meant presumably for warrior spirits and not goddesses. The numerous weapon hoards may be an indication of the warlike character of the Bronze Age where people like the Ob-Ugric people were especially in need of a warrior protector spirit. Spirits also led a human-like life. They had wives, family and even worked in many cases (Gemuev *et al.* 2008). Therefore, deposits with a mixed composition containing tools as well as valuables might have served 'family' needs.

The hoards involving valuables, special weapons and jewels could have been offered at communal ritual ceremonies. Treasures with male and female artefacts could have been intentionally mixed in order to be offered to the Earth and Sky, both of whom were of different sexes in many myths or during a Spring ceremony like a Yakut festival. Among the Yakut, the male 'celestial or white shaman' wore a white woman's fur coat and a tall woman's headgear at the yearly prayers held in honour of the sky and the earth. Mixing the masculine and feminine features, they were meant to express the union of the two principles and also the union of the Sky and the Earth representing the Harmony of the Cosmos (Hoppál 1993, 272).

An interesting aspect of many deposits is that traces of prehistoric destruction mostly occurred on the useable, finished products (Tarbay 2014, 227). Intentional destruction in the archaeological record has a significant number of references. I do not intend to deal with it now, but only mention an ethnographic record to prove its existence in traditional societies as well. Possession has a unique position in the tribal worldview of the Amur Basin in north-eastern Asia and the American Indian. The spirits of the deceased had the right of possessing all the objects they owned in their life. As the deceased was already a spirit, they needed only the spirit of the objects. Therefore, they were either broken or burnt at the grave so that the spirit of objects could more easily follow their master to the Netherworld (Lopatin 1935, 136).

Ritual breakage or offering unusable objects to the supernatural world is also well-known in myths of the Romano-Celtic Europe as a kind of rite of passage or as a spirit-gift (Green 1993,70–71). Fragments or unique broken artefacts in the hoards are also evidence they were left for the spirits. The defective, damaged items were not broken because they were useless in the world of living. They were 'dead' for human use, and being so, perfect for the spirits. Usable objects in the world of living had to die in order for their spirits to be able to enter the world of spirits. Therefore, the objects, after their death, were often buried as well. In the Carpathian Basin where urn burial was common, deposits were often hidden ('buried') in a pot (possibly meant as an urn meant for the spirits).

Shared practices and similar compositions of deposits create certain patterning in a smaller region (Yates & Bradley 2010; Brandherm & Moskal-del Hoyo 2014; Melheim & Horn 2014) which could indicate a common ritual practice and beliefs concerning deposition. A high diversity of objects in a deposit could be due to the smaller or larger differences in the beliefs and local traditions.

The geographical distribution is inconsistent in every period, which could indicate a fluctuating economic background and changing attitude towards transcendental powers, even within one period. People made frequent sacrificial offerings during times of hardship. The different accumulations can show the actual ritualistic needs of a certain region such as during a drought, sickness, or epidemic, etc. It can indicate a 'local trend'. For example, there are barely any deposits from Danish island in the IIIrd period of Nordic Bronze Age (chronology established by Oscar Montelius (1843–1921)) while it is one of the richest periods in Central Europe. However, the number of deposits containing special, exotic objects grew significantly in Denmark by the Late Bronze Age.

Conclusion

Archaeological studies show that ritual deposition was practised throughout the Bronze Age. It was increasingly common from the end of Middle Bronze Age and reached its peak by the Late Bronze Age. It seems, however, the practice was born much earlier together with the emerging beliefs at the dawn of the formation of the human mind. It survived for a long-time in Europe. The deposition of valuable metal artefacts existed in some regions even in the Migration Period. However, other types of deposition such as ceramics, tools, coinage and animal products persisted in some rural regions up until the 20th century (Herva & Ylimaunu 2009).

Therefore, it seems to be plausible to assume that such belief system already existed in the Bronze Age (or at least for most of the period), something which could have been similar to the beliefs of traditional social groups that took up Christianity quite late. Bronze Age social groups in the Carpathian Basin were especially more likely to be tribal societies, with some having limited instances of social ranks and prestige or stratified ones led by chieftains, rather than highly hierarchical town-states with organized religion. Among these people, as anthropology records, shamans were primarily the mediators towards the spiritual world (but always in community ceremonies), or the shamanic jobs were divided between people selected from the communities.

Although depositional practices were also performed in the Mediterranean or Near East, there the majority of deposits or offerings were left in temples and houses with the foundation enclosing the deposits, not outside or in nature like in Europe. This is a strong indication for the difference in their beliefs. For them, divinities populated the transcendent world while inside Europe spiritual beings still dominated.

If we accept the idea of spirit or non-human, animated landscape for Bronze Age Europe, each variation of deposition can find its ethnographic analogy. There is no universal rule for Bronze Age deposits, at least not for the whole of Europe, nor one for an archaeological culture. This would also contradict ethnographic observations.

Acknowledgements

The author thanks Professor George Nash, Herman Bender and Professor Dragos Gheorghiu for their useful comments. Many thanks also to Ruslan Stoytsev and Director Oksana Sergeyevna Gorbatova and the research associate Leonid Vasilyevich Gorbatov from the Museum 'Khurtuyak tas' Khakassia, who helped with the old photographs.

References

Bailey, M. D. 2007. *Magic and Superstition in Europe: a Concise History From Antiquity to the Present.* Lanham ML: Rowman & Littlefield.

Bradley R., 2000. *An Archaeology of Natural Places.* New York: Psychology Press.

Brandherm, D. & Horn, C. 2012. Die Zwei in der Drei, oder: Ein Zwilling kommt selten allein. In B. Ramminger & H. Lasch (eds) *Hunde - Menschen - Artefakte: Gedenkschrift für Gretel Gallay.* Internationale Archäologie Studia Honoraria 32. Leidorf: Rahden, 99–141.

Brandherm, D. & Moskal-del Hoyo, M. 2014. Both sides now: The Carp's-Tongue Complex revisited. *Antiquaries Journal* 94, 1–47.

Czaplicka, M. A. 1914. *Aboriginal Siberia - a Study in Social Anthropology.* Oxford: Clarendon.

Dowden, K. 2000. *European Paganism.* London and New York: Routledge.

Eliade M. 1958. *Patterns in Comparative Religion.* Translated by R. Sheed. New York: Sheed and Ward.

Eliade M. 1987. *The Sacred and the Profane - The Nature of Religion.* Translated by W. R. Trask. New York: Harcourt, Brace & World.

Eluère C. 1999. The world of the gods in the Bronze Age. In K. Demakopoulou, C. Eluere, J. Jensen, A. Jockenhövel & J. P. Mohen (eds) *Gods and Heroes of the Bronze Age.* London, Thames and Hudson, 132–137.

Fekete, M. 2008. A kincs, a lelőhely, a védett terület és a cross-pálya. *Vasi Szemle* 62(5), 525–540.

Falkenstein, F. 2005. Zu den Gewässefund der älteren Urnenfelderzeit in Süddeutschland. In B. Horejs, R. Jung, E. Kaiser & B. Teržan (eds) *Interpretationsraum Bronzezeit. Festschrift für Bernard Hänsel.* Bonn: Universitätforschungen zur prähistorischen Archäologie 121, 491–504.
Fontijn, D. 2008. Everything in its right place? On selective deposition, landscape and the construction of identity in later prehistory. In A. Jones (ed.) *Prehistoric Europe – Theory and Practice.* Malden: Wiley-Blackwell, 86–106.
Gemuev, I. N., Baulo, A. V., Lyutsidarskaya, A. A., Sagalaev, A. N., Sokolova, Z. P. & Soldatova, G. E. 2008. *Mansi Mythology.* Budapest: Akadémiai Kiadó/Helsinki: Finnish Literature Society.
Green M. 1986. *The Gods of the Celts.* Gloucester: Sutton.
Green M. 1989. *Symbols and Image in Celtic Religious Art.* London and New York: Routledge.
Green M. 1993. *Celtic Myths.* London: British Museum Press.
Hall, E. 2016. Hoarding at Tel Megiddo in the Late Bronze Age and Iron Age I. M.A. Thesis. Tel Aviv University.
Hampel, J. 1886. *A bronzkor emlékei Magyarhonban* I. Memories of the Bronze Age in Hungary. Budapest: Országos régészeti és embertani társulat.
Hampel, J. 1892. *A bronzkor emlékei Magyarhonban II. A leletek statisztikája.* Budapest: Országos régészeti és embertani társulat.
Hansen, S. 1994. *Studien zu den Metalldeponierungen während der alteren Urnenfelderzeit zwischen Rhônetal und Karpatenbecken.* Bonn: Universitätsforschungen zur prähistorischen Archäologie 21.
Hansen, S. 2005. Über bronzezeitliche Horte in Ungarn – Horte als soziale Praxis. In B. Horejs, R. Jung, E. Kaiser & B. Teržan (eds) *Interpretationsraum Bronzezeit. Festschrift für Bernhard Hänsel.* Bonn: Universitätforschungen zur prähistorische Archäologie 121, 211–230.
Hansen, S. 2013. Bronze Age hoards and their role in social structure: A case study from south-west Zealand. In S. Bergerbrant & S. Sabatini (eds) *Counterpoint: Essays in Archaeology and Heritage Studies in Honour of Professor Kristian Kristiansen.* Oxford: British Archaeological Report S2508, 179–191.
Harding A. F. 2000. *European Societies in the Bronze Age.* Cambridge: Cambridge University Press.
Herva, V-P. & Ylimaunu, T. 2009. Folk beliefs, special deposits, and engagement with the environment in early modern northern Finland. *Journal of Anthropological Archaeology* 28, 234–243.
Honko, L. 1965. *Finnische Mythologie. Wörterbuch der Mythologie.* Stuttgart: H. W. Haussig.
Hoppál, M. 1993. Studies on Eurasian shamanism. In M. Hoppál & K. D. Howard (eds) *Shamans and Cultures.* Budapest: Akadémiai Kiadó/Los Angeles: International Society for Trans-Oceanic Research, 258–288.
Jockenhövel, A. & Kubach, W. 1994. *Bronzezeit in Deutschland.* Stuttgart: Theiss.
Johansen, Ø. K. 1993. *Norske depotfunn fra bronsealderen. – Norwegian Hoards from the Bronze Age.* Oslo: Universitetets Oldsaksamlings Skrifter Ny rekke.
Jósa, A. 1893. Jósa András a Szabolcs megyei bronzleletekről. *Archaeológiai Értesítő,* 165–170.
Kacsó, C. 1998. Das Depot von Satu Mare. Kacsó Károly: A temesnagyfalusi/Satu Mare, raktárlelet. *Jósa András Múzeum Évkönyve* 36–40, 11–32.
Kállay, F. 1841. Az Erdélyben, Orbaj székben legújabban talált aranyművekről. *Magyar Akadémiai Értesítő* 1, 72–75.
Kelly, E. P. 2006. *Kingship and Sacrifice: Iron Age bodies and boundaries.* Archaeology of Ireland. Heritage Guide 35. Dublin: National Museum of Ireland.
Kemenczei, T. 1979. Új bronzsisak-lelet a Magyar Nemzeti Múzeum őskori gyűjteményében. *Folia Archaeologica* 30, 79–89.
Kemenczei, T. 1996. Zur Deitung der endbronze- und früheisenzeitlichen Depotfunde Ungarns. In P. Schauer (ed.) *Archäologische Forschungen zum Kultgeschehen in der jüngeren Bronzezeit und frühen Eisenzeit Alteuropas.* Regensburg: Regensburger Beiträge zur prähistorischen Archäologie 2, 451–480.

Kingston Bjorkman, J., 1994 Hoards and Deposits in Bronze Age Mesopotamia. Dissertations available from ProQuest. Paper AAI9427503. http://repository.upenn.edu/dissertations/AAI9427503. Accessed 15 August 2017

Kristianssen, K. 2002. The tale of the sword – swords and swordfighters in Bronze Age Europe. *Oxford Journal of Archaeology* 21(4), 319–332.

Krohn, Gy. 1908. *A finnugor népek pogány istentisztelete.* (Pagan worship of Finno-Ugric peoples). A Magyar Tudományos Akadémia Könyvkiadó Vállalata. Új folyam 73. Budapest: Magyar Tudományos Akadémia.

Kulemzin, V. M., Lukina, N. V., Moldanov, T. A. & Moldanova, T. A. 2006. *Khanty Mythology.* Budapest: Akadémia Kiadó. Helsinki: Finnish Literature Society.

Lopatin, I. A. 1935. *The Cult of the Dead Among the Natives of the Amur Basin.* Ann Arbor MI: ProQuest LLC.

Lynn, C. J. 2006. Suggested archaeological and architectural examples of tripartite structures. *Journal of Indo-European Studies* 34(1 & 2), 111–273.

Melheim, L. & Horn, Ch. 2014. Tales of hoards and swordfighters in Early Bronze Age Scandinavia: The brand new and the broken, *Norwegian Archaeological Review* 47, 1–24.

Mozsolics, A. 1972. Újabb kardleletek a Magyar Nemzeti Múzeumban. *Archaeológiai Értesítő* 99, 188–200.

Mulk, I-M. & Bayliss-Smith, T. 2006. *Rock Art and Sami Sacred Geography in Badjelénnda, Laponia, Sweden.* Umeå: Department of Archaeology and Sami Studies/Kungl. Skytteanska Samfundet.

Munkácsi, B. 1902. *Regék és énekek a világ teremtéséről. Vogul népköltési gyűjtemény I. (Legends and songs on the creation of the world. Vogul Folk Collection I).* Budapest: Magyar Tudományos Akadémia.

Nebelsick, L. 2000. Rent asunder: ritual violence in Late Bronze Age hoards. In C. F. E. Pare (ed.) *Metal Make the World Go Round. The Supply and Circulation of Metals in Bronze Age Europe.* Oxford: Oxbow, 160–175.

Neumann, D. 2014. Changing patterns – depositions and their sites during the Middle Bronze Age and earlier Late Bronze Age in the Eastern Alpine area. In D. Ložnjak Dizdar & M. Dizdar (eds) *The Beginning of the Late Bronze Age Between the Eastern Alps and the Danube.* Zagreb: Institut za arheologiju, 7–16.

Osborn, R., 2004. Hoards, votives, offerings: the archaeology of the dedicated object. In R. Osborne (ed.) *The Object of Dedication. World Archaeology* 36(1), 1–10.

Pásztor, E. 2009. A szakrális depóleletek szerepe a bronzkori ember világképének tanulmányozásában. In Gy. Kaposvári & J. Tárnoki (eds) *Csányi Marietta köszöntése, Tisicum* 19, 197–208.

Petres, É., 1982. Neue Angaben über die Verbreitung der spätbronzezeitlichen Schutzwaffen. *Savaria* 16, 57–79.

Randsborg, K. & Christensen, K. 2006. *Bronze Age Oak-coffin Graves: Archaeology and Dendro-dating.* Acta Archaeologica 77, Acta Archaeologica Supplementa VII. Oxford, Copenhagen: Blackwell Publishing.

Rómer, F. 1865. A két házában talált régi arany műemlékekről, különösen a szarvasszói- Marmaros megyei – arany kincsről. *Archaaeológiai Közlemények.* 5 (Új Folyam 3). 29–46.

Soroceanu, T. 1995. Die Fundumstände bronzezeitlicher Deponierungen – Ein Beitrag zur Hortdeutung beiderseits der Karpaten. In T. Soroceanu (ed.) *Bronzefunde aus Rumänian.* Prähistorische Archäologie in Südosteuropa 10. Berlin: Spiess, 15–81.

Sperber, L, 2006. Bronzezeitliche Flussdeponierungen aus dem Altrheim bei Roxheim, Gde Bobenheim – Roxheim, Lkr. Ludwigshafen – ein Vorbericht. *Archaologisches Korrespondenzblatt* 36, 195–214.

Stjernquist, B. 1998. The basic perception of the religious activities at cult-sites such as springs, lakes and rivers. In L. Larsson & B. Stjernquist (eds) *The World-View of Prehistoric Man.* KVHAA Konferenser 40. Stockholm: KVHAA, 157–178.

Tarbay, G. 2014. Late Bronze Age depot from the foothills of the Pilis Mountains. *Dissertationes Archaeologicae ex Instituto Archaeologico Universitatis de Rolando Eötvös nominatae* 3(2), Budapest: Eötvös Loránd University, Institute of Archaeological Sciences, 179–298.

Tarzia, W. 1989. The hoarding ritual in Germanic epic tradition. *Journal of Folklore Research* 26(2), 99–123.

Teržan, B. 1996. Sklena beseda - conclusion. In B. Teržan (ed.) *Depojske in posamezne kovinske najdbe bakrene in bronaste dobe na Slovenskem - Hoards and Individual Metal Finds from the Eneolithic and Bronze Age in Slovenia* II. Ljubljana: Narodni muzej, 243–258.

Váczi, G. 2007. Adatok az urnamezős kultúra fémművességéhez és deponálási szokásaihoz. Ősrégészeti Levelek 8–9, 130–140.

Vandkilde, H. 1998. Metalwork, depositional structure and social practice in the Danish late Neolithic and earliest Bronze Age. In C. Mordant, M. Pernot & V. Rychner (eds) *L'Atelier du Bronzier en Europe du XXe au VIIe siècle avant notre ère*. Actes du colloque international Bronze '96. Paris: Comité des travaux historiques et scientifiques, 243–270.

Vandkilde, H. 2007. *Culture and Change in Central European Prehistory: 6th to 1st Millennium BC*. Aarhus: Aarhus University Press.

Verlaeckt, K. 1998. Metalwork consumption in Late Bronze Age Denmark: depositional dynamics in northern hoards. In C. Mordant, M. Pernot & V. Rychner (eds) *L'Atelier du Bronzier en Europe du XXe au VIIe siècle avant notre ère*. Actes du colloque international Bronze '96. Paris: Comité des travaux historiques et scientifiques, 259–270.

Vértes, E. 1990. *Szibériai nyelvrokonaink hitvilága. (Mythology of our Siberian Language Relatives)*. Budapest: Tankönyvkiadó

Yates, D. & Bradley, R. 2010. The siting of metalwork hoards in the Bronze Age of south-east England. *Antiquaries Journal* 90, 41–72.

Chapter 8

Landscape Transformation and Continuity in Shamanic Rock Art of Northern Asia

Ekaterina Devlet

Abstract *The chapter raises the questions of why and how particular places were chosen for rock art. From the analysis of several sites with rich motifs, it can be argued that they are core sites forming the centre of a sacral landscape. The most significant shamanist activities were held near cliffs marked by petroglyphs. The sites also have a long-lasting tradition of veneration and ritual activity. These factors support the argument that many scenes on the rock, the juxtaposition and even superimposition could be interpreted along with a shamanistic worldview and activities.*

Introduction

Distribution of the rock art sites in the landscape gives us an opportunity to discuss an important subject matter: why particular places were chosen; why petroglyphs appeared at certain places and whether the places had been used through generations for a long period of time; whether it was necessary to travel long distances to make petroglyphs in a particular place or, the choice was arbitrary and depended on the artist idiosyncrasy; whether it was essential for cultures with shamanic practices to come to special sites or it was possible to make images anywhere. It is hardly possible to find a single answer for these questions as well as to clarify who decided that rock art had to be made on a particular rock surface.

It is evident that particular landscapes were chosen for rock art activity and this activity even strengthened and maintained the importance of the place. Although there is still vague understanding of who the witnesses and recipients of skilful rock art compositions were, what kind of ceremonies and how often they may have occurred at rock art sites. It should be also considered whether or not there were any rules of updating rock art panels and the reason why satellite, peripheral rock sites appeared in the vicinity of the central most elaborate sites sharing the same symbolism. It is hardly possible, whereas these questions should be proposed to explain the emergence and transformation of sacral shamanic landscapes and their spatial features.

Rock art is a unique historical source. The rock is the most lasting natural material in the landscape and became the mechanism for transmitting permanent messages which overtime would have been altered, obliterated or superimposed from season to season, year to year and from generation to generation. As a material manifestation of spiritual life of the people, a sort of frozen myth', they brought the realities of everyday life and world-view; these would have been transmitted onto the rock surface.

Approaches in modern rock art studies with primary concern of rock art symbolism in the context of landscape itself and rock art site position in the landscape have been made with consideration to the interaction between landscape and people becoming valuable in understanding the shamanic practices in Eurasia and sacral landscapes (e.g. Nash & Chippindale 2002).

Core Sites and Extension of Shamanic Landscapes

The idea of special value ascribed to a particular rock art landscape is based on the universal rule of longevity of rock art sites (Fig. 8.1). What was auspicious for such a landscape to receive long-term engagement in social activity related with the production of art? Did chronological gaps break the tradition of making rock art or even continuity of the tradition result in the deterioration for the sacral essence of a place and inevitably lead to its destruction? There is evidence coming from different regions which show long-lasting shamanic activities that may clarify the problem.

Fig. 8.1: Zalavruga. North-West Region (image by I. Georgievsky)

General observation of hierarchy and spatial correlation of the rock art site makes it essential to explain the reason why certain sites accumulate the majority of rock art motifs usually with very special iconography and skills in their production. These are core sites which formed the centre of a sacral landscape, from where it emerged and expanded. However, this landscape may have a very limited or have an extended chronology. These core sites are connected with other smaller satellite sites – of the almost the same time span or even those which later emerge were inspired by earlier metaphors within the art.

In every rock art province there are sites of the primary importance that are considered as core sites, those that would have drawn artists and communities together. Several core rock art sites, in one particular area show peak activity occurring at roughly the same time. Iconic narratives expressed through the artistic imagery accumulated the most significant ideas related to the communities' world-view. It is true for core sites of every rock art enclave,[1] for example the site of Tomskaya Pisanitsa within the the Tom' River Area, Bolshaya Boyarskaya in the Middle Yenisei, Mugur-Sargol on the Upper Yenisei (Tuva), Kalbak-Tash within the Russian Altai, the Pegtymel at Chukotka and Sikachi-Alian sites within the Amur-Ussury rock art province, Onega, Zalavruga and Kanozero within the Russian North-West Region, to name but a few significant sites (Fig. 8.2) (Okladnikov & Martynov 1972; Okladnikov & Mazin 1976; Devlet 1980; Kubarev & Jacobson 1996; Dikov 1999; Devlet & Devlet 2005).

Sacral essence of the landscape in its core places involved rock art activity and probably coincided with the most important ceremonies such as calendar rituals, initiations or other occasions that claimed to connect different spheres of *their* universe. These places were at the crossroads of this universe, which is why the location is often connected with the idea of going from the terrestrial world into a Lower world (i.e. via the rivers, cracks, caves, etc.) or the Upper sphere of the universe. This complex symbolism of the landscape extrapolated the symbolism from the depicted art and the activity associated with it.

For the most of the rock art regions, it is typical that core sites normally have satellite rock art panels around them. For example, within the Tom' River region the core site of Tomskaya Pisanitsa is accompanied by Tutalskaya, Novoromanovskaya, Visiachy Kamen sites. These smaller sites surround the core site. For the Bolshaya Boyarskaya site it would be true to mention it as a core site and its satellites – those of Malaya Boyarskaya and Novaya Boyarskaya. For this particular region it is clear that the core site was deliberately chosen in order that communities could move around a known landscape and into peripherals areas such as neighbouring Onega Lake where rock art activity was distributed widely across the landscape. From here, communities appear to have explored and settled further with rock art being made on new sites located on peninsulas and small islands within the Upper Yenisei Region and beyond towards Mugur-Sargol and Aldi-Mozaga. It is possible to identify patterns of rock art activity and structuring of the sacral landscape that can be identified within these particular enclaves. It is within these areas that researchers have begun to witness spatial/temporal patterns within the rock art narrative.

However, do the core site motifs encourage the production of the similar images at satellite sites? It is difficult to find a single answer as the rock art chronology is still not fully understood, although the local and regional styles suggest that it is very likely. It should be mentioned that for most of the core sites (and peripheral sites as well) information regarding the frequency of rock art production and the quantity

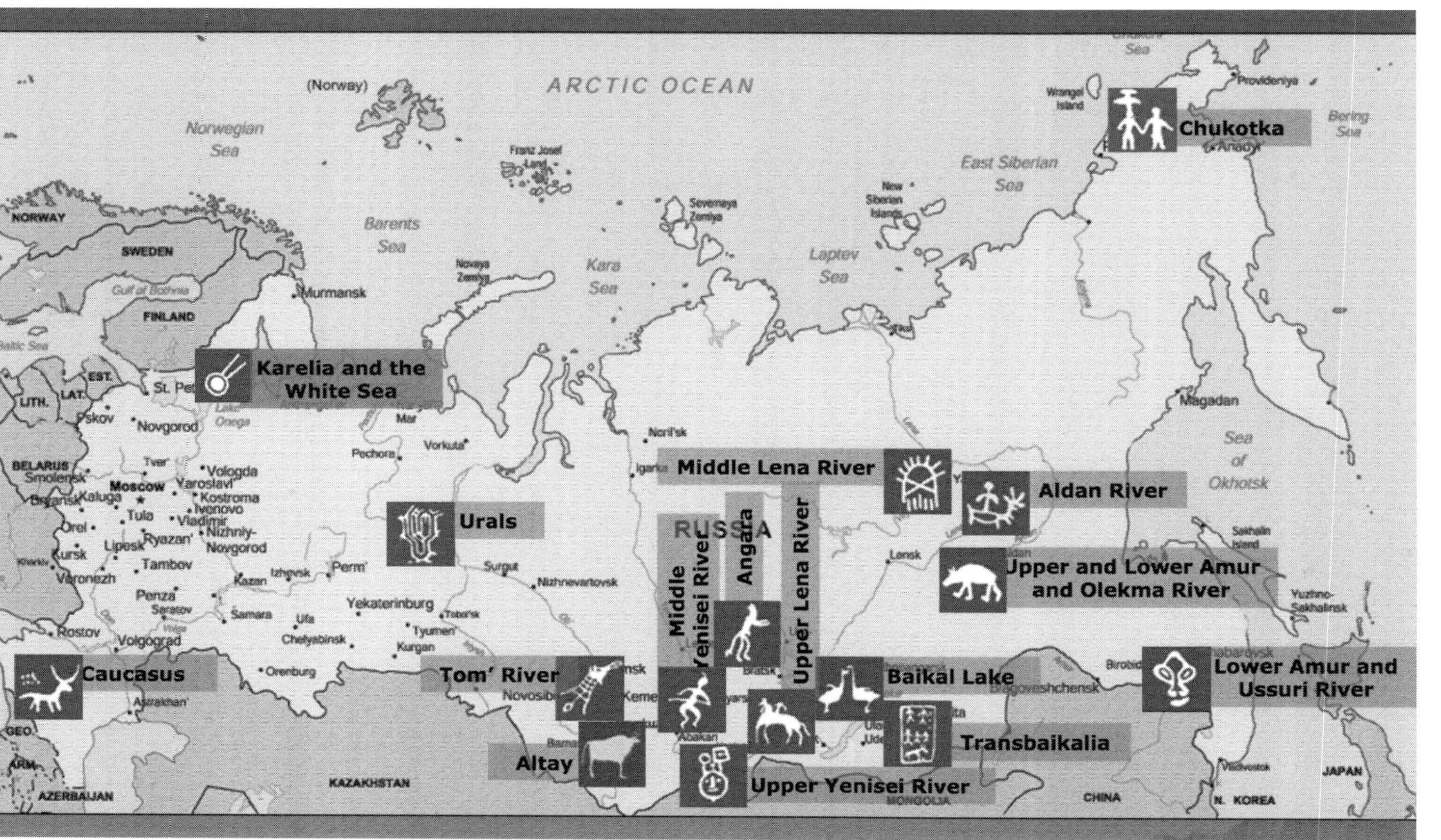

Fig. 8.2: Map of rock art areas in Russia (image by E. Devlet)

of the episodes still remains unknown. Whereas at the core sites with their central compositions seem to be well-organised and planned in advance. It may be supposed that for the core site petroglyphs were made intentionally by skilful artists, and that this activity was regulated and settled according to social planning, probably as well as their updating with new images. The shaman was considered to be the most experienced individual within the group; he or she would have been strong-will and politically powerful, probably forming part of a shaman family dynasty (Popov 1947; Prokofieva 1971). The sites with their long-lasting tradition of veneration and ritual activity would have allowed shamans to yield levels of physical energy for ceremonial use. This activity would have occurred many times and over a number of generations. This may explain the persistence and tolerance in making images in juxtapositions and even superimpositions at the same place. This perniciousness in maintaining of the myths in stone appears to have been a typical trait for the core sites.

What was the reason to have a satellite sites? Was it essential to switch from the core site to another less important one? Furthermore, was the relationship between core and satellite sites similar to, say, the functional relationship between the medieval Cathedral and surrounding chapels? The sites of Bolshaya, Malaya and Novaya Boyarskaya Pisanitsa may be examples of the metaphysically and physically transported ideas from core to peripheral sites (Fig. 8.3). The style and form of the central motifs from both site types are the same, although the Bolshaya Boyarskaya Pisanitsa (*pisanitsa* – is a local Siberian word for rock art sites, both paintings and petroglyphs) presents much more complicated narrative.

Bolshaya Boyarskaya Pisanitsa is an important engraved site with images located on a sub-vertical panel in the intra-montane valleys of the Boyarskiĭ Mountain ridge (the middle Yenisei rock art province). Depicted on this panel is a traditional calendar ceremony. The rock art panel measures 9.8 × 1.5 m and is covered with a plethora of patinated engravings that shows signs of deterioration. The panel has numerous images of dwellings shown from side-on; nomadic *jurts* and others made from timber (Fig. 8.4). Regional peculiarities are very definite and contribute greatly to the understanding of the architectural traditions. Although the materiality of rock art motifs is very important, the explanation of the entire composition appears to show the remnants of a settlement scene (probably unreal) involving its occupants involved in seasonal festivities. Rectangular motifs with extensions in their upper part, shown on the Bolshaya Boyarskaya petroglyphs, are, most likely, containers for the *koumiss* (a drink of Asian nomads made from fermented milk). The receptacle comprises a wooden or earthenware barrel and is probably a leather flask. On the Yakut *koumiss* holiday, the *koumiss* was poured into special ritual *choron*, a three-legged goblet. Food for those celebrating the holiday was evidently prepared in the large cauldron depicted on the rock surface, and from the small vessels they drank the *koumiss*.

In an elucidation of the semantic import and associations of petroglyphs, the data on seasonal holidays and rites connected with human and animal fertility-magic and the cult of the reproductive forces of nature are of particular significance. For

Fig. 8.3: Bolshaya Boyarskaya Pisanitsa (fragments). Upper Yenisei area (photo by E. Miklashevich)

instance, the Yakuts had two annual holidays (*ysyakha*), those of spring and of autumn. These were the '*Koumiss* holidays', since the centre of attraction for participants in the rite were the tubs of *koumiss* which symbolised wealth, abundance and prosperity.

Fig. 8.4: Malaya Boyarskaya Pisanitsa (fragments). Upper Yenisei area (tracing and photo by E. Devlet)

Koumiss was regarded by Yakuts as a drink of heavenly origin, sent down by the bright, heavenly deities who brought the *koumiss*-leaven to the earth.

Between the houses shown on the Bolshaya Bojarskaya petroglyphs are people standing with upraised arms, a ritualistic gesture which, it is generally agreed, signifies a prayer directed towards the heavens. In the upper part of the rock art panel is depicted a man who in one hand holds a bow shown with the bow-string and in the other hand, a staff. It could be supposed that this is a shaman, the bow and staff being his religious regalia (Devlet & Devlet 2005).

The Bolshaya Boyarskaya petroglyphs reflect complicated ideological notions. It may be assumed that the site was a primitive sanctuary where ritualised activity was related to seasonal holidays. The magic actions and ceremonies performed near the rocky frieze covered with petroglyphs were probably not individual, rather, a collective event. Prosperity and abundance or resources were besought not for the individual participant but for the whole group and shamanism was essential for maintaining the social well-being and cohesion of the group.

Nearby the Bolshaya Boyarskaya site are two further sites which portray a similar iconography, but these are more modest in their composition with the core site. Satellite sites include Malaya Boyarskaya and Novaya Boyarskaya rock art panels. Both sites have petroglyphs that share a similar style. Satellite sites clearly form part of the same sacral landscape, the iconography of rock art appears to be similar in style and construction but they were more or less smaller and simple copies of those from the core sites. Traditional mysteries begin to give shape to the major turning-points in the life cycle of both individuals and the community, creating a sense of harmony with the supreme forces which governed their world, thus strengthening bonds of unity between members of the community.

To Bond the Memory

In different traditions some rocks and stones may have become ritual objects, particularly those with unusual shapes, as well as those panels covered with rock art or inscriptions. The resistance of stone to disintegration and decay may have been a venerated attribute. Natural stones and cliffs of special shape (geoglyphs) were perceived as a sort of repository of some mystical power which made it valuable and endowed with an exclusive meaning. Unmovable in the generation's memory stones and rock outcrops was an antithesis to the temporality of human life. The sacred nature of stone's timely immunity to destruction was strengthened by the rock art images (Devlet 2001).

Being part of the landscape, the richness of the rock art imagery may be a reliable background and valuable source for understanding of landscape function and exploration. The approach to structure a landscape shows much flexibility; the emergence of satellite sites may coexist with the superimposition and juxtaposition activity. In certain regions there were preferred strategies to update sacral memory. Superimpositions and juxtapositions of rock art images often emerged at those surfaces that were central sacral narratives of the place. The most significant shamanist activity was held near cliffs using petroglyphs. Here, the rock at became a legacy of these ceremonies, as well as an indication of the mystical essence of the stone.

Superimpositions and juxtapositions often lack the intention to diminish rock art symbolism and decay the importance of the place. Was the act of juxtaposition evidence of religious tolerance or just an instrument of dialogs, communication and coexistence of successive generations? Superimposition quite often is interpreted as symbolical destruction and domination, may be from later communities or by local but exclusive social groups (for example, the Karakol burials from Altai) (Kubarev 1988). There are examples of ritual destruction of the sacral essence of the image, especially when new world-views were introduced by later communities (Fig. 8.5). They are valuable inferences determined by the evidence of long traditions that were involved in maintaining distinct ritual landscapes. One may see the evidence of renewed interest to the same shamanic landscape in the rock art site of Bichiktu-Boom in Russian Altai, where in the middle of the 20th century newly made images of shamans appeared. We know the exact period because the artist had dated one of the compositions (Fig. 8.6). It is important to keep in mind that it was not a period when neoshamanism flourished, as it did during the 1990s; on the contrary, it was during the preceding period when the cult of shamanism was persecuted by the State.

How a particular rock art site could maintain its importance or the reason to abandon such a site is wholly down to the physical evidence. In the recent past, though, anthropologists could interview participants and ask how spirits corresponded with a shaman. Archaeologically-speaking, certain sites may not yield enough evidence to reveal the potential mystical abilities. Only by being involved in ritual activity can the site keep its essence and significance. There are stories related to reverence of the

Fig. 8.5: Besov Nos (fragment), Onego Lake. North-West Region (photo by E. Girya)

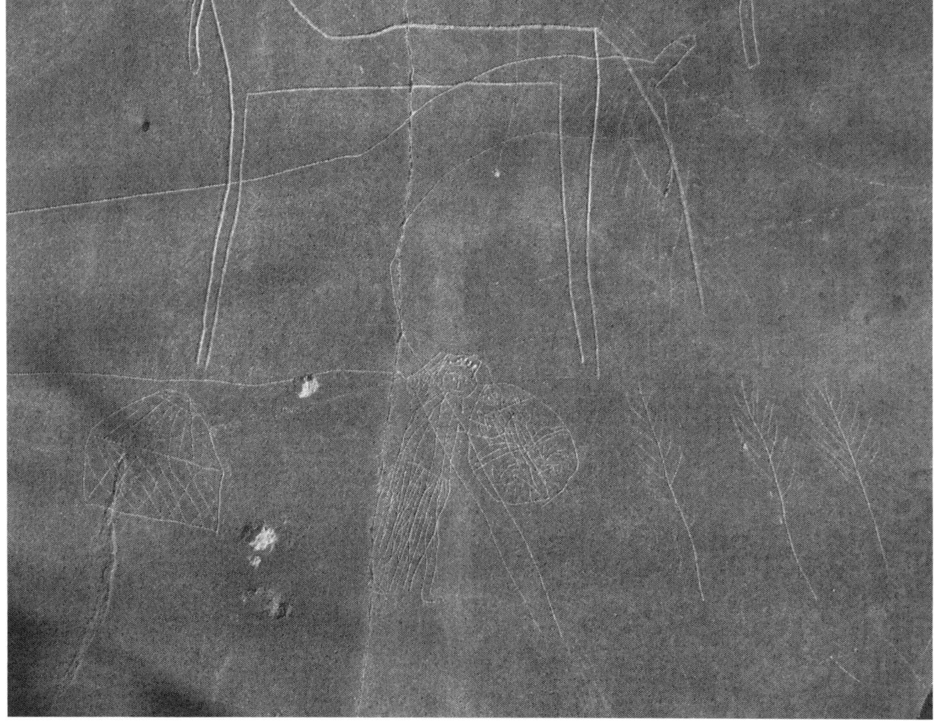

Fig. 8.6: Shaman with a drum and other recent graffiti. Bichiktu-Boom, Altai (photo by E. Devlet)

Getkan rock art site, which was recognised among the Evenk people as a repository of the animal-master. From the very ancient past this site was deemed important and, before the hunt for game, the hunter asked the spirit-master of the site for permission by bringing him offerings. If someone stole these donations, that would make the animal-master angry and leave the rock. Nowadays local people still try to ask for support in exchange for offerings but the cliff has lost its magic essence (Khlopin 1981). The evidence that new images may appear on the surface as indications of magic activity by a spirit contributes to tolerance for repainting and active involvement of juxtapositions and superimpositions at the same site. Were rock art sites with juxtaposed images considered to be a continued narrative, a long-term dialogue or any other kind of phenomenon? For many people the rocks and cliffs themselves became sacred objects, especially those which bore ancient images, or had legends attached to them. Cliffs could be worshipped as embodiments of real ancestors, as symbolic substitutes for mythical forefathers or protectors of the tribal communities, or as receptacles for the deities and various spirits, including spirits of ancestors and souls of living people. Those places, with the greatest foci for worship by a given ethnic group, are defined by ethnographers as the *habitats* or *zones* of activity of ancestors or spirits.

A particular feature of Siberian rock art sites are the remnants of ritual offerings brought to the cliffs which can be found in cracks and natural depressions in the rock. They may include both ancient and modern materials. Among the objects found are stone arrow-heads and other stone tools, shell cartridges, coins, buttons, cigarettes, matchboxes, etc. Unfortunately sacral landscapes generally lack directly-related documented archaeological evidence; however, the site of Kucherla-1, within the Altai region, is a rare exception. Kucherla-1 is one of the few known rock art sites with well-documented deposition, excavated and related to the rock art activity in the shelter. A fragment of decorated wall was found, along with stone arrow-heads, bone items, etc. The material gives ground to interpreting the site as an ancient sacral place; its importance in the landscape has continued and nowadays it is a typical sacral site used by local people. Metaphorically and (still) typical for the area, the site can easily be recognized because of the tree decorated with ribbons and strips of cloth (Fig. 8.7). At Kucherla-1 rock art images are known as superimpositions (Molodin & Efremova 2010).

Fig. 8.7: A tree with ribbons – typical sacral place for Altai (photo by E. Devlet)

In this context materials related to the understanding of a rock art surface, with all its natural physical features such as cracks, fissures, relief, intrusions, collectively as a landscape is important. A panel was intentionally considered as a mental landscape and particular cracks or natural relief features were deliberately used as a frame for the rock panel and as a means to organise the universe.

Mugur-Sargol is a core site at the Upper Yenisei rock art province (Devlet 1980). This Bronze Age sanctuary was central in the area, although the Aldi-Mozaga rock art site, as well as other numerous rock art sites, formed the sacral landscape of the area (Devlet 1997; 1998). At Mugur-Sargol there are a number of panels, with the central one densely covered with petroglyphs. This concentration demonstrates the idea of a three-levelled universe that was also typical of a shamanic world-view (Devlet 1980). The whole panel is divided by fissures into three horizontal zones, the natural frames separating groups of petroglyphs with probable special meaning.

On the upper section of the rock panel, facing skywards, are hollow dots which possibly symbolise celestial bodies, including the depiction of a constellation, presumably Orion. The highest celestial sphere inhabited by the celestials themselves was probably depicted. At the top of the panel, in a deep groove, there was an image depicting a woman in childbirth; perhaps the figure was metaphorically representing the people and their mythical ancestors.

On the upper part of the main inclined surface are numerous mysterious creatures; they are represented by human faces (masks) which are several times larger than the human figures engraved on the surface (Fig. 8.8). The supreme deity is recognisable by its size – it is the largest of the mask-images not only in the altar complex but in the place as a whole.

It would appear that an ancient artist has chosen the surface with a natural projection, so that the nose of the mask protrudes, causing the image to appear as in bas-relief. The second largest mask-image, which bears a malicious grin, possesses a most terrible appearance. It is possible that these two images reflect the myth of the two demiurges, a god and the devil; a concept widespread among followers of Asian shamans (Devlet 1997).

In the central area of the rock surface is shown a settlement, in which houses connected to cattle-fences are depicted from above. In the middle of this area of the surface are strange zoomorphic creatures which possess legs that grow broader from the top down. The largest of these fantastic figures, its head in three tiers, has an anthropomorphic person astride its back.

In the lower part of the panel can be seen pictures of life among mortals – people conducting domestic chores such as animals on a lead, a hunter-archer shooting a goat surrounded by hounds; a man in a wide-brimmed hat squatting with legs wide apart; a deer pursued by an old hunchback of a man, clad in a long garment and with footwear resembling high fur or felt boots, supporting himself all the while on a staff.

The images on the main panel can probably be regarded as a reflection of that complex of ideas offering an explanation of the structure of the universe. Inhabiting

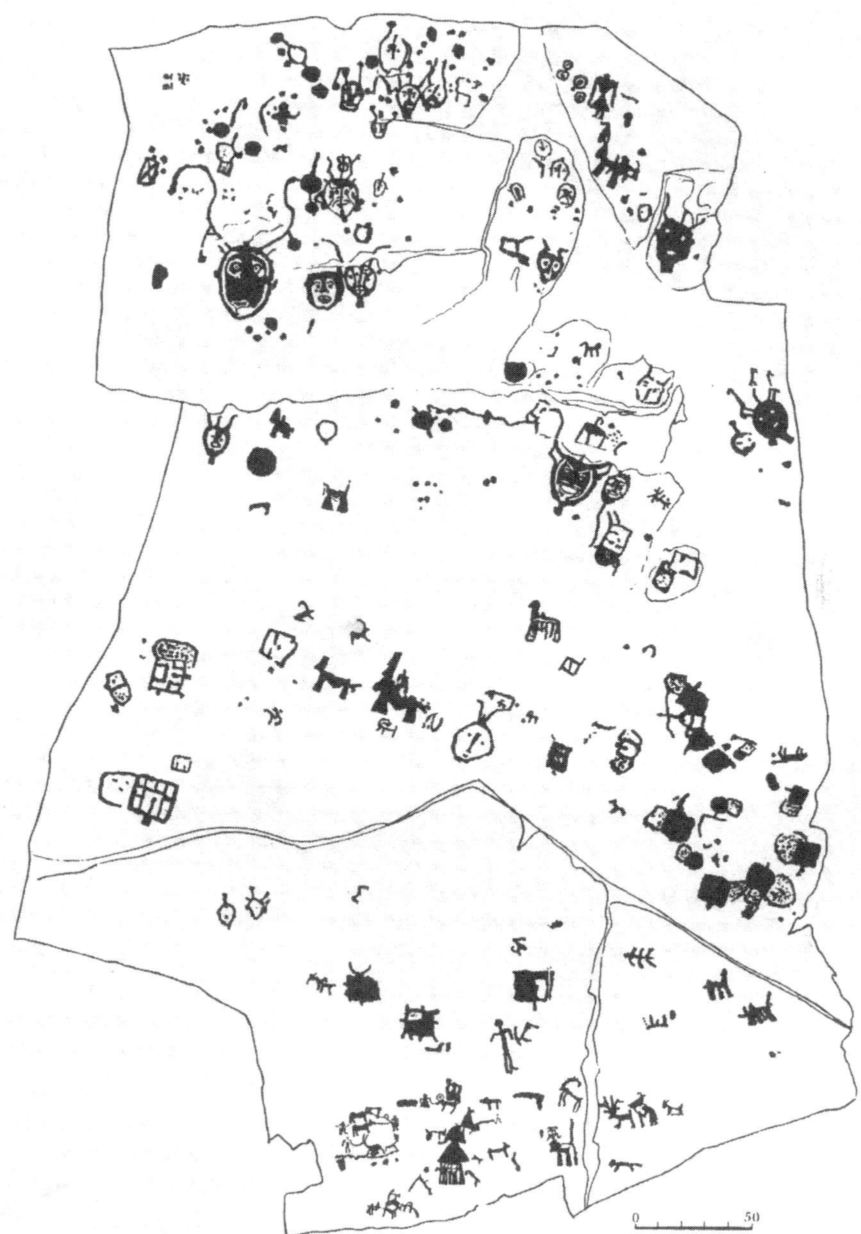

Fig. 8.8: Main panel of the Mugur-Sargol rock art site. Upper Yenisei area (tracing by M. Devlet, 1980)

the top in the upper or celestial world are ancestor spirits; whilst below this is the middle or earthly world; and below that again is the supposed underworld or lower world, which was not usually depicted.

One further interpretation could be offered, namely that the division of the main panel into zones signifies the division of the 'upper world' which is divided into separate spheres; the dwellings representing the homes of the celestial beings, while the small figures engaged in human activity, which are depicted in the lower section of the panel, are the inhabitants of the celestial realm.

Attractive Landscapes

There were obviously local cultural preferences, in particular, rock art motifs. Within this assemblage are images of crucial importance for understanding of the sacral landscapes. Sites with a prevailing concentration of human faces are of primary significance for interpretation of site function.

During the archaic period (*c*. 4000 to 2000 BCE), in traditional society, the major focus of worship appears to have been the ancestors, both in physical form and mythical (Tokarev 1990). The worship of ancestors, upholding in public perception the idea of continuity in blood relationship, consolidated the tribal community and guaranteed both the continuity of tradition and the stability of the primitive society. A deceased kinsman acquired the status of ancestor and became the object of worship. Various anthropomorphic images were being created by primitive communities in order to maintain their relationship with the ancestors, who were regarded as guarantors of the tribe's continuing existence and success.

In the rock art repertoire of the ancient population of northern and central Asia, human faces became quite widespread; however, there are many local variants, for example the heart-shaped masks sometimes with antenna-like engraved lines on top of the head and sometimes with a radiating halo of rays round the head. On petroglyphs of the southern taiga and forest-steppe regions, extending from the Urals to the lower reaches of the Amur River, there are faces of a specific heart-shaped form. Rock art faces with the so-called antenna are present further to the south, in the zone of steppes and foothills. These figures possess a line which extends upward from the crown of the head and ends in a small circle or dot. The antenna is often combined with a variety of horned headgear. These particular images are found at the Mugur-Sargol rock art site (Fig. 8.8). Faces with antennae often have a handle under the chin, in a form of a short line and are obviously masks with a handle by which participants would use to hold the mask in front of their faces.

Rock art images of sun-faced creatures are found throughout the very wide-ranging steppe and foothill territories of the Asian continent. A series of such figures was discovered in the Altai. For the most part they are dated to the Neolithic and Bronze Ages.

The more complicated head-gear of the mask-images, together with an intensive painting/tattoo of the face may be taken as an indication of a social (and political) hierarchy. The crucial importance of the core sites for understanding of the shamanic landscape cannot be exaggerated, and sites with carved masks (human-faces) are of especial importance in sacral landscapes.

Fig. 8.9: Sikachi-Alyan rock art site. Far East Region. 1–2: mask-images (photo by I. Georgievsky); 3: figure of elk in X-ray style (orthophoto by A. Pakhunov)

Sikachi-Alyan is an outstanding rock art site known for its intrinsic character, cultural context and natural surroundings. The site is located on the right bank of the Amur River (see descriptive texts by Okladnikov 1971; Devlet 2008; 2012; 2015; Laskin 2007; Devlet & Laskin 2015). Sikachi-Alyan petroglyphs are dated to the later prehistoric period, in particular, to the Early Iron Age. An artistic tradition of ornamentation exists and dominates the Amur-Ussuri region rock art style with a large number of decorative, elaborated elements such as spirals, concentric circles and recognisable ornaments. This imagery has been used as an essential indicator for some chronological periods. Human faces (mask-images) prevail; these number (so far) 145 human faces, that is about 30% of all the images at the site. They are abstract, conventionalised images of human faces, yet each possesses an individual, characteristic shape. Outlines of the mask-images are diverse with oval, round, heart-shaped, even trapezoidal or square shapes being used (Fig. 8.9, 1–2).

Anthropomorphic figures drawn in a conventionalised manner are extremely rare and not typical for the art of the Amur-Ussuri region. Nevertheless there is a small assemblage that is located on the most important boulders with the most interesting examples being depicted in an X-ray style. Zoomorphic figures in X-ray style are depicted in static postures. Two images of elk are noteworthy, with their bodies being decorated with spirals and curls (Fig. 8.9, 3). The central and most important boulder has a composition on the plane surface and on the edges and side junctions. At the junction of certain surfaces there are X-ray anthropomorphs and a simple mask and circles (Fig. 8.10). This particular boulder is still considered by the local population to be the main place for performing ritual.

Images with spirals and vertical curl decorations are quite numerous throughout Asian rock art. The interpretation may be seen in tradition of cutting or painting of solar symbols on the bodies of a special animal (Devlet & Devlet 2005). Spirals, circles, curls on the corps of a solar animal signify its divine status, indicating that the animal belongs to the Upper World (Devlet & Devlet 2005). An important material for interpretation of X-ray anthropomorphic images may be found in the Siberian ethnographic records that involve the shamanic view on the first 'out-of-body' experience and obtaining the gift of shamanism (Ivanov 1954). A shaman had to pass an initiation in order to obtain his capacity to receive visions from spirits. The ceremony would involve the shaman receiving assistance from his spirits-helpers. Being the mediator between the world of the living and the world of dead, the shaman had to be marked by supernatural powers and was subjected to special rituals representing mystic death and rebirth. The common belief was that shaman's supernatural powers and abilities are concentrated in a bone of his skeleton. One of the bones in his body was considered as being special. The bone was a sign of his great vocation, as the most resistant parts of his body and material embodiment of his high mission. In different parts of the world, this idea resulted in the similar anthropomorphic images in X-ray style.

Fig. 8.10: Sikachi-Alyan rock art site. Far East Region. X-ray anthropomorphic figure (photo by A. Pakhunov)

The most detailed description of body dismemberment as a part of shaman's initiation survived among Yakuts (Ksenofontov 1930). The idea is that the mystical death touches only the body, but not the shaman's soul. The shaman sees and feels all the ordeals he or she had to encounter. At the same time, the spirits would have been training his soul to endure the ordeals. Then the shaman awakens, as though he were a sleeping man. The (metaphysical) dismemberment of the shaman's body may be interpreted not only as a terrible torment, but could be overcome only by a worthy death. From death came rebirth and a new role; however, the old body, metaphysically, would have become a sacrifice to spirits. The shaman thus gains the experience of death as he or she descends to the world below (in his ritual death and the dismemberment of a shaman's body) which signifies his acquaintance with the initial chaos death brings. It was an essential step that should have been passed in order to rid oneself of the mundane, profane essence of daily life and to be reborn, not only into new role but also for a new life. Within the rock art assemblage, anthropomorphic figures in the X-ray style could represent the intermediate condition between death and rebirth, a concept which later persisted in the iconography associated with shaman costume design (Prokofieva 1971). The central position of X-ray anthropomorphic and zoomorphic images confirms the special importance of the core site Sikachi-Alyan of the far eastern shamanic landscape.

Some explanation of the ongoing veneration of the rock art landscape in current ritual practices comes from traditional cultures of Russia's far eastern provinces. In spite of attempts to find other rock art sites, petroglyphs in Chukotka are still known only as the rock outcrops of the Pegtymel River – the major site is at Kaikuul Bluff. Currently, there are about 1700 known figures from almost 300 rock art panels that probably date from the 1st millennia AD (for the Western Chukotka, where the rock art site is located there are no reliable chronological sequences of cultures, while the Beringia got more archaeological attention: Friesen & Mason 2016). Over hundreds of years, many generations visited Kaikuul Bluff, creating petroglyphs on rock outcrops and thus marking the sacred nature of outcropping (Fig. 8.11). It is disputed whether this rock art activity was regulated and connected with some rituals (Dikov 1999). In my experience, and based on four expeditions to this remote site, the landscape is annually visited in late August to early September by indigenous people coming from various coastal areas to celebrate the New Year (fixed by lunar calendar). Elders would spend between 8 and 10 days travelling by foot from the coastal area in order to stay in the vicinity of the Kaikuul Blaff for seasonal events. Distance in traditional cultures is measured by the need to transport people and commodities between points within a landscape; time is not an issue. There are numerous ethnographic observations that record seasonal activity of northern peoples and include long-distance annual travel (Bogoras 1904–9; 1909). For example, seasonal hunting for wild reindeer at the river crossing which occurs once a year at the same place is mentioned by Bogoras, who refers to the season movement of that Yukagir people (Bogoras 1904–9, 133–134). Interestingly, the same ethnic group appears to have used the wild narcotic-inducing mushroom fly-agaric. The fly-agaric would have assisted in the effectiveness of people moving across harsh and inhospitable landscapes.[2]

Fig. 8.11: Pegtymel. Chukotka (photo by I. Georgievsky)

Fig. 8.12: Pegtymel. One of the central panels with fly-agaric female figures (photo by I. Georgievsky)

Though the essence of the ritualised landscape are the rock art motifs associated with anthropomorphic fly-agaric female creatures. These emulate from the local mythology that is associated with shamanic activity and possible altered state of consciousness (ASC) inducement by intoxication. These images are represented as either standalone or as part of a composition. The anthropomorphic figures are usually full-faced figure with a mushroom-shaped headdress (Fig. 8.12). The head was depicted in a form of a mushroom-cup which appears to have been placed over the head. The feet of figures were turned inside and even jointed in such a way to represent a mushroom stalk. These anthropomorphic figures are probably female, deduced from their coats (fur *kerker-coveralls*) and hanging braids or pendants. These figures were identified as representations of a mythological anthropomorphic fly-agaric mushroom that is known within the oral storey telling record among Chukchi and some other northern peoples. Usually they are described as male figures although Jochelson (1908) referred to female fly-agaric as well. Jochelson notes that in the Chukchi description, the transformation of inanimate objects into human beings as 'Eme'mquit and his wives put on wide-brimmed, spotted hats, resembling fly-agaric, and turned into those poisonous fungi' (Jochelson 1908, 17).

The evidence of fly-agaric consumption in the area is well-documented (e.g. Bogoras 1907). Bogoras provides various stories regarding the essence of fly-agaric. These figures are not spirits but are a 'special tribe' called *ya'řnra-va'rat*. The results of fly-agaric ingestion are visual hallucinations. The mushroom-eaters would be transported by a fly-agaric *creature* into another world where they were shown around by the mushrooms. Here, they would be stimulated by the hallucinogen and ignite into uncontrollable activity. The spirits of fly-agaric would have had an outward appearance similar to that of actual mushrooms. It would be necessary for the fly-agaric eater to imitate them. For example, I saw one man suddenly snatch a small narrow bag and pull it over his head, trying to break through the bottom. He was evidently imitating the mushroom when it bursts forth from the ground. Another walked around with his neck drawn in, and assured everyone that he had no head. He would bend his knees and move very quickly, swinging his arms violently about; clearly both examples were in varying states of Altered State of Consciousness (ASC). The poises of each man was, arguably, an imitation of the spirits of the fly-agaric, who are supposed to have no necks or legs, but stout cylindrical bodies which move about swiftly. The spirits associated with fly-agaric are fond of playing practical jokes on men who are under their influence of trance-induced hallucinogens. They begin with asking for homage either for themselves or for surrounding objects, such as the surrounds hills, the river or the moon, etc. (Bogoras 1904–9, 206).

To demonstrate the power of the fly-agaric and the intoxication of shamans, Bogoras published a sketch made by a person following consumption (Fig. 8.13, 2). Bogoras testifies that the toxins form fly-agaric are strong and powerful. According to ethnographic accounts, the hallucinogens may assist in crossing (metaphysical) boundaries between the worlds of the living and the dead. More importantly, as the narcotic wears off, the shaman is *allowed* to return. However, dependent on the mushroom dosage, the return journey can either be passive or aggressive. This specie of mushroom grows through the heart of a stone and breaks it into minute fragments. Mushrooms appear to intoxicate men in certain ways, somewhat related to the shape of the mushroom; for example, a man recalls only having one hand and one foot whilst in ASC; another had a shapeless body. According to ethnographic records, if a shaman has eaten just one mushroom, then he will see one mushroom-man; if he has eaten two or three, he will see a corresponding number of mushroom-men. They will grasp him under his arms, and lead him through the set of different worlds, showing him real things, and deluding him with many unreal apparitions. The pathways in which they follow are very intricate and stimulating; for example, they delight in visiting the places where the dead live (Bogoras 1907, 282).

In the film *Pegtymel* produced in 2000 by Andrei Golovnev the central story was told by a native elder named Natalko. He was an annual visitor to the landscape around Kaikuul Bluff camp. Natalko would get angry of those people who used fly-agaric. Yuri Symchenko recorded use of fly-agaric for communicating with the dead relatives among Chukchi, stating:

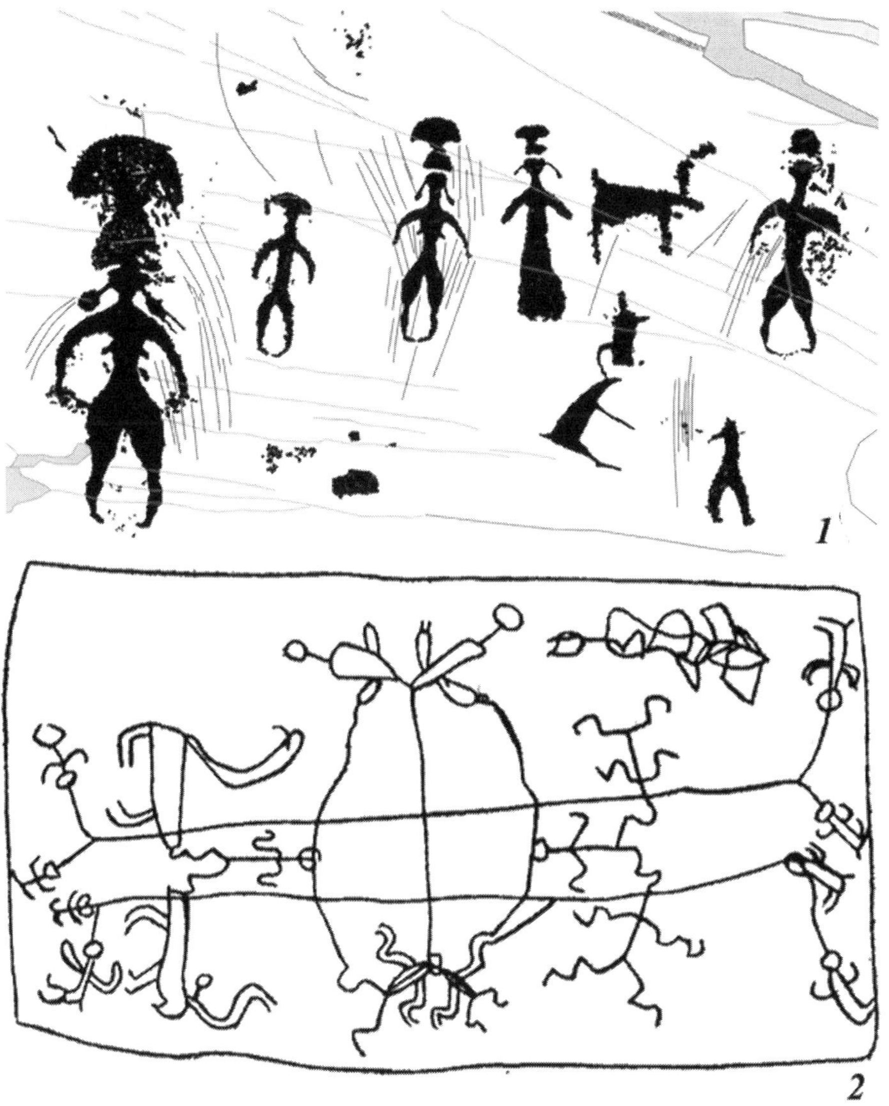

Fig. 8.13: 1. Female fly-agaric figures, intentionally covered by scratches (Pegtymel, Chukotka, by E. G. Devlet); 2. Chukchee sketch illustrating the paths followed by mushroom-men (Bogoras1907, 282, fig. 200)

> ... a fly agaric would ask you in a sleep: Eh, where shall we go? Where shall I drag you? And it will always listen to you. Then you tell him: take me to my father ... It would know everything himself. Would know where your father would be and would drag you along the road to the dead people. (Symchenko 1993, 50–52)

Symchenko was a very experienced ethnographer working among Chukchi and even tried fly-agaric himself with the strong effect of poisoning that is typical for a person unaccustomed to their use. He described that the ritual of mushroom-consumption

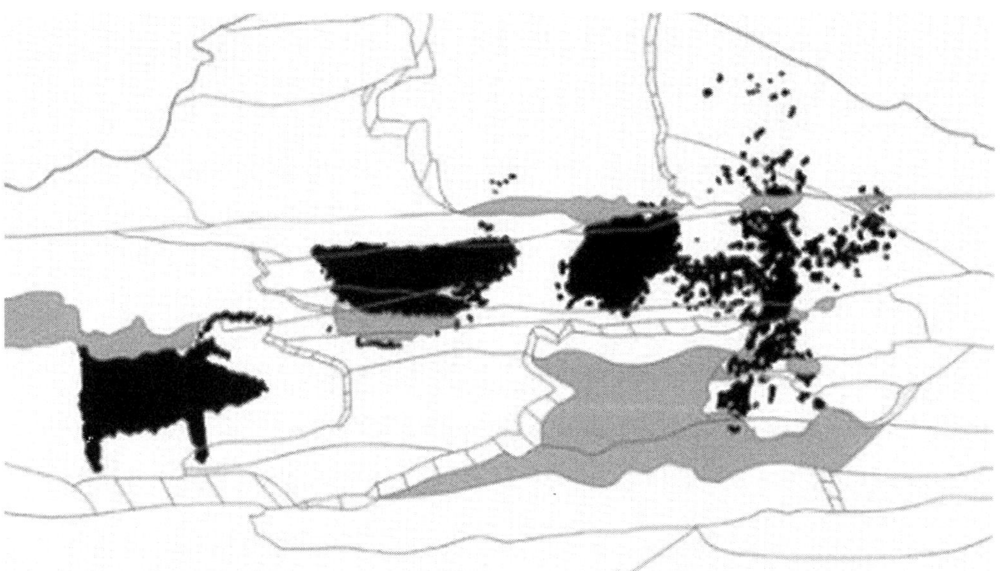

Fig. 8.14: Shaman with a drum, Pegtymel, Chukotka (image by E. Devlet)

was free for ordinary people and was not limited only to specialised shamanic practice. He describes a fly-agaric as a 'shaman for everyone', meaning anyone may obtain it to gain some visions.

A remarkable detail is the scratching-over of the central most attractive anthropomorphic fly-agaric figures (Fig. 8.13, 1). The position of the panels with mythological anthropomorphic fly agaric figures and the detailed skilful compositions made it possible to assume that on the Kaikuul Bluff they were related to the ritual practices, part of which was the use of fly-agaric (Devlet 2008, 120–137). A new discovery – a schematic image of an anthropomorphic figure with a drum – was yet further evidence of possible shamanistic traditions related to Pegtymel rock art (Fig. 8.14).

The Pegtymel petroglyphs also raised a question about whether every rock art site could be perceived as a public place allowing people to witness the art, or whether they represented open air sanctuaries (sacral places) always implied public access of the site and the images it hid. The study demonstrated that some panels with rock art were apparently intentionally made accessible for large groups of people and visible from several convenient points. A unique scene was represented on the lateral face of a massive stone lying on the bank. In addition to the numerous deer figures the central place was occupied by a hunting figure – a special deer that was marked with a symbolic circle with a point in the centre (Fig. 8.15). This was the only specially-marked animal figure among the hundreds of Pegtymel reindeer images. In many northern cultures an unusually coloured deer was dedicated to the gods. The stone, on the lateral face of which an ancient artist pecked this group, in all probability

Fig. 8.15: Panel with a figure of 'solar' reindeer, Pegtymel, Chukotka (photo by E. Devlet)

stood out for its unusual hourglass-shape, which could make it attractive as a kind of a natural altar. The shamanic practice to choose an animal of unusual colour or spotted is still known in indigenous traditions in Northern Asia.

Notes

1 As a result of the efforts of several generations of researchers throughout our country, many hundreds of rock art sites have been discovered and investigated. Specially singled-out have been local centres of rock art which consist of areas characterised by petroglyphs and paintings of a particular type. At these sites it is believed that the art reflects a world-view and aesthetic ideals of the ancient population of these regions. Each of these areas of rock art is unique and embodies local environment and related adaptive strategies, history of the region, ethno-cultural traditions and other collective experiences. The main enclaves of rock art comprise local rock art traditions (Fig. 8.2). In the western part of Russia there is a province where a large corpus of rock art exists (i.e. Karelia, White Sea and Kola Peninsula) as in the Caucasus region in the south. Special areas where painted images are located are typical for the Urals Mountains, which separate Europe from Asia. In the Arctic regions of Asia, specific areas of rock art are found in the tundra zone, in particular, in the area known as Chukotka. At the zone of the Siberian taiga, petroglyphs and paintings are very diverse and split into different groups of rock art. The art is huge both in size and in its chronological range, extending from the Stone Age to modern times. Generally, rock art areas are found towards the basins of the great Siberian rivers. In eastern Siberia rock is distributed liberally along the rivers Lena, Angara, Aldan and Olekma and also on the shores of Lake Baikal. Here the image of the elk – the master of taiga –dominates.

Further south, in the mountain-steppe and forest-steppe zones, concentrations of rock art sites can be identified in the far eastern part of the basins of the Amur and Ussuri rivers, in the Trans-Baikal steppe and north-east Mongolia. Of particular interest are the Great Steppe zone and mountain-steppe areas of Central Asia and the adjacent territories, including west and north-west Mongolia and Tuva. A special area of rock art lies on the boundary dividing these two vast territories, the taiga and forest-steppe zone of northern Asia on the one hand and central Asia, which includes petroglyphs of the middle Yenisei and the Tom' River basins and the Altai Mountains. Needless to say, in these areas where rock art is found the zones of cultural influence was fluid, even during historic times.

2 Russian scholar Krasheninnikov, who travelled to Kamchatka in the early 18th century, reported that a soldier consumed a reasonable portion of fly-agaric before setting out on a march and went a great part of the way without fatigue (Krasheninnikov 1755, 110).

References

Bogoras, W. 1904–9. The Chukchee. Material culture. In F. Boas (ed.) *Jesup North Pacific Expedition* 7(1). Memoirs of the American Museum of Natural History 11. Leiden: E.J. Brill/G.E. Stegert, 1–276.

Bogoras, W., 1907. The Chukchee. Religion. In F. Boas (ed). *Jesup North Pacific Expedition* 7(2). Memoirs of the American Museum of Natural History 11. Leiden: E.J. Brill/G.E. Stegert, 277–536.

Bogoras, W. 1909. The Chukchee. Social Organisation. In F. Boas (ed.) *Jesup North Pacific Expedition* 7(1). Memoirs of the American Museum of Natural History 11. Leiden: E.J. Brill/G.E. Stegert, 537–733.

Devlet, M. A. 1980. *Petroglify Mugur-Sargola*. Moscow: Nauka.

Devlet, M. A. 1997. Ancient sanctuaries in Tuva and the origin of shamanism. In J. Van Alpen (ed.) *Spellbound by the Shaman. Shamanism in Tuva*. Antwerp: Continental printing, Deurne, 37–51.

Devlet, M. A. 1998. *Petroglify na dnie Sayanskogo moria (gora Aldy-Mozaga)*. Moscow: Pamyatniki istoricheskoy mysli.

Devlet, E. G. 2000. X-ray style anthropomorphic rock art images and the mythological subject of obtaining the gift of shamanizing. *Archaeology, Ethnology and Anthropology of Eurasia* 2, 88–95.

Devlet, E. G. 2001. Rock art and the material culture of Siberian and Central Asian shamanism. In N. Price (ed.) *The Archaeology of Shamanism*. London: Routledge, 43–55.

Devlet E. G. 2008. Rock art studies in northern Russia and the Far East, 2000–2004. In P. Bahn, N. Franklin & M. Strecker (eds) *Rock Art Studies. News of the World 3*. Oxford: Oxbow Books, 120–137.

Devlet, E. G. 2012. Rock art studies in northern Russia and the Far East. In P. Bahn, N. Franklin & M. Strecker (eds), *Rock Art Studies. News of the World 4*. Oxford: Oxbow Books, 124–148.

Devlet E. G. 2015. Rock art from the Russian Far East: The Sikachi-Alyan tentative World Heritage Site. In N. Sanz (ed.) *Human Origin Sites and the World Heritage Convention in Eurasia*. World Heritage Series. 41(4/1). Paris: UNESCO, 128–141.Devlet, E. G. & Devlet, M. A. 2005. *Myths in Stone: World of Rock Art in Russia*. Moscow: Institute of Archaeology of the Russian Academy of Sciences.

Devlet, E. G. & Laskin, A. R. 2015. Petroglyphs of Khabarovsk territory: the impact of the 2013 Amur and Ussuri flooding. *Archaeology, Ethnology and Anthropology of Eurasia* 43(4), 94–105.

Dikov, N. N. 1999. *Mysteries in the Rocks of Ancient Chukotka (Petroglyphs of Pegtymel')*. Translated by R. L. Bland. Anchorage AK: U.S. Department of the Interior, National Park Service, Shared Beringian Heritage Program.

Direnkova, N. P. 1930. Poluchenie shamanskogo dara po vozreniam turetzkih plemen. *Sbornik muzeia antropologii y etnographii* AN SSSR 9. Leningrad: Nauka, 267–291.

Friesen, T. M. & Mason, O. K. 2016. *The Oxford Handbook of the Prehistoric Arctic*. New York: Oxford University Press.

Ivanov, S. V. 1954. *Materialy po isobrazitelnomu iskusstvu narodov Sibiry XIX - nachala XX v*. Moscow–Leningrad: Izdatelstvo AN.

Ivanov, S. V. 1979. *Skulptura altaitsev, khakasov i sibirskikh tatar (VIII – pervaja chetvert XX v.).* Leningrad: Nauka.
Jochelson W. 1908. The Koryaks, Part I. Religion and myths, Part II. Material culture and social organization. In *The Eskimo of Siberia; Publications of the Jesup North Pacific Expedition* 7(2). Leiden, New York: E.J. Brill, G.E. Stegert. 842 p.
Khlopin I. N. 1981 Obraz byka u pervobythykh zemledeltsev Sredney Asii. In *Drevnii Vostok i mirovaya kultura.* Moscow: Nauka, 26–31.
Krasheninnikov, S. P. 1755. *Opisanie zemli Kamchatki 2(3,4).* Saint Petersburg: Imperatorskaya Akademia Nauk.
Ksenofontov, G. V. 1930. *Legendi i rasskazi o shamanakh u yakutov, buriat i tungusov.* Moscow: Bezbozhnik.
Kubarev, V. D. 1988. *Drevniye rospisi Karakola.* Novosibirsk: Nauka.
Kubarev, V. D. & Jacobson, E. 1996. *Répertoire des Pétroglyphes d'Asie centrale. Sibérie du Sud 3: Kalbak-Tash I (République de l'Altaï).* V.3. Mémoires de la Mission Archéologique Française en Asie centrale. Paris: De Boccard.
Laskin, A. R. 2007. The rock art of Sikachi-Alyan: Future study and preservation. *Archaeology, Ethnology and Anthropology of Eurasia* 30(2), 136–142.
Nash, G. H. & Chippindale, C. (eds). 2002. *European Landscapes of Rock-Art.* London: Routledge.
Mikhailov, T. M. 1987. *Buriatskiy shamanism: istoria, struktura i sotsial'nie funktzii.* Novosibirsk: Nauka.
Molodin, V. I. & Efremova, N. S. 2010. *Grot Kuilu – kultovyi kompleks na reke Kucherle (Gorny Altai).* Novosibirsk: Izdatelstvo Instituta archeologii i etnografii SO RAN.
Okladnikov, A. P. 1971. *Petroglify Niznego Amura.* Leningrad: Nauka.
Okladnikov, A. P. 1974. *Petrogligy Baikala – pamiatniki drevney kul'tury narodov Sibiri.* Novosibirsk: Nauka.
Okladnikov, A. P. & Martynov, A. I. 1972. *Sokrovisha Tomsikh pisanits.* Moscow: Iskusstvo.
Okladnikov, A. P. & Mazin, A. I. 1976. *Pisanitsi reki Olekmy i Verkhnego Priamurya.* Novosibirsk: Nauka.
Popov, A. A. 1947. *Polutchenie shamanskogo dara u viliuiskikh tatar.* Moscow-Leningrad: Izdatelstvo AN.
Prokofieva, E. D. 1971. Shamanskie costumy narodov Sibiri. *Religioznye predstavlenia i obriady narodov Sibiry XIX – nachale XX v. Sbornik Muzeya archeologii i ethnographii AN SSSR* 27. Leningrad: Nauka, 5–112.
Symchenko, Y. B. 1993. Obichnaya shamanskaya zhizn'. Ethnographicheskiye ocherky. *Rossiyskiy ethnograph* 7. Moscow: Center prikladnoy etnographii IAEA RAN.
Tokarev, S. A. 1990. *Rannie formi religii.* Moscow: Nauka.

Chapter 9

Shamans' Landscapes: note sur la psychologie du shaman pre et protohistorique plus particulièrement en Eurasie

Michel Louis Séfériadès

Abstract *The essential aim of this paper is related to the shaman's psychology surrounded by his proper landscape, more especially in Eurasia, the Balkan area during Prehistoric and Proto-historic times. My purpose here is to try to put in evidence – from an anthropological and also archaeological point of view – the way of thinking of a shaman during the earliest times. For example, the case of levitation and its consequences is debated here through the deep complexity of a long exchange between nature and culture.*

Introduction

La psychologie propre au shaman et le rapport nature-culture qui en découle, teinté sur un fond de paysages multiples mais très différents, sont au centre de notre contribution à cet ouvrage. Vie et mort du shaman sibérien sinon amazonien dans son environnement comme plus particulièrement du shaman protohistorique balkanique sur un passé préhistorique occidental, à l'échelle du temps, à peine plus ancien.

Les témoignages archéologiques, à regarder de plus près, foisonnent ou tout au contraire sont rares au regard de l'interprétation et de l'analyse qu'on en fait des vestiges archéologiques (préhistoire et protohistoire): art des grottes paléolithiques d'Europe occidentale, sanctuaires comme celui de Parta dans le Banat au Néolithique (Lazarovici *et al.* 2001), bucranes (Séfériadès 2005) «proto-écritures» (tablette de Tartaria, disque de Karanovo ou fusaïole de Dikili Tash) à l'Enéolithique, obsession pour un coquillage (spondyle) qui de l'Egée et de l'Adriatique atteint la Manche et la Mer du Nord (Séfériadès 1995a; 1995b; 1995–96; 2000; 2009; 2010; 2011; 2013) «trésors cachés» d'Omurtag, Csoka-Kremenjak, Ariusd ou Carbuna (Banner 1960; Dergachev 1998; Gaydarska *et al.* 2004; Sztancsuj dans Dumitroaia *et al.* 2005), figurines humaines et zoomorphes au Néolithique et à l'Enéolithique ou stèles anthropomorphes au début de l'Age du Bronze (Séfériadès 1985), pétroglyphes des pays scandinaves à l'Angara et jusqu'en Chine (Séfériadès 2002), champignons hallucinogènes de la culture néo-énéolithique de Vinca, mythes liés à l'ours (Paproth 1976), shamans dansant ou en extase néolithiques de Thessalie ou de la Tisza (Theocharis 1973) cannibalisme rituel à Bolgrad en Bessarabie (Dambricourt Malassé *et al.* 2010) et ailleurs etc. La liste peut sembler hétéroclite, mais il n'en est rien: il suffit de nous interroger, de tenter de reconnaître, de choisir et de classer dans une documentation à nos yeux à la fois pauvre ici et conséquente ailleurs. Parvenue à ce stade, l'hétérogénéité se transforme en ordre.

La psychologie liée au shaman trouve ici – hypothèses de recherches – entièrement sa place et particulièrement la plus ancienne en l'absence d'écritures proprement dites et de traditions orales. Shaman (homme ou femme) ancien et récent, la continuité ne fait aucun doute. Continuité ininterrompue des états de conscience d'*Homo sapiens sapiens* en situation, depuis la nuit des temps et que les recherches à la fois archéologiques sur le terrain et ethnographiques accumulées, anciennes et récentes, tendent de plus en plus à rendre compte.

Sur les bases des documents actuels, on peut proposer un certain nombre d'hypothèses sur la psychologie (voire la psychopathologie du shaman) liée à la transe et /ou à l'hypnose et même une approche psychanalytique du shaman depuis la préhistoire – en dépit toujours de l'absence de textes, de traditions orales, de récits ethnographiques divers – et cela jusqu'aux temps modernes.

L'approche du shamanisme en tant que religion «sans âge» est multiple voire infinie. Le shaman appartient à une culture, à des centaines sinon à des milliers de cultures qui depuis des temps immémoriaux se succèdent partout dans le monde. La complexité est d'autant plus grande que la culture est indissociablement liée à l'environnement, à des écosystèmes, des biotopes et niches écologiques, en un mot, à des paysages; la toundra sibérienne n'est pas la steppe mongole et les plaines nord-américaines ne sont pas l'Amazonie. En un mot encore, l'Eurasie n'est pas le continent africain ni le continent américain ni l'immensité de l'Océan Pacifique dans une grande transversale (Nouvelle-Guinée, aborigènes australiens, peuples contemporains de la Nouvelle-Calédonie et jusqu'à l'Ile de Pâques).

Ainsi, faut-il se limiter, ici, à quelques exemples pris parmi d'autres du comportement du shaman, de son action sur le monde qui l'entoure, humain comme naturel. De fait, le couple nature-culture ou inversement, dans une dialectique dynamique joue à fond.

Insistons une fois encore: on s'interrogera ici, uniquement sur la psychologie voire la psychopathologie (sous l'angle en filigrane de la psychanalyse) du shaman pré et protohistorique. Il est toutefois extrêmement difficile de tenter de révéler «les limites de l'opposition entre le fonctionnement normal et le fonctionnement pathologique» et les raisons «des modifications de la conscience et du comportement» (J. de Verbizier dans Michaux 1995). C'est avant tout la transe qui - comme semble en témoigner les rares documents archéologiques les plus anciens – retiendra notre attention. Celle-ci peut être définie comme «un état de conscience modifié» (Michaux 1995).

Bras baissés, bras levés, shaman dansant

Du temps de la préhistoire, on peut identifier comme étant celles de shamans la plupart des rares représentations humaines associées à un bestiaire omniprésent dans «l'art des cavernes». A titre d'exemples: le personnage à «ramures de cervidé» et le «sorcier et animaux hybrides» des Trois Frères (Fig. 9.1a et b), le «personnage cornu» du Gabillou (Fig. 9.2) celui «au bras levé» de Hornos de la Pena (Fig. 9.3), l'homme de Péchialet (Fig. 9.4) et celui associé à un mammouth de Cougnac (Fig. 9.5) ou encore le «personnage ithyphallique» du Portel. Enfin le «thème de l'homme et du bison» comme à Roc-de-Sers, Lascaux (Fig. 9.6), Laugerie-Basse (Fig. 9.7) ou Villars (Fig. 9.8) (Breuil 1952; Leroi-Gourhan 1965; 1992).

Notons, en digression, qu'une possible représentation de shaman (shamane), répétée une seconde fois, date du Gravettien. Il s'agit de la dite Vénus de Predmost (Moravie), gravée sur une défense de mammouth (Fig. 9.9) (Iakovleva dans Otte 2013). Ce

a

b

Fig. 9.1 a. «personnage à ramure de cervidé»; b. «sorcier et animaux hybrides» des Trois Frères (d'après Leroi-Gourhan 1992)

Fig. 9.2: «personnage cornu» du Gabillou (d'après Leroi-Gourhan 1992)

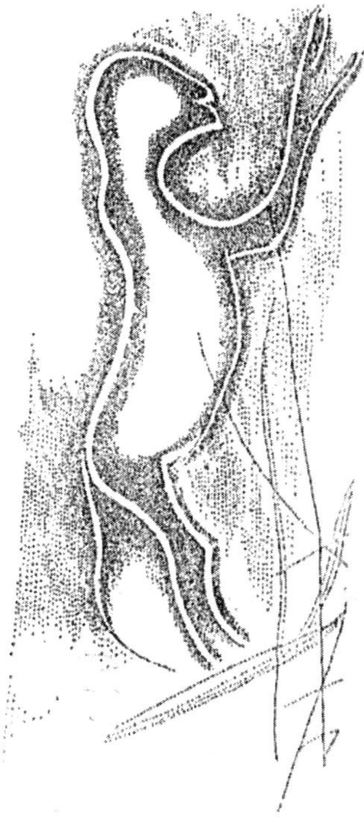

Fig. 9.3: «personnage aux bras levés» de Hornos de la Pena (d'après Leroi-Gourhan 1992).

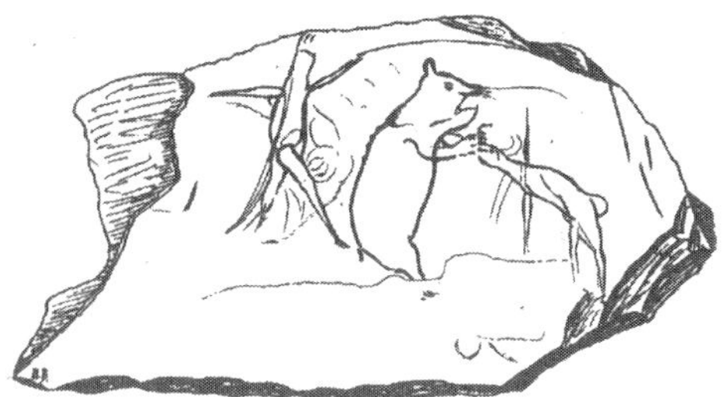

Fig. 9.4: «plaquette gravée» de Péchialet (d'après Leroi-Gourhan 1992).

personnage, comme une shamane, porte un masque (?). L'ensemble du corps associe des traits incisés géométriques rectilignes et curvilignes dans des combinaisons que l'on retrouve sur les céramiques et bien d'autres objets tout au long du Néolithique et jusqu'à l'Age du Bronze.

Avec le début de l'Holocène, aux temps protohistoriques, bien que relativement rares, les représentations de shamans sont particulièrement instructives quant à son comportement. A titre d'exemples:

- Shamans dansant peints sur des bords de vases de la culture néolithique thessalienne de Sesklo, bras baissés (Fig. 9.10) (Théocharis 1973).
- Shaman peint sur un fragment d'autel de Szentes-Ilinopart (culture de la Tisza), bras baissés, le sexe apparent, les jambes agitées comme les shamans dansant de Sesklo (Raczky 1987) (Fig. 9.11).
- Shamans dont un incisé sur un fragment de vase de Szegvar-Tuzköves (culture de la Tisza), bras baissés (J. Korek dans Raczky 1987).
- Shamans peints ou en relief sur un fragment de couvercle et de coupe à piédestal les bras levés de Szegvar

Fig. 9.5: «figure lardée de sagaies» de Cougnac (d'après Leroi-Gourhan 1992).

– Tuzköves et d'Öcsöd-Kovashalom (cultures de la Tisza, de Herpaly) (Kalicz & Raczky 1987).

- Shaman les bras baissés en relief sur un fragment de céramique de Tiszavasvari-Paptelekhat (céramique linéaire de l'Alföld, AVK) (Kalicz 1970) (Fig. 9.12).
- Shaman les bras levés incisé sur un vase de Borsod-Derékegyhaza (culture de Bükk) (Kalicz 1970) (Fig. 9.13).
- Shamans les bras levés ou baissés associés à des animaux, de la Scandinavie à l'Asie centrale, la Sibérie du Sud (Sher 1994).
- Shamans dansant de l'art rupestre de Chine (Cao *et al.* 2014 ; You & Cao 2014).
- shaman les bras levés en relief sur un fragment de céramique de Dikili Tash I (Néolithique Moyen) (Macédoine orientale grecque) (Fig. 9.14).
- Shaman les bras baissés en relief sur la panse d'un vase de Dikili Tash I (Néolithique Moyen) (Macédoine orientale grecque) (Fig. 9.15).
- Shaman les bras levés incisé à «M à triple spirales» sur un vase de Dilili Tash I (Néolithique Moyen, importation Szakalhat de l'Alföld?) (Fig. 9.16).
- Shaman les bras levés peint au graphite sur fond noir sur un fragment de vase chalcolithique de Dikili Tash II (Néolithique Récent/Enéolithique) (Macédoine orientale grecque).

Fig. 9.6: «thème de l'homme et du bison» de Lascaux (d'après Leroi-Gourhan 1992)

Fig. 9.7: «thème de l'homme et du bison» de Laugerie-Basse (d'après Leroi-Gourhan 1992)

La «scène du puit» à Lascaux montre un shaman et son «emblème à tête d'oiseau» en relation avec un bison; on songe immanquablement à l'identification de «l'homme-bison» du «panneau du sorcier» de la grotte Chauvet (Clottes 2001; 2010). «Le chasseur regarde l'animal au moins comme son égal. Il le voit chasser, comme lui pour se nourrir, lui suppose une vie semblable à la sienne, une organisation sociale du même modèle. La supériorité de l'homme s'affirmera seulement dans le domaine technique, où il apporte l'outil. Dans le domaine magique, il attribuera à l'animal une force non moindre que la sienne. D'un autre côté, l'animal est supérieur à l'homme par un ou plusieurs caractères: par sa force physique, son agilité, la finesse de son ouïe et de son flair, toutes qualités

Fig. 9.8: «thème de l'homme et du bison» de Villars (d'après Leroi-Gourhan 1992)

Fig. 9.9: «Venus de Predmost» gravée sur ivoire de mammouth (Otte 2013)

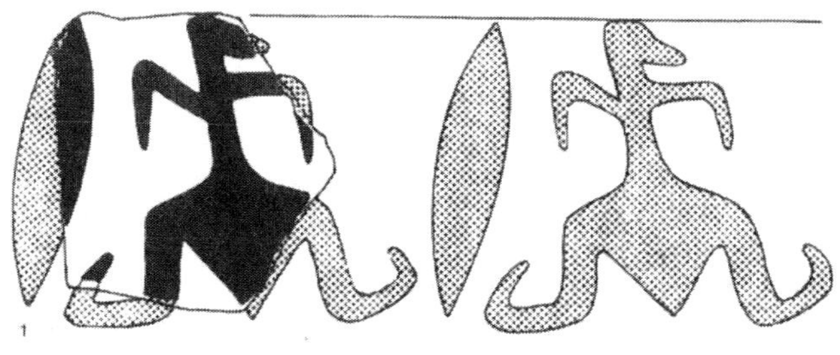

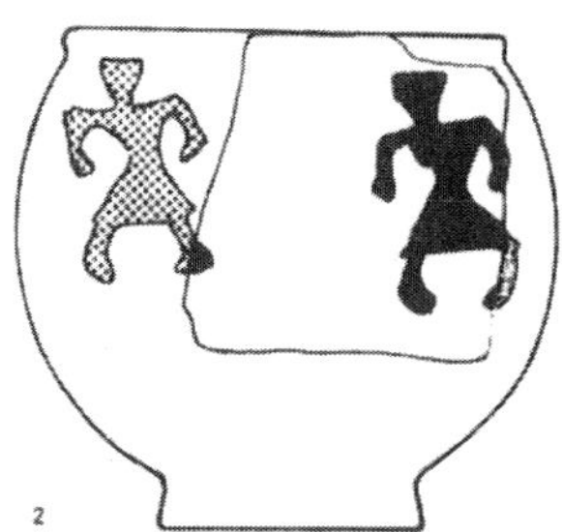

Fig. 9.10: Shamans dansant de Sesklo (d'après Théocharis 1973)

Fig. 9.11: Shaman de Szentes-Ilinopart (d'après Raczky 1987)

Fig. 9.12: Shaman les bras baissés de Tiszavasvari-Paptelekhat (d'après Kalicz 1970)

que le chasseur appréciera. Il accordera plus de prix encore aux pouvoirs spirituels qu'il associe à ces qualités physiques. Comme l'homme, la bête possède une ou plusieurs âmes et un langage. Bien mieux, elle comprend souvent le langage humain; or la réciproque n'est vraie que pour les chamans. L'ours pourrait parler, mais il préfère s'en abstenir et les Yakoutes voient là une preuve de sa supériorité sur l'homme. L'ours écoute, se tait et de cette façon ne donne pas prise sur lui» (Lot-Falk 1953). Aussi nous ne suivrons pas André Leroi-Gourhan lorsqu'il oppose (affrontement) l'homme au bison qu'il s'agisse non seulement de Lascaux mais de Roc-de-Sers, Villars ou de Laugerie-Basse. La scène de Villars révèle au contraire une grande intimité, une communion décisive entre le bison et le shaman en tant que «Maître des Animaux» (Leroi-Gourhan 1992). Les deux sujets sont face à face, le shaman lève le bras, il «salue» le bison cependant qu'à Laugerie-Basse il le suit, se laissant traîner en s'accrochant à lui. Disons qu'il vole. Ainsi, depuis toujours, le shaman est un «diplomate». Précurseur

Fig. 9.13: Shaman les bras levés de Borsod-Derékegyhaza (d'après Kalicz 1970)

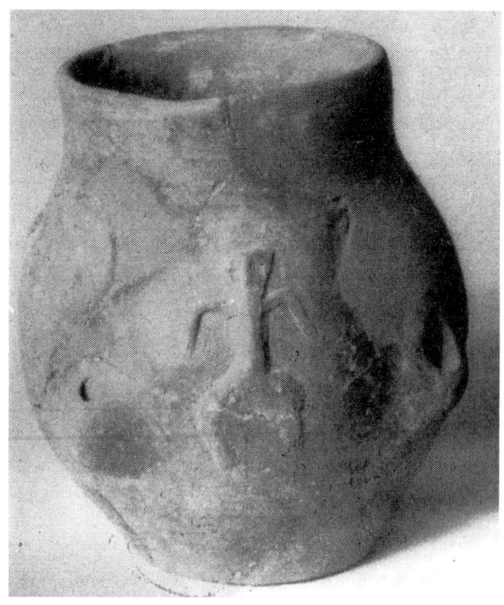

Fig. 9.15: Shaman les bras baissés de Dikili Tash (photo Jean Deshayes)

Fig. 9.14: Shaman les bras levés de Dikili Tash (photo Jean Deshayes)

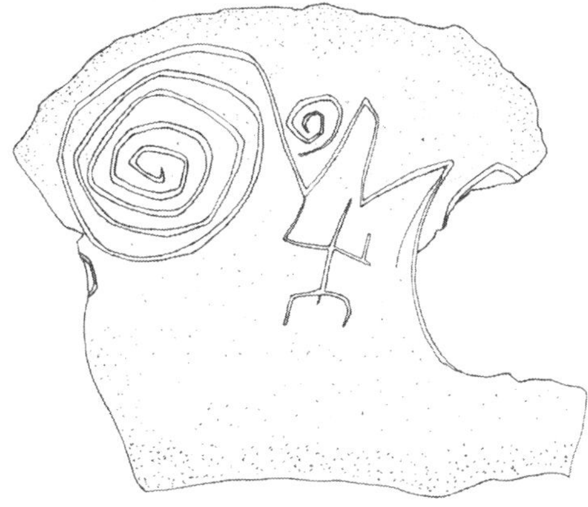

Fig. 9.16: Shaman les bras levés «à M spiralé» de type Szakalhat de Dikili Tash (photo M. Séfériadès)

dans ce domaine, il pèse le pour et le contre, se lance, recherchant la confiance, dans des tractations souvent difficiles dont il souhaite pour la survie de sa communauté l'aboutissement. Plus exactement à Villars, il subjugue l'animal en même temps qu'il est subjugué par lui. On est dans une relation caractéristique, dans une dialectique où le shaman contrôle étroitement son environnement. Il ne fait qu'un avec ce dernier qu'à chaque instant il ordonne.

Lévitation

Bras baissés, bras levés, on peut, chaque fois que le shaman est représenté, parler de lévitation liée à son comportement particulier, à l'état de transe, d'extase qui notamment l'accompagnent. Il est intéressant de noter de plus près que, dans le cas du shaman de la grotte des Trois Frères, le shaman semble s'élever au dessus du sol, que son corps est transparent (détails anatomiques intérieurs) et par là même exprime la légèreté. A propos de la définition du shamanisme, Michael Witzel fait allusion, entre autre, au «spirit flight» (Witzel 2012). Vol «spirituel» dont semble rendre compte le «thème de l'homme et du bison» de Laugerie-Basse.

Psychologie du shaman

La psychologie du shaman a rarement fait l'objet d'études approfondies si l'on excepte les travaux dont certains en partie très récents de A. Leroi-Gourhan, M. Perrin, Y.Lambert, Ph. Descola, A. Métraux, St. Gumper et Fr. Rausky, E. J. Michael Witzel etc. La pensée intime du shaman est en liaison avec des phénomènes complexes qui l'accompagnent tout au long de son existence et de ses «voyages». Le tout baigne dans une nature définie, dans un paysage particulier où le shaman organise un monde qui, au bout du compte, lui est propre comme il en est du groupe humain dont il a la responsabilité. Le paysage (terrestre et céleste), les plantes et les animaux qui l'entourent, le cernent dans une dialectique très stricte, en même temps se soumettent et s'oppose à lui.

On sait ce que l'on doit à Mircea Eliade (Eliade 1951; 1959; 1970; 1976–83) qui a longuement étudié la psychologie ainsi que la psychopathologie du shaman, inscrites dans la sphère de l'*homo religiosus* bien que le terme chamanisme soit d' «une grande confusion définitionnelle»; le shaman, qu'on le désigne comme «personnalité religieuse centrale, sorcier, thérapeute, prêtre, devin et magicien», est «intermédiaire entre le monde des hommes et le monde des esprits» (Franklin Rausky). On peut parler de déséquilibre nerveux souvent héréditaire chez le shaman. Par ailleurs, comme le fait remarquer Franklin Rausky: «certaines souffrances physiques rappellent une mort symbolique initiatique: morcellement du corps, suivi d'un renouvellement des organes intérieurs et des viscères». Organes intérieur et des viscères que révèle le shaman des Trois Frères et bien des pétroglyphes scandinaves. A eux seuls ils illustrent le chemin typique du shaman en quête du Graal.

Se référant à Mircea Eliade, Franklin Rausky toujours, note que le «retour au chaos» équivaut pour l'homme des cultures archaïques à la préparation d'une nouvelle création. Le même symbolisme se laisse déchiffrer dans la «folie» des futurs chamans. C'est le signe que l'homme profane et en train de se dissoudre et qu'une nouvelle personnalité se prépare à naître au monde et que «les prédispositions d'un futur chaman semblent constituer une véritable «maladie-vocation», qui s'inscrit dans des expériences délirantes très élaborées et intégrées dans une tradition culturelle». Le shaman est conduit à se dépersonnaliser, à prendre du recul, à réfléchir en s'isolant dans un premier temps du monde qui l'entoure et qu'il se doit dans un second temps d'ordonner. D'où des comportements qui, à nous «Occidentaux modernes» nous ont échappé trop longtemps. Comme le dit encore Franklin Rausky: «La psychologie et la psychopathologie des religions, après avoir épousé longtemps la première lecture, négative, réductrice et dévalorisante, semblent s'orienter de nos jours vers la deuxième lecture, plus positive, complexe et sensible à la multiplicité des expériences de l'âme» (Gumper & Rausky 2013).

La psychologie propre au shaman est inséparable des «états modifiés de conscience». Comme le rappelle Christine Le Scanff (dans Gumpper & Rausky 2013), «le changement d'état de la conscience n'est perçu qu'en référence à l'«Etat Ordinaire de Conscience» (ECO), c'est-à-dire celui dans lequel on se trouve le plus souvent et auquel le Moi s'identifie généralement. De là naît le concept d'«Etat Modifié de Conscience» ou EMC, ou *altered states of consciousness* dans les années 1960 aux Etats-Unis». «Danses, bras baissés et levées» et autres attitudes (particulièrement dans les pétroglyphes des régions nordiques et plus à l'Est) sont, dans ce sens, les seuls témoignages archéologiques dont on dispose ici. On peut y ajouter les «vases à bras levés» également caractéristiques. C'est en passant d'un état à l'autre que se distingue le shaman.

Certains dessins dits «aux rayons X», montrant le squelette et les organes internes de l'animal, ont été mises en relation avec le chamanisme. Il s'agit d'un art spécifique au culte des chasseurs, mais l'idéologie qui l'imprègne serait, pour Mircea Eliade, chamanique. En effet, seul le chaman, grâce à sa vision surnaturelle, est capable de «voir son propre squelette» (Eliade 1951, 1959, 1970, 1976–1983).

La perte de conscience chez le shaman se confond avec un long voyage semé d'embûches vers l'ailleurs: selon Horst Kirchner, il y a de celà plus de cinquante ans, à propos du shaman de Lascaux: «L'homme, apparemment mort, serait en fait, en transe devant le bison sacrifié, tandis que son âme voyagerait dans l'au-delà. L'oiseau sur la perche, motif spécifique au chamanisme sibérien, serait son esprit protecteur. Selon Kirchner, la «séance» était entreprise afin que le chaman se rende en extase auprès des dieux, et leur demande la bénédiction, c'est-à-dire le succès de la chasse». Nous adhérons ici à cette hypothèse qui nous éloigne de la pensée trop liée au bestiaire de A. Leroi-Gourhan et distante de toute présence décisive en rapport avec le shamanisme (Leroi-Gourhan 1964 ; 1992). On peut considérer dans le même sens le «shaman entraîné» par le bison et qui «vole» de Laugerie-Basse, la communion étroite du shaman avec le bison de Villars comme d'ailleurs à Roc-de-Sers.

La caractéristique de la psychologie du shaman est, avant tout, en état de transe, d'avoir des visions ouvertes à son monde. On sait que selon Mircea Eliade (Fr. Rausky) «Le chamanisme n'est pas seulement la culture religieuse de populations de Sibérie et d'Extrême-Orient, il constitue une forme présente dans des sociétés primitives de l'Ancien et du Nouveau Monde. Le chaman est un spécialiste de la transe extatique, il s'efforce d'abolir l'actuelle condition de déchéance de l'être humain et de réintégrer la condition paradisiaque de l'homme des origines. L'expérience de décorporation ou état de hors-corps est une composante essentielle de la transe chamanique, au cours de laquelle le chaman quitte son corps et accomplit un voyage mystique dans des régions cosmiques: vol chamanique ou ascension vers les sphères célestes, voyage chamanique ou départ vers des terres lointaines, descente chamanique ou entrée dans les demeures infernales souterraines». On voit que le paysage est toujours présent et qu'il est, sous des actions différentes mais paradoxalement identiques, à l'origine d'une perception authentique.

Une étude comparative raisonnée de la psychologie du shaman peut nous entraîner en Amérique du Sud, en Amazonie et ailleurs, plus exactement où l'on dispose d'éléments d'études particulièrement riches sur la base avant toute chose des travaux, par exemple, maintenant anciens d'Alfred Métraux et de ceux au contraire actuels de Philippe Descola et surtout de Michael Witzel (Métraux 2013; Descola 2005; Witzel 2012).

Alfred Métraux insiste sur la variété des cultes sud-américains et la complexité qui les caractérise dès qu'il s'agit de les appréhender. On ne peut ici entrer dans les détails à partir du «Créateur ou d'un Grand Ancêtre». «L'être Suprême» peut parfois être une «déesse» comme il en est particulièrement dans les cultures néolithiques et énéolithiques d'Europe centrale et des Balkans au sens large notamment (abondance des figurines). Il note, au passage, que les chamans sont décrits comme «des hommes particulièrement talentueux et intelligents; seules quelques allusions pourraient inciter à les considérer comme des personnes névrosées». Les shamans s'entourent d'accessoires (hochets, tambours etc.), de talismans tout comme en Europe centrale et balkanique mais qui en archéologie protohistorique ne nous sont pas restitués exceptées parfois les «trousses de shamans» contenant des objets inhabituels ou exotiques comme, par exemple une pierre ponce dans le «trésor» d'Omurtag en Bulgarie accompagnée de coquillages (spondyles d'origine égéenne) (Gaydarska *et al.* 2004). Viennent s'ajouter les «rites de fertilité» conduisant «les esprits à veiller à la croissance des plantes»: on fera allusion à une découverte isolée, celle d'une valve de spondyle brute trouvée par Dragoş Gheorghiu dans un champ actuel de la Roumanie méridionale (Vădastra), champ exploité sans doute depuis le Néolithique (culture de Boian) (Gheorghiu 2011). Enfin, tandis que nous avons fait allusion plus haut aux shamans dansant de Sesklo, Alfred Métraux (2013) note que «Bien que la pratique de la médecine fût la fonction principale des chamanes, celle-constituait rarement leur seule activité ... en outre, ils étaient chargés d'organiser les fêtes magico-religieuses et de mener les danses».

On doit à Phillipe Descola dans «Par-delà nature et culture» de nous éclairer sous un jour nouveau, tâche originale et par là même difficile parce que le concept de complexité cher à Edgar Morin intervient à chaque instant de manière intensive (Morin 1994). «C'est dans l'aval du Kapawi, une rivière limoneuse de la haute Amazonie, que j'ai commencé à m'interroger sur l'évidence de la nature». Tout au long des pages, le biotope ou la niche écologique apparaissent régulièrement en filigrane sinon en pleine lumière. L'imbrication étroite entre l'homme et la nature est un fait incontournable, indiscutable et vieux de milliers d'années qu'il nous faut, scientifiques, dissocier actuellement des interventions politiques «écologiques» presque exclusivement peu avouables. La question est posée d'un diffusionnisme du shamanisme à partir de la Sibérie et des régions adjacentes en direction des deux Amériques. Déplacements d'Est en Ouest de populations au moins dès le «Néolithique», au début de l'Holocène sinon avant. Descola, avec de solides arguments, tergiverse sur le point diffusionniste cependant que, quant à nous, nous croyons, a contrario, à de très probables possibilités d'expansion du shamanisme sibérien si l'on se réfère aux récentes découvertes archéologiques: les momies de l'Ancien Pérou sont à rapprocher des sépultures de Tamsagbulag en Mongolie (Séfériadès 1999). Vouloir dissocier les shamans d'Amazonie de ceux sibériens n'est possible que parce que Philippe Descola a vécu durant plusieurs années avec femme et enfants, isolé en Amazonie au milieu des Achuar dont les chamans sont «ces médiateurs cosmiques auxquels la société délègue la gestion des rapports entre les différentes communautés du vivant». Ces caractéristiques du shamanisme sont attestées dès la Protohistoire, qu'il s'agisse, par exemple, de l'Europe centrale ou des Balkans, avec les représentations de shamans cernés de spirales (repli sur soi-même en même temps que poses de limites). Le shaman, en Amazonie, est en même temps enseignant et comptable; il explique le pourquoi cependant qu'il «gère» les espèces végétales et animales de son «paysage» et sans doute bien mieux que ne le font les agriculteurs, pêcheurs ou chasseurs actuels «occidentaux», de la même manière que son «confrère» d'Eurasie. Comme le note Descola «le chaman, capable de métamorphose, est proche des animaux sauvages et de leur gamme d'aptitudes spécifiques» et ce, toujours de la même manière que le shaman éleveur de rennes ou chasseur d'ours du Nord de notre vieux continent.

Tout au long de ses recherches dans le cadre de sa théorie publiée récemment sur *The origins of the world's mythologies*, Michael Witzel est parfaitement conscient des difficultés que l'on rencontre s'agissant d'appréhender et de définir le shamanisme:

> The problem of defining shamanism instantly indicates that both the word shaman and the concept of shamanism have been employed in a multiplicity of ways in scholarly as well as in popular literature. It may be advantageous to start with a definition. Walter and Neumann Fridman stress the current broad interpretation of the term shamanism as designating any kind of ecstatic behaviour including spirit possession, witchcraft, and even cannibalism and a narrow one that stresses initiatory crisis, vision quest, an experience of dismemberment and regeneration, climbing the sacred (world) tree, spirit flight, the role of the shaman as healer, and the use of trance (Witzel 2012).

Et Witzel de se référer à V. N. Basilov (Basilov 1999). Il est évident que de la série de «critères» propres au shamanisme mis en avant par Basilov, il n'en subsiste en préhistoire et en protohistoire que des lambeaux. En l'absence de textes, de traditions orales, de récits, d'observations d'ordre ethnographique, nous avons toutefois tenté, de manière en fait très hypothétique, d'étudier certains d'entre eux à partir en premier lieu des rares représentations de shamans.

Conclusion

Tout cela nous conduit à conclure provisoirement sur plusieurs faits sociaux et culturels indissociable de la sphère du religieux:

- Le shaman, présent dès la préhistoire (du temps des Néandertaliens sinon bien auparavant) peut paraître à première vue «étrange» dans son comportement du point de vue d'un «Occidental moderne». Cependant à regarder de plus près – et c'est le sens de notre modeste contribution – il en est tout autrement.
- Son comportement que l'on pourrait croire imprévisible est construit, ordonné dans un cadre rigide, structuré et se poursuit jusqu'à aujourd'hui.
- Le shaman est le dernier gardien d'une symbiose totale entre l'homme et la nature (le monde qui l'entoure, le paysage).
- Par là même, son comportement, sa psychologie et l'analyse qu'on peut en faire sont d'une profonde et étonnante complexité.

En préhistoire et protohistoire, aux temps des Balkans néolithiques et énéolithiques, sinon dans toute l'Eurasie, le shaman est représenté dansant ou volant, seuls témoignages avec les artéfacts volontairement brisés (inversion des mondes) qu'il nous a laissé.

Nous conclurons, ici de manière toute provisoire, sur les dernières lignes de l'étude du shamanisme de Michel Perrin qui «nous a fait découvrir et comprendre comment des hommes dépourvus de nos sciences ont élaboré un système intellectuel et religieux cohérent pour expliquer l'ordre des choses et les évènements qui le perturbent, pour justifier l'aléatoire ou l'irréparable, pour répondre aux angoisses et aux souffrances humaines, pour instituer une alliance honorable avec la nature. Dans un monde à deux faces, dont chacune est un miroir déformant pour l'autre, et entre lesquelles il n'y a pas la «béance» que supposent les grandes religions, les chamanes, aidés de leurs partenaires surnaturels, doivent reconnaître des signes qui donnent sens à tout, qui notifient les faits à venir et expliquent l'advenu. Ils sont tenus d'en donner une lecture infaillible. Il leur faut convertir les aléas en certitudes. Dans un univers absolument déterminisme, qui exclut le hasard, on leur demande d'avoir réponse à tout» (Perrin 2001).

Autant de barrières dressées face à une mondialisation forcenée qui tend à perdre, chaque jour qui passe, davantage ses repères. A ce sujet, dans les dédales de la psychologie du shaman, les écrits successifs principalement de Iouri Rythkéou quant au shamanisme ancien et actuel demeurent (Rythkéou 1974; 1978; 2000; 2001; 2003; 2004).

Reférénces

Banner, J. 1960. The Neolithic settlement on the Kremenyak Hill at Csoka (Coka). *Acta Archaeologica Ungarica* 12, 1–56.

Basilov, V. N. 1999. Cosmos as everyday reality in shamanism: An attempt to formulate a more precise definition of shamanism. In R. Mastromattei & A. Rigopulos (eds) *Shamanic Cosmos: From India to the North Pole Star*, New Delhi: D. K. Printworld, 17–39.
Breuil, H. 1952. *Quatre cents siècles d'art pariétal*. Montignac, Paris: Editions Max Fourny; Art et Industrie (1985).
Cao, B., Zhang, P., Dambricourt Malassé, A., Shen, G. & You, Q. S. 2014. Les danses chamanes du site rupestre de Dahongyan, province du Ghizou, Chine du Sud. *Plastir, Revue Transdisciplinaire de Plasticite Humaine* 17, 1–16.
Clotte, J. (ed.) 2001/2010. *La grotte Chauvet. L'art des origines*. Paris: Editions du Seuil.
Dambricourt Malassé A., Dolukhanov, P., Séfériadès, M. & Subbotin, L. 2010. Funeral meal and anthropology in the Gumelnita Chalcolithic civilization in the North-western Black Sea area. In J. Šuteková, P. Pavúk, P. Kalábková & B. Kovár (eds) *Panta Rhei. Studies on the Chronology and Cultural Development of South-Eastern and Central Europe in Earlier Prehistory Presented to Juraj Pavuk on the occasion of his 75th birthday*. Bratislava: Comenius University in Bratislava and Archaeological Centre, Olomouc, 159–168.
Dergachev, V. 1998. Kerbunskij klad (*Carbuna Deposit*). Kichinev.
Descola, Ph. 2005. *Par-delà nature et culture*. Paris: Editions Gallimard.
Eliade, M. 1951. *Le chamanisme et les techniques archaïques de l'extase*. Paris: Payot.
Eliade, M. 1959. *Initiation, rites, sociétés secrètes. Naissances mystiques. Essai sur quelques types d'initiation*. Paris: Gallimard.
Eliade, M. 1970. *De Zalmoxis à Gengis-Khan. Etudes comparatives sur les religions et le folklore de la Dacie et de l'Europe orientale*. Paris: Payot.
Eliade, M. 1976–83. *Histoire des croyances et des idées religieuses*. Paris: Payot.
Gaydarska, B., Chapman, J., Angelova, I., Gurova, M. & Yanev, S. 2004. Breaking, making and trading: the Omurtag Eneolithic spondylus hoard. *Archaelogia Bulgarica* VIII, 11–34.
Gheorghiu, D. 2011 Insignia of exotica: skeuomorphs of Mediterranean shells in Chalcolithic south Eastern Europe. In A. Vianello (ed.) *Exotica in the Prehistoric Mediterranean*, Oxford: Oxbow Books, 13–25.
Gumpper, St. & Rausky, Fr. (eds). 2013. *Dictionnaire de psychologie et psychopathologie des religions*. Paris: Bayard.
Kalicz, N. 1970. *Dieux d'Argile. L'âge de pierre et de cuivre en Hongrie*. Budapest: Hereditas, Editons Corvina.
Kalicz, N. & Raczky, P. 1987. The Late Neolithic of the Tisza region. A survey of recent archaeological research. In P. Raczky (ed.) *The Late Neolithic of the Tisza Region*. Budapest-Szolnok: Kossuth Press, 11–30.
Lambert. Y. 2007–9. *La naissance des religions de la préhistoire aux religions universalistes*. Paris: Armand Colin.
Lazarovici, Gh., Drasovean, Fl. & Maxim, Z. 2001. *Parţa*. Timisoara: Editura Waldpress.
Leroi-Gourhan, A. 1964. *Les religions de la Préhistoire (Paléolithique)*. Paris: PUF.
Leroi-Gourhan, A. 1965. *Préhistoire de l'art occidental*. Paris: Mazenod.
Leroi-Gourhan, A. 1992. *L'art pariétal. Langage de la Préhistoire*. Paris: Jérôme Million.
Lot-Falck, E. 1953. *Les rites de chasse chez les peuples sibériens*. Paris: NRF Gallimard.
Métraux, A. 2013. *Ecrits d'Amazonie. Cosmologie, rituels, guerre et chamanisme*. Paris: CNRS Editions.
Michaux, D. (ed.). 1995. *La transe et l'hypnose*. Paris: Imago.
Morin, E. 1994. *La complexité humaine*. Paris: Flammarion.
Otte, M. (ed.). 2013. *Les Gravettiens*. Paris: Editions Errance.
Paproth, H-J. 1976. *Studien über das bärenzeremoniell. I. Bärenjagdriten und bärenfeste bei den tungusischen völkern*. Skrifter utgivna av Religionshitoriska Institutionen I Uppslala, Uppsala: Tofters Tryckeri/ Kommission/Klaus Renner.
Perrin, M. 2001. *Le chamanisme*. Paris: PUF.
Racsky, P. (ed.). 1987. *The Late Neolithic of the Tisza region*. Budapest-Szolnok: Kossuth Press.

Rytkheou, Y. 1974. *Contes de la Tchoukotka*. Paris: Publications Orientalistes de France.
Rytkheou, Y. 1978. *Un rëve au début du brouillard*. Paris: Pygmalion.
Rytkheou, Y. 2000. *Unna*. Paris: Actes Sud.
Rytkheou, Y. 2001. *L'étrangère aux yeux bleus*. Paris: Actes Sud.
Rytkheou, Y. 2003. *La bible tchouktche ou le dernier chaman d'Ouelen*. Paris: Actes Sud.
Rytkheou, Y. 2004. *Le miroir de l'oubli*. Paris: Actes Sud.
Sефériadès, M. 1985. *Matériaux pour l'étude des sociétés du Nord-Est égéen au début du Bronze Ancien*. Editions Recherches sur les Civilisations, Paris: A.D.P.F.
Séfériadès, M. 1995a. Le commerce des spondyles de la Mer Egée à la Manche. *Archéologia (Dijon)* 309, 42–50.
Séfériadès, M. 1995b. *Spondylus gaederopus*: the earliest European long distance exchange system. A symbolic and structural archaeological approach to Neolithic societies. *Porocilo o raziskovanju paleolitika, neolitika in eneolitika v Slovenia* 22, 233–256.
Séfériadès, M. 1995–96. La route néolithique des spondyles de la Méditerranée à la Manche. In M. Otte (ed.) *International Colloquium 'Nature et Culture'*, Liège University, Dec. 1993, ERAUL 68. Liège: Université de Liège, 291–358.
Séfériadès, M. 1999. A Tamsagbulag, les premiers paysans de Mongolie. *Archéologia (Dijon)* 354, 56–65.
Séfériadès, M. 2000. *Spondylus gaederopus*: some observations on the earliest European long distance exchange system. In St. Hiller & V. Nikolov (eds) *Karanovo III. Beitrage zum Neolithikum in Südosteuropa*. Wien: Sonderdruck, 423–437.
Séfériadès, M. 2002. La représentation de l'élan de la Mer Baltique au Lac Baïkal. In Russie, carrefour de l'Homo Sapiens, les révélations de l'archéologie russe. *Dossiers d'Archéologie (Dijon)*, 32–37.
Séfériadès, M. 2005. Note shamanique: à propos du bucrane de Dikili Tash (Macédoine orientale grecque). In *In Honorem Silvia Marinescu-Bilcu 70 de ani, Cultura si Civilizatie la Dunarea de Jos XXII*. Calarasi: Muzeul Dunarii de Jos, 97–114.
Séfériadès, M. L. 2009. Spondylus and long-distance trade in prehistoric Europe. In D. W. Anthony (ed.) *The Lost World of Old Europe. The Danube Valley, 5000–3500 BC*, Princeton NJ: Princeton University Press, 179–190.
Séfériadès, M. 2010. A propos d'un spondyle de Nitra (fouilles J. Pavuk). Shamanisme protohistorique en Europe centrale et sud-orientale. In J. Šuteková, P. Pavúk, P. Kalábková & B. Kovár (eds) *Panta Rhei. Studies on the Chronology and Cultural Development of South-Eastern and Central Europe in Earlier Prehistory Presented to Juraj Pavuk on the Occasion of his 75th birthday*. Bratislava: Comenius University in Bratislava and Archaeological Centre, Olomouc, 593–599.
Séfériadès, M. L. 2011. Protohistoric *Spondylus gaederopus L.* shell: some considerations on the earliest European long-distance exchanges related to shamanism. In A. Vianello (ed.) *Exotica in the Prehistoric Mediterranean*. Oxford: Oxbow Books, 3–12.
Séfériadès, M. 2013. Spondyles roumains, spondyles américains. In *Facets of the Past. The Challenge of the Balkan Neo-Eneolithic. Proceedings of the International symposium Celebrating to the 85th Birth anniversary of Eugen Comsa*. Bucharest: Publishing House of the Romanian Academy, 247–272.
Sher, J. A. 1994. *Répertoire des pétroglyphes d'Asie Centrale. Fasc. 1: Sibérie du Sud 1: Oglakhty I–III (Russie, Khakassie)*. Paris: Diffusion de Boccard.
Sztancsuj, S. J. 2005. The Early Copper Age hoard from Ariusd (Erosd). In Gh. Dumitroaia, J. Chapman, O. Weller, C. Preoteasa, R. Munteanu, D. Nicola, & D. Monah (eds) *Cucuteni 120 ans de recherches. Le temps du bilan*. Bibliotheca Memoriae Antiquitatis XVI. Piatra-Neamt: Constantin Matasa, 85–105.
Theocharis, D. R. 1973. *Neolithic Greece*. Athens: National Bank of Greece.
Walter, M. N. & Neumann Fridman, E. J. (eds). 2004. *Shamanism: An Encyclopedia of World Beliefs, Practices, and Culture*. Santa Barbara CA: Abc Clio.
Witzel, E. J. M. 2012. *The Origins of the World's Mythologies*. Oxford & New York: Oxford University Press.
You, Q. & Cao, B. 2014. *L'art rupestre du Guizhou*. Guiyang, China: Guizhou Science and Technology Publishing House.

Chapter 10

The Mystery of the Bird-Nester: The Shaman Which Lévi-Strauss Did Not Recognise

Enrico Comba

Abstract *The author advances a hypothesis that the bird-nester myth from the Bororo Indians of Central Brazil, called a reference myth by Lévy-Strauss, actually describes the initiation of an apprentice shaman with the variants representing a general pattern common to most of the shamanic experiences of Amerindian peoples. Other variants describe the cosmological structure of a multi-layered universe that are strictly related to the practice of shamanism and shared by most Native Americas cultures.*

Lévi-Strauss and the Study of Myth

In the first volume of his monumental work on the mythology of the Americas, *Le Cru et le Cuit* (*The Raw and the Cooked*, Lévi-Strauss 1964[1]), Lévi-Strauss takes as his starting point a myth from the Bororo Indians of Central Brazil, which he calls the reference myth. His admitted purpose is to begin the analysis with myths pertaining to a particular society, which he knows well because he has conducted a fieldwork among them during the period he spent in Brazil, in 1935–36, then widening progressively the horizon, he takes into consideration other myths, from neighbouring tribes, and then from peoples more distant, extending the perspective until the entire continent turns out to be covered by his investigation. Since the initial pages of his first volume, Lévi-Strauss announces that the analysis shall be extended to the northern part of the American continent, which shall be realised in the third and fourth volumes (Lévi-Strauss 1968; 1971). The Author's theoretical premise is that the rules which preside to the formation of myths are unconscious mechanisms, analogous to the linguistic rules operating in the functioning of human speech. His main object is to demonstrate that myths are not the products of the free exercise of fantasy and imagination, but are constructed following a set of logical mechanisms, which can be traced by his structural analysis. The reference myth, thus, is revealed to be the transformation, more or less pronounced, of other myths, coming both from the same society and from nearby and far-off societies. Starting from a myth, for every sequence is built the group of transformations of which it is a part, drawing a series of relationships linking the sequences which pertain to different myths. In this way one reaches a higher level of analysis, from the singular myths to a system of frameworks placed on the same axis (Lévi-Strauss 1964, 10). The scope is to reconstruct a 'syntax of South American mythology'.[2]

Lévi-Strauss has the great merit of having emphasised the fact that the mythology of the Americas constitutes a single, huge web of tales and narratives, where the strands link in unpredictable ways peoples which are geographically contiguous and groups which are far away one from the other. But he creates some perplexities in his readers when he declares that the subject of the narratives is thoroughly unimportant, and that the myths have no meaningful content. Every myth exists only as the restricted application of a scheme which the comparative analysis can help to elucidate.[3] So the mythological analysis does not show how men think through their myths, but rather how the myths think themselves through men and without their knowledge (Lévi-Strauss 1964, 20). So, the Bororo reference myth constitutes the starting point only because of purely contingent reasons, as part of a set of logical transformations, but lacks any intrinsic meaning in itself.

This stubborn refusal of taking into consideration the content of the myths notwithstanding, the present article tries to demonstrate that Lévi-Strauss has pointed at a very important aspect of Amerindian mythology. The problem is not to substitute to the wide-ranging comparative perspective of the French anthropologist a strictly contextual point of view, according to which the structure of myth is conveyed by the relationships the symbolic elements of a single myth can reveal among themselves, as Terence Turner has proposed with regard to the same myth of the 'bird-nester' (Turner 1980). The fecundity of Lévi-Strauss's proposal lies properly in having individuated a recurrent theme in the mythology of the Americas, which can be discovered both among the peoples of the Gê linguistic family in South America and among several other groups in the northern part of the continent. But, far from being a meaningless set of formal structures, this group of myths reveals important aspects of the cosmology and shamanic worldview which was shared by most of the ancient peoples of the Americas. To show the possible meanings which can be detected in the myths, we have to follow a little yet on Levi-Strauss's footsteps.

The bird-nester

The so-called reference myth is the Bororo narrative of Toribugu, who in another version is called *Geriguiguiatugo* (Wilbert & Simoneau 1983, 198–209). In synthesis, this tale begins with the discovery, on the part of a Bororo male, that his son had intercourse with one of his wives, the boy's stepmother, thus breaking the clan rules of exogamy. He tries to kill his son by sending him on various dangerous enterprises, stealing magic musical instruments in the land of the dead, guarded by spirits. On his grandmother's advice, the boy assures himself the aid of some animals (hummingbird, dove and locust), which are able to accomplish the task. Then, the father takes the boy hunting macaws and, after the son has climbed the rock wall to get the birds' nest, the father leaves him hanging from the rock. The boy manages to kill some lizards, to quiet his hunger, and ties the rest to his belt. They begin to decay and to smell so bad that he faints. Vultures are attracted by the smell and eat his buttocks, then realise he is a living being and help him to descend on the ground. After a long search, he finds his village again and appears before his grandmother and brother in the form of a lizard. To take revenge of his father he organises a deer hunt, transforms himself into a deer and attacks his father with his horns, plunging him into a lake where he is devoured by piranhas. According to one version, reported by the Salesian missionary Antonio Colbacchini and cited by Lévi-Strauss, the protagonist decides to live no more with the Indians and to go with his grandmother in a far-away place, from which he shall come back only to bring over them wind, rain and cold (Colbacchini 1925, 236; Lévi-Strauss 1964, 45).

In his comment on the text, Lévi-Strauss emphasises some aspects of the social organisation of the Bororo (the division into two moieties and in numerous clans with matrilineal descent and matrilocal residence), the name of the protagonist (which contains the term *adugo*, 'jaguar,' and *geriguigui*, 'land turtle', a name which defines also the constellation of the Raven), the presence of animals and birds. With regard to the macaws he says only that they have a double importance: on the one hand they give the feathers with which ceremonial ornaments are made, on the other hand the birds are involved in a complex cycle of soul transmigration: in a certain period, the souls of the deceased are believed to incarnate themselves into *ara* macaws[4] (*Ara chloropterus* or *Ara ararauna*). He makes a reference to the initiation ritual for young males, because some of the versions of the myth begin with the evocation of the women going to collect the leaves of a palm with which the penis sheaths for the newly initiated boys shall be made. No other mention is made by the French anthropologist regarding the ritual life of the Bororo and, significantly, he never hints at the figure of the shaman.

Such an attitude is not new for Lévi-Strauss. When he described for the first time the results of his observations made on the field, during the expedition of 1935–36 among the Bororo, he declared explicitly having let aside thoroughly all that concerned the spiritual powers and religious life,[5] focusing only on the subject of social organisation. Some years after, rethinking to his ethnographical experiences, Lévi-Strauss admitted that he remained surprised by the unceremonious attitude displayed by the Bororo with regard to the supernatural, contrasting it with his own experiences in infancy towards the Hebrew religion of his parents.[6] In his extended analysis of myths Lévi-Strauss has scarcely emphasised their character of 'sacred histories', of revelations of concepts which were believed by those who narrated or listened to them. According to Godelier, the notion of 'sacred' is badly absent from the analyses devoted by him to the myths and religions of the Amerindian peoples.[7] It is also surprising that Lévi-Strauss makes no mention of the special relationship that the Bororo had with the macaws, well known since the 19th century, when the German ethnographer Karl von den Steinen reported that the Bororo asserted to be 'red *araras*' (Steinen 1894, 352–353).[8] From the detailed analysis made by Crocker (1977, 150 ff.), we apprehend that for the Bororo the variegated colours of parrots, and in particular of macaws, is interpreted as the manifestation of spirit. Macaws are connected with the soul's metamorphoses after death: during the funerary rites the soul is deemed to enter in turn in a jaguar, a macaw, an otter and a hawk. This is the base of Levi-Strauss's assertion that the birds are related to the destiny of souls after death. Furthermore, and appropriately, the caves on high cliffs where the macaws nest are regarded as apertures leading directly to the other world, where the *aroe* spirits dwell (Crocker 1977, 182). In his comment on the myth, Lévi-Strauss says nothing on Bororo shamanism, which seems, from his treatment of the subject, thoroughly irrelevant to the understanding of the narrative.

The particularity of the Bororo is that they had two types of shamans: the shamans of the *aroe* and the shamans of the *bope*. These are distinct but complementary principles of the Bororo cosmology. The *aroe* represent a modality of existence of every physical thing as it existed primarily in the underworld, where the ancestors of the Bororo came from, they are the representation of immutable categorical forms. The *bope* are what causes all things to reproduce, are the principle of all organic transformation and metamorphoses (Crocker 1985, 33–37). Lèvi-Strauss describes rather summarily these two kinds of practitioners as the 'priest' and the 'sorcerer'[9] No shamans of the aroe, *aroe etawarare*, exist today among the Bororo (Crocker 1985, 235), but we have several information on them through the documents recorded by the Salesian missionaries.

According to Antonio Colbacchini, the shaman of the *aroe* is chosen by the spirits who produce in him visions of strange phenomena: he sees a hummingbird which flies around him, or flocks of parrots and macaws which soar above him; when he returns to his village he crouches near the fire, in the grip of tremors and whispering incomprehensible words. He feels a deathlike stench, and is harassed by gusts of wind, which are produced by the *aroe* who come to speak through him (Colbacchini 1925, 77). If we add that the *aroe* represents the soul of the ancestors, and that the macaws have multiple associations with the *aroe* (Crocker 1985, 56, 277), we have a lot of elements to suggest that the story of the bird-nester has many things to do with the Bororo shaman. To be more precise, the hypothesis advanced in the present article is that the focus of the bird-nester myth is the initiation of an apprentice shaman, and this can explain why this myth is diffused all through the American continent.

Let us come back to the narrative text. The story begins with an episode of incest between a boy and his stepmother, which triggers the attempts of the father to take revenge on his son. The incest is not a common theme in the series of variants of the myth, and even in the Bororo myth it seems treated with particular indifference, so much so that the tale seems to concentrate rather on the revenge which the boy takes on his father as the logical conclusion of the story. Such a detail seems to suggest that the incest is not a meaningful subject of the narrative, but is only a literary expedient to represent the abrupt removal of the boy from the social conventions and from the domestic milieu in which he has lived until that moment. It is to be remembered that often the shaman 'breaks, threatens or transforms the social order' in which he/she is immersed (Parman 1991, 9). What are presented as attempts on the part of the father to kill the boy, sending him on various dangerous enterprises, are really tests where the ability and powers of the boy are verified. He has to bring some ceremonial objects from the land of the souls, the world of the *aroe*. The hero looks for the advice of his grandmother and thus obtains the help of assistant animals. The first one is the hummingbird, the little bird which comes in the visions of the prospective shaman of the *aroe*, according to the Colbacchini text cited above. The boy is sent to the world of the *aroe* to get one of their rattles, called *bapo*. These musical instruments are intimately associated with the *aroe* spirits and are used to accompany the songs especially concerned with them.[10] The apprentice shaman of the *aroe* is officially given the *bapu rogu* ('small rattles'), during the course of a ceremony. 'To be given the rattles' is both an honor and a test of the apprentice's esoteric knowledge. Soon after beginning to sing, in fact, the new shaman suddenly collapses into a deathlike trance (Crocker 1985, 294). This seems exactly the meaning of the adventure described in the myth, which is repeated thrice (with slightly differing instruments as target: the rattles, the little rattles, *bapu rogu*, and the string rattle, *buttore*[11]) and which is followed by the more widespread episode of the climbing to the macaws' nest. Since the caves and rocky niches in which the macaws nest are regarded by the Bororo as openings into the underworld inhabited by the *aroe* spirits (Crocker 1985, 277), the previous adventures are introductory episodes to the main enterprise, which, like the others, implies a visit to the world of the spirits, in which the boy's courage and ability are put to test by his angry father.

But who is this father, and why decides he to endeavour to kill his son through so strange a subterfuge? Some commentators have tried to find into this kind of stories the projection of real conflicts between social or kinship categories which characterises the social organisation of Native peoples. For instance, Terence Turner insists that the Kayapo myth of the bird-nester reveals a conflict between the sister's husband and the wife's brother, which is part of the developmental cycle in the life of every young male. Marriage means the transfer of the husband into the wife's household, while consequently the young boys are gradually induced to withdraw from the domestic group and to reside in the men's house at the centre of the village (Turner 1980, 89 and passim). Analogously, one could suggest that the Bororo myth contains a similar message, alluding to the distancing of the adolescent boy from the domestic group, characterised by matrilineal descent and matrilocal residence,[12] but it is doubtful that in such society the role of the father should be perceived in so an outstanding position, since the son does not belong to his father's own kinship group. However, North American variants, on which we are going to return, present still other relationships, for example brother-brother, or no kinship relations at all, as in the case in which the role of the villain is played by the Trickster. So the plot of the story remains unchanged while the relationship among the protagonists varies greatly: as Lévi-Strauss has appropriately observed, the only invariant properties in the group of myths of the bird-nester seem to be an alliance relationship and the age difference between the two men (Lévi-Strauss 1964, 78). This is a too much unspecific feature of social organisation to be interpreted as the focus around which the meaning of the narrative revolves. Perhaps, an alternative way of looking at the problem could be to emphasise the metaphoric potential of kinship terminology. Affinal relationships have been frequently used in many cultures to define the link between individuals not primarily united by any kinship tie, as Lévi-Strauss himself discovered in his field investigations among the Brazilian Indians (Lévi-Strauss 1943, 407–408). Kinship provides a series of links which can be used to establish a wider spectre of relations, of social as well as ceremonial or spiritual nature. In particular, the term for 'father' is employed with symbolic and metaphorical extensions in several cultures, including the contemporary Western countries. Incidentally, among the Bororo, the shaman (*bari*) calls the spirit he is addressing to, during the ritual offerings, as 'my father', since they are generally the spirits pertaining to the opposite moiety (Lévi-Strauss 1944, 266).

If the situation described in the myth could be interpreted as an initiation test in which a young apprentice is subjected to a series of trials by a symbolic 'father', an initiatory spirit or a human instructor, it is absolutely irrelevant to search the clue of the story in the actual relationships among specific social actors or kinship categories. They are not real relatives who act in fantastic and unnatural ways, but symbolic or metaphorical relatives who interact in a real and potentially dangerous situation, the apprenticeship to the shamanic profession. Passing the test signifies to overcome fear and to show ability and power: the hero of the myth demonstrates his powers transforming himself into a deer and killing his father. He throws him into a lake, that is he makes him return in the world of the spirits of the dead, which according to Bororo cosmology abide in the waters.

But there are still other elements in the story which point to the initiation of an apprentice shaman. When he finds himself abandoned on the top of the cliff, the young bird-nester, feeling hungry, began to hunt the lizards, which were numerous in that place. He eats some of them and ties the rest to his belt and armbands. They begin to decay and to smell so bad that the boy faints and falls unconscious on the ground (Wilbert & Simoneau 1983, 206). The stench attracts the vultures, which eat the rotten lizards but also part of the hero's buttocks. Then they grab him by his belt with their beaks and carried him through the air until they put him on the ground. At this juncture, a phrase of the text is significant: 'When the boy came to he felt as though he had awakened from a long sleep' (Wilbert & Simoneau 1983, 207; Colbacchini 1925, 235). Here the story involuntarily reveals that the adventure has been experienced in an ecstatic, dream-like condition. According to Crocker's description, Bororo shamans are possessed by the *bope* spirits during ceremonial food offerings. 'Shamans say possession is much like a dream. They are 'conscious' but passive spectators of a distorted world filled with bizarre activity ...; several shamans confirmed this, comparing their usual experience of possession to a feverish dream or a conscious-less sleep. Only occasionally are they aware of that distorted world just described' (Crocker 1985, 222–223). During the night following the offering, the shaman's familiar come to him during his sleep and causes his *bope*-soul to mount upon its back, and rises with it into the sky and all the *maereboe* (bad spirits) flock around, often in the shape of vultures and hawks. After having gone up to where the mother and father of all shamans live, the shaman's soul rides his familiar back down to earth and the soul returns to the shaman's body. 'The several shamans I discussed the topic with said they seldom could remember upon waking all details of this dream-like experience' (Crocker 1985, 225).

The act of putting on himself the corpses of the dead lizards is not a strange and irrelevant detail, but it signals the transformation of the hero into a corpse, his near-death experience, also represented in other variants of the myth by the covering of the hero with birds' dejections. The motif of the dismemberment of the body of the neophyte and his successive reconstitution is recurrent in the shamanic initiations of many peoples (Eliade 1968, 48 and passim). Among the Bororo, the shaman of the *aroe*, nowadays disappeared, when he received for the first time the ceremonial rattles, collapsed in a deathlike trance. He was treated like he was really dead and the funeral ceremony was begun. According to Bororo theory, the *aroe* actually took away the novice shaman's soul, just as they did when someone died (Crocker 1985, 294). 'During this time the *aroe* alternately 'kill' and resuscitate their new shaman. While he is 'dead', they take his soul around to visit the eight sectors where dwell the *aroe* forms of each clan and to the other-worldly rivers where live the true *aije* [the most powerful spirits], so generally instructing him in the ways of the *aroe* world' (Crocker 1985, 295). One of the signals in the initiation of a *bari* (shaman of the *bope*) is that he smells rotting corpse and that he becomes insensibly possessed (Crocker 1985, 316), a situation that is extraordinarily similar to that of the hero in the myth, who faints for the smell of rotting lizards and is brought, in a dream-like experience, by the vultures in the sky.

At his return to the village, the hero demonstrates the new powers he has acquired showing his ability to turn into animals. First he transforms himself into a lizard, before his grandmother and brother can recognise him, then he turns into a deer, after having organised a deer hunt, with the intention to kill his father. Among the main mystical abilities attributed to Bororo shamans, there is the power to change themselves into certain animals. 'In popular belief, every mature shaman can, through the good offices of his familiar, change himself into a jaguar, alligator, or rattlesnake whenever he chooses, both in dreams and while in trance' (Crocker 1985, 243). Furthermore, the shaman of the *aroe* was thought to be able to change himself into a tapir, or sometimes into a wild pig or certain kinds of fish. 'In this form he either drives game to the hunters or allows his animal form to be killed. He does this only during those collective hunts in which men represent deceased Bororo' (Crocker 1985, 298). The final episode of the myth describes one of this collective ceremonial hunts in which the hero transforms himself into the animal prey and attacks the 'father', the initiatory figure to whom he demonstrates his new powers and his lack of fear.

A Nest of Eagles

Lévi-Strauss has demonstrated that the bird-nester motif was widely diffused both in South and in North America. In particular he has identified a group of myths in the north-west, at the foot of the Rocky Mountains, among the Klamath, Chinook and Interior Salish (Lévi-Strauss 1971, 30). In the present discussion reference shall be made to similar documents from the Northern Plains and the North-Eastern Woodlands.[13]

Among the Crow of Montana, the story of Big-Iron is fit for this purpose, because it presents many points of contact with the Bororo myth. A boy is taken by his stepfather on a steep hill, from which an eagle nest could be seen, on the middle of the way. The boy is lowered with a rope, but when he has reached the nest the stepfather threw the rope, so that he was unable to get up again. At last the eagles took pity on him and brought him down on the ground. He killed a buffalo, cut it open and left it as an offering for the eagles. Then he killed his stepfather and declareed that nobody could go near his body. When one of the man's relatives tried to take his bones and bury them, it suddenly rained on him, though there were no clouds, and lightning struck and killed him. The story reveals at this juncture that the boy was a medicine-man that is a shaman (Lowie 1918, 288–290). Another, longer version of the same tale shows further important details. The boy is thrown down a precipice, while he was looking for deer following the instructions of his stepfather, and remains on a ledge at the middle of the precipice and is abandoned there. The boy cried all day and some animals came to visit him 'in a vision': a sparrow hawk, a squirrel and an eagle. All of them say in turn: 'I was going to have you for my adopted child, but now I won't' (Lowie 1918, 291). At last he is saved by four mountain sheep[14], which say '[y]our father told us to come here and rescue you' and which bring him to an island where he is put in front of an old man. The boy was reduced to a skeleton from hunger. The old man dives in the water four times and comes out first as a young man and then older. These performances meant that the boy was to live four times. The old man's name is Big-Iron, the same name taken by the hero of the story (Lowie 1918, 292). In the successive episodes the hero demonstrates his powers in defeating a shaman, and then reviving him breaking wind in his face, and in conveying to the Crows prophecies about the future coming of the white man. When he was old, he told the people to throw him into the water and he became young again. He played with the most dangerous things, and he enjoyed making fun with Thunder, who was called by him 'my brother' (Lowie 1918, 294).

The situation is thus rather similar to that described by the Bororo reference myth: the initial relationship is a link between a boy and his stepfather. The first version does not even try to furnish a meaningful reason for the stepfather's action, but simply states that '[h]e was always angry with his stepson' (Lowie 1918, 288). As we have seen, it is futile trying to envisage in this fact some peculiar aspect of social life among the Crow: it is rather the necessary first step of every initiatory adventure. The story, then, duplicates the bad father figure with the 'good' father, the old man living on the island, who gave his name and his powers to the boy. But also the animals, coming to visit the boy 'in a vision', are willing to adopt him as a child, that is they wanted to be their 'stepfathers'. The myth explicitly evokes the setting of a vision quest, with the implicit assumption that it is the important undertaking of a man of power, of a prospective shaman. In the vision quest, the supplicants show themselves to be incomplete beings, looking like orphans, seeking completeness and help from the spirit powers. The quester had to remain in an isolated spot, without food and water, in a pitiless and helpless condition, just like a boy abandoned in the middle of a cliff, on a hill or on an island. The main instrument for obtaining a vision is fasting, remaining without food and water for some days. 'A faster is destitute, alone, in need of help, like an "orphan", *akéeleete*, meaning "one with no possessions, one who has nothing". One of the most commonly used expressions in prayer during a sweat, before a meal, or during a Sun Dance is, "I am poor, pitiful, in need" (*biiwaatcheeshkáatak*)' (Frey 1987, 80–81). If the supplicant's gift of himself is deemed worthy, some spiritual power takes pity on him or her and sends a vision and instructions for the acquisition of knowledge and power. The vision establishes a father-child relationship between the quester and the spirit, which is called *iilápxe*, 'my father', spiritual mediator (Frey 1987, 85, 184). The acquisition of powers through the vision produces a transformation in the supplicant; the faster returns as a new self, as a transformed being. The killing of the stepfather signals his abandonment of his previous existence, his acquisition of new powers and confidence.

But we can pose a further question: who is this old man who gave his name of Big-Iron to the hero of the tale? The name Big-Iron (*ū'wut-isā'c*) is of obscure meaning: literally it refers to a material which was not known at the time in which the myth takes place, and alludes to the prophetic capacities developed by the hero. The old man says that '[a]ll the animals are my children', presents himself with a painted shield and a spear and the boy is given by him a war-club-stone tied to a sheep's tail (Frey 1987, 292). All these elements seem to indicate that this personage has something to do with Thunder, the spirit power related to war and whose weapon is often a war-club. Furthermore, the old man says to the boy: 'You are my child and may make all the fun you like' (Frey 1987, 292). And the story narrates that he was eager to make fun of Thunder, who he regarded as his brother. It is possible that this account hinted at the function of the ritual clowns (*akbī'arusacarica*) (Lowie 1913, 207–211; Lewis 1982), that in most of the Plains tribes acquired their powers and behaviour by a contact with the Thunder spirit. During the performance to which Lowie attended, the clowns expressed by gestures that they had come from the sky (Lowie 1935 [1983, 97]). The episode in which the boy defeated a shaman and then revived him breaking wind on his face could well be assigned to a ceremonial clown. Furthermore, when he killed his stepfather and forbade everyone to move the corpse, the individual who tried to bury him was punished by rain and lightning. Incidentally, we have to remember that the Bororo hero, when he at last left the human world, turns himself into a spirit, whose manifestations are wind, rain and storm. So, it is at least plausible that the name Big-Iron could allude to the gloomy colour of the dark stormy clouds. If this is so, then it becomes more clear why the stepfather's name of the hero is Good Clouds (*a'bā'x-ítsic*), since he is a sort of a duplicate of the 'father' who adopts the boy after the ordeal.

In several Plains versions of this story, the role of the villain who sent the protagonist on errand and then abandons him is played by the Trickster. For example, in an Arapaho story, the Trickster (*nih'oothoo*) advises a hunter to climb up a peak in order to get the young eagles from a nest. While he is up there, the Trickster commands the peak to increase its height so that the hunter cannot get down. The Trickster takes the weapons and clothes of the hunter and goes to the other man's tipi where he takes his place as husband and father. The villagers moved in search of the hunter, discover him and ask the geese to bring him down on their backs. Returned home he kills the Trickster, who afterwards comes back to life again (Dorsey & Kroeber 1903, 78–81). An analogous story is told by the Canadian Dakota, among whom the Trickster takes the name of 'Spider' (*iktomi*). The hero of the Dakota story is born from a girl brought up to the sky to marry Thunder, who then fell from the sky and crushed on earth, giving birth to the child, who takes on the name of Thunder Boy (Wallis 1923, 85–88). The name is particularly meaningful, because if Spider was regarded as the most powerful creature on earth, Thunders were the heads of everything above and ruled over everything that flies in the air. Particularly, shamans were instructed by the Thunders, which transmitted to them the instructions given by the Great Power (*wakan tanka*) (Wallis 1923, 57). According to a document collected by Wallis (Wallis 1923, 45):

> A medicine-man said the Thunders told him that the Great Power had given them the fire and instructed them not to tell or show anyone where they kept it, but to keep this information to themselves. Therefore, no one knows where or how they keep the lightning. This medicine-man had asked the Thunders for fire. The Thunders told him that the Great Power had given them the fire with which to set fire to anything they might select, and had given them water also.

This element is of particular interest, in so far as the Bororo reference myth is related to a series of myths from the Gê speaking tribes, which focused on the origin of fire (Wilbert 1978, 160–171). The bird-nester was saved by the jaguar, the master of fire, who brought him to his house, where he lived with his wife. The jaguar gave the hero both the first hunting weapons and the knowledge of fire, which humans still did not possess (Lévi-Strauss 1964, 74–86).

But returning to the Canadian Dakota, they asserted that nearly all shamans were with the Thunders before they came to earth and were born here. While with the Thunders, they travelled about with thunderstorms, searching for a place to be born (Wallis 1947, 81). Though the ceremonial clowns are widely diffused among North American Native peoples, the Canadian Dakota attribute to them special shamanic powers. They are considered the most powerful medicine-men (Wallis 1947, 111). The mythical trickster figure is the narrative personification of the ceremonial clown and reveals also several relationships with the shamanic experience.

> The Ojibway recognize that it is possible for a person to be overwhelmed by personalistic powers, yet they consider that the pursuit of personalistic power is a means of alleviating the inherent weakness of the human condition. The ideal personality is one who becomes so powerful that he can claim to embody the Manitou himself, like Nanabozho [the Ojibwa Trickster], who boldly pursued power and brazenly claimed equal status with the Manitou. (Grim 1983, 88)

So it is understandable that the Trickster could be used in the narratives to represent what an apprentice had to confront with and had to demonstrate having being able to overcome, to 'kill,' in order to become a shaman.

Alone on an Island

An old version of a similar story, recorded among the Ojibwa by Henry R. Schoolcraft and published in 1839[15], reveals a peculiar combination of motifs. The young protagonist is an orphan who is kidnapped by a 'magician' and brought in an island in the centre of a lake, where he is presented to the two daughters of the magician as their prospective husband. Then the boy is taken by his captor on another island where he is expected to gather gulls' eggs, and is left there to be killed by the birds. The boy managed to overpower the gulls and asked them to bring him on their backs to the magician's lodge. The next day he is again abandoned on an island with the pretext of gathering pebbles (a duplicate for eggs?) and destined to be killed by fish, but he is able to make the fish carry him home on his back. At last, he is brought on an island and has to climb a tree in order to reach a nest with young eagles. The magician made the tree become taller and taller and left him up there. The eagles are persuaded to bring him on their backs to the lodge of the magician's daughters. At last the boy decides 'to try his own power', and the defeated magician is transformed into a sycamore tree, while the hero marries his two daughters.

This tale is remarkable in so far as it presents a repetition of the same situation, in some way analogous with that shown in the Bororo reference myth: in the Ojibwa story, too, the adventure of the hero implies both an horizontal displacement, in which he has to cross a body of water, and a vertical displacement in which he remains perched on a tree. It is plausible to suppose that the two modalities are really only different expressions of the same topic: the abrupt and potentially dangerous crossing of a border separating this world from another world, a world inhabited by spiritual powers and potential helpers, if they are willing to take pity of the forsaken hero.

This perspective can be corroborated by a myth from the Hidatsa, which pertains to the group of the so-called 'Potiphar versions' (Lévi-Strauss 1968, 458), in which the motivation for the abandonment of the hero is caused by the false charges advanced by his brother's wife. The boy is abandoned after having crossed a watercourse, during a war expedition. With the instructions of a spirit, who is really the Thunder, the hero asks a Water Serpent to take him across the water. During the crossing he had to feed the monster with cornballs. When the serpent reached the land, the boy jumped down and immediately the Thunder sent down two strokes of lightning that killed the serpent. Thunder was usually depicted as a bird, but this time appeared as an ordinary man, and gave the boy a knife with which he had to chop the serpent's body and offer it to the birds, because the Thunder was the 'head of all the birds' (Beckwith 1938, 81–91). So again, the protagonist of the narrative gains the protection of Thunder, which is represented by the birds, and in particular by the eagle. In fact, 'Indians are of the opinion that the thunderbirds are eagles or at least have the shape of eagles' (Hultkrantz 1979, 50). This confirms again that the Crow hero Big-Iron, who is pitied and saved by the eagles, obtains the powers of Thunder and storm.[16] Incidentally, these are the same powers represented by the Bororo protagonist of the reference myth. It is still more surprising that Lévi-Strauss does not recognise this fundamental element of shamanic origin in the story, since he had observed, during his second ethnographic expedition in Central Brazil, among the Nambikwara, that supernatural communication could occur usually during storms and tempests. Such visions were attributed to Thunder, under his semi-personal appearance. Every individual among the Nambikwara could establish contacts with these cosmic forces, though the shamans were those who possessed the specialised function of intermediaries between the human group and the supernatural world.[17] A long Mandan version of this tale insert the episode in a sequel of adventures attributed to Stiff-Robe, the son of a buffalo-man and a human woman, a fact which explains the hero's capacity to call the buffalo and supply game when his people is in need of food. The boy is abandoned across a river and is saved by the eagles (Beckwith 1938, 161–164).

A myth of the Oglala Lakota focuses on a protagonist who is called Iron Hawk, a name recalling that of the hero in the Crow myth, Big-Iron, and which can possibly have the same meaning. Iron Hawk was found when still a child in a stump, by a couple of elders who reveal themselves to be two meadowlarks. These particulars connect this tale with the group of stories about the boy fallen from the sky, called Fallen Star or Shooting Star, but the implications of these relationships cannot be followed in the present paper.[18] However, the boy begins his adventure helping four men, who are in reality the personifications of Lightning, and kills a bad old woman, who is part of the *unhcegila*, the Rock People. But the Lakota name refers specifically to the Water Monsters living in rivers and streams, who are continually at war against the Thunders. Then again the hero seems to be identified with the Thunder powers or having been able to acquire the powers of Thunder. Subsequently, he jumps into a pit, to catch some objects of value which should permit him to marry the daughter of the chief, but an impostor leaves him on the bottom of the pit, takes on his clothes and goes away to the village. The hero is saved by an old woman who takes him in her tipi, and at last he reveals his powers procuring buffalo using the hoop and stick[19] (Beckwith 1930, 379–391). This version shows another transformation in the general plot: this time the hero is not required to climb on a tree or on a rock but to descend into a pit. However, the significance is always the same: a vertical displacement which brings the hero momentarily in another world, separates him from his family or his acquaintances. As in the versions from the Plateau and Rocky Mountains utilised by Lévi-Strauss (1971), the Oglala hero undresses himself before going into the pit, in this way depriving himself of his social status and he becomes a 'naked man', a helpless being seeking for the benevolent advise of a spiritual power. The meaning of the nakedness of the medicine-man has been aptly observed more than a century ago by Francis La Flesche:

> This nudity is not without significance, it typifies the utter helplessness of man, when his strength is contrasted with the power of the Great Spirit, whose power is symbolized by the horns upon the head of the priest. (La Flesche 1905, 13)

Furthermore, the pit in which the hero descends and where he is abandoned recalls the space in which the supplicant has to dwell when he goes on vision questing. 'In the vision quest, a man is placed on a sacred hill and a pit is dug where he will stay while crying for a vision' (Powers 1977, 182). Explicitly some Lakota have reflected on how much the vision pit was like a grave. 'People often joked about going in your grave on the vision quest' (Powers 1982, 90).[20]

Conversely, among the Ojibwa, the boy had to climb on a tree to fast and obtain a vision. An Indian described in this way, in the XIXth century, his experience when he was a young lad:

> The grandfather then took me by the hand, and led me deep into the forest. Here he selected a lofty tree, a red pine, and prepared a bed for me in the branches, on which I should lie down to fast. We cut down the bushes, and twined them through the pine branches ... I was also permitted to fasten a few branches together over my head, as a sort of protection from wind and rain. (Kohl 1860, 234)

This usage was still remembered among the Canadian Ojibwa of Big Trout Lake during the 1980s. Around the age of 10–12 years, the boys as well as the girls were taken into the woods. Here they had to climb a tree, generally a spruce particularly tall, where a sort of platform had been previously built, almost at the top. There they had to remain, exposed to the elements and in absolute loneliness, fasting and waiting to experience a vision, for four or sometimes ten days, according to the informants.[21] This was particularly important for the future shamans and such an initiatory ordeal was described as a 'nest': *wa'dissan*, 'bird's nest' (Hilger 1951, 42; Barnouw 1977, 136). It was an evident ritual reproduction of the mythical motif of the bird-nester (Désveaux 2001, 73).[22] The experience of the young boy left on a tree, in the middle of woods, when the father or grandfather went away and he remained for days without food nor water, should have been very similar to that described in the myths of the cycle of the 'bird-nester'. But this sense of desperation, of impotence, was necessary because it could rouse the pitiful attention of a spiritual helper, who 'adopted' the faster and decided to bestow on him his own powers and knowledge. This kind of experience is recorded by the Crow chief Plenty Coups:

> When I was sixteen years old I went up onto Bear Tooth Mountains. I went alone and climbed to the highest point. I stayed up there four days without food or water. The days were very hot and the nights were very cold. I waited and watched and nothing came to me. Then, when I was very weak and suffered from hunger and thirst so I could not walk any more I lay down on a rock and gazed up into the Blue. And soon, while I looked, many eagles -maybe so ten, maybe so twenty - flew above me and gave me medicine - strong medicine - you know?. (Wagner & Allen 1933 [1987, 290–291])

The same Plenty Coups has narrated the story of The Fringe, 'one of the most powerful men I ever knew' (Linderman 1930 [1961, 299]). This powerful shaman had his great dream near a spring, called by the Crows Medicine Water, because it healed the sick. The spring lied at the foot of a little hill, and in the centre of the water there was a small island. The Fringe went there to dream, reaching the island by walking a pole which two friends helped him place from the shore. When he had reached the island, his friends, at his request, went away and left him on the island. On the third night a person came to him and asked him to follow, when he sank into the boiling Medicine Water. He found himself into a lodge where there were an Otter and a White Bear, both angry toward him. But the person who had invited him said that he was 'his son'. When he awakened he found himself not on the island but on the shore. He became a powerful and respected healer and was requested often to treat serious wounds received in battle (Linderman 1930 [1961, 299–304]).

Thus, the different versions which constitute the group of myths containing the 'bird-nester motif' and which are diffused all through the American continent, are not only logical transformations on the basis of a system of coordinates, like above/below, vertical/horizontal, up-on-a-tree/down-in-a-pit, and so forth, as Lévi-Strauss has tried to brilliantly show. They rather describe a set of modalities in which the fundamental shamanic experience of communication with another reality can be enacted. Such an experience requires a sort of leap in the unknown, which is represented by the abandonment of the apprentice, who has to rely thoroughly on the help of spiritual powers who take pity of him, who feel compassion for his lamentable condition and provide him with encouragement and support.

There is still a particular of the tales that merits to be taken into account. In the Bororo reference myth, the vultures first eat the protagonist's buttocks and then turn into saviours and bring him down on the ground. He replaces the eaten part with a tuber and carries on his adventures. Lévi-Strauss (1964, 56) signals that the mythical motif of the 'anus stopper' can be found in the mythologies of Oregon and Washington, but these are in reality tales of the Trickster cycle which have little to do with the story of the bird-nester. Fabian suggests that the motif finds his explanation in the initiation rituals for youths. The initiates are 'closed' physically but 'opened' spiritually. Among the Barasana of Colombia the initiates have to adhere to strict food taboos, in order not to have their anuses opened (Fabian 1992, 60). However, the most important element in the episode is not the anus, but the vultures. In most

South American cultures, the vulture has a special affinity with the shaman, and sometimes appears to him in human form, by removing its feather cloak. As carrion eaters, vultures have a special connection to death and the Underworld, the land of the dead, which is one of the other worlds visited by the shamans in their out-of-the-body journeys. But vultures, like other raptors as the eagles, are also birds which can soar high in the sky, until they seem to disappear to human sight, as they were passed through the celestial vault. 'The vulture is itself a shaman, because like the shaman it can travel through the different planes of the multilayered cosmos and is gifted with the special sight by which the human shaman looks into other worlds' (Furst 1991, 104). This is confirmed by a group of myths among the Gê speaking peoples, which narrates of a sick man who is abandoned by his villagers and is helped by vultures, which heal his wounds and take him to the sky. In an Apinaye version he is received by Thunder, who gives him a sword-club before the vultures bring him down on earth. He demonstrates his power by transforming himself into an animal and has to defeat his adversary in a contest of magical skill (Wilbert 1978, 385–399).

In the Bororo myth, the vultures first regard the hero as a dead corpse, which stinks like the dead lizards which he has put on his body, then take pity on him and help him to come back on the ground. This corresponds to the death-like experience which is faced by the apprentice shaman and is represented in different ways in the stories. However, among the Ojibwa (or Chippewa) of North America it is possible to find a tale which shows many points of contact with the Bororo myth. Once again it is a story of the Trickster, which in the Ojibwa world is called Wenebojo. The turkey buzzard (*Cathartes aura*) showed Wenebojo how he could use his arms as they were wings and thus flying in the air like a bird, but then he left him up in the sky. He managed to jump down and decided to take his revenge on the buzzard. He turned into a caribou or a moose and feigned to be dead. When the turkey buzzard, believing he was carrion, began to eat Wenebojo's anus, he closed his rectum and caught the head of the buzzard inside, leaving it go only after some time. That is why the turkey buzzard has a scabby red neck and head and why he smells so bad (Barnouw 1977, 89–90).

Though transformed by the hyperbolic adventures of the Trickster, the common scheme is still recognisable: the vulture is the master of the sky and can teach to its protégé the art of flying as a bird. To attract the attention of the vultures one has to transform himself into a corpse, to experience a death-like transformation. In the story, the vulture is treated disrespectfully by Wenebojo, because the Trickster does not recognise any other power than his own, and he has not to ask the protection or help of anyone, since he already has, or believes to have, all the power he wants. I have not found any document about the role played by the buzzard in the Ojibwa world-view, but an old article, that contains an interesting reference. It is reported here that during fasting the Chippewa practiced many rites 'to excite the feelings to a proper degree of susceptibility'. 'The guardian Manitou finally appears in a dream, assuming the shape of some animal, which is during life the object of adoration, and governs the future life of the dreamer. If it be an eagle, he must be a warrior, if a wolf a hunter, if a turkey buzzard a prophet or physician' (Ranking 1828, 335). Though in a simplistic way, it reveals a relationship of the turkey buzzard with the arts of the shaman (healing the sick and seeing into the future), which comes very close to that described by the group of Gê myths quoted above.

Conclusions

From the above discussion, the 'pivotal' function of the myths containing the motif of the 'bird-nester', proposed by Lévi-Strauss (1964, 17) is largely confirmed. However this function is not due to the position they occupy within a transformation group, but rather to the fact that they include some basic ideas about the way in which an apprentice shaman acquires his knowledge and power. According to Lévi-Strauss's interpretation, the relationship between the Bororo reference myth and the group of Gê myths on the origin of fire is that the first myth shows the motif of the origin of rain and wind, thus transforming the element fire in its opposite, 'a sort of anti-fire' (Lévi-Strauss 1964, 147). The present discussion has revealed that the spirit being presiding to rain, storm and wind is often involved into the process of acquisition of power by the shaman, and the same thing can be affirmed about the jaguar, master of fire for the Gê myths, but also one of the more powerful spirits which can transfer their power to the shaman and into which the shaman himself can be transformed (see Reichel-Dolmatoff 1975; Wright 2013).

The wide distribution of this myth both in South and in North America suggests that the tale has its roots in a long-distant past. The different variants describe a general pattern common to most of the shamanic experience of Amerindian peoples. They are not to be regarded as the specific representation of shamanic institutions typical of this or that particular cultural group. For example, the Bororo reference myth does not emphasise the peculiar Bororo subdivision of shamans into two groups: the *bari* and the *aroe etawa-are*, rather it represents certain common features which could be applied to the experiences of both kinds of shamans. In a similar vein, the Ojibwa variants we have examined do not say anything about the specific shamanic figures of the Ojibwa: the *tcisaki* (shaking tent diviner), the *wabeno* (fire-manipulator) or the *nanandawi* (tube-sucking curer). The bird-nester myth shows a general scheme, into which the experience of the apprentice shaman can be moulded.

Furthermore, the variants of the tale present a series of transformations regarding the dislocation of the hero: in the more 'classical' versions he has to climb a tree, or a rock or steep hill; in other versions, particularly in North America, he has to cross a stream or to reach an island; in other still he descends into a pit or a cave. Far from being only logical variations on a common theme, these variants describe a cosmological structure, shared by most Native cultures of the Americas and strictly related to the practice of shamanism, which shows the image of a multi-layered universe. Most of the Amerindian worldviews are based on the central feature of the search of personal empowerment through dreams and visions, which is embedded in a mythic description of the world inseparable from the natural and social environments. The world constitutes an undivided wholeness, whose centre is the earth itself, described as a life-giving female being. The middle ground, represented by the earth, is related to other interpenetrating strata: the above realm and the below realm. 'The relationship between these realms can best be described topologically as a distinctive contrast, more or less emphasised, between the above and the below, with the middle representing the mysterious realm in which all beings meet and interact' (Irwin 1994, 30). For example, the Ojibwa worldview was constituted by a flat piece of earth, like a log floating in a lake; below the water there was another world similar to the earth, and above the dome of the sky a third world was located. In all of these strata lived the *manitos*, spirit beings similar to humans but having more power. Every individual, but particularly the future shaman, could enter a personal relationship with any of the *manitos* through the puberty vision fast (Vecsey 1983, 72–73). The human world was thus reduced to the earthly realm, a kind of precarious middle ground, in which the human subject inhabited an island at the centre of a dialectical cosmos, subject to protection and assault from above and below by powerful spirit beings (Smith 1995, 3).

The myths of the 'bird-nester' group, taking all the variants together, describe the configuration of this cosmographic structure of a multi-layered universe, as well as the bewildering experience the apprentice shaman had to accomplish: trespassing the boundaries between the realms of the world and coming into contact with powerful beings, who were potentially benevolent and helpful, but could be at the same time dangerous and threatening. Being abandoned and going without food and water, the hero of the tale, like the youths undertaking a visionary quest or a shamanic initiation, makes himself 'poor' and helpless, pitiable to the spirit powers, in order to evoke in them a compassionate response. He places himself in a liminal condition, devoid of normal social relationships, in the hope of establishing more powerful kinship relations with the dream or vision spirits (Irwin 1994, 110). In this sense, the hero of the myth, at the beginning abandoned by a 'father' or other relative, at the end of the story finds another 'father', willing to give him power and knowledge, transforming him into a new person, with the powers of turning himself into an animal or to provoke rain and wind. The poor boy has become a powerful shaman.

Notes

1 In the following pages I make reference to the original French editions of Lévi-Strauss's works. The Anglophone reader can easily find most of these works translated into English.

2 '*Or, c'est bien une syntaxe de la mythologie sud-américaine dont nous avons voulu faire l'ébauche*' (Lévi-Strauss 1964, 16). A more developed presentation of Lévi-Strauss's theory and analysis of myths can be found in a previous work: Comba 2000.

3 'Chaque mythe pris en particulier existe comme application restreinte d'un schème que les rapports d'intelligibilité réciproque, perçu entre plusieurs mythes, aident progressivement à dégager' (Lévi-Strauss 1964, 21).

4 'Les Bororo croient en un cycle compliqué de transmigrations des âmes; pendant un temps, celles-ci sont censées s'incarner dans les aras' (Lévi-Strauss 1964, 55).

5 'Nous laissons complètement de côté tout ce qui se rapporte au pouvoir spirituel et à la vie religieuse' (Lévi-Strauss 1936, 285, n. 1). For a review of the ethnographical contributions given by the two expeditions conducted by Lévi-Strauss in Central Brazil, see Benzi Grupioni (2005).

6 'Ce sans-gêne vis-à-vis du surnaturel m'étonnait d'autant plus que mon seul contact avec la religion remonte à une enfance déjà incroyante' (Lévi-Strauss 1955, 260).

7 'La notion de «sacré» est cruellement absente des analyses que Lévi-Strauss a consacrées aux mythes et aux religions, presque toutes tribales et polythéistes, qu'il a étudiés' (Godelier 2013, 430).

8 A lot of literature has accumulated about this example, since the times of Lévy-Bruhl and Durkheim. A useful compendium is furnished by Crocker (1977) and Smith (1978).

9 '[Le] monde surnaturel est lui-même double, puisqu'il comprend le domaine du prêtre et celui du sorcier' (Lévi-Strauss 1955, 174).

10 They are made with an empty gourd, decorated with red and yellow plumes and with seeds inside to make the rattling sound, see De Palma (2004, 132–133).

11 Boar's hoofs put on a string, which are worn around the ankles and shaken to the rhythm of dance, see De Palma (2004, 122).

12 According to Lévi-Strauss, the motif of the stepmother's rape in the reference myth is attributable to a representation of the boy's refusal to join the men's house and his desire to remain in the domestic group, 'le viol de la mère traduit le refus de rejoindre la maison des hommes et de quitter l'univers infantile et féminin' (Lévi-Strauss 1971, 30). Analogously, Fabian (1992, 32, and *passim*) sustains that the Toribugu myth describes the social growth and maturation of the hero, illustrative of the development of the Bororo male in general.

13 It is presented here a synthesis of a wider discussion of the theme of the bird-nester myth in the Plains which has been advanced in Comba (2012, chap. X)

14 Among the Paviotso of Nevada, 'When animals such an eagle, owl, deer, antelope, bear, mountain sheep or snake, come to a person a number of times in a dream, he knows that he is to become a shaman' (Park 1934, 99).

15 Schoolcraft 1839, vol. 2, 91–104, republished in Williams 1956, 163–168.

16 Among the powers obtained by the young Ojibwa by fasting in his 'nest' is reported the capacity to produce rain and winds (Hilger 1951, 44).

17 'Ces communications surnaturelles se produisent habituellement à l'occasion des tempêtes et des orages ... Ces visions sont attribuées au tonnerre qui les envoie aux hommes sous sa forme semi-personnelle *amõ* ... Chaque individu peut, dans une certaine mesure, établir des contacts avec ces forces, néanmoins ce sont les shamans qui détiennent la fonction spécialisée d'intermédiaires entre le groupe humain et le monde surnaturel' (Lévi-Strauss 1948, 101).

18 For further details on these aspects, see Comba (2012, chap. X).

19 The game of the hoop and pole was diffused throughout the entire continent North of Mexico. It consisted in throwing a spear or a stick at a hoop or ring, see Culin (1907, 420–527). In most of the Plains tribes it was related to the hunting ceremonies.

20 John Fire Lame Deer described the anxiety and restlessness of a young boy spending the night in the vision pit (see Irwin 1994, 128).

21 'Vers l'âge de dix ou douze ans, les garçons ainsi que les filles, sont emmenés dans la brousse. Ils doivent grimper à un arbre, en général un épicéa particulièrement élevé, et ce, jusqu'à une sorte de plate forme qui a été installée au préalable, pratiquement au sommet. Là, exposés aux éléments, dans la solitude absolue, ils sont censées jeûner afin d'avoir des hallucinations, abstinence qui doit durer quatre ou dix jours, selon les informateurs' (Désveaux 1988, 190).

22 Similarly, among the Gros Ventre of the Plains, the fasting place was called a 'nest' (Irwin 1994, 109).

References

Barnouw, V. 1977. *Wisconsin Chippewa Myths and Tales and Their Relation to Chippewa Life*. Madison WI: University of Wisconsin Press.

Beckwith, M. W. 1930. Mythology of the Oglala Dakota. *Journal of American Folk-Lore* 43(170), 339–442.

Beckwith, M. W. 1938. *Mandan-Hidatsa Myths and Ceremonies*. Memoirs of the American Folk-Lore Society 32. New York: J. J. Augustin.

Benzi Grupioni, L. D. 2005. Claude Lévi-Strauss parmi les Amérindiens: deux expéditions ethnographiques dans l'intérieur du Brésil. In L. D. Benzi Gruponi (ed.) *Brésil indien: Les arts des Amérindiens du Brésil*, Paris: Réunion des Musées Nationaux, 313–352.

Colbacchini, A. 1925. *I Bororos Orientali 'Orarimugudoge' del Matto Grosso (Brasile)*. Torino: Società Editrice Internazionale.

Comba, E. 2000. *Introduzione a Lévi-Strauss*. Roma-Bari: Laterza.

Comba, E. 2012. *La Danza del Sole: Miti e cosmologia tra gli Indiani delle Pianure*. Aprilia, LT: Novalogos.

Crocker, J. C. 1977. My brother the parrot. In J. D. Sapir & J. C. Crocker (eds) *The Social Use of Metaphor: Essays on the Anthropology of Rhetoric*. Philadelphia PA: University of Pennsylvania Press, 164–192.

Crocker, J. C. 1985. *Vital Souls: Bororo Cosmology, Natural Symbolism, and Shamanism*. Tucson AZ: University of Arizona Press.

Culin, S. 1907. Games of the North American Indians. *24th Annual Report of the Bureau of American Ethnology 1902-1903*. Washington: Smithsonian Institute.

De Palma, M. C. (ed.). 2004. *Io sono Bororo: un popolo indigeno del Brasile tra riti e 'futebol'*. Cinisello Balsamo: Silvana Editoriale.

Désveaux, E. 1988. *Sous le signe de l'ours: mythes et temporalité chez les Ojibwa septentrionaux*. Paris: Éditions de la Maison des Sciences de l'Homme.

Désveaux, E. 2001. *Quadratura Americana: Essai d'anthropologie lévi-straussienne*. Genève: Georg.

Dorsey, G. A. & Kroeber, A. L. 1903. Traditions of the Arapaho. Collected under the auspices of the Field Columbian Museum and the American Museum of Natural History. *Anthropological Series* Vol. V, Publication 81. Chicago: Field Columbian Museum.

Eliade, M. 1968. *Le chamanisme et les techniques archaïques de l'extase*. 2nd edition. Paris: Payot.

Fabian, S. M. 1992. *Space-Time of the Bororo of Brazil*. Gainesville Fl.: University Press of Florida.

Frey, R. 1987. *The World of the Crow Indians: As Driftwood Lodges*. Norman OK/London: University of Oklahoma Press.

Furst, P. T. 1991. Crowns of power: Bird and feather symbolism in Amazonian shamanism. In R. E. Reina & K. M. Kensinger (eds) *The Gift of Birds: Featherwork of Native South American Peoples*. Philadelphia PA: University Museum of Archaeology and Anthropology, 92–109.

Godelier, M. 2013. *Lévi-Strauss*. Paris: Seuil.

Grim, J. A. 1983. *The Shaman: Patterns of Siberian and Ojibway Healing*. Norman OK: University of Oklahoma Press.

Hilger, M. I. 1951. Chippewa child life and its cultural background, *Bureau of American Ethnology Bulletin* 146, 1–204.

Hultkrantz, Å. 1979. *The Religions of the American Indians*. Berkeley CA: University of California Press.

Irwin, L. 1994. *The Dream Seekers: Native American Visionary Traditions of the Great Plains*. Norman OK/ London: University of Oklahoma Press.

Kohl, J. G. 1860. *Kitchi-Gami: Life Among the Lake Superior Ojibway*. London: Chapman & Hall.

La Flesche, F. 1905. *Who Was the Medicine Man?* Hampton VA, Hampton Institute Press.

Lévi-Strauss, C. 1936. Contribution à l'étude de l'organisation sociale des Indiens Bororo. *Journal de la Société des Américanistes* 18(2), 269–304.

Lévi-Strauss, C. 1943. The social use of kinship terms among Brazilian Indians. *American Anthropologist* 45(3), 398–409.

Lévi-Strauss, C. 1944. Reciprocity and Hierarchy. *American Anthropologist* 46(2), 266–268.

Lévi-Strauss, C. 1948. La vie familiale et sociale des Indiens Nambikwara. *Journal de la Société des Américanistes* 37, 1–132.

Lévi-Strauss, C. 1955. *Tristes Tropiques*. Paris: Plon.

Lévi-Strauss, C. 1964. *Le cru et le cuit (Mythologiques 1)*. Paris: Plon.

Lévi-Strauss, C. 1968. *L'origine des manières de table (Mythologiques 3)*. Paris: Plon.

Lévi-Strauss, C. 1971. *L'homme nu (Mythologiques 4)*. Paris: Plon.

Lewis, T. H. 1982. Traditional and contemporary ritual clowns of the Crow. *Anthropos* 77(5–6), 892–895.

Linderman, F. B. 1930. *American: The Life Story of a Great Indian, Plenty Coups Chief of the Crows*. New York: John Day [reprinted as *Plenty-coups Chief of the Crows*. Lincoln NE/London: University of Nebraska Press, 1961].

Lowie, R. H. 1913. Societies of the Crow, Hidatsa and Mandan Indians. *Anthropological Papers of the American Museum of Natural History* 11(3), 145–358.

Lowie, R. H. 1918. Myths and traditions of the Crow Indians. *Anthropological Papers of the American Museum of Natural History* 25(1)1, 1–308.

Lowie, R. H. 1935. *The Crow Indians*. New York: Rinehardt [new edition, Lincoln NE: University of Nebraska Press, 1983]

Park, W. Z. 1934. Paviotso Shamanism. *American Anthropologist* 36(1), 98–113.

Parman, S. 1991. *Dream and Culture: An Anthropological Study of the Western Intellectual Tradition*. Westport CO: Greenwood Publishing Group.

Powers, W. K. 1977. *Oglala Religion*. Lincoln NE/London: University of Nebraska Press.

Powers, W. K. 1982. *Yuwipi: Vision and Experience in Oglala Ritual*. Lincoln NE/London: University of Nebraska Press.

Ranking, J. 1828. Remarks on the ruins of Palenque in Guatemala, and on the origin of the American Indians. *Quarterly Journal of Science, Literature, and Art* 25 (January-June), 323–355.

Reichel-Dolmatoff, G. 1975. *The Shaman and the Jaguar: A Study of Narcotic Drugs Among the Indians of Colombia*. Philadelphia PA: Temple University Press.

Schoolcraft, H. R. 1839. *Algic Researches, Comprising Inquiries Respecting the Mental Characteristics of the North American Indians*, 2 vols. New York: Harper & Brothers.

Smith, J. Z. 1978. I am a parrot (red). In J. Z. Smith (ed.) *Map Is Not Territory: Studies in the History of Religions*. Leiden: Brill, 265–288.

Smith, T. S. 1995. *The Island of the Anishnaabeg: Thunderers and Water Monsters in the Traditional Ojibwe Life-World*. Lincoln NE/London: University of Nebraska Press.

Steinen, K. von den, 1894. *Unter den Naturvölkern Zentral-Brasiliens*. Berlin: Dietrich Reimer.

Turner, T. 1980. Le dénicheur d'oiseaux en contexte, *Anthropologie et Société* 4(3), 85–115.

Vecsey, C. 1983. *Traditional Ojibwa Religion and Its Historical Changes*. Philadelphia PA: American Philosophical Society.

Wagner, G. D. & Allen, W. A. 1933. *Blankets and Mocassins: Plenty Coups and His People, the Crows*. Caldwell ID: Caxton [new edition, Lincoln: University of Nebraska Press, 1987].

Wallis, W. D. 1923. Beliefs and tales of the Canadian Dakota. *Journal of American Folk-Lore* 36(139), 36–101.

Wallis, W. D. 1947. The Canadian Dakota. *Anthropological Papers of the American Museum of Natural History* 41(1), 1–225.

Wilbert, J. (ed.). 1978. *Folk Literature of the Gê Indians*. UCLA Latin American Studies 44. Berkeley/Los Angeles CA: University of California Press.

Wilbert, J. & Simoneau, K. (eds). 1983. *Folk Literature of the Bororo Indians*. UCLA Latin American Studies 57. Berkeley/Los Angeles CA: University of California Press.

Williams, M. L. (ed.). 1956. *Schoolcraft's Indian Legends*. East Lansing MI: Michigan State University Press.

Wright, R. M. 2013. *Mysteries of the Jaguar Shamans of the Northwest Amazon*. Lincoln NE: University of Nebraska Press.

Chapter 11

Bear Myths and Traditions: The Moon and Mounds in North America

Herman Bender

Abstract *The Kolterman Mound site, a premier petroform and archeoastronomy site overlooking the vast Horicon Marsh, is located 20 miles (32 km) south and east of Fond du Lac, Wisconsin (USA). Viewing of the long anticipated 2006 lunar maximum moonset event from this site enabled the author to connect the singular bear effigy mound at Kolterman with other (lunar) aligned bear effigy mounds in the area. Looking farther afield in Ohio by extension of known bear cult imagery and lunar maximum alignments, combined bear and moon symbolism was also established at the prominent Newark giant earthworks site with links to another at High Banks, the two sites connected at one time by the Hopewell Road. Physical expressions on the cultural landscape, the sites are likely related to ancient bear cult shamanistic traditions and inherent cosmologies, and although modified by time and distance, appear to exhibit shared beliefs and function of design.*

Introduction: The Lunar Maximum and Bear Effigy Mounds

At one time there were approximately 15,000–20,000 earthen mounds in southern Wisconsin USA, but during the last 175 years agricultural cultivation and development have greatly reduced the number to about 4000 that now remain. Composed of heaped and piled earth, distinctive mound shapes include animals, birds, reptiles (lizards and turtles), conical and linear forms. The mounds can vary greatly in size. Conical or round mounds can measure a few metres in diameter while linear and elongated effigy mounds can extend up to 100 m and more in length (Hurley 1986). Considered cemeteries because half or more of the effigy mounds contained burials (Lenzendorf 2000, 103), the remaining mounds are now protected by the State of Wisconsin (Birmingham & Eisenberg 2000, 2–4, 30).

The Kolterman Mounds complex is a prehistoric petroform and earthen effigy mound site located on the east side of the renowned Horicon Marsh in Dodge County,

Wisconsin. Like most of the effigy mounds in southern Wisconsin, the mounds are approximately 800–1200 years old (Birmingham & Eisenberg 2000, 100–101). Remaining mound shapes include conical, otters (many times misidentified or described as panthers) and a bear (Fig. 11.1). Even though bear effigy mounds have been mapped in other mound groups, the connection between them and the moon or, more precisely, the 18.61 years lunar maximum (Krupp 1991, 154–157; Meeus 1997, 26–28) had rarely if ever been conjectured (even if detected through careful mapping) much less confirmed until the 2006 viewing of the long anticipated event at Kolterman (Bender 2017a).

It was in June, 1994 at the Kolterman Mound complex that, after extensive mapping of all the deeply embedded rocks and the bear effigy mound, the association between the bear effigy mound and lunar maximum and minimum moonset alignments was first detected (Fig. 11.2b). As mentioned previously, the lunar maximum occurs every 18.61 years when the moon goes to its far north and south rise and set points. At the latitude of the Kolterman site, 43.5°N latitude, the Lunar Maximum northernmost moonset azimuth (at 0° elevation) is 311.5°±0.5° depending on factors such as the terrain, elevation above the horizon, atmospheric extinction and the epoch (Bender 2011). The southernmost full moonset, the direction the bear effigy is aligned to face, is at azimuth 228.5°±0.5° (Fig. 11.2). The visual confirmation of the northernmost lunar maximum moonset event came in December, 2006 after a long, 12.5 year wait when, as predicted in 1994, the moon was observed to set over the bear effigy mound, the event viewed from the shaped rock platform in-line with the rocks of the (conjectured) lunar maximum alignment of spaced rocks (Figs 11.2 and 11.3).[1]

Bears and Crescents

While observing the full moon setting as it approached the horizon, the shape unexpectedly shifted from full to a thin crescent with only the sun lit edge of the moon visible (Fig. 11.3b), the noticeable effect due to atmospheric extinction or the thickening of the atmosphere at the horizon (Bender 2011 & 2017a). The fundamental and very noticeable shape shift or change from the full disk of the moon to a crescent within less than a half hour would have been recognised by the indigenous people as *transformation,* a fundamental part of Native American beliefs and cosmologies generally associated with bears, spirits, shamans and shamanistic abilities (Howard 1955, 170; Conway & Conway 1990, 32–33, 72–73; Rockwell 1991, 64–66; Bender 2004, 17; 2009, 142, 150; Berres *et al.* 2004, 7–9; Comba 2014).

Even if unexpected at the time (because of the clear sky and short amount of time in which it happened), the crescent shape is a normal part of the lunar monthly waxing and waning cycles. A person observing the lunar maximum (or any moon cycle) would see a waxing crescent moon setting in the northwest in the summer and, six months later, in the south-west during the winter. If drawing or picturing the moon, the crescent phase or shape is what most people generally use to differentiate it from the full disk image of the (rayed) sun (Krupp 1991, 43). Somewhat like the

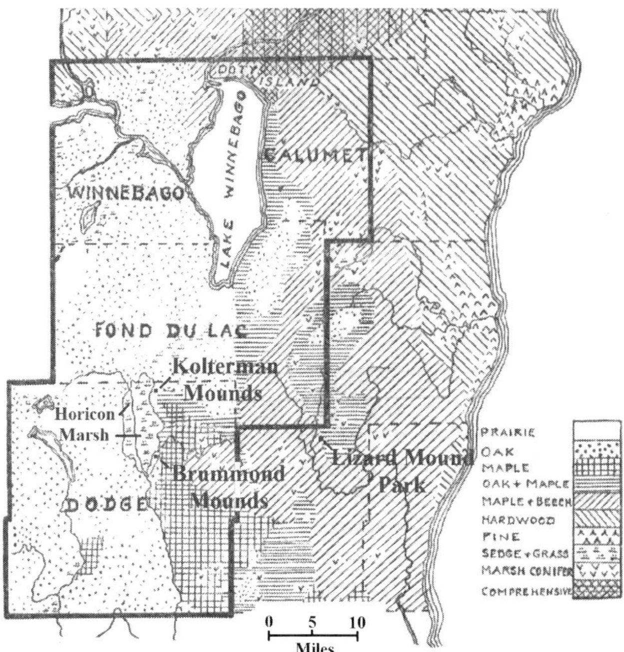

a

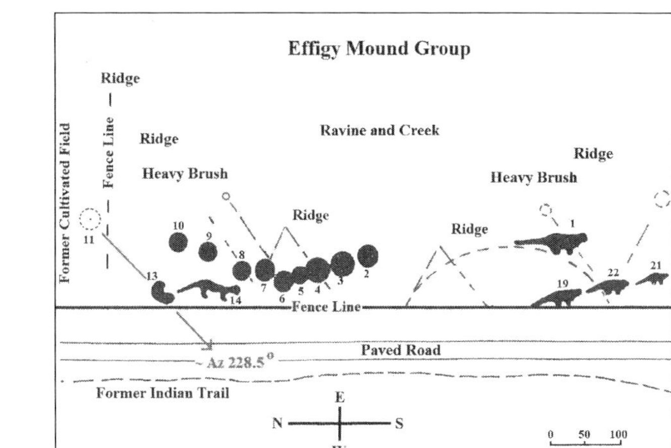

b

Fig. 11.1: a) Original vegetation map of southern Wisconsin with the location of the Kolterman Mounds and Brummond Mounds sites, both constructed on the east edge of the Horicon Marsh in Dodge County, and Lizard Mound Park in Washington County. Before settlement in the 1840s a tall grass, treeless prairie and oak savannah extended from the southern tip of Lake Winnebago south to the Horicon Marsh and further west; b) Kolterman Effigy Mound map adapted after Dr E. C. Bruder's map c. 1951 (Bender 2017a). Mound nos 1 & 19–21 likely represented otters, but were conventionally referred to as panthers. The bear effigy mound is No. 13. Mound nos 15–18, all otter or so-called 'panther' mounds, were destroyed by road and ditch work in the mid-1950s. No. 12, a short linear mound, & No. 20, a conical mound, were also destroyed by the road work. Dashed lines and circles are petroform discovered and mapped between 1994 and 2002. The straight line segments along with lithic bison effigy rocks are aligned to solstice sunrises and sunsets (Bender 2013)

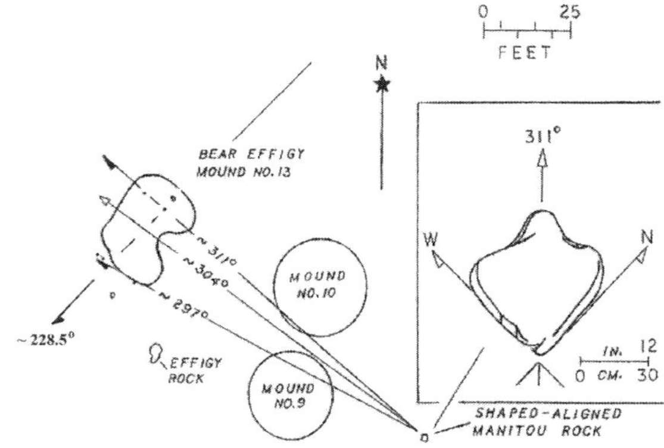

a

b

Fig. 11.2: a) Sketch map of the shaped-aligned Manitou rock (at right) which appears to have been placed and carefully aligned as an observation platform. The line of symmetry marked by the arrow, i.e. azimuth ~311°, marks the lunar maximum northernmost moonset at latitude 43.5° N, the site latitude. Of note, the bear effigy mound (No. 13) is aligned to face the lunar maximum southernmost set point at azimuth ~ 228.5°. The lunar alignment bisects the bear lengthwise with the moonset event appearing to have been viewed from Mound no. 11 (Fig. 11.1b). The small 'dots' located on the bear effigy mound and along its south-eastern edge are rocks. These rocks and additional spaced rocks that once formed a part of both the lunar maximum and lunar minimum alignments are now gone, their apparent locations marked by deep depressions in the grass between the bear effigy mound and Mound nos 9 and 10 (Fig. 11.3a). Azimuth 297° (±0.5°) is the Lunar Minimum moonset azimuth for the site latitude and, like the lunar maximum alignment, was indicated by an alignment of space rocks including those remaining on the bear mounds south-eastern edge; b) Photo overlooking the Horicon Marsh, bear effigy mound and shaped rock in the foreground (Fig. 11.2a). The backpack on the bear mound at azimuth 311° marks the Lunar Maximum and aligned rocks (Figs 11.2a & 11.3a). The elevation to the western horizon overlooking the Horicon Marsh is at 0° elevation when viewed from (or standing on) the shaped rock. Approximate azimuth 297° is the Lunar Minimum bearing at the site latitude (Figs 11.2a & 11.3a)

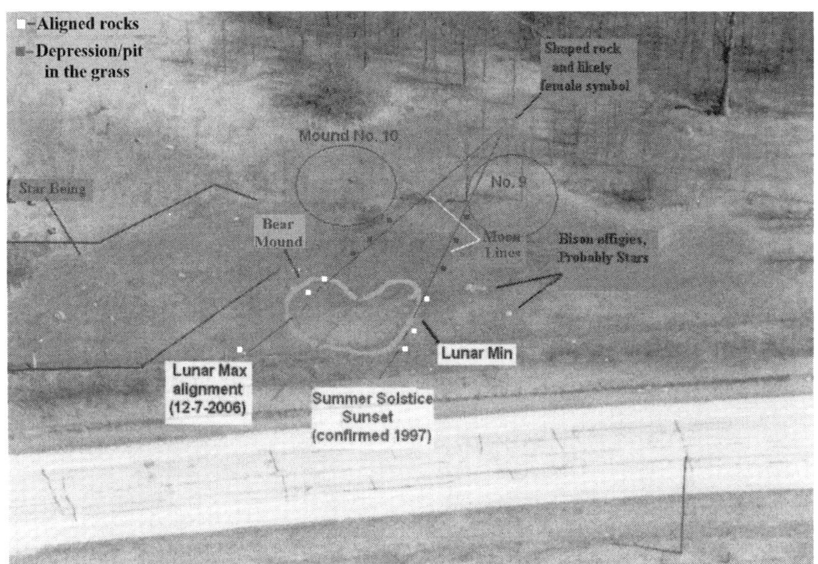

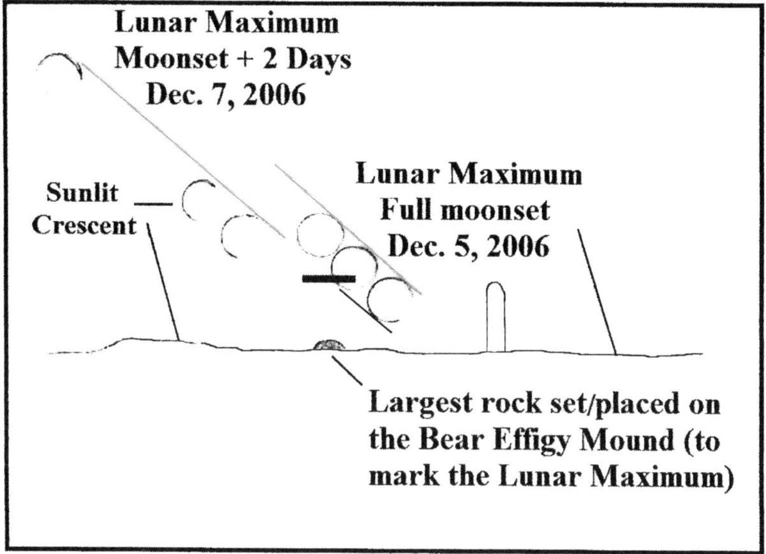

Fig. 11.3: a) Annotated aerial photo illustrating the shaped rock, spaced alignments of rock, mound Nos. 9 & 10 and bear effigy mound. Note that the observed summer solstice sunset alignment detected in 1994 and later confirmed in 1997 bisects the bear (see Fig. 11.2a). The direction north is to the left; b) Sketch based on photos connecting timed intervals of the lunar maximum +2 days full moonset over the bear mound (Figs 11.2 & 11.3a). The horizontal line marks the approximate naked-eye limit of the moonset in the bright daylight due to atmospheric extinction, i.e. the thickening of the atmosphere at the horizon (Bender 2011), and causes it to assume a crescent shape as it approaches the horizon with only the bright, sun lit edge actually visible to the naked eye (Bender 2017a)

moon, the same may be said about the bear. It is generally depicted in most Native American sculptures, carvings and images as crescent-shaped with a head's down posture (Fig. 11.4). What the observation at Kolterman did, though, was to firmly link the moon (whether crescent-shaped or not) and the crescent-shaped bear mound with moon/bear traditions found in the northern latitudes of North America and the ancient, circumpolar bear cult (Bender 2017a).

Additional Bear Mounds and Lunar Alignments

Even though feeling personally vindicated after the 12.5 years wait I was, however, not the first person to realise there may be a connection between an ancient (bear) effigy mound and the moon (crescent-shaped or not). Nor is the Kolterman bear effigy a lone example of a bear effigy mound aligned to the lunar maximum. Approximately seven miles south of the Kolterman mounds is another mound group known as the Brummond Mounds (Fig. 11.1a). The Brummond mound group has the distinction of being the first mound group in Wisconsin (and perhaps all of North America) where the lunar maximum alignment or, more precisely, a link to the moon was conjectured to be present with the aligned mound or mounds constructed as an integral and likely intentional part of the mound group overall design or layout (Ulrich 1980).

The year was 1950 when Dr Edgar Bruder first located and then began mapping the Brummond Mounds (Ulrich 1980). The timing was pivotal as it was also a lunar maximum year (Meeus 1997, 26–27). While mapping with a professional surveyor, he began to suspect that the possibility of a lunar alignment was present and began to regularly consult with an astronomer on lunar cycles and azimuths. According to Bruder's notes and map, two parallel mounds in the group were aligned between azimuths N48° 36′E and S228° 36′W (Fig. 11.5), the respective north-east and south-west lunar maximum rise and set points (Fig. 11.2a).[2] One of the mounds is a long linear approximately 500 ft (150 m) long, the other a 200 ft (61 m) long-tailed effigy mound with an open crescent-shape above the body. The axis of symmetry of the effigy mound and head are aligned to face the lunar maximum southernmost set point, the same as the bear effigy at Kolterman (Figs 11.1 & 11.4d). The mound's distinctive crescent shape of a robust animal with its head down strongly suggests a bear either already in or going to its den (Bender 2017a). Its tail is stretched straight out to form the alignment (Fig. 11.5).

Remains of another long-tailed, bear-like effigy that was approximately 150 ft (40 m) long before being disturbed was mapped north-east of and directly in-line with the larger, long-tailed effigy mound. The combined length of these two long-tailed bear alignments would have approached 350 ft (106 m) which, along with the linear mound, is far longer than is needed for ±0.5° accuracy and parallax correction if observing the rising or setting of the disk of the moon on the horizon (Bender 2011). In addition, another feature Bruder mapped as a 'Little Bear' mound *c.* 50 ft (15 m) long was also apparently aligned to incorporate the lunar maximum, this

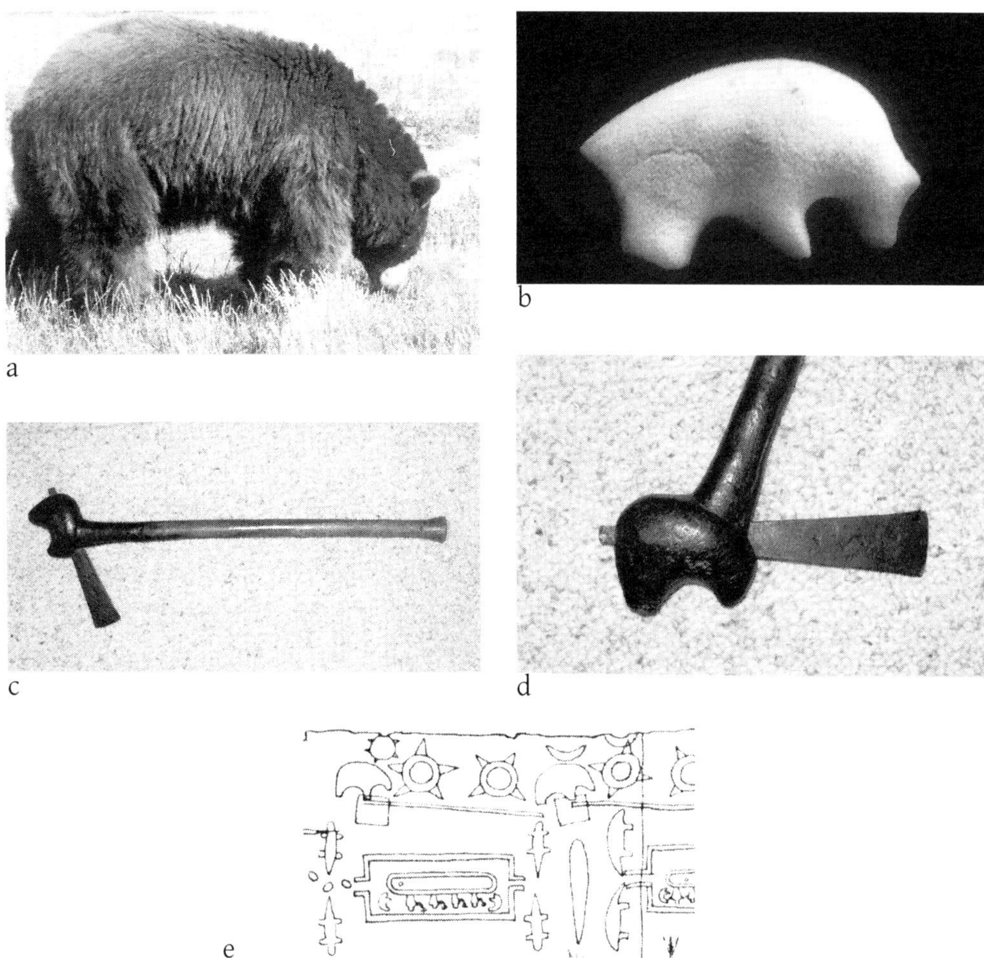

Fig. 11.4: a) Black bear assuming a crescent shape with its head down posture while browsing (photo: Herman Bender); b) a crescent-shaped bear figurine depicted in a typical head's-down posture. The figurine measures c. 5.5 in (14 cm) in length (Herman Bender collection); c) a 300–400 year-old bear effigy club from New England. It is c. 18 in (45 cm) in length and made of hickory, a very hard wood. The bear effigy end was heated in a fire to shrink the wood, thereby tightly holding the highly prized iron bit (Herman Bender collection); d) close up view of the crescent-shaped bear effigy which closely resembles the bear effigy mound shape at the Kolterman mounds (Figs 11.1b & 11.2a) and those seen in the Midé scroll (Fig. 11.3a). The head is to the right. In addition to the crescent bear, what appears to be a crescent moon resembling the shape of the moon that is mirroring the bear (at right) seen in the Midé scroll mirror is carved into the handle; e) a portion of a Midé master scroll from Dewdney (1975, 96, fig. 80) showing the progression of the crescent-shaped bear (as a sky Manitou) on the processional path travelling west along with the sun and moon (the direction east is at left). Note the mirrored crescent moon above the crescent-shaped bear. The box the bear is standing on or entering into is its nest or den

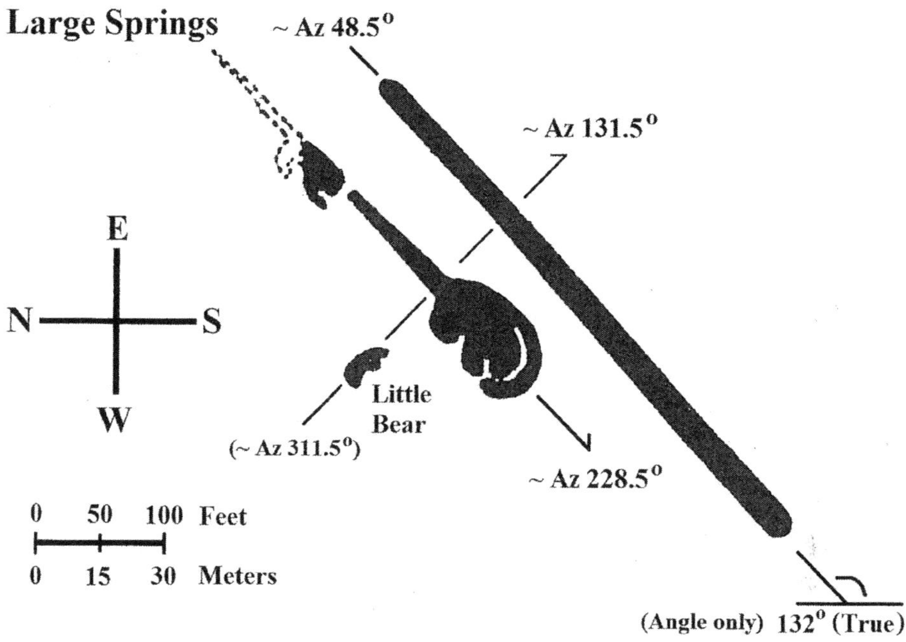

Fig. 11.5: Mounds aligned to the Lunar Maximum at the Brummond Mounds. Bruder was aware of the lunar maximum angle (~41.5° ±0.5° north or south of the east-west line) when he emphasised the angle in the notation '132° True' in the draft of his map (Ulrich 1980)

effigy facing the lunar maximum (full) moonrise at ~Az 131.5°. Based on personal observation and experience, the length of the mound is long enough to establish an accurate sight line (Bender 2011). Perhaps as important as the mounds and alignments are the large springs northeast of and directly in-line with the two long-tailed bear effigy mounds. Among the Algonquin and Siouan speaking tribes in Wisconsin, bears were said to reside in springs during the winter (Overton 1928, 217). Both effigies would appear to have been emerging from the springs, a link to the bears' den underground in the womb of the earth and water which is the medium of birth (Bender 2017a).

Due to factors beyond his control, such as the fickle Wisconsin winter weather, deep snow, general cloudiness that prevails during the entire month of December (Bender 2011) and, perhaps, an incomplete understanding of the complexity of the lunar maximum cycle over the 18.61 years period, Bruder was never personally rewarded with a direct observation of the moon rising or setting in-line with the aligned mounds.[3] His map and effort did, however, have another benefit he may not have recognised or intended, and that was to eventually link the long-tailed effigy mound with the ancient northern Algonquin bear and moon traditions together with

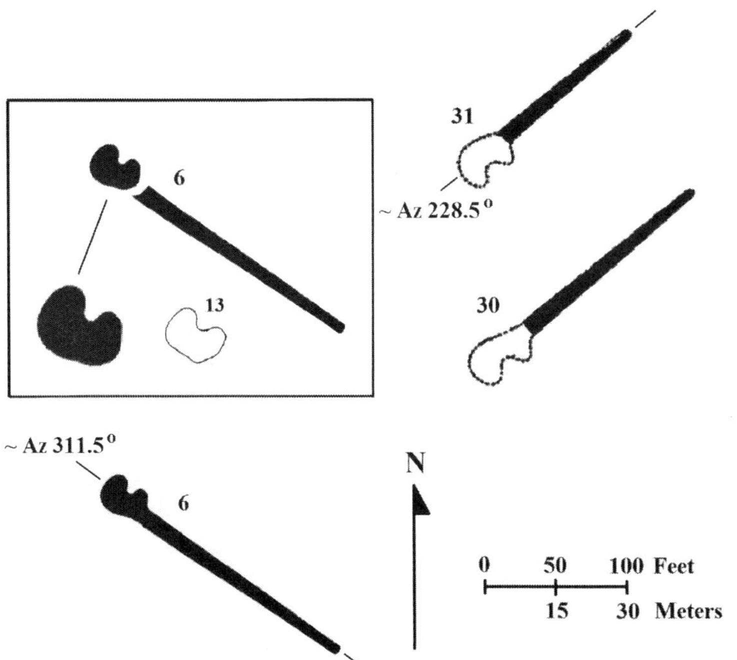

Fig. 11.6: Long-tailed bear effigy mounds at the Lizard Mound (formerly the Hagner mounds). Mound no. 6 is aligned to the lunar maximum far north set azimuth with mound nos 30 and 31 aligned to face the far south lunar maximum set azimuth. The inset shows mound no. 6 separated from the tail revealing the robust bear shape with mound no. 13 from Kolterman juxtaposed for comparison of shape.

other long-tailed effigy mounds in the not-too-distant area that were also aligned to the lunar maximum moonset.

The crescent shape of the bear is again encountered at Lizard Mound Park *c.* 15 miles (25 km) due east of the Brummond mounds (Fig. 11.1a). Sometimes described as 'panther' mounds, the crescent shape of the mounds, each with a robust front quarter and shoulders as seen in mound nos 6, 30 and 31, suggests a 'long-tailed' bear in the head's down posture far more than a panther or otter (Figs 11.6 & 11.7). Because each mound is aligned to face a lunar maximum moonset azimuth at either azimuth 228.5° (±0.5°) or azimuth 311.5° (±0.5°) and they are almost identical in shape to the crescent-shaped bear mound (No. 13) at Kolterman, identifying them as bear mounds makes far more sense than a panther or otter which they in no way resemble (Fig. 11.1b & 11.2a).

Corona Borealis – The Bear's Den and the Midé

What then, is the connection or association between the crescent-shaped bear, the bear's den (Figs 11.4d & 11.5), the lunar maximum, the shaman's journey, the

Fig. 11.7: Leola One Feather with friend Michelle Salvatore standing by mound no. 6 at Lizard Mound Park, one of three likely crescent-shaped bear effigy mounds (see Fig. 11.6). Both women live on the (Lakota) Pine Ridge Reservation, South Dakota. Leola's ancestors were noted Bear women and midwives, a hereditary tradition she has retained. View in the photo is looking approximately west (photo: Herman Bender).

background of stars, the cosmos or space itself? An ethnoastronomy link to the *nest* or den and the attendant bear/star stories can be found by examining Micmac, Lenni Laenape (Delaware), Anishanaabe (Ojibwe), Munsee-Mahican and other eastern North American Indian traditions. To them, the constellation we call *Corona Borealis* was known as the 'Bear's Den', the 'Bear's Lair' and sometimes the 'Bears Head' (Langford 2007, 32; Miller 1997, 37, 292; Stewart 1978, 166).[4]

Corona Borealis is an arc or crescent-shaped constellation (Fig. 11.8a) reminiscent of the crescent-shaped bear effigy mound (Figs 11.1b, 11.4a–c, 11.5 & 11.6). When observed setting in the night sky slightly above the horizon at the mid-latitudes, its azimuth (~311° ±0.5°) and position, at Kolterman for instance, mirrors that of the crescent-shaped bear effigy mound lunar maximum alignment (Fig. 11.8b). Furthermore, the setting of Corona Borealis, i.e. the 'Bears Den', in late fall/early winter mimics the time and season when the bear begins its hibernation. Therefore, the observed crescent-shaped moon setting slightly above the horizon during

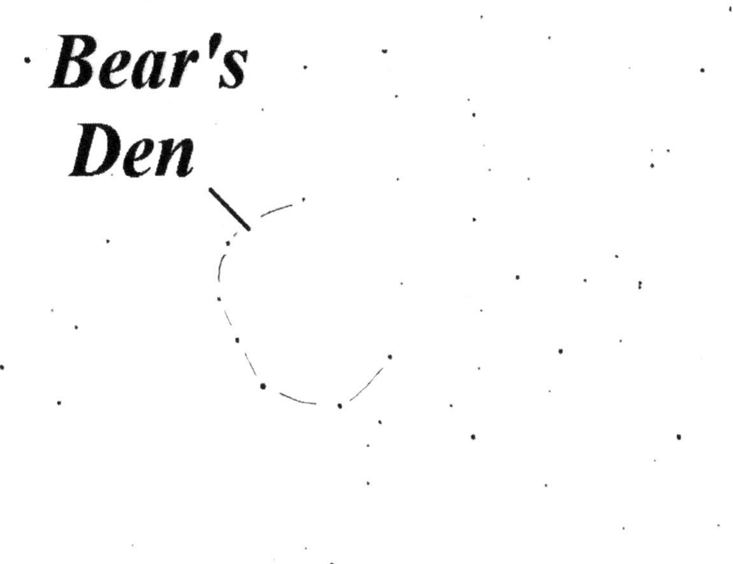

a

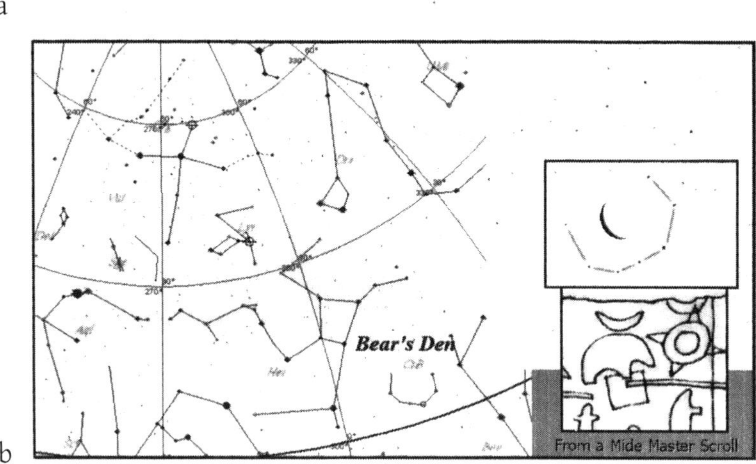

b

Fig. 11.8: a) The arc of the seven bright stars in Corona Borealis formed the bear's den. Corona Borealis would not be seen rising in the eastern sky until early spring, the time of the year when the bear comes out of hibernation; b) at left, a night sky map c. December, AD 1000–1200 (but little changed to this day) with the crescent-shaped 'Bear's Den' or Corona Borealis as it sets at the same azimuth as the Lunar Maximum Moonset, i.e. azimuth 311°- 312°. This alignment is a likely metaphor for the crescent-shaped bear, represented by the (crescent-shaped) moon as it sets (Fig. 11.3a), entering into the den, i.e. Corona Borealis. The sky phenomenon is a mirror-image of the bear effigy mound and setting moon above it, both seen together in the illustration from the Midé master scroll (Fig. 11.4d and inset at right). This alignment only occurs during the Lunar Maximum every 18.61 years when the moon is seen to rise and set at its far northern extremes (Fig. 11.8c)

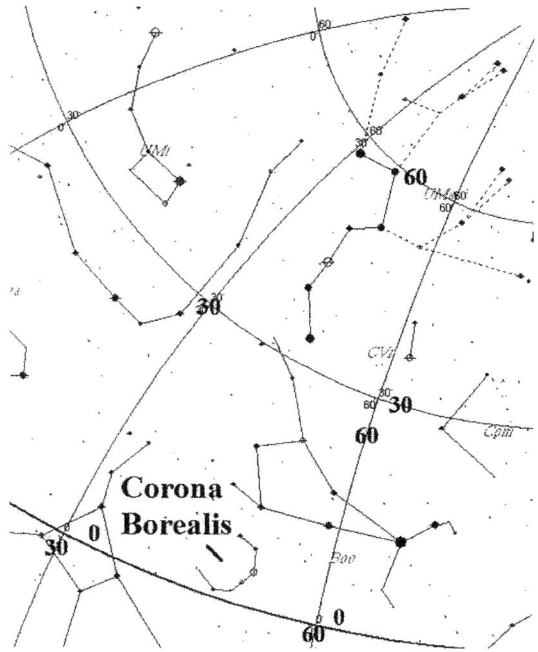

Fig. 11.8: c) Corona Borealis as the crescent-shaped 'Bear's Den' rising at ~Az 49° late in the evening in March, c. AD 1000–1200, the same azimuth as the northernmost lunar maximum moonrise.

the lunar maximum would be seen to directly enter into same part of the sky the crescent-shaped constellation Corona Borealis was seen to set and occupies at that time of the year, i.e., the place of the bear's 'den' (Fig. 11.8b). By extension, it thus becomes an earth womb metaphor. In the spring of the year when the bear comes out of hibernation and is ready to leave its den, Corona Borealis is seen rising in the northeast at the same approximate azimuth as the lunar maximum northernmost moonrise (Fig. 11.8c).

The pairing of the crescent moon (and bear) with Corona Borealis is a cosmic representation of the dualism between the womb and the den where the female bear gives birth. There is historic evidence that supports the premise. The Jesuit priests and French traders who lived among the Algonquin-speaking people in the 17th century recorded many customs and traditions concerning bear beliefs tied to the womb of the (deep) earth. They stated that, '[t]hey have besides many other divinities to whom they pray, and who, they claim, *reside in the air, under the land, and beneath the earth.* The gods beneath the earth, [especially] are *bears* who pass the entire winter without eating, nourishing themselves only from substance they extract from their navel (umbilicus) sucking' (Campbell 1988, 147; Heming 1896, 119; Kinietz 1965, 287–288).

Adding credence to early historic bear and den associations, there are also Ojibwe legends and stories about the '*spiral-tail bear in* [the] *abyss of the earth*' (Fertey 1970, 266; Schoolcraft 1853, 352). Describing the legend of the spiral-tail bear, Mallery (1894) stated, '... the tail ... is of great length and extends completely around the body ... this spirit lives in the earth ... [and is] sometimes seen above ground' (Fig. 11.9a).

These descriptions are likely of a deep earth (or den) reflection of part of the night sky, sometimes thought to be where the (curved celestial bear) tail stars of what we call the constellation *Ursa Major* revolve around the North Star (*Polaris*) forming a spiral shape in the northern night sky. However, the constellation we call Corona Borealis is not only seen as the bear's den or lair, i.e. the *abyss*, but together with its somewhat dimmer stars the complete pattern of stars can easily be interpreted as a spiral shape (Fig. 11.9b).

Important in Algonquin and Chippewa culture, the long or spiral-tailed bear was more than a legend. The Chippewa totem or clan of the Long-tailed Bear was famous for its leaders, warriors (and shamans), sometimes described as 'fabulous' because of its mythical base (Schoolcraft 1853, 418–419). Their members were represented by a crescent-shaped bear with a long tail, 'the peculiar feature in which [it] differs from the northern black bear, is formed of copper, or some bright metal' and was shown curving around the bear like that in the image of the spiral-tailed (Fig. 11.10a).

Moreover, there is a place in south-eastern Wisconsin named Mukwonago, a word or place name which has two translations. One translation is '*bear constellation* or *constellation of the bear stars*', the other is '*bear's hole*' or '*bear's lair*' (Gard & Sorden 1988, 186; Vogel 1991, 140). Therefore, a definite correlation can be made between the 'abyss' or 'hole' of the underworld, certain 'bear stars' of the upper world and the bear itself. In the Algonquin cosmological base, the abyss or underworld is viewed as a reflection of the night sky (Hall 1993, 28–300).

At the Brummond mounds there are large springs (Fig. 11.5), a perceived underground entrance to the abyss, i.e. the womb or den of the underworld and place where bears were said to hibernate (Overton 1928, 217). The long-tail bear effigies may well be physical, earthly representations of the 'spiral-tail bear' with its long, coiled tail straightened, the bears aligned to face the southernmost lunar maximum moonset. The alignment would seemingly indicate the place or 'portal' on the horizon where the moon sets at its far south point on the southwestern horizon (i.e. ~Az 228.5°±0.5°). The two bears are, in essence, on a journey between the lower world and upper world moving from the north-east to the south-west, the direction determined by the lunar maximum rise and set points. What then, was the purpose of the journey and to where or what in the south-west?

After a person died, the soul was said to journey for 4 days on what the Anishinaabe or Ojibway, Menomimee and other Algonquin-speaking Indians called the *Jibekana* meaning 'the path of the dead' or 'the path of souls' (Keesing 1987, 51; Bender 2009, 147–149). The path has its counterpart in the night sky, the Milky Way, and the Ojibway and others who practiced the Midé had precise rites and ceremonies to help direct

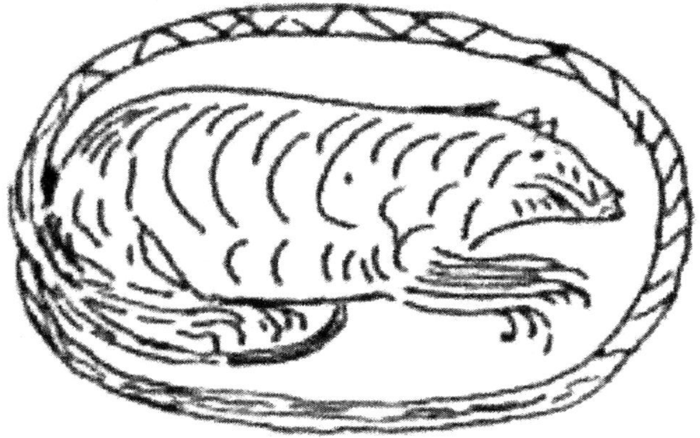

a

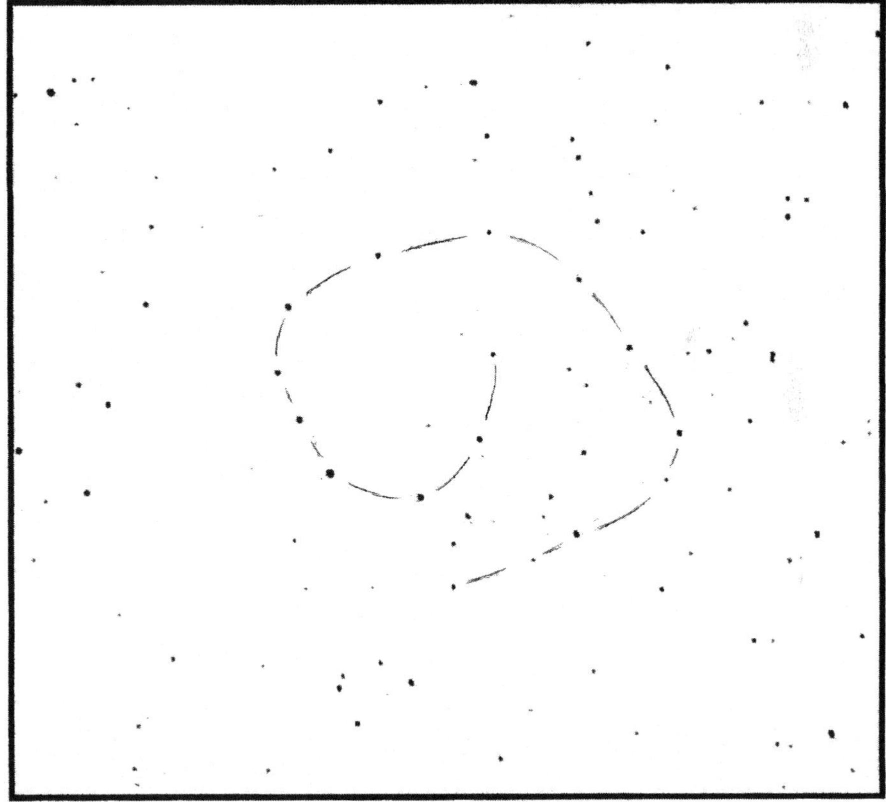

b

Fig. 11.9: a) Illustration of the spiral-tail bear from Schoolcraft (1853, 352); b) Corona Borealis configured as a spiral, perhaps a celestial mirror of the spiral-tailed bear in its den, the abyss of the earth

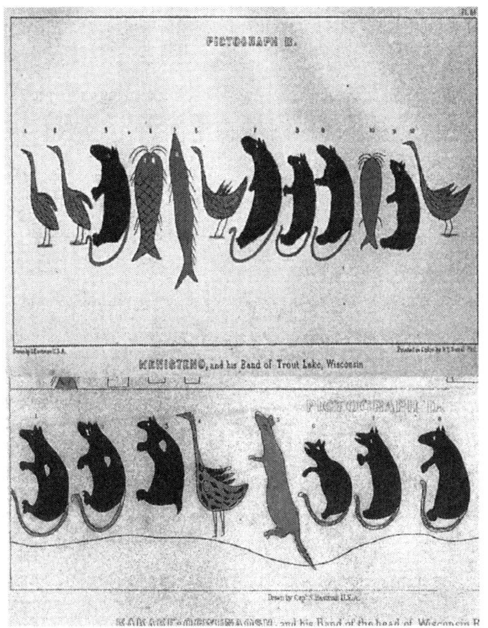

a

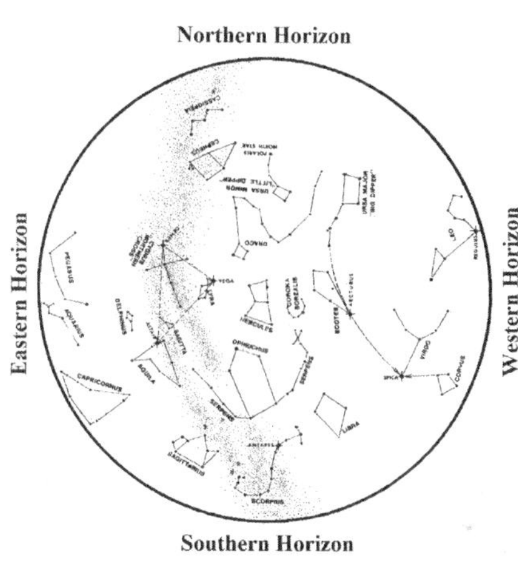

b

Fig. 11.10: a) Pictograph B and portion of Pictograph D from Schoolcraft (1853, 418–419). Nos 3 & 7–9 represent individual warriors of the clan of the fabulous Long-tailed Bear who were named, in their order: Pa-na-shee (no. 3) Wa-gi-ma-wash (no. 7) or would-be-chief, Ka-be-tau-wash (no. 8) or Mover-in-a-circle, and Sha-tai-mo (no. 9) or Pelican's excrement. Note the crescent shape of the bear body and long tail (which is approaching a spiral crescent shape) and the lack of the long tail in no. 11, O-ta-gau-me or the Fox Indian of the Bear totem; b) A conventional star map showing the Milky Way stretching overhead from north-east to south-west in the mid-latitudes of North America during the late spring and early summer. At this time of the year the southern end of the Milky Way is at its brightest and most spectacular (and later as it rotates to the south and south-west during the summer months). Both the north-east and south-west ends are at the same approximate azimuths as the lunar maximum northernmost moonrise and southernmost moonset. Corona Borealis lies just above the horizon in the north-west at the same azimuth as the lunar maximum northernmost moonset (Fig. 11.8b).

the dead along it. The Milky Way was seen by many tribes as a bridge stretching across the night sky toward the south or south-west, i.e. the 'Ghost road' (Heming 1896, 135), along which the souls of the deceased travelled on their way to paradise (Russel 1980, 46–47; Hadingham 1984, 94; Krupp 1991, 272–273; Goodman 1992, 22–23, 38; Schwartz 1997, 93–96; Langford 2007, 201–215).

The midewiwin or Midé Society, i.e. the 'Grand Medicine' (lodge) ceremonies of the Ojibway and other northern tribes (Keesing 1987, 48–50) hold additional clues that may help define both purpose and function. As Grim (1983, 156) says, 'The midewiwin ceremony draws extensively upon the psychic techniques of earlier forms of Ojibway shamanism ... the trance states both structured and spontaneous ...' where the candidate for a Midewiwin degree or patient to be healed 'participates in the cosmic symbolism of the Ojibway origin stories'. One of the 'earlier forms of Ojibway shamanism' with roots in that 'cosmic symbolism' was known as the *Wabeno*, a shamanistic society whose members included both men and women (Grim 1983, 144). The name *Wabeno* translates as 'men of the dawn sky' or 'red dawn sky' (Grim 1983, 67, 113). Thought to descend from the northern Archaic culture, *Wabeno* ceremonies and practices would then predate the Midé by millennia (Kinietz 1965, 291; Miller 1982, 282; Schlesier 1987, 71–72; Brehm 1996, 690–692). The *Wabeno* were said to manipulate fire, danced until dawn in their ceremonies, were capable of transformation, specialised in the regulation of the natural order on earth, fertility, reincarnation of souls, studied the stars and moon, and during the day gained spiritual power from the sun (Grim 1983, 67, 113; Conway & Conway 1990, 70). The moon and star knowledge together with their traditions were very likely passed on and incorporated by the Midé and other medicine lodges (Conway 1992, 236–240, 252).

Many times the services of a shaman were sought to act as a psychopomp (Murray 2004, 59, 107) whose job it was to help guide the soul to the land of departed spirits (Smith 1995, 58; Leeming & Page 1998, 116–117).[5] According to the Midé, that land was said to be located 'somewhere – as though in space' (Densmore 1979, 75). It is at this place '... in space' near the horizon, sometimes referred to as 'portals' or 'sky holes' (Langford 2007, 52, 224, 226–232), that the soul could pass over when, during certain times of the year, e.g. the solstices, the veil was thinned between this reality and the spirit world. The lunar maximum far north and south rise and set points were most noticeable during the time of the solstices using the extreme declinations of the sun for comparison (Bender 2011; 2017a). To help make the journey, the shaman was said to be assisted by a bear spirit guide able to penetrate all the layers of the cosmos, moving from the bottom-most level of the abyss to the top layer of the sky (Grim 1983, 77–78).[6] The landscape and placing of the bear mounds at Brummond were likely meant to represent a physical representation of the cosmic journey and to assist the soul of anyone interred in the mound.

Of interest, the Midé 'Ghost scrolls' may offer further insights into what was to be encountered at the end of the journey or, perhaps more importantly, how to get there and the purpose for the journey. In two of the Midé 'Ghost scrolls', a circular 'village of the dead' is pictured at the (west) end of the 'path of the dead'. Within the village on one illustration is a slightly north-east to south-west oriented 'Ghost Midewagun' while the second scroll shows the 'Ghost Midewagun' with a west/north-west–east/south-east axis (Dewdney 1975, 103, 105). The north-east–south-west and west/north-west–east/south-east orientations seen in both of the 'Ghost Midewagun' scrolls are almost certainly veiled indications of the seasonal movement of the Milky Way as it rotates from a north-east–south-west orientation in the late Spring of the year to a west/north-west–east/south-east one in late autumn. In the late Summer to late Fall, when the Cygnus rift in the Milky Way lays on the western horizon, its Y-shape is seen as the head of the open-mouth serpent with its coiled body stretching back to the east. Like many Native American traditions, this conceptual view of the Milky

Way is not new. Furthermore, the arc along the western horizon from the south-west to the north-west is consistent with the parameters which bracket both the Lunar Maximum moonsets and the Milky Way or Ghost road from late Spring to early winter. In the Midé scrolls, it is the same processional path the bear is traversing on its way to its (celestial) den (Fig. 11.4e).

Bear Mounds and Cosmic Function

Although none of us will ever truly know why the mounds were constructed or can state so with any degree of certainty, I propose that the bear mounds at Brummond may have been carefully laid out to be utilised as a metaphor which represents the long (spiral) tail bear in the abyss or womb of the earth on its journey between worlds. On the surface is the crescent-shaped bear shown within a crescent or the womb (Fig. 11.5), built and aligned to reflect the direction of the bear's journey between the lower and upper worlds. In the earth and earth mound metaphor, the springs represent the entrance into or, more likely, from the earthly womb with the moon alignment to the south-west (the direction the bears are facing) establishing the direction of journey. Bearing all in mind, the entire scene would, along with the setting moon at the lunar maximum, act to complete the transformation of the landscape into the sacred, a profound transmutation needed to aid the journey of souls and shamans at a critical time of the year when souls can more easily pass between worlds. Intrinsic in all are the pervasive feminine attributes associated with the bear, the womb, the moon and birth or rebirth after death (Bender 2017a).

The Newark (Ohio) Giant Earthworks, Moon and Bear Connection

Perhaps the most ancient site known in North America where there is a confirmed lunar maximum alignment and associated bear imagery is at the Newark (Ohio) Giant Earthworks. This site and what was discovered there were key elements in linking the moon, bear and shamanism (Bender 2017a). The Newark Earthworks (Fig. 11.11a) were the largest set of geometric earthworks ever built in Ohio (Lepper 1998; 2006). They were constructed by the Hopewell people sometime between 200 BC and AD 400 (Seeman 1979, 237; Birmingham & Eisenberg 2000, 84–86). Two elements stand out at the Newark Earthworks, the first being the alignment of the axis of symmetry of the circle and octagon to the 18.61 year lunar maximum moonrise northernmost extreme (Fig. 11.11b). The alignment was confirmed at the Newark Earthworks in December, 2005 by Dr Michael Mickelson (Fig. 11.12a). The second is the bear shaman carving or figurine discovered in 1881 at the base of the largest burial mound at the Newark Earthworks (Fig. 11.12b). The bear shaman in the figurine may be either a male or female, but because of its association with the lunar aligned earthworks and the moon's link to women, its discovery helped to suggest a further connection between the moon, the bear and the feminine (Bender 2017a).

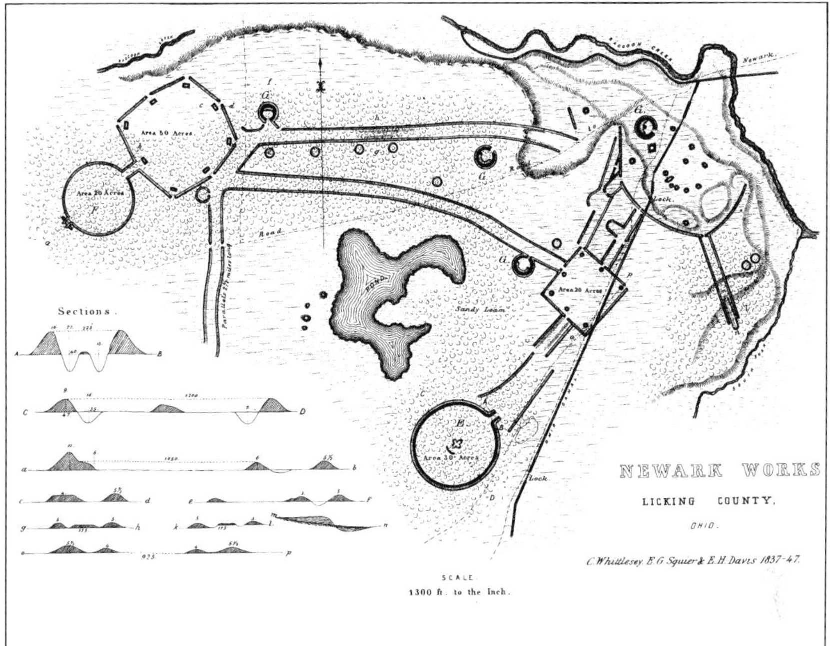

a

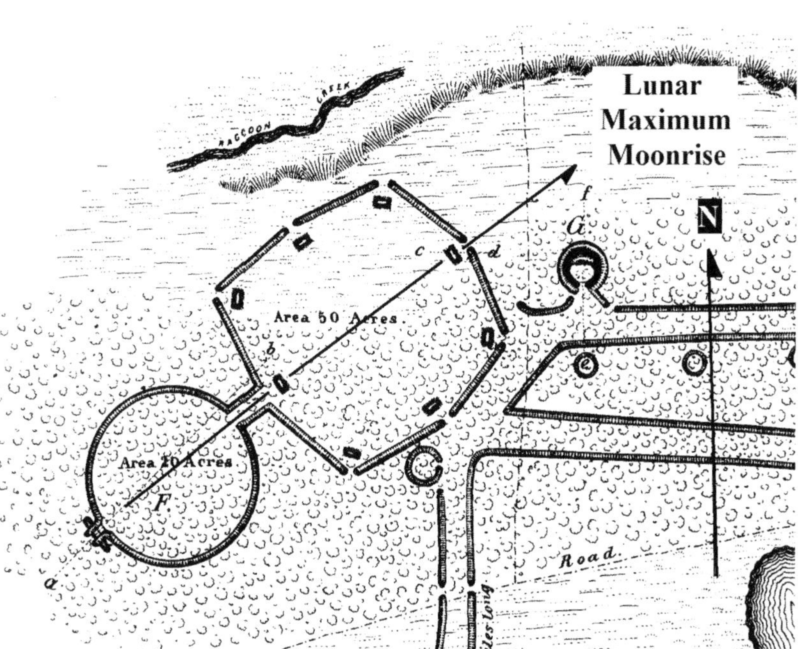

b

Fig. 11.11: a) The Newark giant earthworks located near Newark, Ohio (Squire & Davis 1848 pl. 67); b) the 18.61 year Lunar Maximum Moonrise alignment symmetrically bisecting the Newark Octagon and Circle

a

b

Fig. 11.12: a) Photograph of the Lunar Maximum Moonrise alignment at the Newark Octagon (Fig. 11.11b) taken on 16 Dec. 2005, a lunar maximum year (photo courtesy Michael Mickelson); b) the approximately 2500 year-old bear shaman carving, sometimes called the Wray figurine, discovered at the lunar maximum aligned giant earthworks at Newark (Berres et al. *2004, 17). It is owned by the Ohio History Museum*

The High Bank Earthworks and Hopewell Road

There is, however, another remarkable Octagon and Circle giant earthwork that may share far more than its shape with the one at Newark. Nearly 60 miles (96 km) south-east of the Newark earthworks, the High Bank Works was constructed near present day Chillicothe, Ohio (Fig. 11.13). Unlike at its almost identical counterpart at Newark (the circles share a nearly exact diameter), the main axis of symmetry of

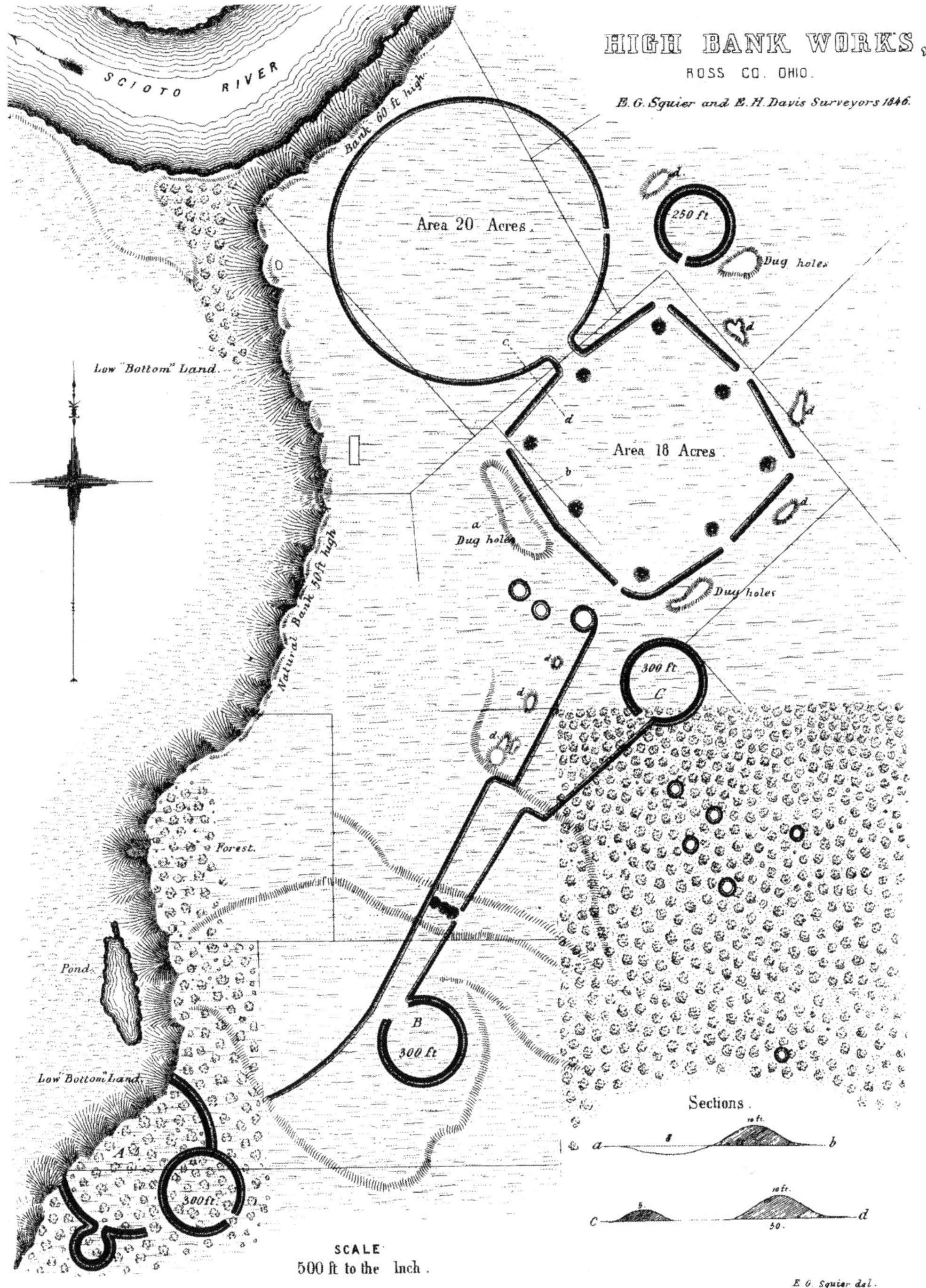

Fig. 11.13: High Bank Works located near Chillicothe, Licking County, Ohio (Squire & Davis 1848, pl. 67)

the octagon and circle at the High Banks Works is aligned perpendicular to Newark's axis of symmetry, i.e. to the south-east. Furthermore, it has also been demonstrated that the High Banks Works circle and octagon incorporated not only both the summer and winter solstice sunrise and sunset alignments but, more importantly, alignments to all eight Lunar Maximum and Minimum rise and set points (Hively & Horn 1984).

In addition to sharing Lunar Maximum alignments, the two giant earthworks also appear to have been connected by the 'Hopewell Road' (Lepper 1995, 52–56; 2006), a straight track composed of parallel walls that, at one time, linked the two sites over the distance (Fig. 11.14). The High Banks Works anchored the south-west end of the Hopewell Road and the Newark earthworks anchored the north-east end. Remarkably, the 1848 map of the Newark earthworks compiled by Squire & Davis showed the road as 'Parallel's 2½ miles long' running due south from the octagon (Fig. 11.11).

Lepper (1995, 56) suggested that the Hopewell Road may be a long earthly reflection of the Milky Way and, because of a directional similarity both share, I concur with his assessment. As we have seen with the long-tail bear effigy mounds aligned north-east to south-west which connect the lunar maximum moonrise and moonset azimuths at both the Brummond mounds and Lizard Mound Park, a credible argument can be made to support Lepper's hypothesis. A tentative link exists with the Newark earthworks at the northern terminus of the road which is aligned to the north-east azimuth where the moon rises at its far northern declination (Fig. 11.11b). There is also a Milky Way seasonal component associated with the declination.

The Milky Way, Star Portals, Moon and The Bear

Because the Milky Way is seen in the same seasonal alignments overhead throughout the mid-latitudes of North America, a fundamental question may therefore exist (as proposed for the bear effigy mounds in Wisconsin similarly aligned to the lunar maximum incorporating a Milky Way component) of whether or not the Milky Way could have played a role in the shaman's journey in Ohio a millennium earlier? Beginning in the early spring of the year, the Milky Way, i.e. the spirit's path, shifts from the western night sky and begins to reappear in the north-east with the rising of the constellation Cygnus. As the months progress from spring through summer and into early fall, the Milky Way rotates along the eastern horizon from the north-east to the east stretching overhead from the south to the south-western horizon. In the fall through early winter, it arches directly overhead from east to west, and in late fall and early winter from the south-eastern to the north-western horizon. It is during the late spring and early summer when the Milky Way is at its brightest, stretching from the north-east to the south-west, that the 'ends' of the arc are bracketed by the extreme declinations of the moon at its northern rise and southern set points during 18.61 year Lunar Maximum cycle. It is this bright, seasonal alignment arching toward the zenith that almost perfectly mirrors the alignment of the Hopewell Road connecting the giant earthworks at Newark and High Bank Works (Fig. 11.15a).

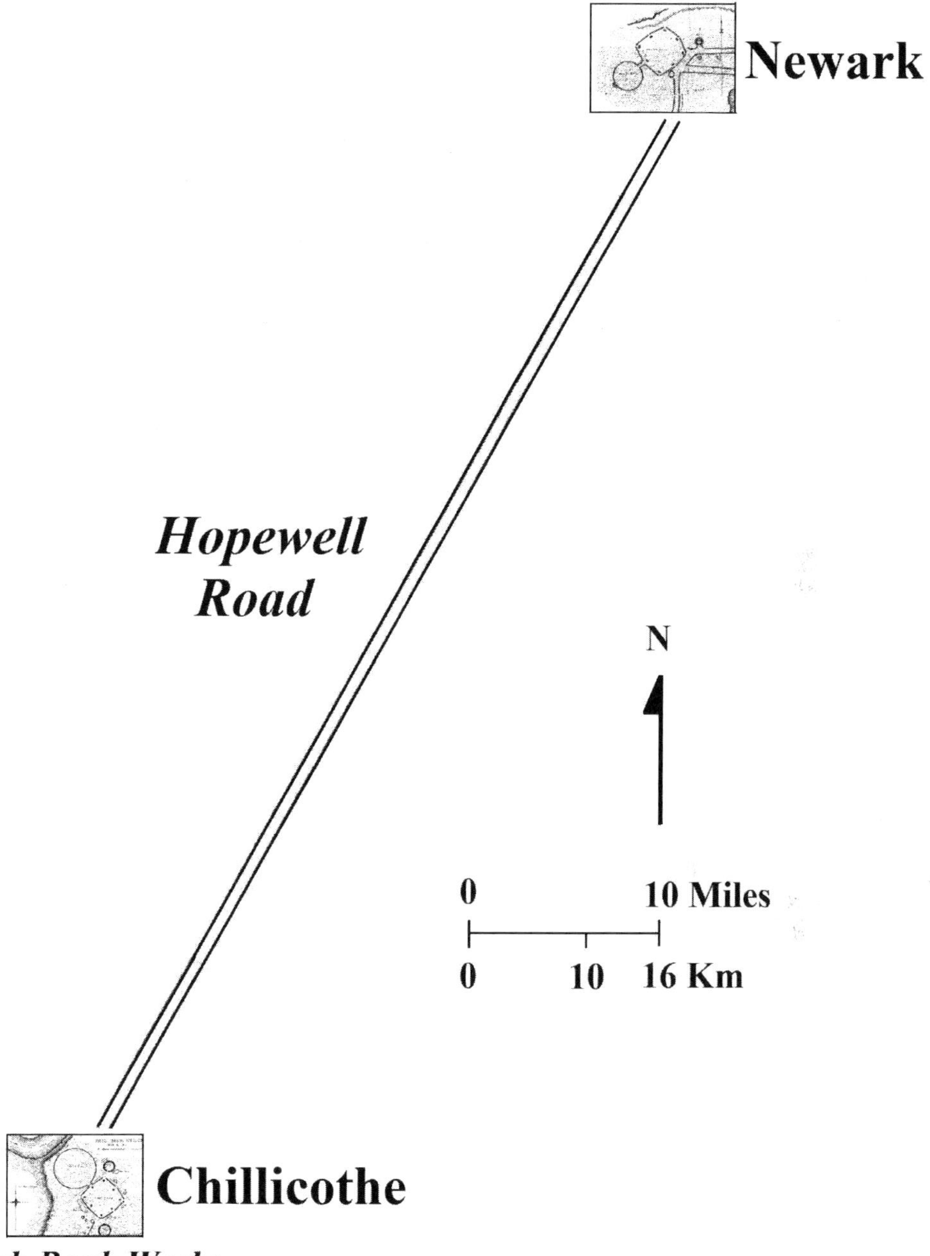

Fig 11.14: Map of the Hopewell Road as it may have existed c. AD 1 stretching from the Newark giant earthworks with Octagon and Circle aligned to the Lunar Maximum moonrise (Figs 11.11 11.12a) on the north-east end to High Bank Works (Fig. 11.3) on the south-west end

Was this a favoured time of the year after a long winter when the 'portals' seen just above the horizon (Langford 2007, 52) that souls or a shaman needed to travel between worlds would be in the proper alignment (or alignments)? The bear shaman could have symbolically travelled along the Hopewell Road that ran from the north-east at Newark to the High Banks Works at Chillicothe in the south-west or, mirrored above it, to the south-west along the bright Milky Way where Scorpius and Sagittarius are low on the horizon. The bright part of the Milky Way in Sagittarius where the 'puff of steam' comes out of the spout of the 'teapot' may then have acted as Langford's (2007, 52, 240–242) portal or sky-hole at the south-west at the end of the Milky Way (Fig. 11.15b), a doorway accessed by shamans who escorted the souls to the other side before the doorway closed when its stars set below the horizon (Fig. 11.15a). As we have seen, it is also where the moon sets at its far south point during the lunar maximum (Fig. 11.16).

Both Sagittarius and Scorpius rise in the south-east near the Lunar Maximum far south rise point (Fig. 11.17) and, approximately 6 months later, set in the south-west near the Lunar Maximum far south set point. In either case and perhaps importantly for identification of the place on the horizon whether rising or setting, the azimuths are well south and north of the winter solstice azimuths and very close to those of the Lunar Maximum.

Sagittarius is the constellation of interest as it travels along the southern horizon from early spring to late fall before disappearing, the timing much the same as the bear's hibernation cycle. A natural question is if there was an awareness or association between these stars and the bear in Hopewell thought? A large bear effigy mound was once located near Fullerton Field on the south side of the Ohio River near the mouth of the Scioto, a Fort Ancient settlement (Hyde 1962, 158). High Banks Works is also on the Scioto River, but it is not known if the bear mound shared a cultural connection with it. However, a tentative connection between the bear and the stars of Sagittarius may have existed in ancient times surviving to early historic times.

To a number of tribes on the central and northern Plains, the pattern of stars in Sagittarius that form the body and dome of the 'teapot' (Fig. 11.15b) may have represented a 'humped animal' (Leola One Feather and Ralph Redfox, pers. comm.). Only two animals in North America have a hump: the buffalo and the bear. Von Del Chamberlain (1982, 129–130) surmised that Sagittarius was the bear constellation of the Pawnee, an idea I highly concur with for two reasons. One is the 'humped animal' identification of Sagittarius by traditional elders of the Lakota and Northern Cheyenne, both of whom are (or were) responsible for the keeping of traditional and star knowledge.[7] The other is that the late Ralph Redfox (personal communication), a Northern Cheyenne spiritual elder, one of the last surviving members of the ancient Wolf Lodge and grandson of the last traditional priest of the Massaum or Crazy Animal Dance (Bender 2017b) by whom he was raised, remarked that 'people came to earth [or can go back to the stars] through that part of the sky at the end of the Milky Way ... you know that one, I think it is sometimes called the teapot', i.e. Sagittarius. Ralph

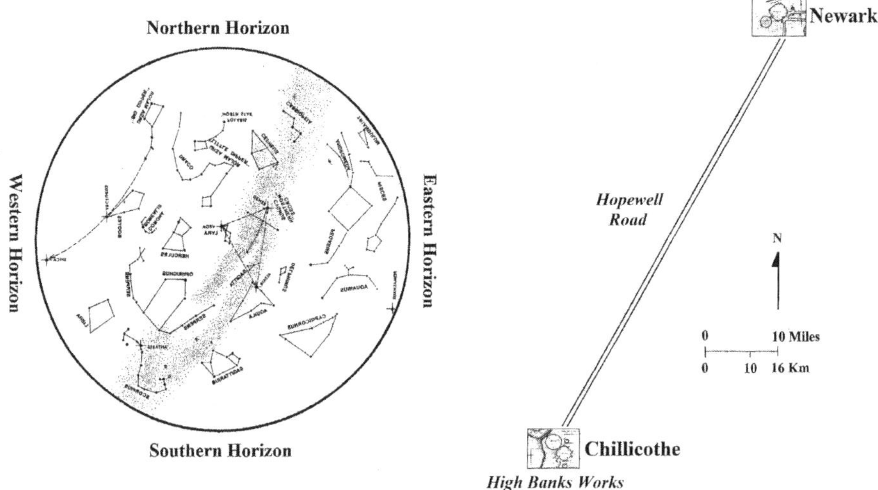

a

b

Fig. 11.15: a) Reversed star map showing the Milky Way stretching overhead from the north-east to the south-west during the late spring and early summer juxtaposed with the map of the Hopewell Road north-east to south-west angle for comparison; b) photo of Milky Way 'portal' with the 'teapot' of Sagittarius and a portion of Scorpius with the red star Antares (at right)

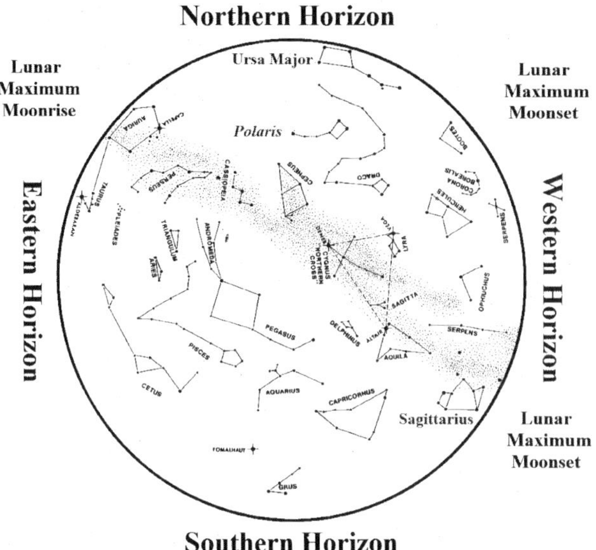

Fig. 11.16: The Milky Way with Sagittarius in the south-west shortly before it sets at the same approximate azimuth as the Lunar Maximum southernmost moonset.

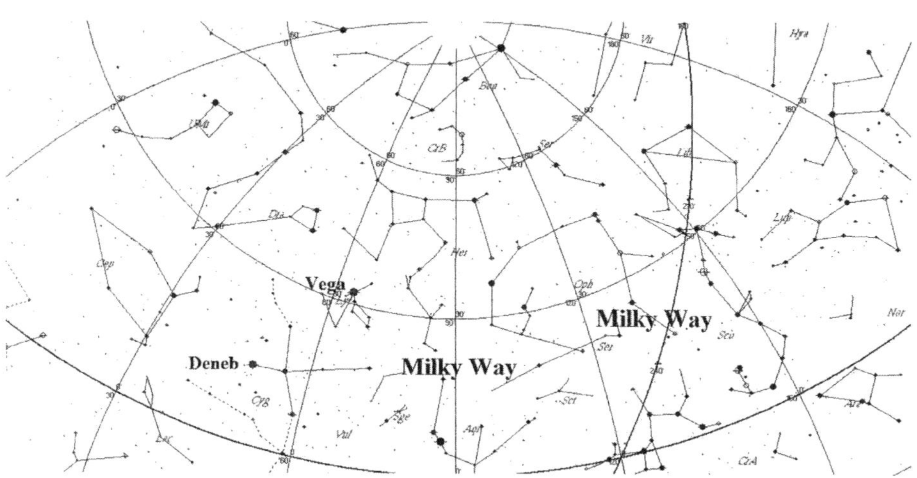

Fig. 11.17: Star chart showing Sagittarius and Scorpius rising in the south-east in late winter and early spring. Both constellations rise at the same approximate azimuth as the southernmost Lunar Maximum moonrise. Note the bright stars Deneb and Vega, which both rise at the same approximate azimuth at the northernmost Lunar Maximum moonrise, and the Milky Way hugging the eastern horizon between the bright stars in the north-east and constellations in the south-east. The two 'ends' of the Milky Way form an approximate 90° arc, the same as that bracketed between the Lunar Maximum moonrise azimuth aligned to the north-east at Newark and to the south-east at High Banks.

Redfox often called the Pawnee 'the borrowers' because of traditions they shared with the Cheyenne (pers. comm.), but in the case of the 'teapot' as a portal, the Pawnee may have been the lenders.

The Pawnee were a Caddoan-speaking people who migrated north from what is now Texas and may have been one of the earliest tribal groups to permanently move to and live on the Great Plains. They later divided into the four major bands: the Skidi or Wolf Pawnee, the Chaui or Grand Pawnee, the Kitkehahki or Republican Pawnee, and the Pitahauerat or Tapage Pawnee (Waldman 1988, 179–180; Johnson 2000, 137). The Pawnee are intriguing because they possessed cultural traits related to the Temple Mound culture and Mound Builders of the south-eastern United States including the Hopewell (Waldman 1985, 20–22). Through sacred medicine bundles, shrines and priests, their ceremonies were rich in symbolism connected to the supernatural cosmic forces of the night sky and other heavenly bodies including the sun and moon (Murie 1981; Waldman 1988, 147–150, 181; Johnson 2000, 137).

When the Pawnee migrated north to the Plains, they may well have taken the tradition of Sagittarius as a bear with them and, from there, disseminated the belief to other tribes and people. Alice Fletcher (1902, 730) had no doubt of a 'network of exchange [which] lies over the whole country' and after interviewing Siouan-speaking people (who, along with the Cheyenne, lived north of the Pawnee), '... met with evidence which seemed to indicate that ... the Pawnee had been instrumental in the spread of certain cults among their neighbours, and that this tribe still possessed in considerable detail many of their ancient ceremonies'. As Taylor and Sturtevant (1996, 136) stated, '[m]uch of the Plains Indian cosmos centred on ... the recognition of an intangible power of the universe ... in varying forms from one linguistic group to the next and was embedded in ancient beliefs which, while modified by the Plains environment, can be traced back to the[ir] original Woodland homelands ...' There can be little doubt that traditions, e.g. the Milky Way as a soul's path, songs, music and ceremonies were shared over distance for millennia, transcending both language and cultural barriers with many of the traditions and ceremonies likely existing as shamanic practices (Heming 1896, 145; Langford 2007; 220–224).[8]

Adding credence to the shared and widespread belief of a north-east to south-west travel of souls travelling on the Milky Way are surviving traditions of apparent ancient origin. In North America the Pawnee and a host of other tribes (Langford 2007, 205) say that the souls of the dead, pushed by the wind, are received by a star at the northern end of the Milky Way which guarded the pathway and started the souls on their journey toward the south or south-west (Chamberlain 1982, 113; Miller 1997, 224; Murie 1981, 42). Near this star the (Milky Way) path divides into a short fork and long fork. To quote from Dorsey (1904, 57):

> The star that receives the Pawnee after they are dead stands at the end of the Milky Way, in the north. He receives them upon the earth, takes them on a long journey to the north, and after he gets to this place he places them upon the Milky Way. If the dead man was a warrior, he was put on the dim Milky Way; if he died of

> old age, or if it was a woman, they were put on the wide traveled road. Then they started on the journey toward the south. There, at the end of the Milky Way, in the south, stands another star, who receives the spirits of the departed, and there they make their home.

From this description it is clear there were two stars which received the spirits at the ends of the Milky Way. One was in the north, the other in the south. The argument of exactly which star in the south was the 'spirit star' has been debated although anthropologist S. Hagar thought the Spirit Star was Antares.[9] Antares (Fig. 11.15b) has been identified by other tribes as 'the brightest star in the southwest' near the end of the Milky Way (Langford 2007, 208). Furthermore, Antares is very near Sagittarius, the likely bear constellation at the 'end' of the Milky Way in the southern sky (Fig. 11.15b). But is there a stellar bear link at the north end? In order to answer this question we must raise the question of what star was or is the spirit star in the north bearing in mind there is a difference between the bear constellation (a pattern of stars) and what were identified as individual 'bear stars'. Accounts suggest that the area of Cygnus and the Cygnus rift in the Milky Way is the place where the spirit star that receives souls stands at the 'end' of the Milky Way (Chamberlain 1982, 129; Miller 1997, 224). But is there a bear connection with this area or any particular stars?

There are two bright, first magnitude stars found in this area, Vega and Deneb. Both have tentatively been identified as 'Black' stars in Pawnee cosmology; Vega likely the Black Meteoric Star, Deneb the Second Black Star (Chamberlain 1982, 126, 134). In Pawnee and Plains Indian cosmology, the colour was black associated with the north-east direction and, perhaps more importantly, the bear (Wedel 1977, 136–137; Miller 1997, 226). Therefore, the 'best fit' candidate for the Bear or spirit star that '... that receives the Pawnee after they are dead [and which] stands at the end of the Milky Way, in the north' is Deneb, the Second Black Star, at the north end of the Milky Way Cygnus Rift (Figs 11.15a, 11.16–18).

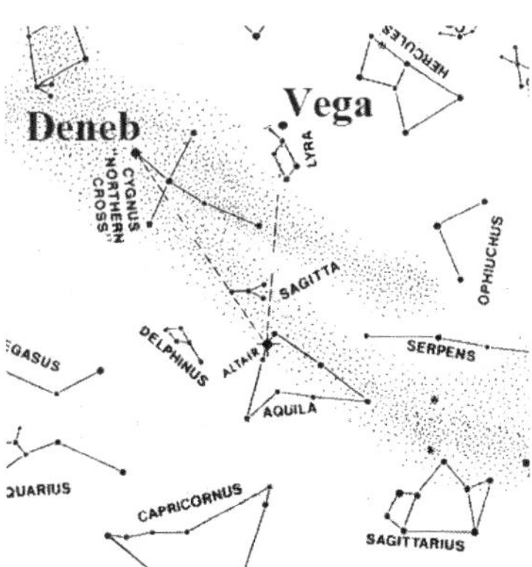

Fig. 11.18: Partial star map of the Milky Way showing Deneb where the Cygnus Rift begins, the two branches of the Milky Way and Vega near the edge of the Milky Way

Deneb should not be confused with nearby Vega, the Black Meteoric Star. They are distinctly different stars. The medicine bundles for each separate star and village where kept were apparently associated with animal powers, but different animals. The Black Meteoric Star represented animal powers and, in particular, the buffalo (Murie 1981, 39, 42). The Second Black Star bundle and village was associated with left-handedness, conveyed cosmic power and the ability to directly communicate with the animals (Murie 1981, 39), classic bear cult traits (Bender 2017a). Shamanic feats were also learned through the Second Black Star bundle (Murie 1981, 39, 42, 155; Chamberlain 1982, 124–125), another likely link to ancient bear cults and shamanic healing (Bender 2017a). Furthermore, Cygnus and the bright star Deneb were seen in the western high plains and basin as a 'part of a Grizzly bear' (Milller 1997, 296).

What should not go unnoticed is the possible association between Deneb, the bear shaman figurine from Newark, the Hopewell Road and the Milky Way. Perhaps the bear shaman was placed at Newark on the north-east end of the Hopewell Road and, like the bear star Deneb in the north, meant to help act as an 'escort' or psychopomp for the souls received by the star Deneb where the Milky Way divides in the constellation Cygnus (the Cygnus Rift), and from there travelling on the bright branch of the Milky Way to the area of Sagittarius in the southern sky (and near it, Antares, possibly the southern spirit star)? Moreover, like the 'ends' of the Milky Way, i.e. Deneb and Sagittarius (both celestial bears?), connected on the eastern horizon by the Milky Way (Fig. 11.17), the giant earthworks alignments found at Newark in the northeast and High Banks to the southwest were connected by the Hopewell Road, the Milky Way's apparent mirror image on the ground. The earthly reflection of the Milky Way, its ends defined by the rise points of the moon at lunar maximum observed from the giant earthworks at Newark and High Banks, may have been profound when taken together with the Hopewell Road connecting the two, the road that souls and shamans accessed when travelling on their journey between worlds. Like the Milky Way whose brilliance has been diminished by another society's wonders (the electric light), the shamanistic traditions of the giant earthworks and Hopewell Road have been greatly diminished in importance and all but vanished, surviving as slivers of information, remnants and conjecture.

Final Comments

When trying to recover ancient traditions that may have been practised at sites steeped in antiquity where there is no record of rituals, shamanistic practices, inherent cosmologies or the ceremonies performed, the answers to questions of what, why or how, function, use or purpose itself can be and most likely are all mainly modern conjecture. In North America, unless recorded by missionaries or travellers, identification and knowledge of Native American constellations, asterisms, individual stars and the traditions that were inherent within the beliefs of the sites builders can be murky. It is made even more so where the cultures and spoken languages have vanished. Adding insult to injury, the heinous policy of government and Christian denominations actively involved in purging Native American traditional beliefs, languages and culture during the late 19th and early 20th centuries caused great harm. Fortunately, tribal elders and holy men, traders, and some missionaries did make great efforts to preserve indigenous traditions and ceremonies despite the pressures of colonisation (Ralph Redfox and Leola One Feather, pers. comm.).

It is from this record we can hypothesise and present ideas based on both scientific and historic fact with additional thanks to the work of dedicated ethnologists and anthropologists who recorded invaluable stories in the late 19th and early 20th centuries. These historic records contain tantalising accounts that help connect some Native American sites with shamanistic traditions related to the stars, portals or 'sky holes' and, in a round about way, the bear and moon. As the inevitable passage of time continues to take its toll on not only the sites, but those who help to preserve the scraps of information available to us, the information and thoughts recorded centuries ago still reverberates and may well be the last surviving remnants from the slim editions and oral records of the past.

Notes

1 For a fuller explanation of the event, the mapping process, anticipation and problems, see Bender (2017a).

2 Four azimuths are of importance if a lunar maximum alignment is thought to be present and computed dependent on the latitude and elevation above the horizon. The lunar maximum rise and set azimuth values computed for the latitude of the sites (43.5°N) are 41.5° (±0.5°) north and south of the east–west line (Bender 2011). Therefore, simple addition or subtraction to 90° and 180° produces the four azimuths for a 0° elevation or flat horizon observation of the lunar maximum far north and south rise and set points (which is why the mound sites themselves were likely chosen in what was treeless and open, flat country). The values for the rise lunar maximum azimuth rise azimuths in the north-east and south-east are 48.5° and 131.5° (or 132°±0.5°), and the lunar set azimuths are (as mentioned previously) 228.5° in the south-west and 311.5° in the north-west (Bender 2011). The 311.5° azimuth as a far north set point was confirmed at Kolterman in December, 2006 (Bender 2017a).

3 Because the alignment of the two parallel mounds had been computed by an astronomer as a lunar maximum azimuth (Ulrich 1980), E. G. Bruder visited the Brummond mounds during the approximate time of the winter solstice (when the full moon had swung to its northernmost rise and set points along the eastern horizon). Beginning in 1952 and then following for the next 9 years in a row, Bruder's attempt to confirm and document the moonrise alignment at the Brummond mounds was continuously ruined by cloud cover (Mayville News, 21 Dec. 1961). He would likely have had better luck and clear skies by returning to the site about the time of the summer solstice, a season when the skies are far less likely to be cloud covered for weeks at a time, in order to document the moon at the 'back azimuth'. If so, he would have observed it setting a 180° in the opposite direction of the lunar maximum moonrise in the north-east during the winter, i.e. the lunar maximum moonset in the south-west and, moreover, the actual direction the bear effigy mound is aligned to face, perhaps an accurate indication which direction the viewer was meant to be facing to observe the event.

4 In the western Great Lakes area, the Ojibwe identified bright stars near Corona Borealis or sometimes the constellation itself as the 'Bear's Head' (Kohl 1860, 118–119; Fertey 1970, 35). Other sources list the Pleiades as the 'bears head' and this confusion may be explained by time and distance from its origins like the general confusion with these asterisms themselves. It may have its roots in antiquity, but many times it is the misidentification and confusion (caused by a lack of basic astronomy or star knowledge) of those who recorded the traditions.

5 Ghosts were highly and universally feared by many of the Indian tribes and culture as 'the dread of spirits unappeased ...' The ghost could become separated from the soul or personality of the deceased and would hopefully accompany the soul on the four day journey to the land of departed spirits (Keesing 1987, 45, 51–52; Langford 2007, 207).

6 According to Chippewa accounts, the earth has four layers or levels. It is always night in the bottom layer and where the Manitou (spirit) who is 'boss' rules the bottom of the earth (and

all four layers). There is no special name for him or the four layers. The bear is said to be the 'boss' or Grandfather. Like the earth, the sky has four layers. The Manitou who lives in the top layer is equal in power to the Manitou at the bottom. The opposite of the bottom layer, it is always light there and never night. There is no special name for these layers or Manitou although some refer to him as the *Gicimanitou* (Great Spirit). The flat earth of humans is in the middle, between the four layers of the earth and four layers of the sky.

7 Through environmental modification and acculturation like that seen in the Midé scrolls where the Algonquin horned-serpent and Michipeshu or the 'Great Lion' (Conway & Conway 1990, 24–27) were replaced by the horned bison over time (Dewdney 1975, 96), it is likely that the Lakota, once they were acculturated on the Plains, eventually equated the humped animal with the bison and not the bear (Bender 2013).

8 One such example is the Calumet or 'tobacco pipe' dance and belief that '... the sun gave it to the Panys (Pawnee), and that since then it has been communicated from village to village' including to the Menominee in Wisconsin sometime in the early to mid-17th century (Keesing 1987, 51). Many times, however, the origin of a tradition or belief is uncertain because of its wide-spread occurrence and depth of time itself. The tradition of Sagittarius as the bear constellation and its origin may have been forgotten and lost, much like the sacred bundles and traditional knowledge that was buried with prominent medicine men after they had passed on (Murie 1981, 195–197).

9 In North America the Pawnee and Cherokee say that the souls of the dead are received by a star at the northern end of the Milky Way. There the path divides. 'He [God] directs the warriors on the dim and difficult path, and women and those who die of old age upon the brighter and easier path. The souls journey southwards; at the end of the celestial path they are received by the Spirit Star.' The anthropologist S. Hagar thinks the Spirit Star is Antares. (https://sites.google.com/a/spirit-web.org/spirit-web/veda/astronomy-and-antiquity-of-vedic-culture)

References

Bender, H. E. 2004. Star beings and stones: Origins and legends. In F. Giordano & E. Comba (eds) *Indian Stories Indian Histories* Torino: Otto Editore, 7–22.

Bender, H. E. 2009. Caring for creation: A hierophany at Strawberry Island. In G. H. Nash & D. Gheorghiu (eds) *The Archaeology of People and Territory.* Budapest: Archeolingua Alapitvany, 137–156.

Bender, H. E. 2011. Archeoastronomy investigations on petroform sites in the mid-continent (& latitudes) of North America: A common sense approach with commentary. Part 2: Practical or 'naked-eye' astronomy. Unpublished manuscript.

Bender, H. E. 2013. Bison effigy stones in Wisconsin. IFRAO 2013 Proceedings. *American Indian Rock Art* 40, 43–80.

Bender, H. E. 2017a. Bear myths and rituals: The moon, women, stars and possible ancient links to Eurasia in North America. In D. Gheorghiu, E. Pasztor, H. Bender & G. Nash (eds) *Archaeological Approaches to Shamanism: Mind-Body, Nature, and Culture.* Newcastle-upon-Tyne: Cambridge Scholars Publishing, 68–91.

Bender, H. E. 2017b. Star-beings and stones. *Journal of Lithic Studies* 4(4), 77–116.

Berres, T., Stothers, D. M. & Mather, D. 2004. Bear imagery and ritual in northeast North America: An update and assessment of A. Irving Hallowell's Work. *Midcontinental Journal of Archaeology* 29(1), 5–29.

Birmingham, R. A. & Eisenberg, L. E. 2000. *Indian Mounds of Wisconsin.* Madison WI: University of Wisconsin Press.

Brehm, V. 1996. The metamorphoses of an Ojibwa Manido. *American Literature* 68(4), 677–706.

Campbell, J. 1988. *Historical Atlas of World Mythology Volume 1: The Way of the Animal Powers - Part 1: Mythologies of the Primitive Hunters and Gatherers* and *Part 2: Mythologies of the Hunt*. New York: Perennial Library, Harper & Row.

Chamberlain, V. D. 1982. *When the Stars Came Down to Earth.* Los Altos CA: A Ballerina Press/Center for Archaeoastronomy Cooperative.

Comba, E. 2014. Amerindian cosmologies and European prehistoric cave art: Reasons for and usefulness of a comparison. *Arts* 2014(3), 1–14.

Conway, T. 1992. The Conjurer's Lodge: Celestial narratives from Algonkian Shamans. In R. A. Williamson & C. R. Farrer (eds) *Earth and Sky.* Albuquerque NM: University of New Mexico Press, 236–259.

Conway, T. & Conway, J. 1990. *Spirits on Stone. The Agawa Pictographs. Heritage Discoveries.* San Louis Obispo CA: Heritage Discoveries.

Densmore, F. 1979. *Chippewa Customs.* St Paul? MN: Historical Society Press.

Dewdney, S. 1975. *The Sacred Scrolls of the Southern Ojibway.* Toronto/Buffalo NY: University of Toronto Press.

Dorsey, G. A. 1904. Traditions of the Skidi Pawnee. *Memoirs of the American Folklore Society* 8, 00–00.

Fertey, A. 1970. *The Journals of Joseph N. Nicolet.* St Paul MN: Minnesota Historical Society.

Fletcher, A. C. 1902. Star cult among the Pawnee – a preliminary report. *American Anthropologist* 4(4), 730–736.

Gard, R. & Sorden, L. G. 1988. *The Romance of Place Names in Wisconsin.* Minocqua WI: Heartland Press.

Goodman, R. 1992. *Lakota Star Knowledge.* Rosebud SD: Sinte Gleska University.

Grim, J. A. 1983. *The Shaman.* Norman OK/London: University of Oklahoma Press.

Hadingham, E. 1984. *Early Man and the Cosmos.* New York: Walker & Company.

Hall, R. L. 1993. Red Banks, Oneota, and the Winnebago: Views from a distant rock. *Wisconsin Archeologist* 74(1–4), 10–79.

Heming, H. H. 1896. *The History of the Catholic Church in Wisconsin.* Milwaukee WI: Catholic Historical Publishing Company.

Hively, R. & Horn, R. 1984. Hopewellian geometry and astronomy at High Bank. *Archaeoastronomy* supplement to *Journal for the History of Astronomy* 15(7), S85–S100.

Howard, J. E. 1955. The tree dweller cults of the Dakota. *Journal of American Folklore* 69(268), 169–174.

Hurley, W. M. 1986. The Late Woodland stage: Effigy mound culture. *Wisconsin Archaeologist* 67(3–4), 293–301.

Hyde, G. E. 1962. *Indians of the Woodlands.* Norman OK: University of Oklahoma Press.

Johnson, M. 2000. *Encyclopedia of Native Tribes of North America.* New York: Gramercy Books.

Keesing, F. M. 1987. *The Menomini Indians of Wisconsin.* Madison WI: University of Wisconsin Press.

Kinietz, V. W. 1965. *Indians of the Western Great Lakes 1615–1760.* Ann Arbor MI: University of Michigan Press.

Kohl, J. G. 1860. *Kitchi-Gami: Wanderings Round Lake Superior.* London: Chapman & Hall.

Krupp, E. C. 1991. *Beyond the Blue Horizon.* Oxford/New York: Oxford University Press.

Langford, G. E. 2007. *Reachable Stars.* Tuscaloosa AL: University of Alabama Press.

Leeming, D. & Page, J. 1998. *The Mythology of Native North America.* Norman OK: University of Oklahoma Press.

Lenzendorf, D. 2000. *A Guide to Effigy Mounds National Monument.* Fort Washington PA: Eastern National.

Lepper, B. T. 1995. Tracking Ohio's Hopewell Road. *Archaeology* 40(6), 52–56.

Lepper, B. T. 1998. The archaeology of the Newark Earthworks. In L. Sillivan & R. Mainfort (eds) *Ancient Enclosures of the Eastern Woodlands.* Gainsville FL: University Press of Florida, 114–134.

Lepper, B. T. 2006. The Great Hopewell Road and role in the pilgrimage in the Hopewell Interaction Sphere. In D. Charles & J. Buikstra (eds) *Recreating Hopewell.* Gainesville FL: University Press of Florida, 122–133.

Mallery, G. 1894. *Picture-writing of the American Indians.* Smithsonian Institution Tenth Annual Report of the Bureau of Ethnology. Washington DC: Smithsonian.

Meeus, J. 1997. *Mathematical Astronomy Morsels.* Richmond VA: Willman-Bell.

Miller, J. 1982. People, berdaches and left-handed bears: Human variations in Native Americana. *Journal of Anthropological Research* 38(3), 274–287. Albuquerque: University of New Mexico.

Miller, D. S. 1997. *Stars of the First People.* Boulder CO: Pruett.

Murie, J. R. 1981. *Ceremonies of the Pawnee* (ed. D. R. Parks). *Smithsonian Contributions to Anthropology* 27. Washington DC: Smithsonian Institution.

Murray, A. S. 2004. *Who's Who in Myth & Legend.* London: CRW.

Overton, G. 1928. The sacred springs of the Lake Poygan region. *Wisconsin Archaeologist* new series 7(4), 211–218.

Rockwell, D. 1991. *Giving Voice to Bear.* Niwot CO: Roberts Rinehart.

Russel, H. S. 1980. *Indian New England Before the Mayflower.* Lebanon NH: University Press of New England.

Schlesier, K. H. 1987. *The Wolves of Heaven.* Norman OK/London: University of Oklahoma Press.

Schoolcraft, H. R. 1853. *Information Respecting the History, Condition and Prospects of the Indian Tribes of the Unites States: Collected and Prepared Under the Direction of the Bureau of Indian Affairs*, Vol. 1, Philadelphia PA: Lippincott, Grambo & Co.

Schwartz, M. 1997. *A History of Dogs in the Early Americas.* New Haven CO/London: Yale University Press.

Seeman, M. F. 1979. *The Hopewell Interaction Sphere: The Evidence for Interregional Trade and Structural Complexity*, Prehistory Research Series V(2), Indianapolis IN: Indiana Historical Society.

Smith, T. S. 1995. *Island of the Anishnaabeg: Thunderers and Water Monsters in the Traditional Ojibwe Life-World.* Moscow ID: University of Idaho Press.

Squire, E. G. & Davis, E. H. 1848. *Ancient Monuments of the Mississippi Valley.* Smithsonian Contributions to Knowledge 1, Washington, DC: Smithsonian Institution.

Stewart, J. D.,1978. A research strategy for the study of star lore. In P. G. Duke (ed.) *Diffusion and Migration: Their Role in Cultural Development.* Calgary: University of Calgary Archaeology Department, Chacmool Proceedings, 144–166.

Taylor, C. F. & Sturtevant, W. C. 1996. *The Native American.* New York: Smithmark.

Ulrich, R. A. 1980. The Brummond time mounds. *Wisconsin Archaeologist* 1(1), 100–110.

Vogel, V. J. 1991. *Indian Names on Wisconsin's Map.* Madison WI: University of Wisconsin Press.

Waldman, C. 1985. *Atlas of the North American Indian.* New York: Facts on File.

Waldman, C. 1988. *Encyclopedia of Native American Tribes.* New York/Oxford: Facts on File.

Wedel, W. R. 1977. Native astronomy and Plains Caddoans. In A. F. Aveni (ed.) *Native American Astronomy.* Austin TX/London: University of Texas Press, 131–145.

Chapter 12

To Re-Enact Is to Remember: Envisioning a Shamanic Research Protocol in Archaeology

Apela Colorado and Ryan Hurd

Abstract *Increasingly, western scientific disciplines and indigenous ways of knowing and being, or* Indigenous science, *are being brought together. Indigenous science refers to the place-based, holistic and spiritual knowledge system and wisdom traditions of indigenous peoples. Issues of climate change, sea rise, extreme weather events, food equity and global health challenges necessitate context-driven research that causal research cannot address on its own. The question is, how to consciously link the ways of knowing to ensure validity, reliability, ethical standards and vigor to both systems. Here, Indigenous Science perspectives are presented in a dynamic and reciprocal relationship of contextualisation with landscape archaeology, performance and community education with the goal being the potential transformation of all parties involved. Like an initiation, this article progresses through several deepening levels of contemporary shamanism, each connected with the honouring of prehistoric sacred sites including the Kurgans (burial mounds) of Karakol Valley, Altai Republic; and petroglyphs in south-eastern Alaska. Our final aim is to present considerations for a shamanic-scientific research protocol.*

Introduction

> To re-enact is to remember
>
> Alphonso Ortiz, PhD. Hopi Pueblo

Up to recent times, science as a practice falls short of its ideals when it comes to the questions that demand embodied participation to collect information. The 'taboo of subjectivity' has reached far into the human sciences and humanities as well, especially concerning questions about the nature of consciousness and perception (Wallace 2000). Ontologically, subjectivity is impossible to truly root out when it comes to topics that demand participation: such are the aims of landscape archaeology, to understand how humans used, altered and were altered by the landscapes they inhabited in the past. As Kris Hirst suggests, in landscape archaeology, there remains a default tendency to 'hide behind scientific objectivity, and ignore the sensual aspects associated with actually living within a landscape and ignore the sensual aspects associated with actually living within a landscape' (Hirst 2017). Christopher Tilley's phenomenological approach is a balm to this tendency; he writes, 'There is no substitute for personal experience' (2008, 271). Yet something more is needed: remembering that we are in a deep relationship with landscape, with an understanding that landscape is alive and dynamic too.

The gravitas of environmental, social and climate change issues requires precisely this – a renewal of relationship with the living landscape. The time has come for *Indigenous science* to stand alongside Western science in a dynamic and reciprocal partnership. Indigenous science refers to the place based, holistic and spiritual knowledge system and wisdom traditions of indigenous peoples (Colorado 2014). Indigenous Cultural Practitioners, ICPs, are our 'master scientists', often referred to as 'shamans' by western researchers. In the last 30 years, policy and practice towards indigenous knowledge has evolved. Although there is still a climate of distrust and exploitation, something to be discussed later in this chapter, individual scientists have been turning to indigenous reportage (oral history, material culture and ceremony) to confirm scientific speculation. For example, Dr Bruce Masse, environmental geologist with Los Alamos National Laboratory, examined thousands of indigenous stories, drawings and historical records, and concluded 'historical information contained in these myths can be transmitted faithfully through successive generations and can be elicited by scientific study' (Masse *et al.* 2007, 9). By comparing dozens of creation myths around the world that involve both celestial and epic flooding events, Masse hypothesises that a massive cosmic impact hit the earth around 2800 BP (1998, 53). Ruth Ludwin, University of Washington Seismographic Institute, also draws on indigenous oral history, traditional stories and pertinent petroglyph sites to extend baseline data, provide personal witness, and raise new questions to better understand and predict tsunami and earthquake cycles (Ludwin *et al.* 2005).

Wade Davis, anthropologist, ethnobotanist, National Geographic explorer, sums up the critical situation and importance of indigenous science:

> Just as there is a biological web of life, there is also a cultural and spiritual web of life – what we at the *National Geographic* have taken to calling the 'ethnosphere.' It's really the sum total of all the thoughts, beliefs, myths and institutions brought into being by the human imagination. It is humanity's greatest legacy, embodying everything we have produced as a curious and amazingly adaptive species. The ethnosphere is as vital to our collective well-being as the biosphere. And just as the biosphere is being eroded, so is the ethnosphere – if anything, at a far greater rate. (Parsell 2002)

We will explore ways in which ICPs and western scientists have practically applied a more holistic and integrated approach and discuss precautions to be considered for future endeavours.

A New Role for Landscape Archaeology – The Danger and Promise

Landscape archaeology employs integrative, multi-layered, multi-disciplinary approaches to study complex issues that shape our landscape; it cuts across traditional subjects and time periods to develop new methods for analysing the physical and intangible aspects of landscape. This interdisciplinary trend comes out of post-processual archaeology and is in line with the larger research questions of cognitive archaeology, which seeks to understand how the material influences cognition and vice versa. Landscape archaeology, with its focus on earthworks, stones and burials, is well suited to investigate how non-normative cognition styles affect the material record, especially in regards to sacred psychology, belief and religion (see Fagan 1998; Pearson 2002; Hayden 2003; Romain 2009). The interest in the sacred or non-normative in cognitive archaeology is also drawn from values first discussed in the anthropology of the extraordinary. Here, researchers interested in altered states of consciousness include their own personal experiences as relevant sources of data – including dreams and visions (Laughlin *et al.* 1983; Tedlock 1992; Young & Goulet 1994; Hurd 2015).

Underlying these more inclusive anthropologies is a willingness to include multidimensionality in the research design. As anthropologist Charles Laughlin points out, it can take a lot of unlearning: 'In modern materialistic western cultures, children are typically taught to disattend their dream states and focus on adaptational interactions with the exterior physical world' (Laughlin 2011, 62). The relevancy of the extraordinary in anthropology is that many cognitive artefacts and landscapes were crafted by people who live or lived in cultures that value information from trance, dreams and other ecstatic states. In this context, recent experiential work that integrates the subjective experiences of archaeological researchers, including non-normative states of consciousness, into valid research protocols (Tilley 1997; Hurd 2011; Gheorghiu 2011; Devereux 2013) has begun to chip away at the invisible barrier between objects and subjects.

Archaeology is replicating ancient technology and experiencing mystical – perhaps shamanic – states of mind in the process. From the perspective of Indigenous science, many of the research areas where this work is being done are known as sacred sites for indigenous peoples. Why are archaeologists seeking shamanic experiences? What is their intention and what do they wish to achieve? We suggest that the direct, interactive dialogue in multidisciplinary qualitative research is key to this emerging field. It allows the researcher to enter the world of participants, reduces power differences and encourages disclosure and authenticity between researchers and participants thus inviting a meeting of minds necessary to produce a shared understanding.

Not without its critics, archaeology is moving towards the open door that altered and proto-shamanic states of consciousness can provide for deeper understanding. There is much promise but also pitfalls. It is at this threshold that indigenous sacred site guardians wait.

Indigenous ceremony used to be embedded and accepted in cultural work, but is now in an increasingly Westernised culture that demands explanation and justification. This articulating of the ceremony and the associated networking of

ICPs and appropriate archaeologists is an essential part of making the multicultural research initiative resilient so that it may have a lasting influence on preserving the sustainability and renaissance of traditional knowledge and give rise to a newly linked indigenous–western form of research.[1] From an Indigenous science perspective, preservation is a higher value than excavation, because the sites are valued not for their materials but their living presence. To the extent that archaeologists go into the field to communicate through the landscape, not just to make assessments of ancient cultures, it is helpful for researchers to work closely with embodied wisdom of ICPs to include in their own research, publications and teaching.

Archaeologists at sacred sites are reportedly experiencing shamanic consciousness during their research (see Gheorghiu 2011). Researchers can be taken over during these moments, but without fully losing control, they are just moments (not fully-blown shamanism), which can cause the researcher to explore Shadow, both collective and personal. However, these shamanic experiences, if not supported by sacred site guardians and shamans, are very dangerous as we explore below.

Lys Kruiper, bushman healer, describes the power of trance and the vital role of shamans:

> 'I'd like to take the young boys and the young girls there [to a sacred Bushman site north of Cape Town], so they can see it with their eyes, because I need to teach that when we change into a very dangerous animal, there's a certain bush we need to burn and then how to bring that person back out of that trance'[2]

Kruiper goes on to say that as a person goes into trance, other shamans must hold him back from walking directly into the ceremonial fire. With compassion, women practitioners, comb the energy of the entranced to ground him and bring him back to himself.

In a similar vein, Phil Johnson reiterates, 'There is danger between worlds or in crossing from one to another. We need to develop ceremonies for today.'[3]

To begin the conversation, we present a ceremony written in stone of contemporary indigenous prescription and proscription for entering shamanic consciousness on the rock art of southern Alaska. Then, Danil Mamyev, park director, geologist and Altai shaman, will speak about the Kurgans of Karakol Valley. Finally, considerations for a balanced shamanic-archeaological research model will be explored.

The Petroglyphs of South-eastern Alaska

Altaian shaman Danil Mamyev puts it this way: 'Indigenous knowledge never speaks in direct language, but it is important to know the meaning underneath'. Shamans use metaphor – ways of thinking about one thing in terms of another.[4] Such practices permit the use of sensory, emotional and cognitive information in a way that alters perception.

The most ancient articulation of indigenous shamanic initiation can be found in petroglyphs relating to the water spirit.[5] Water is life; the shaman is its instrument. The ceremony is so important that the ancients inscribed symbols of swirls, curves and uniform grooves on basalt so complex that even modern technology cannot replicate them. The transmission endures for centuries, or perhaps millennia,[6] as a means to convey the proper ceremonial protocols to future generations so far removed as to no longer share a common language.

The antediluvian messages are primary source documents that provide us with a direct link to the thoughts, beliefs and concerns of ancient people. Situated in the tide lines of south-east Alaska is a water spirit petroglyph[7] (Fig. 12.1) that depicts the transformative propensity of standing present to paradox, the very process that births shamanistic consciousness and that now calls to archaeologists. Edward Keithan, first curator of the Alaska Territorial Museum, wrote that the images located in the tide lines were meant to be awash: '... considerable evidence has appeared to suggest that these glyphs were always placed in such a way that each tide, in submerging specific graven supplications (depending on the type of tide), would dispatch the prayer anew, after the manner of prayer wheels, etc' (Keithan 1940).

According to oral tradition, the lizard-like Water Spirit image depicts human consciousness (the head in the jaws) about to be eaten, to undergo profound change. The thunderbird of the higher world of sky (intellect) is in the claws, and the shark of the underworld of water, with lines depicting its electro-sensory abilities, is atop the dorsal fin. The inversion of symbols typifies the encounter with paradox. In Jungian psychological terms, which can be seen as the closest Western psychology has ever gotten to shamanism (Bright 2009), the experience is not just a projection

Fig. 12.1: Water spirit petroglyph, situated in the tide lines of south-eastern Alaska, depicting the transformative propensity of standing present to paradox (Chyna Colorado, 2015, line drawing)

but signals an encounter with *Shadow*, or the part of the personality or collective culture that has been hidden from observation due to an inability to be integrated (Jung 1980, 20). Facing Shadow demands courage, determination and choice. We must consciously choose to integrate the unseen and unknown of ourselves (symbolised in the spiral, the journey of the sun and soul) or else the conscious self becomes a slave of the autonomous Shadow.

The horizontal 'Y's affirm that we are experiencing the watery realm of emotion and spirit; water dissolves and forms. 'When the lizard approaches, it is, according to the late Lakota Medicine Man Pete Catches, a time of great fear.'[8] The circular bubbles constituting the tail are the good news. Enduring the initiatic ordeal results in new life forms. The successful encounter gives rise to vision and creativity, exactly what our species needs now to survive.

Consideration: Karakol Valley, Altai Republic (Mongolia)

The Uch Enmek Nature Park in Altai follows the borders of the Karakol Valley. While the entire valley is considered sacred ground to the contemporary Altai villagers, the most sacred peak is Mount Uch Enmek, traditionally known as the 'cradle to the world' (Dobsen & Mamyev 2010, 245). The glacial history produced the ridge and valley landscape that is home to tundra, mountain steppe and sub-alpine meadow vegetation. There are many prehistoric and historic cultural features, including Kurgan (barrow) mounds, standing stones and petroglyphs. The Kurgans are the most important sites for contemporary Altai people, who treat them with reverence as burial grounds of 'the epic heroes, the spiritual giants of old' (Dobson 2010, 246).

Danil Mamyev, Geologist-Shaman

Danil Mamyev, park director of Uch Enmek, geologist and Altai shaman, struggles to protect the Kurgans of Karakol Valley. Sometimes his struggles are with conventional archaeologists. Mamyev's research combines spirituality, traditional indigenous knowledge and western science to reveal and restore the true meaning of Karakol sacred sites. In his words:

> So we came to the conclusion that the whole system (of Kurgans) was organized with very clear order of geophysics of the Earth. All of them combine as a complex and make a bank, which is database. That is the significance of the sacred sites on the Earth.
>
> Elders and Ancestors (other life forms and past generations) say that sacred sites dictate certain etiquette, attitude and rules towards them. So, we argue that the burial sites in Karakol valley are not just archeological objects for studying history and culture of the past, but they are the existences that keep and transmit the old knowledge and energy. Excavating these sacred sites does not let us find out how

> the ancestors saw the world. The assertions that archeologists make today are just opinions of the individual archeologist who did the digging, trying to explain the issue through his own worldview. So what we read in scientific, archeological books is not the culture of an ancient generation, but just a projection of contemporary archeology.[9]

Ethical Considerations for a Shamanic-Research Protocol in Archaeology

Collaboration and partnership requires constructive action to address ongoing legacies of colonialism by creating more equitable and inclusive research models that close the philosophical, methodological and economic gaps. It requires will, joint leadership, trust building, accountability and transparency as well as investment of and sharing resources.

Hopi physicist Phil Johnson notes that shamanic ways are holistic, embodied, earth-based and spiritual and calls for the establishment of a safe container for researchers – protocols and guidance from sacred site guardians to deal with the chaos of the liminal zone.[10] Unfortunately, the relationship between the west and the non-western indigenous peoples has been built on a foundation of separation and usurpation of indigenous wisdom. Indigenous people are seen and used as a source of data but are not included as co-equal partners (Harry 2006). Up to recent times, western science has looked at indigenous science and seen its own construction of fact-based, 'Indigenous, local or traditional knowledge'. These facts can be exploited but the source not credited. Following the Rio Earth Summit in 1992, ethnobotanist Jeremy Narby observed:

> Everybody was talking about the ecological knowledge of indigenous people, but certainly no one was talking about the spiritual origin of it as claimed by indigenous people themselves ... We, scientists, were not talking about it because we were afraid we would not be taken seriously. (Narby 1998, 31)

Conducting research across any cultural context requires attention to landscape and personal ethics. Cross-cultural research relationships inherently involve a dynamic of power. As members of colonial cultures, researchers have traditionally held power in forms of money, knowledge, and 'expertise' over their human subjects. Cascading from this foundation of power, the research relationship spawns other ethical issues of informed consent, control, research design, and data ownership. A linked model of inquiry incorporating an ongoing process of communication and consent offers an ethical solution that is mutually beneficial. A science that recognises and potentiates the dynamic interaction of complementary pairs of opposites. It honours all phenomena, and fosters creativity and life. It is a bio-cultural science of renewal.

Maria Sabina, *Chjota Chjine* (the one who knows) Mazateca Healer (1894–1985), became an internationally-known figure due to her extensive ceremonial and healing knowledge of peyote. In her book, she reveals that in childhood she and her sister turned to the mushroom to lift the pangs of hunger, 'we had nothing, only hunger and cold'.[11] After eating the mushrooms they felt full and the presence of a good spirit. She might have remained anonymous were it not for the appearance of anthropologist Robert Gordon Wasson. Their encounter is a cautionary tale. Wasson violated his agreement not to publish photos of Maria in trance or of her ceremony by publishing them in *Life*, a popular North American magazine, and went on to write books and even produce an album of her songs. The press trivialised her work and triggered a massive invasion of [Counterculture] *hippies* into Maria's mountains, ceremonies and life.

In the documentary film *María Sabina, mujer espíritu,* Sabina continues:

> From the moment foreigners came ... the holy children (peyote spirits) lost their purity. They lost their strength. They (foreign researchers) broke them down. From now on they will no longer serve. The holy children (peyote spirits) spoke ... I knew the language ... Suddenly I was surrounded by foreigners who came to look for God: they stole everything, even my songs, and I went to jail ... It is true that Wasson and his friends were the first foreigners who came to our town [*c.* 1927] in search of the holy children and who did not take them because they suffered from some illness. His reason was that they came to find God. Before Wasson nobody took mushrooms simply to find God. They were always taken for the sick to heal.[12]

To avoid the pitfalls of Wasson, researchers who find themselves experiencing or witnesses altered states of consciousness could benefit from cultural protocols or ceremony and an Indigenous Sacred Site Guardian with whom to partner. In this way, we can generate deep forms of wisdom that provide factual data, while renewing both western and indigenous ways of knowing – a paradigmatic shift into sustainability.

What Are the Implications of Landscape Archaeology Moving into Shamanic Consciousness?

In correspondence, Brian Bates, psychologist and expert in shamanic consciousness, suggests: 'For indigenous people, lost knowledge may be returned and trigger a renaissance of indigenous sciences. Native cultures, in general, no longer create new stories of history or science'. Perhaps the way forward is a different premise of returning and enlivening data taken from the native communities and framing the research findings to ask, 'What is Indigenous science; how did our people go about it in the past?' In this way, 'Indigenous knowledge inspired by western science may re-ignite the cultural expression of science making again'.[13]

In exchange for Indigenous science 'data' and with respect to the ICPs who shared it, activities and events can be structured within research to help indigenous people know more about our own cultural knowledge base as well as the related western scientific aspects. This is doubly important as indigenous wisdom has been vetted through western lenses without any parameters or checks for reliability, vigour or accountability. The mono-cultural scientific paradigm is failing to protect the earth's bio-culture, yet without meaningful participation in projects and policy formation, Indigenous science is likewise limited to unconnected projects scattered around the world.

For landscape archaeology, Indigenous science can help researchers extend baseline data, provide personal witness, raise new questions and answer critical issues for which science cannot find answers. The ceremonies integral to a shamanic archaeology are iconic bridges between the deep-rooted wisdom of traditional cultures and landscape archaeology and can benefit modern culture which responds to dramatic and image-rich presentation.

Consideration: Ritual at Pech Merle, Lot Valley, France

In 2016, an interdisciplinary team organised by Worldwide Indigenous Science Network (WISN) visited several prehistoric caves in south-west France. The team's expertise was in consciousness research, animal conservation, acoustics and native cosmologies. The team visited the cave of Pech Merle on 27 June 2016. Located in the Lot Valley, Occitania district, Pech Merle is known for large animal murals dating to the Magdalenian era but some of the paintings are almost 10,000 years older, dating to the Gravettian culture (Lawson 2012, 379).

As most of the guides on staff were present for our invited after-hours visit, an unplanned and unanticipated occasion of performance was created. For example, we had a respectful silence and time for prayer and reflection, as well as the burning of sage and copal, before entering the caverns. Later, Maori healer Timoti Bramley began a long series of singing chants and prayers to the caves and ancestors in front of one of the more resonant mural paintings, known as the *Dappled Horses*. It became apparent that members of the staff had never spent as much time in the cave as this particular visit; it had left an impression. Guides said they planned to incorporate aspects of the WISN approach to entering the cave respectfully. They said they now felt they were more than workers, but were 'guardians' to the sacred site.[14] As French Palaeolithic expert Pascal Raux entones, 'We go in the Dordogne caves to see the cave petroglyphs, rock paintings and engravings because we have lost the principal reason of life. We go into the caves to retrieve, to restore this thing'.[15]

Given that hundreds of tourists stream through Pech Merle weekly, this small shift in consciousness may affect change in the way that archaeology tourism is perceived and valued, at least at this one site in the south of France. In an era when the preservation of cultural sites is not guaranteed, the advantage of incorporating public education or active participant/performance is clear. As archaeologists with a community project with school children in Wales found, projects that incorporate ritual, music and performance can be used to 'ask big questions about mortality and religion, providing a new way to approach sensitive topics, without privileging one worldview over another' (Reynolds & Adams 2014, 14). The shift of consciousness occurred in this group by inviting others to change their status from passive observers

of 'art' to embodied participants in respectful relationship with the living cave. Deep participation is necessary for this shift to occur. In this spirit of hopefulness for the continued relevance of the Painted Caves of the Dordogne for all modern peoples, High Sanusi Credo Mutwa, Zulu *sangoma* (traditional healer), has a message to share: 'It's already deep inside you. When you are there, it will come out of you – ancient truths will emerge from you. May the winds of light carry you to the cradle of human awareness and artistry. Let the spirits come out of you – the gods do this, in this way. Feel them, the earth itself will make ideas and prayers from many thousands of years ago come out.'[16]

Consideration: Uch Enmek, a Model of Shamanistic and Western Science Collaboration

In 2005 Danil Mamyev partnered with the Siberian Branch of the Russian Academy of Science and Gorno-Altaisk University to conduct research into the magnetic and radioactivity fields of Karakol kurgans (Dmitriev & Shitov 2005). The results of the exploratory tests were intriguing.

> ... magnetic and weight characteristics of a group of people in a meditative condition significantly influence the different fields at Kurgan sites ... standing in one of the series of Scythian ritual complexes affects the autonomic nervous system. In addition, a small and highly intense 'magnetic dipole' has been discovered in the immediate vicinity of a double kurgan ...] The magnetic field of the dipole displayed variation in the amplitude up to 10,000T (nanotesla) and reacted to the presence of a human being. By comparison, changes in the field during magnetic storms on the earth's surface do not exceed 1,000T. (Dobsen & Mamyev 2010, 249)

The report concludes that the 'complex magnetic and radioactive fields, location and layout of kurgans in relation to the geological characteristics of the landscape partly reveal their hidden meaning' (Dobsen & Mamyev 2010, 250). The report warns that excavating kurgans destroys their magnetic properties and the possibility of recovering the knowledge embedded in this ritual structure and points out the significance, from an indigenous point of view, of this site for the modern world.

Concluding Remarks

After learning of the psychophysical effects of kurgans, one cannot help but be reminded of the oracles of Delphi in ancient Greece, who most likely went into shamanic trance by inhaling hydrocarbons (Spiller *et al.* 2002). Sometimes the mysterious can end up having prosaic correlations. There is much work to be done to isolate geophysical variables, such as radiation, geomagnetic effects, and even psychogeographical effects like landscape simulacra that can affect consciousness through readily explainable mechanisms (Dobsen & Mamyev 2010; Devereux 2013). However, finding the physiological underpinnings of states of consciousness does not mean we should dismiss the holistic and intrinsic value of sacred sites, or the crucial value of ceremony. It's a common western-minded misnomer to equate the entering of shamanic states with taking a drug. Taken outside of ceremony, plant medicine, referred to the west as hallucinogens, will bring on a hallucinogenic experience. Taken in a ceremony, the medicine allows participants to face the Shadow and get clarity and direction.

Thankfully, the values embodied by Mamyev and Dobsen's Karakol project (2010) are paralleled today in a larger shift in archaeological practices towards sustainability, preservation and non-invasive technologies. Archaeology has come a long way since its colonial roots and, through community education, indigenous-led projects and conservation activism, making the past come alive is put back in its proper context: to ensure the survival of endangered knowledge – not for its own sake – but for our children's children. After all, how can humankind plan if there is no past worth remembering? From an Indigenous science perspective, preservation for future generations is a higher value than any information retrieved from the destruction or disturbance of sacred sites and the landscape that supports them. At a time of great global uncertainty, sacred sites are places that re-enchant those who have gone to sleep due to ecological denial or despair. Sacred sites recharge people and communities, creating new relationships with the living ecology and landscape. Further, becoming attentive to and sharing extraordinary experiences – such as dreams, visions and intuitions – normalises them. By doing so, we remember who we are. By re-enacting, we remember.

Acknowledgments

First we thank our ancestors for giving us the opportunity to do this work. We also are deeply grateful for Beth Duncan and Frances Santiago for editing and feedback. Finally, thanks to all those who support the work of the Worldwide Indigenous Science Network.

Notes

1 Bates, Brian. Correspondence with Apela Colorado, 2009
2 Kruiper, L. *Indigenous Mind* Presentation. Maui, HI, November 2017.
3 Johnson, Phil. Correspondence with Apela Colorado, September 1990.
4 Mamyev, Danil. Presentation. 'Cultural landscapes: Preservation challenges in the 21st century', Rutgers University, 12 October 2013.
5 Marie Batiste points out that petroglyphs have multiple layers of meaning including but not limited to oral history, environmental knowledge, sound and navigation aides (1984).
6 Preliminary observations by geologist Cyril Wanamaker, Sealaska Corporation, indicate that the rocks were desposited at the site by two retreating glaciers and that some of the red granite boulders came from the centre of Copper Mountain. It appears that the rocks had to be carved in the period of time after the glaciers retreated and before the sea rise since geological evidence indicates that the rocks remained submerged until the last few hundred years when glacial rebound elevated them to their present tide line position. (Colorado 1983). However Bednarik suggests minor fluctuations in sea level occurred in the early Holocene and may account for

early shoreline petroglyphs that are currently underwater (2014, 200). Still, southern Alaska does have other signs of art from the late Pleistocene, such as the presence of red ochre found in On Your Knees Cave (9200 BP; Mrzlack 2003; Stanford 2011 33).

7 In accordance with the direction of Indigenous Cultural Practitioners a line drawing, not a photo, is provided.
8 Catches, P. Conversation with Apela Colorado. Pine Ridge, South Dakota, 1985.
9 Mamyev, Danil. Interview by Apela Colorado. IUCN, Jeju, South Korea, September 2012.
10 Johnson, Phil. Correspondence with Apela Colorado, September 1990.
11 Sabina, M. (2009). *María Sabina, mujer espíritu.* Documentary film, DVD, original release 1978. Directed by Nicolás Echevarría. México: Instituto Mexicano de Cinematografía.
12 *Ibid.*
13 Bates, Brian. Correspondence with Apela Colorado, 2009.
14 Colorado, A, Hurd, R. & Tucker, M. (2017). Prayer and resonance in Palaeolithic painted caves of Southern France: An Indigenous Science approach. Presented at *Archaeoacoustics III: The 3rd international multi-disciplinary conference on the human experience of sound in heritage, ceremonial and ritual places,* in Macao, Portugal.
15 Raux, Pascal. Interview by Apela Colorado. Dordogne, France, June 2016.
16 Mutwa, Credo. Conversation with Apela Colorado. Kuruman, South Africa, October 2005.

References

Bednarik, R. 2014. Pleistocene palaeoart of the Americas. *Arts* (3), 190–206.

Bright, B. 2009. The Shamanic perspective: Where Jungian thought and archetypal shamanism converge. http://www.depthinsights.com/pdfs/The-Shamanic-Perspective-Jung_and_Shamanism-BBright.pdf (accessed November 2017).

Colorado, P. 1983. Copper Mountain Research Project, A Report Submitted to the Alaska State Humanities Forum. https://library.wisn.org/2018/06/23/copper-mountain-research-project-report-1983/(accessed on June 14, 2018).

Colorado, A. 2014. Scientific pluralism. *The Pari Dialogues: Essays in Indigenous Knowledge and Western Science* 2. Pari: Pari Publishing, 337–361.

Devereux, P. 2013. Dreamscapes: Topography, mind, and the power of simulacra in ancient and traditional societies. *International Journal of Transpersonal Studies* 32(1), 51–63.

Dmitriev, A. N. & Shitov, A. V. 2005. On the geophysical characteristics of kurgan complexes in Gorny Altai. http://www.pulse.webservis.ru/Science/Tumuli/BGeo/index.html. (accessed 05.03.2018).

Dobsen, J. & Mamyev, D. 2010. Sacred valley, conservation management and Indigenous survival: Uch Enmek Indigenous Nature Park, Altai. In B. Verschuuren, R. Wild, J. McNeeley & G. Oviedo (eds) *Sacred Natural Sites, Conserving Nature and Culture*, London: Earth Scan, 244–354.

Fagan, B. 1998. *From Black Land to Fifth Sun; the Science of Sacred Sites.* Reading: Helix.

Gheorghiu, D. (ed.). 2011. *Archaeology Experiences Spirituality?* Newcastle-upon-Tyne: Cambridge Scholars Publishing.

Harry, D. 2006. High-tech invasion: Biocolonialism. In J. Mander & V. Tauli-Corpuz (eds) *Paradigm Wars: Indigenous Peoples' Resistance to Globalization.* San Francisco CA: Sierra Club Books.

Hayden, B. 2003. *Shamans, Sorcerers and Saints: A Prehistory of Religion.* Washington DC: Smithsonian Books.

Hirst, K. K. 2017. What is landscape archaeology? Thought Co. https://www.thoughtco.com/what-is-landscape-archaeology-171551. (accssed 05.03.2018)

Hurd, R. 2011. Integral archaeology: Process methodologies for exploring prehistoric rock art on Ometepe Island, Nicaragua. *Anthropology of Consciousness* 22(1), 72–94.

Hurd, R. 2015. Barometers of the anomalous? Dreams and transpersonal archaeology. *Paranthropology* 5(4), 70–74.

Jung, C. 1980. *The Archetypes and the Collective Unconscious*. Princeton NJ: Princeton University Press.
Keithan, E. 1940. The petroglyphs of southeastern Alaska. *American Antiquity* 6(2), 123–132.
Laughlin, C., McManus, J. & Shearer, J. 1983. Dreams, trance and visions: What a transpersonal anthropology might look like. *Phoenix: Journal of Transpersonal Anthropology* 7(1/2), 141–159.
Laughlin, C. 2011. *Communing with the Gods: Consciousness, Culture and the Dreaming Brain*. Brisbane: Daily Grail Press.
Lawson, A. 2012. *Painted Caves: Palaeolithic Rock Art in Western Europe*. Oxford: Oxford University Press.
Ludwin, R., Thrush, C. P., James, K., Buerge, D., Jonientz-Trisler, C., Rasmussen, J., Troost, K. & De Los Angeles, A. 2005. Serpent spirit-power stories along the Seattle Fault. *Seismological Research Letters* 76(4), 426–431.
Masse, W. B., Barber, E., Piccardi, L. & Barber, P. 2007. Exploring the nature of myth and its role in science. In L. Picardi & W. B. Masse (eds) *Myth and Geology*. Geological Society 273. London: Geological Society, 9–28.
Masse, W. B. 1998. Earth, air, fire, and water: The archaeology of Bronze Age cosmic catastrophes. In B. Peiser, T. Palmer & M. Bailey (eds) *Natural Catastrophes During Bronze Age Civilisations: Archaeological, Geological, Astronomical and Cultural Perspectives*. British Archaeological Report S728. Oxford: Archaeopress, 53–92.
Mrzlack, H. 2003. Ochre at 49-PET-408. M. A. thesis, Department of Anthropology, University of Colorado, Denver.
Narby, J. 1998. *The Cosmic Serpent: DNA and the Origins of Knowledge*. New York: Jeremy P. Tarcher/Putnam.
Parsell, D. 2002. Explorer Wade Davis on vanishing cultures. *National Geographic News* 28 June 2002. https://news.nationalgeographic.com/news/2002/06/0627_020628_wadedavis.html (accessed November 2017).
Pearson, J. 2002. *Shamanism and the Ancient Mind: A Cognitive Approach to Archaeology*. Walnut Creek CA: Altamira Press.
Reynolds, F. & Adams, D. 2014. Sound and performance in public archaeology: Examining the benefits of outdoor learning with creative engagement at the Neolithic Site of Tinkinswood burial chamber, Vale of Glamorgan. *Time and Mind* 7(1), 13–31.
Romain, W. 2009. *Shamans of the Lost World: A Cognitive Approach to the Prehistoric Religion of the Ohio Hopewell*. Plymouth: Altamira Press.
Spiller, H., Hale, J. & De Boer, J. 2002. The Delphic oracle: A multidisciplinary defense of the gaseous vent theory. *Journal of Toxicology* 40(2), 189–196.
Stanford, M. 2011. Shoreline pictographs of extreme southeast Alaska. *Alaska Journal of Anthropology* 9(1), 27–47.
Tedlock, B. 1992. *Dreaming: Anthropological and Psychological Perspectives*. Santa Fe NM: School of American Research Press.
Tilley, C. 1997. *A Phenomenology of Landscape: Places, Paths and Monuments*. Oxford: Berg.
Tilley, C. 2008. Phenomenological approaches to landscape archaeology. In B. David & J. Thomas (eds) *Handbook of Landscape Archaeology*. Walnut Creek CA: Left Coast Press, 271–276.
Wallace, B. A. 2000. *The Taboo of subjectivity: Towards a New Science of Consciousness*. New York: Oxford University Press.
Young, D. & Goulet, J. G. (eds). 1994. *Being Changed by Cross-cultural Encounters: The Anthropology of Extraordinary Experience*. Petersborough, Ontario: Broadview Press.